Pope and Horace: studies in imitation

POPE AND HORACE:
STUDIES IN IMITATION

FRANK STACK

Lecturer in English, University of Southampton

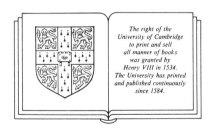

*The right of the
University of Cambridge
to print and sell
all manner of books
was granted by
Henry VIII in 1534.
The University has printed
and published continuously
since 1584.*

CAMBRIDGE UNIVERSITY PRESS

Cambridge
London   New York   New Rochelle
Melbourne   Sydney

Published by the Press Syndicate of the University of Cambridge
The Pitt Building, Trumpington Street, Cambridge CB2 1RP
32 East 57th Street, New York, NY 10022, USA
10 Stamford Road, Oakleigh, Melbourne 3166, Australia

First published 1985

Printed in Great Britain at
the University Press, Cambridge

Library of Congress catalogue card number: 85–4092

British Library cataloguing in publication data
Stack, Frank
Pope and Horace: studies in imitation.
1. Pope, Alexander – Criticism and
interpretation
I. Title
821'.5   PR3634
ISBN 0 521 26695 5

For
FREIDA, JESSICA, *and* JOHN

Contents

Contents

Acknowledgements

I would like to thank Sandy Cunningham, Brian Morris, Jean Robertson, John Birtwhistle, Penny Wilson, Terry Moore, Pauline Leng and Jim Sambrook for guidance and advice at various stages of work on this project. Special thanks are due to Howard Erskine-Hill for his constant help and encouragement, and to Derek Attridge for tirelessly reading and discussing early drafts. Norma Martin and Sally and Graham Johnson expertly typed a complex manuscript, and Helen Langdon and Edmund Papst gave intangible assistance as only friends can. But my greatest debt is to Fred Williams who provided the translations for the Latin and gave selflessly of his time and expert knowledge: without his collaboration this book could not have been written.

F.S.

Southampton, 1984

Abbreviations

Corr.	*The Correspondence of Alexander Pope*, ed. G. Sherburn, 5 vols., Oxford, 1956.
Dacier	*Remarques Critiques sur les Oeuvres d'Horace, avec une nouvelle traduction*, 10 vols., Paris, 1683–97. All references are to this edition unless otherwise indicated. I have not modernized Dacier's French.
'Discourse'	'Discourse Concerning the Original and Progress of Satire' in John Dryden, *Poems 1693–1696, Works*, IV, ed. A. B. Chambers, William Frost, and Vinton A. Dearing, Berkeley and Los Angeles, 1974.
Shaftesbury, 1714	*Characteristics of Men, Manners, Opinions, Times*, 2nd edn, 3 vols., 1714.
Shaftesbury, 1900	*The Life, Unpublished Letters, and Philosophical Regimen of Anthony, Earl of Shaftesbury*, ed. Benjamin Rand, London and New York, 1900.
TE	*The Twickenham Edition of the Poems of Alexander Pope*, ed. J. Butt, *et al.*, 11 vols., London, 1939–69.

All quotations from Pope's poems are from the Twickenham edition, references normally giving line number only. All quotations from the Horatian poems which Pope imitated are from Pope's own Horatian text reproduced in the Twickenham edition (IV) ed. John Butt, with occasional errors silently corrected. Quotations from other Horatian poems are from *Q. Horati Flacci Opera*, ed. Wickham and Garrod, 1901. Dr F. J. Williams and I have provided new translations for all the Latin poetry.

References to other works are made by using the author/date system which enables the reader to find the work in the alphabetically arranged bibliography. This is divided into works written before and after 1800, editions being listed by author rather than editor. Editions of Horace, however, are listed by their editors in order to distinguish those published before from those published after 1800.

Pope's index numbers linking the Latin and English poems are given the first time lines are quoted, but not thereafter.

All Greek quotations have been transliterated.

Imitation has been capitalized when it refers to the formal genre.

Preface

THE POINT OF DEPARTURE for this book is the fact that Pope printed alongside his *Imitations of Horace* the texts of the original Horatian poems on which they were based. By doing this he asked his readers not merely to remember those famous Horatian poems, but actively to re-read them while they were reading his *Imitations*. In the case of each Imitation, two poems were being offered rather than one. Indeed, the texts of the Horatian poems were carefully prepared to encourage this double reading in the closest detail: individual Latin words, phrases, or whole lines were picked out from the italic text in roman type; parts of lines, whole lines, or even whole sections of some poems, were cut; emendations to some of the uncertainties in Horace's text had been chosen.[1] Moreover, an elaborate system of index numbers or letters linked, from beginning to end, particular points in Pope's text to the parallel sections of Horace's poem. The result was that these well-known Latin poems commanded attention in a new way, and at every point begged comparison with the *Imitations*.[2]

The importance of Pope's parallel texts has long been recognized, but there is no study which analyses this practice in detail and assesses its importance in all the *Imitations*. In offering such a study I emphasize the extraordinary complexity of the relationship between each Imitation and the poem on which it is based. Sustained comparison reveals that in each Imitation Pope has here slightly modified and there utterly transformed, here intensely echoed and there ironically undercut the countless minute particulars of Horace's rich poetic language and subtle poetic forms. In addition, I argue that there is a vital and dynamic intertextual relationship between Horace's original poems and Pope's *Imitations*. Criticism of these poems often implies, I think, that the *Imitations* are variations on 'fixed' Horatian texts. I suggest that the relationship between the texts is much more fluid. The key words in the Latin often draw attention to unsuspected or novel details and thus constitute a 'reading' of Horace. Furthermore, Pope's *Imitations* are themselves, in one sense, highly original 'interpretations' of Horace, and next to these *Imitations* those 'traditional' poems actually look different.

In order to appreciate this fully it is necessary to provide an historical context. How was Horace read in the eighteenth century? How were the particular poems Pope imitated read? What was novel or striking about Pope's *Imitations* as versions of those particular poems? How challenging to us now is his treatment of Horace? Some of these questions have been raised before, but not, I think, adequately explored, mainly because it has not been fully realized how complex and difficult the questions are.[3]

It might be useful to set out briefly some of the problems. First, there was no simple or agreed view of Horace in the late seventeenth and early eighteenth century. Dryden's 'interpretation' of Horace was different from André Dacier's which was different from Isaac Casaubon's which was different from the Third Earl of Shaftesbury's. As we shall see, there was as much disagreement as there was agreement about the nature of Horace's political positions, the value of his 'low' style in the hexameter poetry, the strength of his 'forms' in satire and epistle, or the strength of his moral commitments.

Second, Pope's *Imitations of Horace* operate at a level well below, as it were, generalizations about 'Horace', however fine they may be. The group of Horatian poems which Pope imitated is remarkably varied in tone, form, and content, and in itself belies any simple view of Horace. *Satire* II.i. is a sophisticated dramatic dialogue, but *Satire* II.ii. is a simple moral diatribe. In contrast to both, the early *Satire* I.ii. is a notoriously immoral work full of personal allusions. The very late *Ode* IV.i. poses problems concerning lyric form and vision; while the mature *Epistles* II.i. and II.ii. require consideration of the interrelationship between moral vision, poetic structure, and self-consciousness. Different again are the questions about scepticism, 'contentment', and irony raised by the last poems Pope imitated, *Epistle* I.vi., *Satire* II.vi., *Epistle* I.vii., and *Epistle* I.i.

Third, Pope's treatment of these poems is so detailed, so intense, and so original, that he changes our perception of them. It seems to me that Pope, Shaftesbury, and Bentley, in their different ways, were the most challenging and imaginative readers of Horace in the first half of the eighteenth century. As I hope to show, to read the *Imitations* is, ultimately, to reassess traditional views of Horatian satire, Horace's images of 'himself', his moral teaching, and his psychological ideals.

The thrust of this study is to emphasize the radical nature of Pope's treatment of Horace. Pope's extraordinary attention to detail forces us to read Horace in a very concentrated manner. 'Horace' here is

not so much the well-known classical figure as the intense details of
his poetic language. The Horatian text is seen as a dynamic catalyst:
not as containing fixed meaning but as creating new meanings within
the intertextual field of the parallel poems. Pope's language seems at
once to extend Horace's meanings and to discover latent possibilities
within them. Furthermore, Pope's *Imitations* vigorously focus attention on the nature of Horatian self-portraiture; indeed, they explore
all the ideas of the 'self' found in Horace. In this area they reassess the
significance of one of Horace's own favourite themes, the profound
inconsistencies of human feelings and actions which question the
very idea of the unity of self. Finally, if these *Imitations* reassert the
validity of Horace's finely achieved poetic forms, especially the
epistle, they also question it. If they endorse, they also in some ways
deny, the value of Horace's moral and political positions. Ultimately,
they extend Horace's satiric vision to a point at which it undermines
the nature and purpose of satire itself. As a group, Pope's *Imitations*
confirm and question all that 'Horace' is.[4]

Fully to appreciate these aspects of Pope's *Imitations* we must
adopt two critical positions simultaneously, one which is historical
and another which is much more modern. On the one hand, we must
see Pope's reading of Horace in a historical context, and compare his
approach to Horace with those of his contemporaries. Only by doing
so does his real originality emerge. On the other hand we need to
recognize that these perspectives do not do full justice to his achievement. Pope's creative response to Horace in the *Imitations* was more
personal and more challenging than most of his contemporaries
realized. Only now, I think, can we fully appreciate that challenge.

In order to bring the historical perspective to bear on Pope's
Imitations I have used extensively two eighteenth-century readings
of Horace: André Dacier's detailed commentary on each poem Pope
imitated in his *Remarques Critiques sur les Oeuvres d'Horace, avec
une nouvelle traduction* (1683–97), and Shaftesbury's interpretation
of Horace as evident in detailed comments on, and quotations from,
individual Horatian poems in both *Characteristics of Men, Manners,
Opinions, Times* (2nd edn, 1714) and *The Life, Unpublished
Letters, and Philosophical Regimen of Anthony, Earl of Shaftesbury*, ed. Benjamin Rand (1900). Dacier's edition of Horace was the
most respected interpretative edition in the early eighteenth century,
and his comments on individual poems offer the best guide to the
way in which these works were generally read. This edition gives a
full and rich view of the classical Horace: Dacier comments sympathetically, indeed enthusiastically, on the whole of Horace's work,
and tries to appreciate in turn the individual qualities of odes,

epodes, early and late satires, and the two books of epistles. He emphasizes the moral seriousness of *Epistle* I, and comments particularly on the encouragement to virtue in those works, in contrast to the satiric castigation of folly and vice in the satires. To point up this seriousness Dacier draws parallels, when possible, between Horatian passages and a wide range of classical and biblical texts. Throughout, he comments thoughtfully on the structure of Horace's poems, and on his elegant play of tone and irony. Finally, and so importantly, he attempts to put Horace's poems into a specific historical and social context: he identifies the many individuals mentioned in Horace's poetry, tries to date each of the poems, comments on the social mores and customs Horace mentions, and seeks to explain the significance of the historical and political events to which Horace alludes. In doing so, Dacier opened up a rich Roman milieu with which Pope could compare his own times in sharp and often surprising detail.

Shaftesbury's interpretation of Horace was much more personal, at times highly erratic, and yet imaginatively searching, not least when it seems strange and we are tempted to call it simply 'wrong'. If Dacier allows us to measure Pope's originality in his approach to Horace, Shaftesbury permits us to compare one very personal response to Horace with another. There is no doubt that Pope knew and used Dacier's edition, as will become evident. Although I am not specifically concerned with Shaftesbury's 'influence' or otherwise on Pope, the references 'Shaftesbury, 1714' for the *Characteristics* indicate what Pope would have known, while 'Shaftesbury, 1900' indicates Shaftesbury's private writings, such as the personal and speculative 'Philosophical Regimen', a moral and psychological self-examination, not published in the eighteenth century. Modern critical studies of Horace, however, also inform my own readings of Horace, and the headnotes to each chapter provide a basic guide to modern criticism of each Horatian poem, as well as each Imitation. In interpreting the Horatian poems I have drawn primarily on the work of Eduard Fraenkel, M. J. McGann, Gordon Williams, Niall Rudd, and Charles O. Brink.

The first of two introductory chapters considers more generally the ways in which Horace was interpreted and evaluated in the late seventeenth and early eighteenth centuries in order to provide an historical context and to isolate points of reference for later comparison with Pope's *Imitations*. The second outlines briefly the tradition of the theory and practice of the Restoration and 'Augustan' Imitation, and stresses the originality of Pope's practice within those traditions. Thereafter each chapter concentrates on a single Imitation. Pope's first Imitation, the *Imitation of Satire II.i.*, is analysed in full, even though it is well known, in order to demonstrate that these *Imitations* can only be fully understood if they are approached as complete works read at every line in relation to the Horatian originals. Thereafter the poems are treated selectively, except for the Imitations of the two odes and the short *Imitation of Epistle I.vi.* The *Imitations* are treated chronologically and the chapters are divided into three parts to emphasize how Pope's approach to Horace changed and developed during the five-year period in which they were written. If each of the Horatian poems Pope imitated offers a different view of Horace, the *Imitations* as a group seem to be a dynamic and creative struggle with those changing visions. To start we must ask, what were the views of Horace with which Pope himself began?

PART I
Introductions

I

Interpreting Horace

But to come to particulars: *Heinsius* and *Dacier*, are the most principal of those, who raise *Horace* above *Juvenal* and *Persius*. *Scaliger* the Father, *Regaltius*, and many others, debase *Horace*, that they may set up *Juvenal*: And *Casaubon*, who is almost single, throws Dirt on *Juvenal* and *Horace*, that he may exalt *Persius* ...

Dryden, 'Discourse of Satire' (p. 50)

IN WRITING his *Imitations of Horace* Pope was able to allude to a complex tradition of Horatian interpretation, a tradition which is as varied, indeed at times as contradictory, as Horace's poetry itself. Since each single Imitation draws upon so many of these traditions, often with light and telling allusions, it will be useful to set out these main lines of interpretation. This will also enable us to assess the originality and individuality of Pope's treatment of Horace. We will find how vigorously and imaginatively Pope treats the traditional views, by turns energetically endorsing them, rethinking them afresh, or questioning their validity.

Evidence for these seventeenth- and eighteenth-century views of Horace can be drawn from several types of sources. Editions of Horace with their 'Prefaces' and interpretative notes are invaluable: the most important are those of Daniel Heinsius (1629), André Dacier (1683–97), L. Desprez (1694), and Richard Bentley (1711). Central also are the scholarly and critical essays on the nature and history of satire, particularly those which debate the relative merits of Lucilius, Horace, Juvenal, and Persius: the most significant are Isaac Casaubon's *De Satyrica Graecorum poesi, & Romanorum satira* (Paris, 1605), the essays on satire in the editions of Heinsius and Dacier, and Dryden's seminal 'Discourse concerning the Original and Progress of Satire' (1693) which served as a preface to his translation of Juvenal and Persius.[1]

To these we must add references to Horace in other contexts which so often provide sharp and illuminating views of Horace's poetry. As indicated in the preface, the pervasive allusion to Horace, and sustained discussion of his work in the Third Earl of

Shaftesbury's *Characteristics of Men, Manners, Opinions, Times* (1714) and his unpublished writings and letters (Shaftesbury, 1900) constitute an original and important 'reading' of Horace. What we find here on a large scale is repeated in miniature: countless allusions to, or quotations from, Horace in essays, poems, and letters of Chesterfield, Bolingbroke, Swift, Addison, Fielding, Pope himself, hint at how individual lines, passages, or poems were read, and how 'Horace' was interpreted and found significant. Finally, parodies of Horatian odes, satires, epistles, throughout this period suggest many different ways in which Horace was seen and found relevant.

The purpose of this chapter is to isolate the most significant features of this many-sided tradition, and to ask how Pope's *Imitations* might relate to them. The questions raised here will provide the terms of reference for all the chapters that follow.

THE MORAL TEACHER

Probably the single most important assumption about Horace in the eighteenth century was that he was a moral teacher, particularly in the satires and epistles. That this was one of Horace's views of himself is clear from that poetry itself, and is explicit in the *Ars Poetica* with its general contention that poetry should both 'instruct and delight'. Such a view of Horace was asserted by Isaac Casaubon (1605), more fully developed in Daniel Heinsius' essay on satire in his edition of Horace (1629), and re-asserted by André Dacier in his 'Preface sur les Satires d'Horace' in vol. VI of his important interpretative edition (1683–97). It was, furthermore, the keystone of Dryden's interpretation and evaluation of Horace in the 'Discourse concerning the Original and Progress of Satire' (1693). Dryden quite explicitly points to the significance of this tradition and builds his general argument about the relative merits of Horace and Juvenal upon it ('Discourse', p. 74). He asserts himself that this is Horace's singular strength: '*Horace* is teaching us in every Line, and is perpetually Moral' ('Discourse', p. 62).

As this is such an important aspect of the interpretation of Horace it is worth looking more closely at its language and assumptions. A fine example is Dryden's translation of Dacier's general statement about Horace's two books of satires (Dacier, VI, 'Preface'):

In these two Books of Satire, 'tis the business of *Horace* to instruct us how to combat our Vices, to regulate our Passions, to follow Nature, to give Bounds to our desires, to Distinguish betwixt Truth and Falshood, and betwixt our Conceptions of Things, and Things themselves: To come back from our prejudicate Opinions, to understand exactly the Principles and Motives of all our

Actions; and to avoid the Ridicule, into which all men necessarily fall, who are Intoxicated with those Notions, which they have received from their Masters; and which they obstinately retain, without examining whether or no they are founded on right Reason.

In a Word, he labours to render us happy in relation to our selves, agreeable and faithful to our Friends, and discreet, serviceable, and well bred in relation to those with whom we are oblig'd to live, and to converse. To make his Figures Intelligible, to conduct his Readers through the Labyrinth of some perplex'd Sentence, or obscure Parenthesis, is no great matter. And as *Epictetus* says, there is nothing of Beauty in all this, or what is worthy of a Prudent Man. The Principal business, and which is of most Importance to us, is to shew the Use, the Reason, and the Proof of his Precepts.

They who endeavour not to correct themselves, according to so exact a Model; are just like the Patients, who have open before them a Book of Admirable Receipts, for their Diseases, and please themselves with reading it, without Comprehending the Nature of the Remedies; or how to apply them to their Cure.   ('Discourse', pp. 74–5)

This suggests that Horatian satire offers a subtle and coherent view of moral life and personal growth. The aim of this satire is self-discovery, inner contentment, and the richness of personal relationships. The passage, like the satire, assumes that, in some sense, we are all 'sick' and in states of delusion; but it implies that with Horace as our Master, we can, through control and restraint on the one hand and true perception on the other, truly become ourselves, and, indeed, ourselves come to know 'Truth'.

This interpretation of Horace as a moral teacher was unquestionably of great importance to Pope, informing profoundly his treatment of Horace in the *Imitations*, and his view of himself as a poet; indeed, it is part of a tradition which powerfully influences our interpretation of Pope. And yet it does pose some important critical problems. To some extent it represents an imposition of neo-classical Renaissance ideas about the moral value of literature upon the classical poetry itself which will not always easily receive such ideas and is certainly open to other interpretations. Indeed the seventeenth-century attempts to distinguish between corrosive 'satire' and the more moral 'epistle' half recognize this fact (see, for example, Dacier's 'Remarque sur le Titre des Epistres', vol. VIII). In addition, it accepts too much at face value Horace's own portrait of himself as a moral teacher without seeing the ironies and ambiguities of that position in his poetry. It takes no account of the frankly immoral side of Horace, as in *Satire* I.ii., for example. Perhaps most important of all it assumes that Horace's poetry does indeed offer a clear and contained view of what the self is, or could be – the 'aequus animus' – and what 'Truth' is, without exploring how far his poetry is genuinely paradoxical, questioning those very ideas while it asserts them so memorably.

How much do Pope's *Imitations* accept this view of Horace, indeed appeal to it, and reinforce its authority? How much do they question its validity and, indeed, its existence? How much do they offer quite other views of the self, of Nature, and of Truth? How much do they discover in the Horatian poetry itself other ways of reading Horace, other views of the poet and the value of his poetry, other views of social relationships and inner contentment? These are some of the questions to be explored.

THE POLITICAL POET

Horace's relationship with the 'Court' of Augustus, his involvement with Maecenas, his explicitly political poetry, and indeed the general 'political' tenor of all his poetry were fully debated in the seventeenth and eighteenth centuries. Influential critics like Dacier and Desprez give a very positive account of Augustus and Maecenas, and, as we shall see, emphasize Horace's ability to maintain his integrity and independence in his relationships with them. But Howard D. Weinbrot has argued that Augustus was often regarded as a tyrant who despoiled Rome of its liberty and Horace often denigrated as a 'Court slave' and flatterer of Augustus, unlike Juvenal who was regarded as the heroic scourge of vice in Domitian's court and a stern champion of strenuous liberty (1978, *passim*). More recently Howard Erskine-Hill (1983) has stressed the many-sided quality of both the 'Augustan' and 'Horatian' traditions in English literature, and has shown that views on these subjects were, in fact, very varied.

Shaftesbury, as we shall see shortly, gives a complex account of Horace's political commitments, but he, for one, is very critical of Augustus and Maecenas and of Horace's relationship with them in what he regarded as Horace's 'debauched, slavish, courtly state' (Shaftesbury, 1900, p. 360). Indeed, he is scornful of Dacier's own 'Court models of breeding and friendship' under Louis XIV which make him unable to understand Horace when he *is* being honest (1900, p. 356). Dryden is even more critical, offering a striking contrast to his own view of Horace as the moral teacher, when he compares him with Juvenal in impassioned terms:

so that, granting *Horace* to be the more general Philosopher; we cannot deny, that *Juvenal* was the greater Poet, I mean in Satire. His Thoughts are sharper, his Indignation against Vice is more vehement; his Spirit has more of the Commonwealth Genius; he treats Tyranny, and all the Vices attending it, as they deserve, with the utmost rigour: And consequently, a Noble Soul is better pleas'd with a Zealous Vindicator of *Roman* Liberty; than with a Temporizing Poet, a well Manner'd Court Slave, and a Man who is often afraid of Laughing in the right place: Who is ever decent, because he is naturally servile. After all, *Horace* had the disadvantage of the Times in which he liv'd; they were better for the Man, but worse for the Satirist. 'Tis generally said, that those Enormous Vices, which were practis'd under the Reign of *Domitian*, were unknown in the Time of *Augustus Caesar*: That therefore *Juvenal* had a larger Field, than *Horace*. Little Follies were out of doors, when Oppression was to be scourg'd instead of Avarice: It was no longer time to turn into Ridicule, the false Opinions of Philosophers; when the *Roman* Liberty was to be asserted. ('Discourse', p. 65)[2]

Drawing upon accounts of Augustus by Tacitus and Suetonius he emphasizes that Augustus, out of concern for his 'violent Methods' of 'Usurpation' and well-known adulteries, created 'an Edict against Lampoons and Satires, and the Authors of those defamatory Writings, which my Author *Tacitus*, from the Law-Term, calls *famosos libellos*' ('Discourse', pp. 66–7). This, Dryden argues, partly accounts for the nature of Horace's poetry: '*Horace*, as he was a Courtier, comply'd with the Interest of his Master, and avoided the Lashing of greater Crimes, confin'd himself to the ridiculing of Petty Vices, and common Follies' ('Discourse', p. 68).[3]

These perspectives present real difficulties for the interpretation of Pope's *Imitations*: how far did Pope share these views of Augustus, Maecenas, and Horace? How far did Pope explicitly see himself as a satirist and a man in a striking contrast to Horace, as his own epitaph published in 1738 would, as Weinbrot points out, seem to suggest:

> HEROES and KINGS! your distance keep:
> In peace let one poor Poet Sleep,
> Who never flatter'd Folks like you:
> Let Horace blush, and Virgil too.   (*TE*, VI, p. 376)

How far does this account of Horace undermine the authority of Horace as the moral teacher? How much does it colour Pope's treatment of Bolingbroke as a Maecenas figure in the late Imitations?

STOIC, EPICUREAN, OR ECLECTIC?

Closely related to questions of moral teaching and political commitment is the question of Horace's relationship with classical moral philosophy. To the seventeenth and eighteenth centuries this was a more complex issue than we are accustomed to think.[4] Both Dacier and Dryden emphasize the importance of Horace's avowed eclecticism. In his interpretation of Horace's *Epistle* I.i. Dacier underlines Horace's claim that he is neither a Stoic nor an Epicurean; Dryden asserts the same in the 'Discourse'. But this famous eclecticism, which modern 'liberal' critics are inclined to commend, was not always praised in the seventeenth and eighteenth centuries. Indeed Casaubon made Persius' firm adherence to Stoicism the preeminent reason why he rated him higher than either Juvenal or Horace. Casaubon's overall championing of Persius was generally regarded as bizarre, but Dryden himself fully recognized the force of this particular argument. Summarizing and enlarging upon Casaubon he concludes:

> Herein, then it is, that *Persius* has excell'd both *Juvenal* and *Horace*. He sticks to his one Philosophy: He shifts not sides, like *Horace*, who is sometimes an *Epicuraean*, sometimes a Stoick, sometimes an Eclectick; as his present Humour leads him: Nor declaims like *Juvenal* against Vices, more like an Orator, than a Philosopher. *Persius* is every where the same: True to the Dogma's of his Master: What he has learnt, he teaches vehemently; and what he teaches, that he Practices himself. There is a Spirit of sincerity in all he says: You may easily discern that he is in earnest, and is perswaded of that Truth which he inculcates. In this I am of opinion, that he excels *Horace*, who is commonly in jeast, and laughs while he instructs: And is equal to *Juvenal*, who was as honest and serious as *Persius*, and more he cou'd not be.　　　　　　　　　　　　　　('Discourse', pp. 56–7)

This too provides important perspectives on Pope's Imitations: how far does Pope emulate Horace's eclecticism, how far does he strive for greater philosophical consistency and greater moral seriousness? In particular, how far is he drawn to another view of the self and its possibilities explicitly associated with Stoic writing, the idea that the nobility of the self lies precisely in the passion of commitment and in profound inner consistency? This, as I hope to show, provides one of the central tensions in Pope's last Imitation, the *Imitation of Epistle I.i.*, based on a poem in which Horace asserts his 'essential' eclecticism.[5]

But while most seventeenth- and eighteenth-century interpretations of Horace recognize the significance of his overall eclecticism and individuality, they nevertheless give, compared to most modern editors, a great deal of attention to what they considered the philosophical character of Horace's poetry. Dacier and Desprez annotate as fully as they can Horace's allusions to Plato, Aristotle, and Lucretius, and Dacier in particular quotes extensively from Cicero and Seneca to emphasize the philosophical character of the details of Horace's language. Furthermore, though fully aware of Horace's irony, they tended to take very seriously those poems in which Horace spoke of his resolve to give up writing lyric poetry to study philosophy, notably *Epistle* I.i. and *Epistle* II.ii.

Shaftesbury provides an illuminating view of this, and the whole question of Horace's 'philosophy', in a theory that is all the more interesting because it is in part highly individual. In a long and detailed letter to the French critic and translator Pierre Coste dated 1 October 1706, Shaftesbury suggests that Horace's commitment to philosophy fell into three phases corresponding to three periods of his life. 'The first period is that which I call his *original free republican state*. His friend and patron during this time was Brutus, who was head of the cause, and who raised him to command of a legion. His philosophy was suitable thereto; that of Brutus, the old genuine *Academic*, or as Cicero says, in reality, the downright Stoic.' In contrast to Cyrenaic and Epicurean views this philosophy 'recommended action, concernment in civil affairs, religion'; it 'maintained that society, right, and wrong was founded in Nature, and that Nature had a meaning, and was herself, that is to say in her wits, well governed and administered by one simple and perfect intelligence' (Shaftesbury, 1900, pp. 358–9).

After Philippi 'comes Horace's second period or state, for he soon gets to Court, and this I call his debauched, slavish, courtly state. His patron Maecenas, a suitable one, and his philosophy, too, as suitable, being of the second kind I mentioned', i.e. Epicurean, which 'derided all [action, civil affairs, religion], and advised inaction and retreat, and with good reason'. But

"Naturam expellas furca". Nature is powerful, and will return when she has fair play. Horace could not long hold it ... And hence arose his third and last period, viz. his *returning, recovering state*, and his recourse to his first philosophy and principles, sorely against Maecenas and the Court's desire, who would have kept him, and did all they could to do so, but in vain.

(Shaftesbury, 1900, pp. 359–60)

Introducing this account Shaftesbury equivocates nicely as to how far this is 'mythology' and how far it really reveals 'Horace's whole life' which 'is clearly and purposely transmitted to us in his writing, particularly under his apologues' (p. 358). But, as we shall see, in the letter he does go on to interpret individual poems in accordance with this pattern, and provides very striking readings of *Satire* II.vi., *Epistle* II.ii., *Epistle* I.vii., *Epistle* I.i., and *Epistle* I.vi. Shaftesbury regards all these as works from Horace's last period, describing *Epistle* I.vi., for example, in 'Miscellaneous Reflections IV' as 'one of his latest Epistles of the deeply philosophical kind' dealing with the problems of admiration and emotional involvement (Shaftesbury 1714, III, p. 202, footnote). How do Pope's Imitations of all these poems, his last Imitations, compare with Shaftesbury's highly idealistic, Stoic readings of these poems?

'CHRISTIANIZED' HORACE

The question of Horace's relationship to both pagan and Christian religion poses problems even more acute. Straightforward allusions to pagan gods and religious rites are not difficult: commentators like Dacier tend to take them seriously and assume that Horace took them seriously, as suggested, for example, by Dacier's comments on the allusion to the *Carmen Saeculare* in *Epistle* II.i. (IX, pp. 371–6). The problem arises with the common Renaissance tendency to draw parallels between Horatian thought and passages from both Old and New Testaments. Thomas E. Maresca's *Pope's Horatian Poems* (1966) has the merit of pointing to the significance of these parallels, but it over-states the importance of this tradition and presents a very distorted account of both the Horace Pope knew and the *Imitations* themselves. Maresca does not distinguish adequately between a work like Thomas Sagittarius' *Horatius Christianus* (1615) which virtually presents Horace as a Christian moralist, and the editions of Dacier and Desprez and others which, while noting Biblical parallels, give a much more balanced view of Horace. Dacier certainly stresses the moral seriousness of Horace, particularly in *Epistles* I, but he also comments frequently and perceptively on Horace's wit and irony and on the distinctive nature of Horace's personality and moral vision as seen within a very Roman context. What is interesting, indeed, about Dacier's edition is the tension between its appeal to general moral truth and its recognition of distinctive customs and cultural traditions. Jean Marmier's *Horace en France au dix-septième siècle* (1962) presents a much more convincing case than Maresca, arguing that the attempts to present Horace as a proto-Christian writer were generally regarded as bizarre. He notes that even the Jesuit teaching of Horace, and the official Desprez edition, presented a far more well-rounded view of Horace (pp. 37–8).

There is no doubt that Pope was alive to what could be Theistic and Judaic/Christian 'suggestions' in Horace's language. Questions about Horace's 'intention' here are, of course, irrelevant. Pope's own allusive language itself often brings these various traditions together in the very act of imitating Horace, particularly in the last Imitations. But it is doubtful if these religious suggestions provide the primary field of meaning in Pope's *Imitations*, as Maresca argued. Rather, as we shall see, they seem to add depth and resonance to contexts which are essentially personal, moral, social, and political.

And yet the problem remains an important one: how much do the parallel Biblical passages in the seventeenth- and eighteenth-century editions constitute readings of at least individual lines and passages of Horace? What is the significance of Shaftesbury's claim that Horace's Stoicism was actually as 'Theistic' as his own? Shaftesbury argues that Horace's early Stoicism, to which he eventually returned, 'maintained that society, right, and wrong was founded in Nature, and that Nature had a meaning, and was herself, that is to say in her wits, well governed and administered by one simple and perfect intelligence' (Shaftesbury, 1900, p. 359). William Wollaston, as Maresca notes, can quote Horace in his *The Religion of Nature Delineated* (London, 1724) to show that Horace had a deep sense of the divine in nature (see Maresca, 1966, pp. 26–7). Dryden can assert that the Stoicism of Persius was so noble and inspiring that it could well be taught in churches ('Discourse', p. 56). How does Pope treat Dacier's 'religious' interpretation of individual passages in Horace? How Christian or Theistic is the 'Stoicism' of his last two Imitations, of *Epistle* i.vi. and *Epistle* i.i.?

WIT AND RAILLERY

In striking contrast to those interpretations of Horace which emphasize his presentation of philosophical or religious truths are those which value his distinctive urbanity and wit. These of course raise again the nature of Horace's relationship with his society: how far is that delicate wit and subtle play of irony compatible with genuine moral commitment? Yet again there are contrasting views and different evaluations.

Editors like Dacier, Desprez, Baxter and others note very acutely Horace's light tones and wry ironies, and, without fully discussing the issue, generally imply that they are one of Horace's major achievements and an essential part of his civilized urbanity. Dryden's view is more complicated than is usually realized: despite his personal preference for Juvenal Dryden insists that Horatian raillery is, in principle, a finer mode of satire than Juvenalian declaiming. Commenting on Barten Holiday's assertion that '*A perpetual Grinn, like that of* Horace, *rather angers than amends a Man*', Dryden declares:

I cannot give him up the Manner of *Horace* in low Satire so easily: Let the Chastisements of *Juvenal* be never so necessary for his new kind of Satire; let him declaim as wittily and sharply as he pleases, yet still the nicest and most delicate touches of Satire consist in fine Raillery. This, my Lord, is your particular Talent, to which even *Juvenal* could not arrive. 'Tis not Reading, 'tis not imitation of an Author, which can produce this fineness: It must be inborn, it must proceed from a Genius, and particular way of thinking, which is not to be taught; and therefore not to be imitated by him who has it not from Nature: How easie it is to call Rogue and Villain, and that wittily! But how hard to make a Man appear a Fool, a Block-head, or a Knave, without using any of those opprobrious terms! To spare the grossness of the Names, and to do the thing yet more severely, is to draw a full Face, and to make the Nose and Cheeks stand out, and yet not to employ any depth of Shadowing. This is the Mystery of that Noble Trade; which yet no Master can teach to his Apprentice: He may give the Rules, but the Scholar is never the nearer in his practice. ('Discourse', pp. 70–1)

Indeed his admiration for Horace's brilliant rapier-thrusts produces one of the finest compliments Horace has ever received:

Neither is it true, that this fineness of Raillery is offensive. A witty Man is tickl'd while he is hurt in this manner; and a Fool feels it not. The occasion of an Offence may possibly be given, but he cannot take it. If it be granted that in effect this way does more Mischief; that a Man is secretly wounded, and though he be not sensible himself, yet the malicious World will find it for him: Yet there is still a vast difference betwixt the slovenly Butchering of a Man, and the fineness of a stroak that separates the Head from the Body, and leaves it standing in its place. ('Discourse', p. 71)

Dryden, indeed, indicates that he prefers Horace's raillery of his friends to his 'exposure' of his enemies, noting in particular how he 'rallies' Trebatius in *Satire* II.i. ('Discourse', pp. 62–3).

And yet Dryden is also very critical, in terms which are aesthetic, political, and moral: 'His Urbanity, that is, his Good Manners, are to be commended, but his Wit is faint; and his Salt, if I may dare to say so, almost insipid' (p. 63). And Dryden emphasizes the political implications of this style: Horace is 'ever decent, because he is naturally servile' (p. 65). But Shaftesbury, despite his condemnation of Horace's 'Epicurean' period, takes a quite different view: criticizing Dacier's inability to see the moral seriousness in what he takes to be a fine fusion of delicate irony and deep religious faith in *Ode* IV.xi. he comments:

But Mons. Dacier knew little of the simplicity of Horace or measure of his irony. For there is so just a measure of his irony that nothing is more simple or honest. There is a due proportion in irony well known to all polite writers, especially Horace, who so well copied that noted Socratic kind. Go but a little further with it, and strain it beyond a certain just measure, and there is nothing so offensive, injurious, hypocritical, bitter, and contrary to all true simplicity, honesty, or good manners. (Shaftesbury, 1900, pp. 356–7)

And, as we might expect, Chesterfield, quoting *Epistle* I.i., assumes that Horatian urbanity is compatible with the true personal moral integrity (*Letters*, ed. Dobrée, 1932, VI, pp. 2762–3).

There is no doubt that Pope was alive to these different interpretations and evaluations: as Howard Erskine-Hill has pointed out, the 'Friend's' portrait of Horace in the *Epilogue to the Satires Dialogue I* (1738) is a very subtle critique of the 'Court's' admiration for the compliant Horace it would, perhaps, like Pope to be (1975, pp. 272–3). And yet Pope's raillery can be as fine and delicate as Horace's. How do these issues affect our reading of Pope's *Imitation of Satire II.i.*, with its raillery of Fortescue, Pope's Trebatius? What is the moral significance of the brilliant raillery of Pope's *Epistle to Augustus*?

AESTHETIC FORMS

This is a complex subject which involves questions about unity of subject in satire, the nature and significance of Horace's famous epistle form, the unique aesthetic qualities of the odes, and the 'low' style of most of Horace's hexameter poetry. But it involves also consideration of Horace's aesthetic ideals of harmony, order, and purity not only aspired to in the odes themselves, but so fully discussed, subtly present, and richly contemplated in the late epistles.

The question of the unity of subject in satire was an important one in the seventeenth century. Casaubon had praised Persius for writing each of his satires on one principal subject, and Dryden fully endorsed the value of this:

Will you please but to observe, that *Persius*, the least in Dignity of all the Three [Roman satirists], has, notwithstanding, been the first, who has discover'd to us this important Secret, in the designing of a perfect Satire; that it ought only to treat of one Subject; to be confin'd to one particular Theme; or, at least, to one principally. ('Discourse', p. 79)

In his commendation of Juvenal, his critical language suggests a crucial reason for this: the 'unity of subject' is essential for the power of the poetry and for the strength of the emotional response it provokes:

Juvenal is of a more vigorous and Masculine Wit, he gives me as much Pleasure as I can bear: He fully satisfies my Expectation, he Treats his Subject home: His Spleen is rais'd, and he raises mine: I have the pleasure of Concernment in all he says; He drives his Reader along with him; and when he is at the end of his way, I willingly stop with him: If he went another Stage, it wou'd be too far, it wou'd make a Journey of a Progress, and turn Delight into Fatigue. When he gives over, 'tis a sign the Subject is exhausted; and the Wit of Man can carry it no farther. If a Fault can be justly found in him; 'tis that he is sometimes too luxuriant, too redundant; says more than he needs, like my Friend the *Plain Dealer*, but never more than pleases. ('Discourse', p. 63)

On the other hand, admirers of Horace like Heinsius and Dacier insisted that 'true' Roman satire dealt with many subjects and the real art lay in the subtle weaving of those subjects together. The scholarly debate about the origin of the word 'satire' was relevant here, advocates of the Horatian model opting for the Latin 'satura' or 'mixture, medley' rather than 'Satyr' which suggested origins in the Greek Satyr play. Dacier also persistently points to the example of Lucilius, not as the fierce forerunner of Juvenal as Dryden ('Discourse', p. 64) and Weinbrot (1978, p. 139–40, footnote) see him, but rather as the writer who wrote on many different subjects. Dacier sees Horace's *Epistle to Augustus* as a Lucilian poem for this reason (IX, p. 309).

Once again Shaftesbury is particularly provocative, raising questions about Horatian form which left other seventeenth- and eighteenth-century critics, except Dryden, far behind. Recognition of Horace's easy, familiar style was all too common, but only Shaftesbury really attempted to understand and interpret the inner shaping of Horace's hexameter poetry, particularly the epistle form. In 'Advice to an Author' Shaftesbury tries to express the true relationship between 'Method' and 'Ease' in the epistle style which he calls '*The Simple* Manner':

Now tho every other Stile and genuine Manner of Composition has its Order and Method, as well as this which, in a peculiar sense, we call *the Methodick*; yet it is this Manner alone which professes Method, dissects it-self in Parts, and makes its own Anatomy. *The Sublime* can no way condescend thus, or bear to be suspended in its impetuous Course. *The Comick*, or Derisory Manner, is further still from making shew of Method. 'Tis then, if ever, that it presumes to give it-self this wise Air, when its Design is to expose the Thing it-self, and ridicule the Formality and Sophistry so often shelter'd beneath it. *The Simple* Manner, which being the strictest Imitation of Nature, shou'd of right be the compleatest, in the Distribution of its Parts, and Symmetry of its whole, is yet so far from making any ostentation of Method, that it conceals the Artifice as much as possible: endeavouring only to express the effect of Art, under the appearance of the greatest Ease and Negligence. And even when it assumes the censuring or reproving part, it does it in the most conceal'd and gentle way.

(Shaftesbury, 1714, I, pp. 257–8)

His motto and exemplum for this comes, of course, from Horace's *Epistle* II.ii.124: '*Ludentis speciem dabit, & torquebitur*' ('he'll make it look like child's play, although he's in agony' – Shaftesbury, 1714, I, p. 234). In 'Miscellaneous Reflections, Miscellany I' he takes this even further, exploring the relationship between freedom in language and political freedom, and asserting the importance of Horace's habit of addressing epistles to individual named men rather than just the general public as Seneca did in the generation after Horace, Seneca's epistles being only nominally addressed to Lucilius, according to Shaftesbury (1714, III, 17–27).

Criticism of the *Imitations* has often emphasized Pope's capacity to infuse his Horatian forms with the energy of a Juvenal or a Persius, as G. K. Hunter (1960) argued of the *Imitation of Satire II.i.* and Howard Weinbrot (1982) has argued of the *Imitation of Epistle I.vi.* (pp. 287–92). But how much was Pope also aware of the subtle shaping of Horace's *Satire* II.i., and how much did he seek to emulate the fine blending of subjects and much admired 'transitions' of Horace's epistles? How much, furthermore, in poems like the *Epistle to Augustus*, was Pope emulating what Shaftesbury detected as the self-consciousness of the Horatian manner: how far does this poem, or, indeed, the impassioned *Imitation of Epistle I.vi.* 'make its own Anatomy' (Shaftesbury, 1714, I, p. 257)?[6]

Two other points need mention here and are, I think, usefully put together. First, the seventeenth- and eighteenth-century reactions to Horace's 'low-style' in the satires and epistles and, second, interpretations of his aesthetic ideals particularly in the odes and in the epistles which speak of those odes. It is useful to take these together because clearly they point in different directions, and because, as the *Imitations* show, Pope was deeply interested in both.

We have already seen that Shaftesbury found subtle aesthetic beauty and indeed moral purity in Horace's simple style. But Dryden took a different view. Asserting boldly that 'Versification, and Numbers, are the greatest Pleasures of Poetry', Dryden continues, 'when there is anything deficient in Numbers, and Sound, the Reader is uneasie, and unsatisfi'd; he wants something of his Complement, and desires somewhat which he finds not: And this being the manifest defect of *Horace*, 'tis no wonder, that finding it supply'd in *Juvenal*, we are more Delighted with him.' ('Discourse', pp. 64–5). The language of Dryden's praise of Juvenal is very telling:

Add to this, that his Thoughts are as just as those of *Horace*, and much more Elevated. His Expressions are Sonorous and more Noble; his Verse more numerous, and his Words are suitable to his Thoughts; sublime and lofty. All these contribute to the Pleasure of the Reader, and the greater the Soul of him who Reads his Transports are the greater. *Horace* is always on the Amble, *Juvenal* on the Gallop: But his way is perpetually on Carpet Ground. He goes with more impetuosity than *Horace*; but as securely; and the swiftness adds a more lively agitation to the Spirits. The low Style of *Horace*, is according to his Subject; that is generally groveling. ('Discourse', pp. 63–4)

But Dryden makes it very clear he is only speaking of Horace's hexameter poetry and, indeed, goes out of his way to assert the general aesthetic superiority of Horace's odes: 'If it be only argu'd in general, which of them was the better Poet; the Victory is already gain'd on the side of *Horace*. *Virgil* himself must yield to him in the delicacy of his Turns, his choice of Words, and perhaps the Purity of his *Latin*. He who says that *Pindar* is inimitable, is himself inimitable in his *Odes*' ('Discourse', p. 58). And, indeed, Dryden significantly singles out *Epistle* ii.i. as a striking exception to his general argument. Speaking of this low style he adds: 'I question not but he cou'd have rais'd it. For the First Epistle of the Second Book, which he writes to *Augustus*, (a most instructive Satire concerning Poetry), is of so much Dignity in the Words, and of so much Elegancy in the Numbers, that the Author plainly shews, the *Sermo Pedestris*, in his other Satires, was rather his Choice than his Necessity' ('Discourse', p. 64).

Comparison of Latin hexameter with English heroic couplets is, of course, difficult, but there is no doubt, as many critics have said, that Pope often sought to raise the tone of Horace's verse towards greater rhetorical intensity (see Pope, *Works*, ed. Warton, 1822, IV, p. 59). At the same time he often excelled in loosening that couplet style to emulate the casual manner of Horace's easy conversational and colloquial style. But, as we shall see, the whole issue is made more complicated by the fact that Horace's hexameter style, looked at in detail the way Pope does, is in fact much more varied than these generalizations would suggest. The question finally becomes how does Pope treat the distinctive rhetorical force of Horace's language in *Epistle* i.vi., or the mounting rhetoric at the end of *Satire* ii.ii., or the brilliant 'operatic' effects that form the conclusion of *Satire* i.ii.? To return to the odes, how far does he try to emulate the elegant rhythms and linguistic patterns of *Ode* iv.i. in his *Ode to Venus*?

RETREAT AND THE INNER SELF

Questions about aesthetics in Horace lead, significantly, to speculations about the nature of the self and the possibility of achieving inner calm and deeper personal harmony, aspects of Horace explored fully by Maren-Sofie Røstvig (1962) and Maynard Mack (1969). In this area Shaftesbury's 'readings' of Horace are particularly distinguished, as we might expect from the author of 'Soliloquy, or Advice to an Author'. Shaftesbury finds in Horace his own concern with centrality of 'self' but also his own awareness of its elusiveness: a concern for the inner harmony of self as a moral and aesthetic ideal, but also a recognition of the complex relationship between self and passion, self and error, self and inconsistency, self and all forms of property. As we shall see, only Shaftesbury in the eighteenth century explores these Horatian themes with a subtlety comparable to Pope's.

For Shaftesbury this represents, perhaps, the essential Horace: the

Horace of contemplation celebrated in 'Moralists: A Rhapsody', the Horace of the 'obscure, implicit Language' of our deepest thoughts (Shaftesbury, 1714, I, p. 171), the Horace of what Shaftesbury in 'An Essay on the Freedom of Wit and Humour' can only call the *'moral Magick'* of the poetic imagination (Shaftesbury, 1714, I, p. 136). This is the Horace of the 'Philosophical Regimen' who represents for Shaftesbury that inner harmony which constitutes the true self and is utterly and exclusively private. And yet, as we shall see, Shaftesbury himself was also very critical of that 'easy' form of Horatian retreat which encouraged mere self-indulgence, a self-absorption made possible by wealth and property. Did Pope share these doubts, and seek to balance his own Horatian cultivation of the self with a concern for others and a continued public involvement which were characteristic of *Stoic* retreat? This is an important issue: how deeply does Pope interpret the 'visionary' poetry of *Ode* IV.i., and how far does this side of Horace inform Pope's own images of retreat on the 'silver Thames'? How does Pope's *Imitation of Epistle II.ii.* compare with Shaftesbury's 'reading' of that epistle as a profound discovery of the inner self? How far does a concern with the inner self cut across the political focus of Pope's last two *Imitations*?

> So slow th'unprofitable Moments roll,
> That lock up all the Functions of my soul;
> That keep me from Myself . . .   (*Imitation of Epistle I.i.* 39–41)

2

Imitation

Strait *Horace* for some lucky Ode I sought,
And all along I trac'd him, Thought by Thought ...
John Gay, 'A Letter to a Lady', 31–2

IN WRITING his *Imitations of Horace* Pope was working within a tradition of the poetic Imitation which began in the mid-seventeenth century. Yet Pope's handling of this form seems particularly individual and challenging. The purpose of this chapter is to show that Pope not only drew upon but extended and developed the Restoration and 'Augustan' theory and practice of Imitation. Of central importance here is Pope's distinctive development of the parallel text format, where the original poem is printed along with the Imitation, but first we must put this in a wider context.

Imitations of classical and foreign writers were extremely popular from the mid-seventeenth century until at least the end of the eighteenth century. There were no doubt many reasons for this, ranging from the highest to the lowest. On the one hand, imitation of the ancients sprang from immense respect for their value and authority, and was inspired by ancient example itself, Latin literature being so dependent on Greek models and its own traditions.[1] The classical forms of epic, ode, satire, epistle were respected in themselves and were found relevant for a remarkable range of contemporary contexts. In addition, imitation seemed to endorse ideas of general nature and general truth, the conviction that human nature and human experience, despite changes of time and circumstance, had always been the same.

On the other hand, as John Gay suggests, imitation was also an easy way of writing poems for any occasion and on any subject. Despite his own great Imitations of Juvenal's *Satire* III and *Satire* X, Johnson recognized this: in his famous disparagement of Pope's *Imitations of Horace* he said they were 'written as relaxations of his genius' after his more original poems (*Lives*, ed. G. Birkbeck Hill, 1905, III, p. 246). This judgement needs qualification, but there is no doubt it contains some truth about Pope and a great deal of truth about lesser writers. We must recognize, however, that the Imitation as a form was wholly compatible with genuinely creative expression, and the freer the Imitation, the more this was so.

THE TRADITION

It is clear that the form of Imitation, as opposed to the pervasive practice of adapting and borrowing from classical or foreign writers, grew mainly out of the debate about free translation begun by Cowley and Denham in the 1650s. Free translation involved both modernization of classical names, places, and words to make classical poems more readily comprehensible, and general latitude in rendering to avoid what Cowley and Denham and others regarded as the excessive literalism of, for example, Ben Jonson's translation of the *Art of Poetry*. From these free translations grew what would eventually be called 'Imitations'.[2]

Within this tradition two main types of Imitation emerged: one was the careful consecutive modernizing of a single poem which was, in effect, a form of translation designed for those who did not know the original. This type of translation was advocated by Denham in some remarks prefixed to Fanshawe's *Pastor Fido* (1648) and also by Cowley in the preface to his *Pindarique Odes* (1656); but was most fully expounded and practised by Dryden and Oldham. In the preface to his translation of *Ovid's Epistles* (1680) Dryden recommended this as the best mode of translation, between the extreme literalism of Jonson and the extreme freedom of Cowley's practice. Oldham in *Some New Pieces* (1681) explicitly adopted this principle and stated exactly what he strove for in his version of Horace's *Ars Poetica*. He decided to write the translation as if Horace were living at his time:

I therefore resolved to alter the scene from Rome to London, and to make use of English names of men, places, and customs, where the parallel would decently permit, which I conceived would give a kind of new air to the poem, and render it more agreeable to the relish of the present age ... I have not, I acknowledge, been over nice in keeping to the words of the original, for that were to transgress a rule therein contained. Nevertheless I have been religiously strict to its sense, and expressed it in as plain and intelligible a manner as the subject would bear.

(*Works*, ed. Bell, 1854, p. 144)

Oldham's translation of Horace's *Ars Poetica, Satire* I. ix., and two Horatian *Odes* in *Some New Pieces* more or less follow this model, as does Dryden's revised version of Sir William Soame's translation of Boileau's *L'Art Poétique* (1683). (For the interrelationship between Oldham and Dryden in this respect, see Brooks, 1949, pp. 134–7).

By contrast a second form of Imitation involves not just modernization but the deliberate alteration of meaning in order to create a different poem. Crucial works here are Cowley's imaginative transformations of Horace's *Ode* IV.ii. and *Ode* I.v. (1656), his 'paraphrase' of *Satire* II.vi. (1663), his version of *Epode* II (1668), and Sprat's completion of *Satire* II.vi. (1666). In these works details of the original poems are deliberately modified to create contrasts with Horace's meaning, and here the real 'freedom' of the Augustan imitation is pre-figured. Boileau's Imitations come into this category, such as his Epistle addressed to his book which is clearly modelled on Horace's *Epistle* I.xx. In this tradition also come Rochester's *Satyr against Mankind* (1676), an extremely free version of Boileau's *Satire* VIII, and the highly influential 'An Allusion to Horace' (c. 1678) based on Horace's *Satire* I.x. All these works really demand knowledge of the original for full effect.

The boundaries between these two types of Imitations are, however, very fluid, and individual works often defy classification. Two further points are important here. First, Imitations were often based on parts of a poem, as in the case of the Cowley/Sprat Imitations of parts of Horace's *Satire* II.vi. Swift's Imitation of the fable from *Satire* II.vi. and the beginning of *Epistle* I.vii., are examples of this, as are his Imitations of sections of *Ode* III.ii. and *Ode* IV.ix. Second, Boileau's favourite form was a free Imitation which consisted of an eclectic blending together of imitations of different sections of different works. This 'pastiche' form is found in Boileau's *Satire* I which adopts very freely the situation of Juvenal's *Satire* III but incorporates also sections from Juvenal's *Satire* VII. Although this eclectic form was not widely imitated Boileau's generally free approach to subject matter was. Boileau, indeed, shows all the freedom of Cowley and Rochester, contrasting Paris with Rome as well as comparing them, and introducing moral views and Christian conclusions which stand against the Juvenalian model, anticipating Pope's *Imitations* and Samuel Johnson's practice in *London* and *The Vanity of Human Wishes*.[3]

Finally we must consider the antecedents of Pope's parallel Latin and English texts. Restoration Imitations virtually never contained parallel texts, but, as Weinbrot (1966) has demonstrated, one source of this is in the practice of the Restoration Parodists. In Charles Cotton's *Scarronides* ... *Being the First Book of Virgils Aeneis in English, Burlésque* (1664), a parody of the first book of the *Aeneid*, the relevant passages of Latin are at the bottom of the page and 'the reader is desired for the better comparing of the *Latin* and *English* together, to read on forward to the ensuing Letter of Direction' before comparing the two (quoted Weinbrot, 1969, p. 26). This practice very likely inspired a similar procedure for formal Imitation. The first known instance of this is Thomas Wood's *Juvenal Redivivus, or The First Satyr of Juvenal Taught to Speak Plain English* (1683) where the Latin parallels are printed at the bottom of the page.

Complete texts of the original, however, were not always printed with Imitations in the early eighteenth century; very often only relevant passages, or extracts, or just the first few words of each consecutive paragraph of the complete Latin poem were given. Swift sometimes provided no Latin, sometimes only extracts. Johnson printed *London* and *The Vanity of Human Wishes* with just a few words indicating the beginning of the Latin paragraphs, presumably assuming the reader had his own copy of Juvenal to hand if he wished. Very occasionally, whole poems were reproduced: Rochester's 'Allusion to Horace' was published with the complete text in 1714. But in 1731 Charles Carthy came closest to anticipating Pope's practice with his rather infamous Dublin edition of his translation of Horace's *Epistles Book* II, which contained a complete text of the original facing his own lame translation. This however, if Pope even knew it, was not a very illustrious model: Carthy was nicknamed Mezentius as a result, after the King of Caere in Etruria notorious for his torture of living victims by tying them to dead bodies (see Swift, *Poems*, ed. Williams, II, p. 665).

IMITATIONS OF HORACE 1730–40

It is important to realize that between 1730 and 1740 thirty-eight Imitations of Horace were published quite apart from Pope's (see appendix). During this period George Ogle was Pope's chief competitor as 'Imitator of Horace', writing thirteen Imitations (not including the anonymous *Three Odes*, 1739, which may have been written by him). Ogle came to specialize in the Horatian epistle, publishing eleven Imitations of *Epistles* I. Several are impressive in various respects, notably his *Imitation of Epistle I.i.* (1735), as we shall see in Chapter 11. But for the most part they show how difficult it was to imitate the distinctive features of this form. More successful, in fact, are Ogle's Imitations of *Satire* II.v. (*Of Legacy-Hunting*) and *Satire* II.viii. (*The Miser's Feast*). Both of the originals are, of course, particularly aggressive Horatian satires, and Ogle's Imitations underline a general point: that it was easier to imitate the Horace of trenchant satire than the Horace of more refined wit, but it was even harder to re-create the Horace of retreat and the inner self. George Ogle's standard printing device is also significant: he printed only key words and phrases at the bottom of the page of his Imitation with index numbers linking them to the relevant point in his own text. The 'neglected' parts of the Horatian poem were represented by black lines (see an example in note 6 to Chapter 11 below).

Another Imitator of Horace at this time was James Miller, notable for writing two of the three Imitations of the *Ars Poetica*. *Harlequin-Horace* (1731), which uses modern authors in a rough equivalent of Horace's argument in the *Ars Poetica*, is interesting in that it anticipates Pope's practice in his *Imitation of Epistle II.i.* ('To Augustus'), particularly Pope's section on the theatre. Miller's *Art of Life* (1739), however, is striking in that it shows the persistence of the 'pastiche' approach to Imitation. Here Horace's poem on literary criticism is turned into a poem about the nature of moral life. Horace's *Ars Poetica* was, in fact, very often subjected to this kind of pastiche: the most popular were [William King], *The Art of Cookery* (1708), [James Bramston], *The Art of Politicks* (1729), [R. Dodsley] *The Art of Preaching* (?1735), anon., *The Art of Architecture* (1742), anon., *The Art of Stock-jobbing* (1746). Even if the complete Latin poem was printed at the bottom of the page, or if there were merely selected passages, comparison merely revealed that there was no substantial relationship between Horace's poem and the Imitation, there was merely a surface parody. Miller's other Imitation *Seasonable Reproof* (1735) is interesting in that it is a rare example of Boileau's form of mixed Imitation bringing together both *Satire* i.iii. and iv. This was unusual, although Paul Whitehead's *The State of Rome* (1739) was another example of the form, based on passages from Juvenal and Persius. *Seasonable Reproof* shows also the influence of Pope's printing practice: the Latin poetry is printed on the left-hand page in italics with key words in Roman type.

The Imitations of odes form a more varied group. It is notable that most Imitations of odes are on political subjects adapting Horace's public poems to contemporary political situations. Examples are Swift's Imitation of *Ode* i.xiv. (1730), the anonymous [?Henry Hyde] Imitation of *Ode* iv.ii. (1737), and the anonymous Imitations of *Odes* iii.ii. and ii.i., called *Horace's Instructions to the Roman Senate* (1740). Such works often include, of course, panegyric on contemporary public figures, modelled either thoughtfully or obsequiously on Horace's praise of public men. Imitations of Horace's odes on retreat and inner integrity are, of course, also very common, a curious example, with political overtones, being the anonymous Imitation of *Ode* i.xxii. [?1740]. Within this context Pope's Imitations of *Odes* iv.i. and ix. are, as we shall see, quite individual.

Imitations of epodes in this ten-year period form an interesting category. Røstvig's (1962) study of the 'Beatus ille' tradition might suggest that *Epode* II would figure prominently. It is significant that it does not appear at all among these printed Imitations. Instead we find a sardonic Imitation of the mock-heroic *Epode* III (1735) by J. Mitchell, and in 1739 two political Imitations of *Epode* XVI, pleading for the ending of internal disharmony within England and the creation of a new national spirit in the war against Spain. The Imitations of *Epode* XVI should be seen in the context of the Imitations of Horace's other poems about Roman corruption and civil war, notably the two Imitations of *Ode* III.vi. called *England's Sin, and Shame* (1672) and *The Causes of Scotland's Miseries* (1700). We should bear these Imitations in mind when we read Pope's darker studies of the England of his time in his Imitations of 1738.

POPE'S PRACTICE

How do Pope's *Imitations* relate to these traditions? At the simplest level of structure Pope, in the major *Imitations*, treats whole poems as continuous works. Much more significantly, Pope's presentation of parallel texts went much further than any of his predecessors and most of his contemporaries. With the exception of the first editions of the *Imitation of Epistle II.i.* and *II.ii.* Pope printed every Imitation with a complete parallel text of the original on the facing page (or at the bottom of the page in some of the later editions). In addition, as explained in the preface, he 'prepared' the Horatian texts to encourage the closest possible comparison between the texts.

But most important of all Pope's treatment of his Horatian models was at once much more complex and much more intense than his Restoration and 'Augustan' predecessors and contemporaries. There is extraordinary variation in modes of imitation within a single poem: the terms which can more or less describe those practices are inadequate to deal with Pope's highly flexible treatment of the subtleties of Horace's form and the minute details of his language. At one point in a single poem Pope seems to be a free translator modernizing Horace's meaning as Oldham had done; at another point he completely transforms Horace's meaning in the manner of Cowley or Rochester; at another point he alludes to a different Horatian poem or adopts a different Horatian style in the manner of Boileau; and then, suddenly, he returns to close rendering again as if he is after all only 'modernizing' Horace. The parallel texts repeatedly underline the essential point: that as an imitator Pope's relationship with Horace is profoundly paradoxical, involving both the minutest connections of word, tone, and nuance and the greatest freedom and individuality of expression.

Clearly this practice has the closest affinity with the free style of Cowley, Rochester, and Boileau; but what is striking, as we shall see in the very first *Imitation of Satire II.i.*, is the power of this paradoxical play of simultaneous involvement with Horace and divergence from him. The point can be underlined, perhaps, by considering the language of Dryden's famous distinction between the various types of imitation in the 'Preface to the Translation of Ovid's Epistles' (1680). Summarizing the whole debate about free translation, Dryden asserts that there are three ways of 'translating' an author: the first he calls 'metaphrase' or 'turning an author word by word, and line by line, from one language into another'; the second is 'paraphrase' or 'translation with latitude' where the author's 'words are not so strictly followed as his sense'; and the 'third way is that of imitation, where the translator (if now he has not lost that name) assumes the liberty, not only to vary from the words and sense, but to forsake them both as he sees occasion; and taking some general hints from the original, to run division on the groundwork, as he pleases' (*Essays*, ed. Ker, 1926, I, p. 237).

This definition of Imitation admirably describes the free Restoration Imitation: taking 'some general hints from the original' and running 'division on the groundwork' is exactly how Cowley had treated Horace's *Ode* I.v., or how Rochester in *The Satyr against Mankind* (1676) had treated Boileau's *Satire* VIII, and it prefigures how Swift would treat Horace's *Satire* I.vi. and *Epistle* I.vii. But it does not fully account for Pope's characteristic manner in poems which were, after all, written fifty years after Dryden's definition. Compared with these examples Pope's practice is more like 'metaphrase', 'paraphrase' and 'imitation' rolled into one.[4]

Only sustained and detailed analysis of a whole poem can reveal this and that is why I have discussed such tensions particularly fully in the first Imitation. But the dynamic relationship between Pope's parallel texts has further consequences. Pope seems to invite not mere recollection of the original as the Restoration imitators desired, but an active re-reading of those well-known poems. His Latin texts incorporate his own choice of variant readings, and the words in roman type acquire in themselves special force. Furthermore, next to the moving mirror of Pope's Imitation the Latin itself looks different, and certainly, at times, might be excused for not knowing itself. In addition, the original presentation of *Imitations* makes the experience of reading different from that of most poetry. We can read each poem from beginning to end on its own, or we can read, as it were, partly horizontally, back and forth, across the page. Reading the Imitations is an invitation to re-read Horace, and then to read the Imitations again, and to appreciate these poems fully we probably must do all these things: in this world of imitation all reading is re-reading.

These points raise questions which relate to those discussed in the previous chapter. How much is the Horatian text here an authority, and imitating Horace very much speaking in *Horace's* person? How much, by contrast, is the Horatian original merely a foil to Pope's own personality and thought? How much does Pope actually criticize the very poems he 'imitates'? Pope's general 'Advertisement' to the *Imitations* suggests one view: '*The Occasion of publishing these* Imitations *was the Clamour raised on some of my* Epistles. *An Answer from* Horace *was both more full, and of more Dignity, than any I cou'd have made in my own person*' (*TE*, IV, p. 3). Yet it is clear this is not the whole story. As we shall see, Pope's identification with Horace and his texts in the *Imitations* involves at once an appreciation of Horace's forms, language and vision, a criticism of their limitations, and an imaginative and creative extension of their possibilities.

One final point about Pope's *Imitations* must be made before turning to the poems: though it is hard to judge, it seems doubtful whether Pope's contemporaries fully appreciated the originality and the challenge of these poems. Two significant examples can be cited. First, there is no doubt that Pope's contemporaries recognized the need for the closest comparison between the Latin and English texts: the editions of Warburton and Warton, and Johnson's comments on the *Imitations*, make that clear. But their notes urge readers not only to compare but to evaluate which was 'better', the Pope or the Horace. This would seem to involve to some extent a constraint upon the texts. Whereas we tend to be struck by the 'openness' created by the parallel texts, they may have felt the need to 'close' them. Second, there is no doubt that, as Weinbrot (1969, Chapter I) has urged, all forms of imitation were profoundly respected in the eighteenth century in education, aesthetic theory, art, political theory and architecture, precisely because it implied the existence of general truth and the idea that there was such a thing as general human nature. As Dryden put it in 'A Parallel of Poetry and Painting: Prefixed to the Version of Du Fresnoy, *De Arte Graphica*' (1695), 'Nature is still the same in all ages, and can never be contrary to herself' (*Essays*, ed. Ker, 1926, II, p. 134). Johnson's appeal to 'general nature' as the ultimate criterion of aesthetic judgement in the 'Preface to Shakespeare' and *Rasselas*, Chapter 10 suggests the same. Richard Hurd's 'Discourse concerning Poetical Imitation' (1751) justifies borrowing and imitation of the classics in the same terms: '*similarity of mind* ... like that of outward *form* and *make*' has been given to the whole species. 'We are all furnished with the same original *properties and affections*, as with the same stock of *perceptions and ideas*' (1753, II, p. 135).

But is this what Pope's *Imitations of Horace* really suggest? How far in fact do they suggest the opposite: that local 'manners' and minute particulars are more alive and more important for identity than 'general nature'? How far do they suggest that the self is even more complex than Horace thought, or that 'Nature' might, indeed, contradict herself? How much do they imply that no one can ever be 'Horace' again?[5]

PART II
Three Horatian satires (1733–4)

Raillery and energy:
The Imitation of Satire II.i.

Dans cette premiere Satire il y a une plaisanterie continuelle ...
André Dacier (VII, p. 18)

have you seen my imitation of Horace? I fancy it will make you smile; but though, when I first began it, I thought of you; before I came to end it, I considered it might be too ludicrous, to a man of your situation and grave acquaintance, to make you Trebatius, who was yet one of the most considerable lawyers of his time, and a particular friend of the poet. In both which circumstances I rejoice that you resemble him, but am chiefly pleased that you do it in the latter.
Pope to Fortescue, Sunday 18 February, 1733.

IN DECEMBER 1731 Pope's *Epistle to Burlington* caused a major stir for what was taken to be its ridicule of Lord Chandos and Cannons in the portrait of Timon and his villa. The critical reception of this poem made Pope hold back from publication the even more dangerous *Epistle to Bathurst*, with its severe criticism of such powerful figures as Peter Walter and Francis Chartres. By the winter of 1733 however, he must have felt it was time to proceed. It was just at this point, when Pope was ill in bed that Bolingbroke, visiting him, happened to pick up a copy of Horace by his bed, and, turning to *Satire* II.i., remarked how similar Pope's case was to Horace's as described in that poem. This, it seems, was all that was needed: Pope imitated the satire in just two mornings, published 15 January the *Epistle to Bathurst*, and then on 15 February brought out his first *Imitation of Horace* which is in part a defence of that epistle.

Horace's *Satire* II.i. is a lively dramatic debate between Horace and his lawyer friend, Trebatius, ostensibly about whether or not Horace should continue to write satire. The real subject of the poem, however, is finely equivocal: on the one hand it is a very light-hearted defence of Horace's own satire; on the other hand, it contains a challenging portrait of Lucilius, the first Roman satirist, and in this it offers more searching thoughts about satire and the nature of 'the satirist'. The distinctive achievement of the poem, indeed, is to hold these two together, so that throughout the poem the idea of 'Horace' gives rise to 'Lucilius' and the idea of 'Lucilius' gives rise to 'Horace'. Pope's Imitation of this poem began as a defence of the satire of the *Epistles to Burlington* and *Bathurst*, but it became much more. In writing this Imitation Pope discovered at one stroke a whole new world of poetry, and found as well, in the two figures of Horace's poem, a whole new vision of himself.

In order to appreciate this fully we must have some idea of how Horace's satire was read in the eighteenth century, and here André Dacier's commentary provides the most detailed guidance. In his introductory 'Remarques' on this poem Dacier emphasizes its lively raillery which he says had not been sufficiently recognized by earlier commentators:

Dans cette premiere Satire il y a une plaisanterie continuelle, & qui a esté connuë de fort peu de gens. Horace rebuté par tout ce qu'on disoit de ses Satires, va trouver le plus habile Jurisconsulte de son temps, pour luy demander conseil. Il luy propose donc la chose. Ce Jurisconsulte, d'un ton de Legislateur, luy ordonne de n'écrire plus. Horace au lieu de se rendre, combat ses raisons.

(VII, pp. 18–19. Desprez and Baxter also comment on the light tone of this poem and note its many puns.)

But Dacier also sees that there is something ironic in this whole encounter, because, as he points out, neither Horace nor Trebatius actually alters his position in the course of the conversation, and at the end Horace simply goes on writing satire: 'Et la fin de cette Comedie est, que le Jurisconsulte ne démord point de son premier avis, & qu'Horace continuë à faire des Satires' (VII, p. 19). By emphasizing this Dacier has touched on something of this poem's distinctive irony, and his explanation of it is in itself quite shrewd. He suggests that people generally ask advice not to correct themselves but only to confirm themselves in what is natural and habitual to them: 'C'est en vain que les hommes demandent conseil sur les choses ausquelles ils sont portez naturellement. Il n'arrive mesme presque jamais qu'ils le demandent pour se corriger. Ils ne cherchent d'ordinaire qu'à flater leurs inclinations, & qu'à se confirmer dans leurs habitudes' (VII, p. 19).

It is important also that Dacier emphasizes both the theatricality of the poem and its accurate portrayal of particular people and events, blending together so finely, as it were, fiction and fact. He stresses, indeed, that all Horace's satires of the second book are what he calls 'Pieces de Theatre' in which the dialogue is sharply accurate: 'Au reste, si ce second Livre de Satires est plus fort que le premier, il est aussi plus agréable; car toutes ses Satires sont autant de Pieces de Theatre, où la Dialogue est admirablement bien observé' (Dacier adds this comment in his later editions: here, 1709, VII, p. 17). In this respect he comments on Trebatius' reserved style of speaking and his witty use of serious legal language. In describing Trebatius' character as revealed in Cicero's letters, he emphasizes how much the dialogue reflects what Trebatius was actually like; and suggests convincingly that Trebatius was chosen for the dialogue because he liked this kind of raillery, and because he was known to be good at it. 'Tout cela,' he says 'augment la plaisanterie de cette Satire' (VII, p. 22).

Dacier sees the poem as a whole, therefore, as a fine piece of raillery, and in his commentary he focuses perceptively on the poem's overall play of wit and its persistent punning. This interpretation is very similar to that of Niall Rudd who has more recently called the poem 'the most brilliant piece of shadow-boxing in Roman literature' (1966, p. 128). One further feature of Dacier's interpretation is however, for our purposes, important: his treatment of the figure of Lucilius in Horace's poem. Dacier appreciates fully the importance of the play between the Lucilius and Horace as his young follower, noting that much of it is ironical, and he comments intelligently on the poem's two important characterizations of Lucilius. He makes virtually no comment, however, on the one line which Pope saw as being the key to Horace's assessment of Lucilius, and, for his own purposes, the key to the whole of Horace's poem: the remark that Lucilius was 'scilicet uni aequus virtuti atque ejus amicis' (line 70 – 'indulgent to none but Virtue and her friends').

Pope put this line on the title-page of his Imitation, and in doing so, pointed to what would be at the heart of the work: for Pope the central question of *Horace*'s poem, to be explored in his Imitation, was, how far the energy of satiric writing is fundamentally moral. Satiric energy is found both in the vitality of Horatian wit and irony, and in the savage power of Lucilian invective; and Pope discovers both within himself. If the writing of such satire is as 'natural' as Dacier suggests, then is the energy of the self also moral? Or, is the poet's 'true self' created only in the language of his poetry? By raising such questions Pope's Imitation makes us look afresh at the whole of Horace's famous satire, and look again at Pope himself.

The playful character of *Satire* II.i. is clear right from the beginning. Horace, the satirist, explains his predicament to Trebatius with wry wit, and he in turn responds with amusing brevity and sardonic irony:

> HOR. [1]*Sunt quibus in Satyra videar nimis acer, & ultra*
> *Legem tendere opus;* [2]*sine nervis altera quicquid*
> *Composui pars esse putat, similesque meorum*
> *Mille die versus* deduci *posse.* [3]*Trebati!*
> *Quid faciam?* Praescribe.

TREB. [4]*Quiescas.*
　　　　　HOR. *Ne faciam inquis,*
Omnino versus?
　TREB. *Aio.*
　　　HOR. *Peream male si non*
Optimum erat: [5]*verum nequeo dormire.*
　　　　　TREB. [6]*Ter uncti*
Transnanto Tiberim, somno quibus est opus alto,
Irriguumve mero sub noctem corpus habento.
　[7]*Aut, si tantus amor scribendi te rapit, aude*
CAESARIS *invicti res dicere,* [8]*multa laborum*
Praemia laturus.　　　　　　　　　　　　　(1–12)

(HOR. For some I seem too sharp in satire and to stretch what I write beyond the legal limit; others think that everything I have composed lacks muscle, and that a thousand lines like mine could be spun in a day. Trebatius! What am I to do? Give your opinion.

TREB. Keep quiet.

HOR. You say I shouldn't write verses at all?

TREB. I do.

HOR. I'll be damned if that isn't the best course; but I can't sleep.

TREB. Persons in need of deep sleep should anoint themselves and swim three times across the Tiber, or ensure that their bodies are soused with neat wine at nightfall. Or else, if such a great passion for writing seizes you, have the courage to declaim in verse the achievements of Caesar the unconquered; you'd be sure to carry off many rewards for your labours.)

Dacier comments well on the witty ironies of this opening, showing that the details of language are important (VII, pp. 19–24). Horace claims to be concerned with the way in which his satire is received, and yet he does so with delightful irony: some think it is too sharp ('*nimis acer*'), others too feeble ('*sine nervis*'). For some it goes beyond decency and indeed the libel law (a nice pun on '*ultra / Legem*'), while for others it appears weakly spun out ('*deduci*'). Horace's anxiety here appears to be somewhat high-spirited.

When Trebatius is appealed to there is a neat play on the word '*faciam*': '*Quid faciam?*' ('What am I to do?') provokes the reply '*Quiescas*' ('Keep quiet'), and the ironic return '*Ne faciam*' ('I shouldn't write'). And then in response to Horace's amused afterthought that he writes because he cannot sleep ('*verum nequeo dormire*'), Trebatius offers ironical remedies for insomnia, with the heavy third-person imperatives of legal jargon for the verbs ('*Transnanto*' – 'let them swim' and '*habento*' – 'let them sleep') and a generalized subject for the recipient of his official advice ('*quibus est*' – 'Persons in need'). Only after ironically referring to the desire to write poetry as a madness that carries one away ('*rapit*') does he suggest the idea that Horace might write not satire but panegyrics on

Caesar's exploits and gain many rewards ('*multa* . . . Praemia'). This advice might be serious but the tone is still equivocal.

In his opening Pope catches brilliantly the distinctive tones of the Latin, adapts everything in Horace to his own situation, and gives us a winning portrait of both himself and his own lawyer friend, William Fortescue. We know we have heard it all before, and yet it is all fresh and alive – experienced again in a new poet and a new poetry:

> P. There are (I scarce can think it, but am told)
> [1]There are to whom my Satire seems too bold,
> Scarce to wise *Peter* complaisant enough,
> And something said of *Chartres* much too rough.
> [2]The Lines are weak, another's pleas'd to say,
> Lord *Fanny* spins a thousand such a Day.
> Tim'rous by Nature, of the Rich in awe,
> [3]I come to Council learned in the Law.
> You'll give me, like a Friend both sage and free,
> Advice; and (as you use) without a Fee.
> F. [4]I'd write no more.
>   P. Not write? but then I *think*,
> [5]And for my Soul I cannot sleep a wink.
> I nod in Company, I wake at Night,
> Fools rush into my Head, and so I write.
> F. You could not do a worse thing for your Life.
> Why, if the Nights seem tedious – take a Wife;
> [6]Or rather truly, if your Point be Rest,
> Lettuce and Cowslip Wine; *Probatum est.*
> But talk with *Celsus, Celsus* will advise
> Hartshorn, or something that shall close your Eyes.
> [7]Or if you needs must write, write CAESAR's Praise:
> [8]You'll gain at least a *Knighthood*, or the *Bays*.   (1–22)

It is impossible to describe this adaptation of Horace in simple terms, that it is either 'like' or 'unlike' Horace. Every point in Pope has been inspired by Horace, and yet every point is different. And it is this lively, endlessly open, play between the texts which makes reading the poem as an Imitation so invigorating. Each poetry seems to open up the other and give it new vitality. What we are aware of is the endless play of similarity and disparity, re-creation and transgression.

Here the transformations take place in the language of self-portraiture. Pope recreates the bright tone of Horace's opening few lines, but at the same time gives them a new vigour and sharper satiric edge. To Horace's '*nimis acer*' Pope adds a perfect Horatian irony, '(I scarce can think it, but am told)', and then while keeping the surface perfectly smooth, he drives home with back-handed thrusts at '*Peter*' and '*Chartres*', fresh victims of the *Epistle to Bathurst*. Horace's '*sine nervis*' (without muscle, 'weak') in Pope gives rise to a cutting little aside, 'another's pleas'd to say'; and seizing on the 'deduci' ('spin out') of '*similesque meorum* / *Mille die versus* deduci *posse*' Pope audaciously turns the line into a throw-away swipe at Lord Hervey, only reporting, of course, what someone else has said: 'Lord *Fanny* spins a thousand such a Day.' In reading these lines we are at once deep in Horace and deep in the London of 1737 as experienced by Pope. Horace concentrates attention on his clear, dry ironies; Pope instinctively, it seems, makes each irony double-edged. Horace thinks of himself in relation to a general public; Pope's lines bristle with living personalities. From the beginning we realize that the power of Pope's satire lies in its power to offend, and if it is to be defended, it has to be defended in those terms.

As Pope goes on he presents an amusing and engaging picture of himself as personality and as satirist, bringing to the fore not Horace's play on '*faciam*' but on the afterthought, '*verum nequeo dormire*' ('but I can't sleep'). All this is done with the lightest touch, following on from the tongue-in-cheek irony of 'Tim'rous by Nature, of the Rich in awe.' We should not, I think, take too seriously the Juvenalian hints of 'Fools rush into my Head, and so I write.' These lines on writing as the cure for 'thought', insomnia, and the nightly attack of fools, seem to me sheer self-delight, much more lively than the Juvenalian allusions would seem to suggest: 'difficile est saturam non scribere' ('it is difficult *not* to write satire') and 'facit indignatio versum' ('indignation will produce my verse'), *Satire* I, 30 and 79.

Fortescue's advice is exactly in the spirit of Trebatius' sardonic irony, and perfectly adapted to Pope's own life:

> Why, if the Nights seem tedious – take a Wife;
> Or rather truly, if your Point be Rest,
> Lettuce and Cowslip Wine; *Probatum est*.   (16–18)

To Horace's '*mero*' ('wine') Pope adds 'Lettuce' often regarded in the eighteenth century as an anaphrodisiac (see *TE*, IV, p. 5), and then he gives Fortescue his own bit of legal Latin '*Probatum est*'. Fortescue can now slip easily into a Roman context and advise Pope, as Trebatius could well have advised Horace, to 'talk with *Celsus*', the chief Roman writer on medicine, who will advise, however, a fashionable prescription in eighteenth-century London, 'Hartshorn', or, with nice double meaning for a satirist, 'something that shall close your Eyes'. This lively play between the texts is rounded off with a 'straight' translation of 'CAESARIS' in 'CAESAR'S

Praise', and the neat transformation of '*multa* ... Praemia' into 'a *Knighthood*, or the *Bays*'.

In the section that follows Horace plays wittily on the possibility and impossibility of writing panegyric instead of satire, and introduces for the first time the example of Lucilius. He is mentioned, however, rather obliquely, as the praiser of Scipio rather than as the first great Roman satirist. The idea of Lucilius arises here from the notion that Horace might praise Caesar's martial achievements:

> HOR. *Cupidum, pater optime! vires*
> *Deficiunt:* [9]*neque enim quivis* horrentia pilis
> *Agmina, nec* fracta pereuntes cuspide Gallos,
> *Aut* labentis equo *describat vulnera Parthi.*
> TREB. [10]*Attamen & justum poteras & scribere fortem,*
> *Scipiadam ut sapiens Lucilius.*
> HOR. *Haud mihi deero,*
> *Cum res ipsa feret.* [11]*Nisi* dextro tempore *Flacci*
> *Verba per attentam non ibunt* Caesaris *aurem;*
> *Cui male si palpere, recalcitrat undique tutus.* (12–20)

(HOR. I am willing enough, good sir, but I haven't the strength; because it's not everyone who will dare to put down on paper 'battle columns bristling with javelins' or 'Gauls slain, spears shattered', or 'the wounds of a Parthian toppled from his horse'.
TREB. Even so you could write how he is both just and brave, like wise Lucilius did of Scipio.
HOR. I shan't let myself down when the subject matter itself demands it. Not until the right moment will Flaccus's words enter the emperor's pricked-up ear. If you stroke that horse clumsily it kicks back, wary at every point.)

Here we see the first of the many *recusatio* passages we shall find in Horace's texts, i.e. a refusal to do something, made in language which in some sense actually does what is 'refused' (from *recuso* which means 'to object to, to protest against, or refuse'). Stylistically this particular passage is very interesting, because it is a clear blending of serious and amusing *recusatio*. The tone of *recusatio* in Horace always seems to be unstable, its stance always verging on the ironic, but here the comedy is very overt. The tone of Horace's '*pater optime*' is 'sincere', and the idea of Horace's praising Caesar quite possible at this time in Horace's career; but the epic language of what follows is ironically forced: 'horrentia pilis / Agmina' (battle columns bristling with javelins'), the usual Gauls and the usual troublesome Parthian, in the usual epic periphrasis, 'labentis ... vulnera Parthi' (literally 'the wounds of the falling Parthian'). Trebatius quickly changes course, and suggests that, rather than Caesar's military exploits, Horace might praise Caesar's other qualities, as one '*justum* ... *& fortem*' ('both just and brave'), much as wise ('*sapiens*') Lucilius once wrote of Scipio. This again could be serious, but Horace replies with lively irony and outrageous puns: '*Nisi* dextro tempore ... *non ibunt*' is a rather spectacular double negative ('Not until the right moment'); '*Flacci / Verba*' puns on Horace's name, Quintus Horatius Flaccus and 'flaccus' ('floppy-eared', 'a mule') to suggest 'the words of an ass or a Horace'; and then this is suddenly and daringly transformed into an image of Caesar himself who, if stroked clumsily kicks back ('*recalcitrat*'), wary at every point ('*undique tutus*').

Pope certainly responded to these ambiguous tones and these lively and potentially very subversive puns. His text of the first lines of the Horace emphasizes the heavy epic diction of the Latin; and in his imitation he transforms this diction into a bathetic parody of Blackmore and Budgell;

> P. What? like Sir [9]*Richard*, rumbling, rough and fierce,
> With ARMS, and GEORGE, and BRUNSWICK crowd the Verse?
> Rend with tremendous Sound your ears asunder,
> With Gun, Drum, Trumpet, Blunderbuss & Thunder?
> Or nobly wild, with *Budgell*'s Fire and Force,
> Paint Angels trembling round his *falling Horse*?   (23–8)

The contrast between Pope's and Dacier's 'readings' of the Horatian passage here is interesting. What we find, in fact, is that Pope has used Dacier's commentary against Dacier's own interpretation of the text. In his note on 'horrentia pilis / Agmina', Dacier quotes Ennius' line '*Sparsis hastis longe* [*sic*] *campus splendet & horret.*' ('The plain shines and bristles with spears scattered far and wide.') He explains that Lucilius had ridiculed Ennius' use of 'horret' ('bristles') and argues that Horace in fact was using the word seriously. This is not very convincing, and Pope has simply opted for the Lucilian mockery, neatly making Blackmore a new ludicrous Ennius. Dacier also suggests that '*Aut* labentis equo *describat vulnera Parthi*' refers to the defeat of Pacorus, king of the Parthians, by Ventidius, and notes the significance of 'labentis equo' – the Parthians were famous for their cavalry (VII, pp. 25–6). This was too much for Pope: in a wonderful stroke of flagrant mis-translation, 'labentis equo' are yoked together, to parody both Budgell's absurd *Poem upon His Majesty's Late Journey to Cambridge and Newmarket* and the event it enshrined – George II's horse shot under him at the battle of Oudenarde:

> Or nobly wild, with *Budgell*'s Fire and Force,
> Paint Angels trembling round his *falling Horse*.   (27–8)

Here we see Pope playing with Horace's text for his own purposes, but in doing so he is developing possibilities latent in Horace's own audacious ironies. The constant punning that we find in this Horatian satire is more persistent and more infectious than we usually find in Horace's satires, and Pope develops it with even greater energy. We see this in the fine satiric imitation of what follows. Pope interestingly, in the light of what is to come, passes over the allusion to Lucilius; he has Fortescue offer other advice, and gives himself some sharp retorts:

> F. [10]Then all your Muse's softer Art display,
> Let *Carolina* smooth the tuneful Lay,
> Lull with *Amelia's* liquid Name the Nine,
> And sweetly flow through all the Royal Line.
>   P. [11]Alas! few Verses touch their nicer Ear;
> They scarce can bear their *Laureate* twice a Year:
> And justly CAESAR scorns the Poet's Lays,
> It is to *History* he trusts for Praise.   (29–36)

Now the other side of 'Caesar' apparently is Queen Caroline, who, ironically, might be celebrated in weak pastoral poetry. Horace's idea of writing only at the right time ('dextro tempore') produces a brilliant stroke, 'They scarce can bear their *Laureate* twice a Year'; and then Caesar's scorn for poetry is fully explained with dry irony: 'It is to *History* he trusts for Praise.'

The kind of free expansion of Horace's text seen here is found also in Pope's treatment of the next few lines of Horace. In the Latin Trebatius ignores Horace's pun on '*Flacci*' and Caesar as a nervous horse, and continues:

> TREB. [12]*Quanto rectius hoc, quam tristi laedere versu*
> *Pantolabum Scurram, Nomentanumve nepotem?*
> *Cum sibi quisque timet, quanquam est intactus, & odit.*   (21–3)

(TREB. Isn't this more correct than hurting 'Pantolabus the hanger-on, Nomentanus the spend-thrift' in harsh lines? – When each man fears for himself, although he's untouched, and hates you.)

As Dacier realised, Horace has Trebatius quote directly from Horace's own *Satire* I.viii. to make his point (Dacier, VII, p. 29):

> hoc miserae plebi stabat commune sepulcrum,
> Pantolabo scurrae Nomentanoque nepoti ...   (10–11)

(Here was the common burial-place fixed for pauper folk, for Pantolabus the parasite, and spendthrift Nomentanus.)

Significantly these stock names come from Lucilius, but Trebatius suggests, ironically, that the mere mention of these names of the parasite and the spendthrift causes others to be afraid.

Pope sees at once an opportunity to allude again to the *Moral Essays* and to explore in debate the significance of names:

> F. [12]Better be *Cibber*, I'll maintain it still,
> Than ridicule all *Taste*, blaspheme *Quadrille*,
> Abuse the City's best good Men in Metre,
> And laugh at Peers that put their Trust in *Peter*.
> [13]Ev'n those you touch not, hate you.
>
> P. What should ail 'em?
>
> F. A hundred smart in *Timon* and in *Balaam*:
> The fewer still you name you wound the more;
> *Bond* is but one, but *Harpax* is a Score.   (37–44)

For a moment Horace's *Satire* I.viii. becomes the *Epistle to Burlington* and the *Epistle to Bathurst*, and typically Pope twists Trebatius' simple point into intense paradox:

> The fewer still you name, you wound the more;
> *Bond* is but one, but *Harpax* is a Score.   (43–4)

Horace's '*laedere*' ('hurt') and '*odit*' ('hate') are strong; but Pope's 'A hundred smart in *Timon* and in *Balaam*', conveys positive delight in his power to hurt.

It is at this point that Horace, while seeming to veer away onto a new subject, actually picks up Trebatius' idea that Horace might write like Lucilius. We find here the first of two famous passages on Lucilius in this poem, and an assertion by Horace that he does in fact identify himself with that great satirist. But the portrait we are given here of Lucilius is in fact very unusual:

> HOR. [14]*Quid faciam? Saltat Milonius, ut semel icto*
> *Accessit fervor capiti numerusque lucernis.*
> [15]*Castor gaudet equis; ovo prognatus eodem*
> *Pugnis: quot capitum vivunt, totidem studiorum*
> *Millia:* [16]*me pedibus delectat claudere verba,*
> *Lucili ritu, nostrum melioris utroque.*
> *Ille, velut fidis arcana sodalibus olim*
> *Credebat libris; neque si male gesserat, usquam*
> *Decurrens alio, neque si bene: quo fit ut omnis*
> *Votiva pateat veluti descripta tabella*
> *Vita senis. Sequor hunc,* [17]*Lucanus an Appulus anceps:*
> *[Nam Venusinus arat finem sub utrumque colonus,*
> *Missus ad hoc pulsis (vetus est ut fama) Sabellis;*
> *Quo ne per vacuum Romano incurreret hostis,*
> [17]*Sive quod Appula gens, seu quod Lucania Bellum*
> *Incuteret violenta.]*   (24–39)

(HOR. What am I to do? Milonius dances when once the heat rushes to his drink-smitten head and he sees the lanterns spin round. Castor delights in horses; his brother, born of the same egg, in fist-fights. There are as many thousands of enthusiasms as there are individuals living. My pleasure is to confine words in metre in the manner of Lucilius, who was a better man than either of us. He in his time would confide his secrets to books as to trusted friends, neither in misfortune ever turning anywhere else, nor in success: hence it is that the old man's whole life lies open as if written up on a votive tablet. I'm his follower, even though I'm not certain whether I'm a Lucanian or Apulian; [for the settlers of Venusia plough on either side of the boundary; they were sent there when the Sabines were driven out (as the old story goes), so that the enemy could not attack the Romans across uninhabited territory, whether it was the Apulian tribesmen or violent Lucania fomenting war.])

This lively passage raises questions about the origins of the satirist and the origin of his satire. Horace first suggests ironically that writing satire is simply an instinctive delight similar to Milonius' drunken dancing, Castor's joy in horses, and Pollux's pleasure in boxing. Pollux is identified in an extraordinary mock-solemn periphrasis, lightly thrown off: 'Ovo prognatus eodem' ('the one born from the same egg'). The way he speaks about writing satire and Lucilius is in fact doubly ironic: *me pedibus delectat claudere verba, / Lucili ritu, nostrum melioris utroque* ('My pleasure is to confine words in metre in the manner of Lucilius, who was a better man than either of us'). On the one hand, satire is seen as merely an inoffensive exercise in imprisoning ('*claudere*') words in metre (similar in tone to Pope's 'The good man heaps up nothing but mere metre' from the *Imitation of Epistle II.i.* 198). This is hardly the way one normally thought about Lucilian satire, noted for its aggressive power. But it is ironic also for Horace to say of this aesthetic activity '*Lucili ritu*' ('in the manner of Lucilius'), for in all his previous poems on satire he had insisted that artistic perfection was in fact Lucilius' weakest point. He had all the inspirational vigour of a great writer but was careless in his form:

> ... facetus,
> emunctae naris, durus componere versus ...
> garrulus atque piger scribendi ferre laborem,
> scribendi recte: nam ut multum, nil moror.
>
> (*Satire* i.iv. 7–8, 12–13)

(Witty he was, and of keen-scented nostrils, but harsh in framing his verses ... He was wordy, and too lazy to put up with the trouble of writing – of writing correctly, I mean; for as to quantity, I let that pass.)

This allusion to Lucilius then is somewhat tongue-in-cheek, but what follows is not. In a mere five lines Horace gives a memorable picture of the origin, character, and significance of Lucilian satire. Lucilius' satires were like his faithful friends ('*fidis ... sodalibus*'), to them he entrusted the secrets (*'arcana'*) of his private self, and he never turned anywhere else, whether his life was going badly or going well (*'neque si male ... neque si bene'*). The result is that the whole life of the old man is open to view (*'pateat'*) as if inscribed on a votive tablet (*'Votiva ... tabella'*). A highly dramatic hyperbaton separates the *'omnis'* from the *'Vita senis'* to emphasize how total this portrait of the self is: 'the old man's whole life lies open'.

Dacier speaks warmly of this passage and stresses particularly how Lucilius' poetry reveals what was good and bad about his life: 'S'il estoit heureux, il leur disoit le sujet de sa joye; & s'il estoit malheureux, il ne leur cachoit pas ses chagrins' (VII, pp. 32–3). He emphasizes also the importance of the votive tablet simile, noting that it was an apt image because votive tablets could reveal the whole of one's life: 'C'est pourquoy, dit Horace, nous avons dans les Ecrits de ce grand Poëte toutes les particularitiez de sa Vie aussi exactement décrites, que s'il en avoit fait le tableau, pour le consacrer à quelque Dieu' (VII, p. 33). Finally, he stresses that the votive tablet, while a sacred object, was also very public. His note on *'pateat'* ('stand open, revealed') is: 'Est exposée aux yeux de tout le monde, comme les tableaux que l'on expose en public' (VII, p. 34).

Eduard Fraenkel (1957, pp. 145–53) more recently has con-vincingly suggested that this moving passage represents for Horace a very significant re-assessment of Lucilian satire. Previously, he argues, Horace saw Lucilius as the rough but vigorous satirist daring to attack anyone in his lively, improvisational verse. This is the Lucilius who had been Horace's model in his own early satires; but now, as Horace was maturing towards the more inward and contem-plative style of his epistles, he saw a different Lucilius. Here was the writer who was not a narrow satirist, but a man who wrote about all his interests and all his experiences – poetry, friendship, food, politics – and revealed in his poetry all of his inner life. Furthermore, Horace's old and new views together could suggest an important synthesis: that the writing of fierce invective was not in a simplistic way motivated only by malice and anger; rather satiric writing of such power could be part of the life of man who was singularly cultivated, introspective, moral, and candid. He was, indeed, Horace says rather pointedly to Trebatius, *'nostrum melioris utroque'* ('a better man than either of us').

Somewhat cryptically, after this fine appreciation, Horace says *'Sequor hunc, Lucanus an Appulus anceps'* ('I'm his follower, even though I'm not certain whether I'm a Lucanian or Apulian'), sugges-ting humorously that he writes satire so naturally because he comes from frontier stock. It is interesting that he mentions the uncertainty of his origin, Lucanian or Apulian, a dualism kept up in the description of the threat of war from either tribe: '*sive quod Appula gens, seu quod Lucania Bellum / Incuteret violenta*' ('whether it was the Apulian tribesmen or violent Lucania formenting war'). This detail is not of great significance in itself, but is so in terms of what Pope makes of it.

Pope's imitation of this whole passage is a real *tour de force*, a piece of inspired writing in which he assimilates the whole of Horace's portrait of Lucilius and transforms it into a highly dramatic image of himself. To Dacier the passage on Lucilius was Horace's tribute to the rich inwardness of Lucilian writing; to Fraenkel it was, in these terms, a moment of mature Horatian reflection. Who would have imagined that a poet could have found in it an image of his over-flowing poetic power and a justification for all its abundant, truth-telling energies?

> P. [14]Each Mortal has his Pleasure: None deny
> *Scarsdale* his Bottle, *Darty*, his Ham-Pye;
> *Ridotta* sips and dances, till she see
> The doubling Lustres dance as fast as she;
> [15]F – loves the *Senate*, *Hockley-Hole* his Brother
> Like in all else, as one Egg to another.
> [16]I love to pour out all myself, as plain
> As downright *Shippen*, or as old *Montagne*.
> In them, as certain to be lov'd as seen,
> The Soul stood forth, nor kept a Thought within;
> In me what Spots (for Spots I have) appear,
> Will prove at least the Medium must be clear.
> In this impartial Glass, my Muse intends
> Fair to expose myself, my Foes, my Friends;
> Publish the present Age, but where my Text
> Is Vice too high, reserve it for the next:
> My Foes shall wish my Life a longer date,
> And ev'ry Friend the less lament my Fate.
>   My Head and Heart thus flowing thro' my Quill,
> [17]Verse-man or Prose-man, term me which you will,
> Papist or Protestant, or both between,
> Like good *Erasmus* in an honest Mean,
> In Moderation placing all my Glory,
> While Tories call me Whig, and Whigs a Tory. (45–68)

Pope cleverly updates Milonius and Castor and Pollux into contemporary examples. He throws out quick thrusts at Scarsdale, who was known for his love of the bottle, and Dartineuf, famous as an epicure; and he ridicules the Fox brothers by turning the sense of 'ovo prognatus eodem' upside down, in 'Like in all else, as one Egg to another.' He then asserts that his pleasure lies in pouring out himself in poetry. This he puts deliberately in contrast to Horace's delighting in the rhythms of words (the index figures relate these two points), and this, deliberately or not, marks him as a real Lucilian satirist. For '*Lucili ritu*', however, Pope at first finds other examples: his confession is as plain as 'downright *Shippen*' (the leader of the Jacobite group in the House of Commons, noted for his integrity) and 'old *Montagne*'. Lucilius' secrets ('*arcana*') allow Pope to assert their essential candour:

> In them, as certain to be lov'd as seen,
> The Soul stood forth, nor kept a Thought within ...   (53–4)

For Pope these secrets then become the flaws which prove the purity of the medium of poetry;

> In me what Spots (for Spots I have) appear,
> Will prove at least the Medium must be clear.   (55–6)

Lucilius' religious votive tablet brilliantly becomes 'this impartial Glass' in which 'my Muse intends / Fair to expose myself, my Foes, my Friends.' Lucilius turned to his poems as his friends, whether things went badly or well, and his poems reveal the whole life of the old man. In Pope the sacred muse of poetry exposes the poet, his foes and friends, and the whole age as well; but she holds back the worst vice for the poems of the next age, with the result that his enemies wish him to live longer, and his friends worry less about his fate. The muse of poetry is the 'subject' of the lines, but the poetry is, all the same, exuberantly egocentric: 'my Muse', 'my Foes', 'my Text', 'my Life', 'my Fate'.

This intense and paradoxical writing involves an extraordinary series of transformations and cross-references from Horace's text. All details of Horace's language splinter into fragments only to come to life in a myriad of new forms and combinations:

'*Votiva ... tabella*' ('votive tablet') becomes: 'the medium', 'this impartial Glass', and then 'my Muse', 'my Text', 'the next'.

'*pateat*' ('be revealed') becomes: 'expose', and then 'Publish'.

'*fidis ... sodalibus*' ('trusted friends') becomes: 'my Friends', and 'ev'ry Friend'.

'*neque si male*' ('neither in misfortune') becomes: 'Vice too high', and then 'my Fate'.

'*neque si bene*' ('nor in success') becomes: 'Fair to expose', and 'the present Age', and 'less lament my Fate'.

'*omnis ... Vita*' ('the whole life') becomes: 'myself, my Foes, my Friends', then 'the present Age', and then 'the next'.

'*senis*' ('old') becomes: 'shall wish my Life a longer date', and then 'my Fate'.

This is imitation at its most powerful showing just how closely Pope read Horace's text, and at the same time how creative and energizing his imagination found that vivid reading.

Equally exuberant also is the flow of happy contradictions inspired by Horace's '*Lucanus an Appulus anceps*' ('whether I'm a Lucanian or Apulian') and '*Sive quod Appula gens, seu quod Lucania*' ('whether it was the Apulian tribesmen or violent Lucania'): 'Head and Heart', 'Verse-man or Prose-man', 'Papist or Protestant', 'While Tories call me Whig, and Whigs a Tory.' How significant that Pope can only think of himself in terms of contradiction, or as someone able to hold such contradictions together. Throughout his life Pope was a poet of human contradiction as was Horace, and, as we shall see, the contradictions of the self are a recurring theme throughout these *Imitations*. It is significant that in this Imitation Pope finds that he is both Horace and Lucilius: only by being both, it seems, could he express what he felt himself to be, 'My Head and Heart thus flowing thro' my Quill.'

Pope's identification of himself with Lucilius adds an important new dimension to the relationship between the parallel texts, because from this point on both Horace and Pope, in their own ways, 'play' Lucilius. Having humorously claimed that he is naturally aggressive because of his frontier ancestry, and that this is why he takes so readily to satire, Horace asserts that really, of course, he only strikes in self-defence. Again his language is enlivened with comic hyperbole and mock heroic exaggerations, as he plays Lucilius in a very light-hearted vein. The figure of Lucilius now gives way to the figure of 'Horace' again:

> [18]*Sed hic stylus haud petit ultro*
> *Quenquam animantem; & me veluti custodiet ensis*
> *Vagina tectus, quem cur distringere coner,*
> [19]*Tutus ab infestis latronibus?* [20]*O Pater & Rex*
> *Jupiter! ut pereat positum rubigine telum*
> *Nec quisquam noceat* [21] *cupido mihi pacis! at ille,*
> *Qui me commorit (melius non tangere clamo)*
> [22]*Flebit, & insignis tota cantabitur urbe.*   (39–46)

(But this pen of mine does not attack anyone alive without provocation; and it will guard me like a sword, even sheathed in its scabbard. Why should I try to draw it while I am safe from threatening robbers? O Jupiter, Father and King! – if only my weapon might perish from rust unused and no one harm me, who long for peace! But the man who has angered me ('better not touch me,' I yell) shall suffer for it, and his infamy shall be sung throughout the city.)

The tones are struck by the pun on '*stylus*' meaning both 'dagger' and 'pen', the exaggeration of '*O Pater & Rex / Jupiter!*', the comedy of '(*melius non tangere clamor*)' '('better not touch me' I yell)', the sharpness of '*Flebit*' ('he shall suffer for it'), and the idea of the infamous name sung ('*cantabitur*') up and down the whole town ('*tota ... urbe*'). (Dacier comments well on this irony, VII, p. 38.)

In his imitation of this passage Pope catches this tone acutely, and weaves together Horace's lively ironies and sharp contemporary allusions:

> [18]Satire's my Weapon, but I'm too discreet
> To run a Muck, and tilt at all I meet;
> [19]I only wear it in a Land of Hectors,
> Thieves, Supercargoes, Sharpers, and Directors.
> [20]Save but our *Army*! and let *Jove* incrust
> Swords, Pikes, and Guns, with everlasting Rust!
> [21]Peace is my dear Delight – not *Fleury*'s more:
> But touch me, and no Minister so sore.
> Who-e'er offends, at some unlucky Time
> [22]Slides into Verse, and hitches in a Rhyme,
> Sacred to Ridicule! his whole Life long,
> And the sad Burthen of some merry Song.   (69–80)

Pope here twists the Horace into some very contemporary satire. Horace's '*infestis latronibus*' ('threatening robbers') he identifies in the England of 1733 as being 'Hectors, / Thieves, Supercargoes, Sharpers, and Directors'; and Horace's '*ut pereat positum rubigine telum*' ('if only my weapon might perish from rust unused') becomes a superb jibe at the standing army ('Save but our *Army*!'). Pope manages to throw in so casually satiric thrusts at Fleury and Walpole's peace policy; and then to delight, along with Horace, in the poet's power to make any man he wishes 'his whole Life long ... the sad Burthen of some merry Song.' In these last two couplets Pope captures the implications of '*cantabitur*' which usually means to '*celebrate* in song', to praise someone in rhyme, and which contrasts sharply with its subject '*insignis*' ('distinguished', here for 'infamy').

These passages in both Horace and Pope are good-humoured, but in the section which follows the tones of both poets become darker. Horace suddenly asserts that everyone uses what powers they have to frighten those they fear, and he throws out some sinister little sketches to illustrate his point:

> [23]*Cervius iratus leges minitatur & urnam;*
> *Canidia Albuti, quibus est inimica, Venenum;*
> *Grande malum Turius, si quid se judice certes;*
> [24]*Ut, quo quisque valet, suspectus terreat, utque*
> *Imperet hoc natura potens; sic collige mecum.*
> *Dente lupus, cornu taurus petit; unde nisi intus*
> *Monstratum?* [25]*Scaevae vivacem crede nepoti*

Matrem: nil faciet sceleris pia dextra (mirum
Ut neque calce lupus quenquam, neque dente petit bos)
Sed mala tollet anum vitiato melle cicuta. (47–56)

(An enraged Cervius threatens one with laws and the judges' urn; Canidia threatens her enemies with Albutius's poison; Turius threatens you with heavy damages if you go to law over something when he's a judge. Everyone uses his own special strengths to frighten those he mistrusts, and sovereign nature ordains this: work it out with me. The wolf attacks with his tooth, the bull with his horn; how, unless taught by instinct? Entrust to the spendthrift Scaeva ('Lefty') a hale and hearty mother, his reverent right hand will do nothing criminal (amazing? – like the wolf not kicking and the ox not biting), but what will dispatch the old woman will be deadly hemlock in tainted honey.)

Cervius and Turius are shown using the law itself to vent their anger ('*iratus*') and their power. Canidia, one of Horace's persistent *bêtes noires*, uses the poison of Albutius on her enemies. The spendthrift 'Scaeva' ('Lefty') will do nothing at all to an old matron with his pious right hand (a sarcastic little pun on '*Scaevae*' and '*dextra*'), but he will get rid of her with deadly hemlock ('*mala ... cicuta*') in honey.

Pope clearly saw the force of these comic but bitter sketches, and in his imitation he produces the darkest and most cutting lines of his poem by picking up Horace's references to poison and turning them into images of poisonous slander and the corrupted *word*:

[23]Slander or Poyson, dread from *Delia's* Rage,
Hard Words or Hanging, if your Judge be *Page*
From furious *Sappho* scarce a milder Fate,
P–x'd by her Love, or libell'd by her Hate:
[24]Its proper Pow'r to hurt, each Creature feels,
Bulls aim their horns, and Asses lift their heels,
'Tis a Bear's Talent not to kick, but hug,
And no man wonders he's not stung by Pug:
[25]So drink with *Waters*, or with *Chartres* eat,
They'll never poison you, they'll only cheat. (81–90)

The poison of Albutius with which Canidia threatens her enemies ('*Canidia Albuti, quibus est inimica, Venenum*') becomes in Pope a sinister fusion of the physical and the verbal: 'Slander or Poyson', 'P–x'd by her Love, or libell'd by her Hate.' In the devastating couplet on Lady Mary, of course, Pope's own blatant libel is used to sharpen the verbal attack. Scaeva's hemlock in honey is sarcastically reversed by Pope to make another point, now about the physical and the moral:

So drink with *Waters*, or with *Chartres* eat,
They'll never poison you, they'll only cheat. (89–90)

45

Canidia in Horace becomes two women in Pope, '*Delia*' and 'furious *Sappho*'; and the Roman judge Turius lives again: 'Hard Words or Hanging, if your Judge be *Page*.' Now the physical and the verbal/ literal are intensely fused. Horace's open sarcasm, '*mirum*' ('How marvellous') is heard once more: 'And no man wonders he's not stung by Pug.' Pug was a well-known Cornish boxer but also a common nickname for a pet dog. Horace says with irony this aggressiveness is due to the command of '*natura potens*' ('sovereign nature'); but Pope turns that irony into much more intense sarcasm: 'Its proper Pow'r to hurt, each Creature feels.'

In the Latin these darker tones quickly become brighter. Horace concludes this part of the discussion with a comic description of his own situation and a mock-heroic assertion of his strident defiance, only to be brought down by a witty joke from Trebatius:

> [26]*Ne longum faciam; seu me tranquilla senectus*
> *Expectat, seu mors atris circumvolat alis;*
> *Dives inops, Romae seu sors ita jusserit, exul,*
> [27]*Quisquis erit vitae, scribam, color.*
>   TREB. [28]*O puer, ut sis*
> *Vitalis, metuo; & majorum ne quis amicus*
> *Frigore te feriat.*   (57–62)

(To be brief, whether a peaceful old age awaits me, or whether death is hovering on black wings, rich or poor, at Rome or, if fate so orders, in exile, whatever the colour of my life, I will write.
TREB. Young man, I fear you will not be long-lived, and that one of your powerful friends may blast you with a chill wind.)

With a touch of lyric poetry '*mors atris circumvolat alis*' ('whether death is hovering on black wings'), and hints of high melodrama Horace fantasizes on every possible fate, before making his dramatic assertion '*Quisquis erit vitae, scribam, color*', with '*scribam*' ('I will write') emphatically breaking up the line. (Dacier appropriately quotes *Odes* II.vii. 24–5 to underline the drama, VII, p. 42.) One can hardly take this seriously, and Trebatius replies with mock solemnity, warning this boy ('*puer*') that he will soon be dead, killed by a chilling frown from one of his friends in Maecenas' powerful circle ('*Frigore te feriat*'). 'At e'ery Word a Reputation dies' (*The Rape of the Lock*, Canto III, 16.).

Pope captures superbly this quality in Horace's poetry. The venom of his own sarcastic irony gives way to a new version of Horace's poetry of self-delight, even though Pope's world is somewhat more dangerous:

> [26]Then learned Sir! (to cut the Matter short)
> What-e'er my Fate, or well or ill at Court,

> Whether old Age, with faint, but chearful Ray,
> Attends to gild the Evening of my Day,
> Or Death's black Wing already be display'd
> To wrap me in the Universal Shade;
> Whether the darken'd Room to muse invite,
> Or whiten'd Wall provoke the Skew'r to write
> In Durance, Exile, Bedlam, or the Mint,
> [27]Like *Lee* or *Budgell*, I will Rhyme and Print.
>   F. [28]Alas young Man! your Days can ne'r be long,
> In Flow'r of Age you perish for a Song!
> Plums, and Directors, *Shylock* and his Wife,
> Will club their Testers, now, to take your Life!   (91–104)

Pope clearly relishes Horace's touches of comic melodrama, and loves the opportunity to fantasize; again we find a wonderful play of contradictions, Horace's language here inspiring in Pope a vital language of exotic imagery and compelling metaphor. '*Dives inops, Romae seu sors ita jusserit, exul*' ('Rich or poor, at Rome or, if fate so orders, in exile') produces first the lively irony of 'or well or ill at Court' and then 'In Durance, Exile, Bedlam, or the Mint', place and money coming together. Horace's '*seu me tranquilla senectus*' ('whether a peaceful old age awaits me') produces a little moment of luxurious self-indulgence:

> Whether old Age, with faint, but chearful Ray,
> Attends to gild the Evening of my Day ...   (93–4)

while the melodramatic '*seu mors atris circumvolat alis*' opens up into a one-couplet *Essay on Man*:

> Or Death's black Wing already be display'd
> To wrap me in the Universal Shade.   (95–6)

The mere hint of '*color*' ('colour', 'tint') in Horace's '*Quisquis erit vitae, scribam, color*' ('whatever the colour of my life, I will write') produces the lightning-fast contrast of the 'darken'd Room' which gently invites the successful poet to 'muse', and the 'whiten'd Wall' that provokes 'the Skew'r to write'. Pope concludes by going one better than Horace's dramatic '*scribam*': 'I will Rhyme and Print.'

Fortescue's response to this display of high spirits is very much in the Trebatian style: 'Alas young Man! your Days can ne'r be long.' But the treatment of '*majorum ne quis amicus / Frigore te feriat*' is nicely double-edged: in part it is the Horatian joke – 'In Flow'r of Age you perish for a Song!'; but then it points, audaciously, not to outraged friends, but to Pope's real enemies in high places, again reminding us of the *Epistle to Bathurst*:

> Plums, and Directors, *Shylock* and his Wife,
> Will club their Testers, now, to take your Life!   (103–4)

47

In the Horace these witty jokes and playful gestures of defiance lead to the most powerful passage in the poem, the second portrait of Lucilius. Horace's own battles are clearly light-weight affairs, but defending them allows him once more to characterize his predecessor, Lucilius, and to show in particular how that satirist was appreciated by the great. Mock-heroics give way to the genuine heroics of satire and these then provide at least some sort of standard by which Horace himself might be judged:

> HOR. [29]*Quid? cum est Lucilius ausus*
> *Primus in hunc operis componere carmina morem,*
> [30]Detrahere & pellem, nitidus *qua quisque per ora*
> *Cederet,* introrsum turpis; *num Laelius, & qui*
> *Duxit ab oppressa meritum Carthagine nomen,*
> *Ingenio offensi? aut laeso doluere Metello,*
> *Famosisque Lupo cooperto versibus? Atqui*
> Primores *populi arripuit,* populumque *tributim;*
> *Scilicet* [31]UNI AEQUUS VIRTUTI ATQUE EJUS AMICIS.
> [32]*Quin ubi se a* Vulgo & Scena, *in Secreta remorant*
> Virtus Scipiadae, *& mitis* Sapientia Laeli;
> *Nugari cum illo, & discincti ludere, donec*
> *Decoqueretur olus,* soliti.
>   *– Quicquid sum ego, quamvis*
> *Infra Lucili censum, ingeniumque, tamen me*
> [34]*Cum* magnis vixisse *invita fatebitur usque*
> *Invidia, & fragili quaerens illidere dentem,*
> Offendet solido; –
>   [35]*– Nisi quid tu,* docte Trebati,
> Dissentis.   (62–79)

(What? In the days when Lucilius first dared to compose poems in this style, to strip off the skin in which each paraded gleaming before the eyes of the world, though foul within, were Laelius and the man who took his title, deservedly, from the suppression of Carthage (Scipio Africanus) offended by his wit? Were they aggrieved when Metellus was attacked and Lupus buried under a hail of satirical lines? Far from it: he went for the leaders of the people and the people of every estate, being, he'd say, indulgent to none but Virtue and her friends. Indeed, when the valiant Scipio and the wise and gentle Laelius had withdrawn into privacy from the stage of public life, they used to play the fool with Lucilius and to sport with him, relaxed, while their vegetables were cooking. Whatever I am, although I fall beneath Lucilius' class and genius, still, Envy will always have to admit, reluctantly, that I have lived with the great; and expecting to sink her tooth into tender flesh will strike against solid – Unless you disagree at all, learned Trebatius.)

The language of this passage rises to make Lucilius fully alive. Horace proudly calls Lucilius the first ('*Primus*') who dared ('*ausus*') to write satirical verse in this fashion ('*in hunc operis componere carmina morem*'). And when he wrote he stripped off the skin

('Detrahere & pellem') of those who, while they paraded ('*Cederet*') gleaming ('nitidus') before the eyes of everyone, were actually foul within ('introrsum turpis'). But when he did this the leaders of his time Laelius and Scipio, identified with the resonant periphrasis '*qui / Duxit ab oppressa meritum Carthagine nomen*' ('the man who took his title, deservedly, from the suppression of Carthage'), were not offended. They were not hurt when Metellus was hit, or Lupus completely buried under a shower of lampooning verses (the word order shows this happening: '*Famosisque Lupo cooperto versibus*'). He went for ('*arripuit*') both the leaders of the people ('Primores *populi*') and the people of every estate ('populumque *tributim*'). Eighteenth-century editions emphasize the power of this: Baxter, for example, points out that '*arripuit*' means to bite with the teeth, 'dentibus, ceu Canis' (1701, p. 316). But at the same time Lucilius was, in the line which Pope takes to be the key to the whole and puts into bold capitals, '*Scilicet* UNI AEQUUS VIRTUTI ATQUE EJUS AMICIS' ('indulgent to none but Virtue and her friends'). Furthermore, far from disapproving of this vigorous Lucilius, the leaders of the time, virtuous Scipio and wise and gentle Laelius actually took him with them into their private retreat. Horace gives a charming sketch of them together with their formal clothes thrown off ('*discincti*'), playing ('*ludere*') and fooling ('*Nugari*'), while their vegetables were on the boil ('*Decoqueretur olus*'). Dacier takes '*discincti*' very literally as their formal clothes removed (VII, pp. 48–9), but Desprez sees it partly metaphorically, 'Solutis vestibus & animis ab omni curâ' (1694, p. 619).

Thinking of his relationship with the circle of Maecenas at this time, Horace claims that he too is like that ('*Quicquid sum ego*') even if he is less than Lucilius in both rank ('*censum*') and talent ('*ingenium*'). He too can say with some pride that envy ('*Invidia*'), in spite of herself ('*invita*') will have to admit he lives among the great ('*Cum magnis vixisse*'); and, in trying to harm him, will hit something hard while aiming to bite at something soft.

Pope's imitation of this passage is the high point of his poem, and in one sense the *raison d'être* of the whole work. His imitation is at once an interpretation of the portrait of Lucilius, and a brilliant adaptation of it for his own purposes. What struck Pope was clearly that line, '*Scilicet* UNI AEQUUS VIRTUTI ATQUE EJUS AMICIS.' There is no reason why this aspect of Horace's portrait of Lucilius should be given special prominence. Significantly no contemporary edition makes any special comment on what was for Pope the crucial line. Other features of the portrait indeed are more striking – the sheer power and daring of the satire, the charming picture of retreat.

These, in fact, are the points which Dacier emphasizes in his commentary. He argues that the main point of the whole passage was that Lucilius had the approval and enjoyed the friendship of such men as Laelius and Scipio; and he stresses particularly the playful character of their retreat, and the engaging detail of the vegetables they are cooking, which he points out, is an amusing allusion to those laws which restricted the eating of meat on holidays (VII, pp. 44–55). Dacier implies that the approval of such men was Horace's trump card in his defence of satire. But what struck Pope was obviously this mere suggestion that a love of Virtue was the motivating force at the heart of the attacking energy of Lucilius' satire. The hint is there in Horace, and when Pope puts the line into huge capitals, that is then what the whole passage rests on. He demands that we re-read Horace's passage in the light of that one line.

But if we still miss the point Pope spells it out in no uncertain terms:

> P. [29]What? arm'd for *Virtue* when I point the Pen,
> Brand the bold Front of shameless, guilty Men,
> Dash the proud Gamester in his gilded Car,
> Bare the mean Heart that lurks beneath a Star;
> Can there be wanting to defend Her Cause,
> Lights of the Church, or Guardians of the Laws?
> Could pension'd *Boileau* lash in honest Strain
> Flatt'rers and Bigots ev'n in *Louis'* Reign?
> Could Laureate *Dryden* Pimp and Fry'r engage,
> Yet neither *Charles* nor *James* be in a Rage?
> And I not [30]strip the Gilding off a Knave,
> Un-plac'd, un-pension'd, no Man's Heir, or Slave?
> I will, or perish in the gen'rous Cause.
> Hear this, you tremble! you, who 'scape the Laws.
> Yes, while I live, no rich or noble knave
> Shall walk the World, in credit, to his grave.
> [31]TO VIRTUE ONLY and HER FRIENDS, A FRIEND,
> The World beside may murmur, or commend.
> Know, all the distant Din that World can keep
> Rolls o'er my *Grotto*, and but sooths my Sleep.
> [32]There, my Retreat the best Companions grace,
> Chiefs, out of War, and Statesmen, out of Place.
> There *St. John* mingles with my friendly Bowl,
> The Feast of Reason and the Flow of Soul:
> And He, whose Lightning pierc'd th'*Iberian* Lines,
> Now, forms my Quincunx, and now ranks my Vines,
> Or tames the Genius of the stubborn Plain,
> Almost as quickly, as he conquer'd *Spain*.
> [34]*Envy* must own, I live among the Great,
> No Pimp of Pleasure, and no Spy of State,
> With Eyes that pry not, Tongue that ne'er repeats,

Fond to spread Friendships, but to cover Heats,
To help who want, to forward who excel;
This, all who know me, know; who love me, tell;
And who unknown defame me, let them be
Scriblers or Peers, alike are *Mob* to me.
This is my Plea, on this I rest my Cause –
[35]What saith my Council learned in the Laws? (105–42)

This is one of Pope's most imaginative passages written in imitation of Horace. He sees himself as Lucilius, 'arm'd for *Virtue*' and doing in the London of his time all that Lucilius dared to do in his society. His own rhetoric easily matches the power of Horace's high style, and to see the lines as an imaginative transformation of the Latin seems only to increase their energy. Again, as in the earlier Lucilius passage, the references and cross-references are highly charged because of their complexity, and again because he generates from Horace's Latin such a multitude of meanings. 'Detrahere & pellem, nitidus *qua quisque per ora* / *Cederet* introrsum turpis' ('to strip off the skin in which each paraded gleaming before the eyes of the world, though foul within') produces:

Brand the bold Front of shameless, guilty Men ... (106)
Bare the mean Heart that lurks beneath a Star ... (108)
And I not strip the Gilding off a Knave ... (115)

Significant here is the fact that Pope greatly intensifies Dacier's interpretation of 'Detrahere & pellem.' Dacier sees this as a theatrical metaphor: '*Pellem*, le masque. C'est une figure tirée des masques que les Comediens portoient sur le Theatre' (VII, p. 45). Desprez, however, offers a more vigorous interpretation of the expression which emphasizes the revelation of rank hypocrisy: 'Occulta procerum vitia divulgare, ac turpes ostendere eos ipsos qui honesti & probi estimabantur' (1694, p. 618). This is clearly closer to Pope's reading.[1] He brings out the much more violent meanings of 'Detrahere' ('strip off') and 'pellem' ('skin', 'hide'). The 'nitidus' ('gleaming') for Pope becomes 'the bold Front', 'the proud Gamester', 'his gilded Car', 'a Star', 'the Gilding', 'rich or noble knave'. The 'introrsum turpis' ('foul within') becomes 'shameless, guilty Men', 'the mean Heart', 'a Knave'. In Pope's satire there is an intense desire to build up these glittering surfaces, and an equal desire to cut through them to inner corruption. Next to Horace, we see his poetry imagining again and again what it wishes to destroy – truth and virtue here are found in the energy of that imagined stripping away.

It has often been suggested that Pope's lines on the satirist's concern with religion in this passage are an addition to Horace, and show that his conception of the satirist is more moral and more exalted than that of Horace (see, for example, Hunter, 1960, pp. 400–1). But the source for this was the identification of the Lupus here ('*Famosisque Lupo cooperto versibus*') as Publius Rutilius Lupus, a consul who was accused of impiety towards the gods. Dacier's note makes this clear:

C'est Publius Rutilius Lupus, qui fut Consul douze ou treize ans aprés la mort de Lucilius. Ce Poëte l'avoit extrémement mal traité dans ses Satires; jusques à l'accuser d'impieté envers les Dieux, comme il paroit par ce fragment.
> – *Tubulus si Lucius unquam*
> *Si Lupus, aut Carbo, aut Neptuni filius Divos*
> *Esse putasset, tam impius aut perjurus fuisset.*

Si Lucillius Tubulus, si Lupus, si Carbo, & ce fils de Neptune, croyoient qu'il y a des Dieux, seroient-ils si impies? On attribua mesme la mort de Lupus à son impieté, & au mépris qu'il avoit eu pour la Religion, en méprisant les Sacrifices qui luy estoient contraires.

> (VII, pp. 46–7. Desprez makes the same point and quotes the same verse, 1694, p. 619)

It is clearly this interpretation of the Horace which causes Pope to write:

> Can there we wanting to defend Her Cause,
> Lights of the Church, or Guardians of the Laws?
> Could pension'd *Boileau* lash in honest Strain
> Flatt'rers and Bigots ev'n in *Louis*' Reign?
> Could Laureate *Dryden* Pimp and Fry'r engage,
> Yet neither *Charles* nor *James* be in a Rage? (109–14)

Lucilius here becomes first Boileau and Dryden, and then Pope himself, and Laelius and Scipio become Louis XIV, Charles and James, before, in the lines that follow, becoming Bolingbroke and Peterborough. Pope's play on Horace's 'populumque *tributim*' ('the people of every estate') is also ingenious. Dacier points out the significance of '*tributim*': 'Il parcourut les trente-cinq Tribus qui partageoient le peuple Romain' (VII, p. 48). In Pope this becomes an allusion to new social groups; 'Flatt'rers and Bigots', 'Pimp and Fry'r'.

But then the fact that Lucilius attacked both the leaders of the people ('Primores') and the people themselves ('populumque') provides Pope with yet another shift: here the satirist is himself one of the people ('Un-plac'd, un-pension'd, no Man's Heir, or Slave'), and his victims now specifically the great who ''scape the Laws', the 'rich or noble knave', the high who are in fact the low. But then Pope suddenly changes perspective again to make the great central point: all social position is irrelevant when he is 'TO VIRTUE ONLY and HER

FRIENDS, A FRIEND.' Horace's 'AEQUUS' is untranslatable, meaning 'equal', 'fair' *and* 'indulgent', i.e. both 'impartial' and 'partial'. Dacier suggests 'doux, favorable' (VII, p. 48). Pope seems to hold all this together in what is really a superb 'translation' – 'A FRIEND'.

Using this line as a pivot Pope transforms the loose and carefree retreat of Laelius and Scipio into the image of an intellectual and morally cultivated retreat at Twickenham. Horace's '*Nugari*', '*ludere*' have gone, unless they have become the superior play of giving order to the garden. The emphasis is all on 'Virtus Scipiadae' and 'Sapientia Laeli', turned miraculously into 'The Feast of Reason and the Flow of Soul.' The emphasis is also on a new movement '*a Vulgo & Scena*' ('from the stage of public life') to 'Secreta' ('privacy'): 'Chiefs, out of War, and Statesmen, out of Place.' The wise Laelius is now Bolingbroke who 'mingles with my friendly Bowl, / The Feast of Reason and the Flow of Soul', a remarkable contrast to Horace's vegetables. The virtuous soldier, Scipio, who took his name from conquered Carthage, has become Peterborough who so brilliantly took Barcelona in 1705, now with superior wisdom taming 'the Genius of the stubborn Plain, / Almost as quickly, as he conquer'd *Spain*.' Pope, of course, says these companions grace *his* retreat, but for the moment our attention is on these men and their generosity to him.

After this Pope can translate Horace's '*Cum* magnis vixisse *invita fatebitur usque* / *Invidia*' absolutely straight: '*Envy* must own, I live among the Great', but adds with sharp irony, 'No Pimp of Pleasure, and no Spy of State.' In the lines that follow he develops an important new idea for which there is no real source in Horace; that he, a satirist, is as much concerned to be creative and positive in human relationships as to be destructive and aggressive, if not more so:

> Fond to spread Friendships, but to cover Heats,
> To help who want, to forward who excel;
> This all who know me, know; who love me, tell ...   (136–8)

His final defence of himself lies in what his friends know about him, and indeed tell him.

This takes us to another dimension of the whole passage; Pope has turned this section into an image not so much of Horatian retreat as of Stoic retreat. This satirist who is 'Un-plac'd, un-pension'd', and who as a Catholic is debarred from public office, is all the same actively engaged in the nation's civil and moral life. If Epicurean retreat concentrated on cultivation of the self, then Stoic retreat demanded that the excluded person should as a private citizen be committed to public life for the sake of 'Virtue':

Hoc puto virtuti faciendum studiosoque virtutis. Si praevalebit fortuna et praecidet agendi facultatem, non statim aversus inermisque fugiat latebras quaerens, quasi ullus locus sit, quo non possit fortuna persequi, sed parcius se inferat officiis et cum dilectu inveniat aliquid, in quo utilis civitati sit. Militare non licet? Honores petat. Privato vivendum est? Sit orator. Silentium indictum est? Tacita advocatione cives iuvet. Periculosum etiam ingressu forum est? In domibus, in spectaculis, in conviviis bonum contubernalem, fidelem amicum, temperantem convivam agat. Officia civis amisit? Hominis exerceat.

This is what I think Virtue and Virtue's devotee should do. If Fortune shall get the upper hand and shall cut off the opportunity for action, let a man not straightway turn his back and flee, throwing away his arms and seeking some hiding-place, as if there were anywhere a place where Fortune could not reach him, but let him devote himself to his duties more sparingly, and, after making choice, let him find something in which he may be useful to the state. Is he not permitted to be a soldier? Let him seek public office. Must he live in a private station? Let him be a pleader. Is he condemned to silence? Let him help his countrymen by his silent support. Is it dangerous even to enter the forum? In private houses, at the public spectacles, at feasts let him show himself a good comrade, a faithful friend, a temperate feaster. Has he lost the duties of a citizen? Let him exercise those of a man.

(Seneca, 'De Tranquillitate Animi', in Essays, ed. Basore, 1928–35, II, pp. 226–9)

Significantly, this passage on the Stoic retreat from Seneca's 'De Tranquillitate Animi' was to be recalled by Bolingbroke himself in the introduction to his essay *The Idea of a Patriot King*, written for the Opposition during a short visit to England in 1738:

Stripped of the rights of a British subject ... I remember that I am a Briton still. I apply to myself what I have read in SENECA, Officia si civis amiserit, hominis exerceat. I have renounced the world, not in show, but in reality, and more by my way of thinking, than by my way of living, as retired as that may seem. But I have not renounced my country, nor my friends ...   (*Works*, 1754, III, p. 40)

Bolingbroke concludes recalling another passage from Seneca's essay:

In that retreat, wherein the remainder of my days shall be spent, I may be of some use to them (my friends); since, even from thence, I may advise, exhort, and warn them. "Nec enim "is solus reipublicae prodest, qui candidatos extrahit, "et tuetur reos, et de pace, belloque censet; sed qui juven- "tutem exhortatur, qui, in tanta bonorum praeceptorum inopia, "virtute instruit animos; qui ad pecuniam luxuriamque cursu "ruentes, prensat ac retrahit, et, si nihil aliud, certe moratur; "in privato publicum negotium agit."   (p. 41)

For the man that does good service to the state is not merely he who brings forward candidates and defends the accused and votes for peace and war, but he also who admonishes young men, who instils virtue into their minds, supplying the great lack of good teachers, who lays hold upon those that are rushing wildly in pursuit of money and luxury, and draws them back, and, if he accomplishes nothing else, at least retards them – such a man performs a public service even in private life.   (Basore, II, p. 224–5)

These are themes we shall explore more fully in considering Pope's Imitations of *Epistle II.i.* and *Epistle I.i.*[2]

Horace ends his poem by picking up the reference to the libel laws mentioned in the very first lines. Trebatius, in a professional manner, agrees that Horace's plea is quite acceptable; but warns all the same that the laws specifically forbid libel. Horace turns this into a witty pun, hints that Caesar enjoys his poetry, and with that the consultation and the poem are over:

> TREB. [36]*Equidem nihil hinc diffindere possum.*
> *Sed tamen ut monitus caveas, ne forte negoti*
> *Incutiat tibi quid sanctarum inscitia legum.*
> [37]'*Si mala condiderit in quem quis carmina jus est*
> Judiciumque.'
>   HOR. *Esto, siquis* [38]*mala; sed* bona *siquis*
> *Judice condiderit laudatur* CAESARE: *siquis*
> *Opprobrijs dignum laceraverit, integer ipse,*
> [39]*Solventur risu tabulae; tu missus abibis.*   (79–86)

(TREB. I can't find fault with this. Nevertheless, be warned, and beware in case
    ignorance of our hallowed laws inflicts trouble on you. 'If a man has
    composed bad verses against another ... there is the law and the court.'
HOR. So be it, if they are bad, but if a man has composed verses that are good in
    Caesar's judgement, he'll be praised; if a man flays someone who deserves
    rebuke, and his own character is clear, the case will be laughed out of
    court; you're dismissed and walk away.)

It was normal in seventeenth- and eighteenth-century editions to regard the line beginning 'Si mala condiderit' as a direct quotation from the statute books, and certainly the phraseology is precise. This sharpens Horace's pun on 'mala' ('libellous' and 'of poor quality') and 'bona' ('good'). However, Horace's conclusion turns mainly on the idea that his poetry is approved of by Augustus, the equivalent, as it were, of Laelius and Scipio. It is clear that if Caesar approves, any court case would be quite laughable.

Pope emphasizes this point with his 'CAESARE' in capitals; and then turns the idea into irony with a version which at once satirizes Horace and wryly teases Fortescue for his close association with Walpole, the new Caesar:

> F. [36]Your Plea is good. But still I say, beware!
> Laws are explain'd by Men – so have a care.
> It stands on record, that in *Richard*'s Times

A Man was hang'd for very honest Rhymes.
[37]Consult the Statute: *quart.* I think it is,
Edwardi Sext. or *prim. & quint. Eliz:*
See *Libels, Satires* – here you have it – read.
      P. [38]*Libels* and *Satires!* Lawless Things indeed!
But grave *Epistles*, bringing Vice to light,
Such a *King* might read, a *Bishop* write,
Such as Sir *Robert* would approve –
                    F. Indeed?
The Case is alter'd – you may then proceed.
[39]In such a Cause the Plaintiff will be hiss'd,
My Lords the Judges laugh, and you're dismiss'd.   (143–56)

Pope adds the satiric point that 'Laws are explain'd by Men', and the dry allusion to the man 'hang'd for very honest Rhymes'. This detail, however, often seen as providing a contrast to the Horace, was probably suggested by Dacier's comment that the Roman Law referred to actually carried the death penalty: 'C'est la Loy des XII Tables qui établissoit la peine de mort contre ceux qui parloient ou qui écrivoient contre la reputation de quelqu'un' (VII, p. 56). For the Latin statute about redress for libel, Pope cleverly weaves into rhythm the obscure in-talk of legal jargon alluding to the actual English statutes about libel. But his main point is to turn Horace's pun on 'mala' – 'bona' into an ironic distinction between '*Libels* and *Satires*' and what he calls 'grave *Epistles*, bringing Vice to light', a final allusion to his *Moral Essays*. Horace's language at the very end emphasizes the dramatic contrast between the satirist as good man ('*integer ipse*') and the lashings of his verse ('*laceraverit*'). It is significant that in line 85 Pope keeps the violent '*laceraverit*' ('lash') he found in Heinsius, rather than emending it to the '*latraverit*' ('bark') adopted by both Dacier and Bentley, and now generally accepted. This energetic language is reduced to the blandness of 'Such as a *King* might read, a *Bishop* write'. After the extraordinary energy of this poem, this defence can only be disingenuous. Pope knew, as much as everyone else, that Sir Robert, the new Caesar, would be the last person to approve.

    It is interesting that Pope, in the Imitation, concludes by departing from his own printed Latin text which, as was traditional, gave the last line of the poem to Horace. He here adopts Bentley's suggestion, now always accepted in modern texts, that Trebatius has the last word.[3] This enables Pope to allude to Fortescue's association with Walpole and at the same time hint at just how powerful this great man had become. In Horace, of course, this final stroke is his last winning joke; in Pope it becomes the final thrust of double-edged irony.

Pope's first Imitation of Horace is, as an Imitation, an extraordinary *tour de force*: Pope has re-created the whole form and shape of Horace's satire, though abbreviated here, and expanded there; and he has assimilated and imaginatively transformed into something new, alive, and provocative virtually every detail of Horace's text. In the dialogue with Fortescue, he has matched what Dacier saw was at the heart of Horace's poem, its lively raillery and persistent punning; and the new work has all the energy, forward movement, and exuberance of the original. But Pope has not only mirrored Horace's *Satire* II.i.; he has given the whole Horatian satire a new intensity based on his fresh interpretation of Lucilius and his identification with that figure, as well as with Horace.

This Imitation was, in fact, a seminal moment in Pope's poetic development, because of its self-portraiture and its discovery of the possibilities of sustained imitation. The point when a poet turns to self-characterization is bound to be significant, and this was for Pope at forty-five such a moment. Pope had 'appeared' in his earlier major poems only very briefly, as at the end of *Eloisa to Abelard* and in the *Epistle to Burlington*. Here for the first time 'he' appears at the very centre of one of his poems, a full, complex, and subtle personality trying to explore and reveal all that he is. This is the beginning of Pope's quite conscious creation of a poetic persona, doing what Horace had supremely done before him. In this activity the 'real' and the 'fictional' are blended: in this poem a lively, playful dramatic performance ends with a dramatic appeal to his 'true' self: 'This all who know me, know; who love me, tell.' Writing to Pope on 16 May 1733, Aaron Hill said significantly: 'I must own, there is a spirit, in the honest vivacity of that piece, that charmed me to the soul. In your other writings, I am pleased by the *poet*; I am, here, in love with the *man*' (*Corr.* III, p. 370). But this opposition is perhaps too sharp; if this poem is so successful as poetry is it not because Pope's whole personality seems, at least, to live in it? The self of this poetry is the self felt in all the subtle nuances of the verse and in all its arrogant power, a self perhaps ultimately inseparable from the whole achievement of that poetry.[4]

This inspired poem in fact opened up a whole new area of poetry for Pope. The Imitation was an instant success, and Pope wrote to Caryll on 8 March 1733, that 'my last piece of song' had 'met with such a flood of favour that my ears need no more flattery for this twelvemonth' (*Corr.* III, p. 353).[5] Pope had never written a dramatic dialogue before, and from this performance spring, in particular, those other great poems of self-dramatization, *The Epistle to*

Arbuthnot (1735) and the two 'Dialogues' of the *Epilogue to the Satires* (1738). More generally, however, the self in all its moods and all its complexities was to be one of the major preoccupations of all the *Imitations* to follow. The catalyst for this development was not only Horace's self-portraiture, but, most profoundly, Horace's interpretation of Lucilius in *Satire* II.i. as understood by Pope himself.

Of great significance in this respect is Pope's assertion that the motivating power of his satiric poetry was a profound love of 'Virtue'. He had explored this idea in his letters and touched on it in earlier poetry, but never before had he asserted it so boldly. The line he discovered in Horace virtually became his motto for the next six years. He explored the theme again in the *Epistle to Arbuthnot*, again in the *Imitation of Epistle I.i.*, and yet again in *Epilogue to the Satires*. The word 'Virtue' acquired political connotations in the 1730s when it was appropriated by the Opposition in the attack on Walpole's 'Vice', and these, as Paul Gabriner (1973) has shown, only deepened the significance of its meaning for Pope. Pope never tired of asserting that his poetry was inspired by a love of virtue or gave up attempting to understand what that might fully mean.

But if this Imitation is memorable for Pope's first assertion of this idea, the Imitation itself also shows that no such view can in fact account for the complexities of Pope's satire, for the mysteries of its origins, and for whatever might be the results of its brilliant satiric thrusts. The poem indeed confirms P. K. Elkin's (1973) view that the Augustan moral defence of satire is ultimately inadequate. So much of this satire is self-delight and so much poetic fantasy. A whole Lucilian personality is indeed present in this living satiric poetry, with its touches of cruel malice, moments of joyous scorn, and flashes of happy irritation.

Pope's image of himself as it emerges from this work is energetically contradictory, and this is most particularly what we see if we read the poem as an Imitation. Pope is sometimes playing Horace, sometimes Lucilius, sometimes Horace playing Lucilius, and sometimes himself. The whole poem as a poetry of imitation is a reflection of this: the relationship between the texts is perpetually fluid, weaving back and forth along the edge of paradox – it is all from Horace, and it is all different. This is the result of the extreme freedom implicit in the whole idea of imitation, which Pope here exploits to the full. Far from tying Pope to a single vision imitation seems profoundly liberating. The relationship between the texts changes moment by moment and line by line; and Pope's relationship with himself is just as fluid, just as momentary. What makes this first Imitation so alive is its improvisational capturing of the reality

of every moment, and its vigorous acceptance of those contradictions of the self which spring from experience and testify to truth:

> Know, all the distant Din that World can keep
> Rolls o'er my *Grotto*, and but sooths my Sleep. (123–4)

>   Not write? but then I *think*,
> And for my Soul I cannot sleep a wink. (11–12)

4

Horace, moral:
The Paraphrase of Satire II.ii.

Have you seen the last satire of Horace in which You are so ill treated? I could not find any method of sending it to you.

Pope to Bethel, 6 August 1734

POPE must have realized that the triumph of the *Imitation of Satire II.i.* could never be repeated, and in pursuing the possibilities of imitating Horace he wisely turned to another type of Horatian satire, the moral diatribe. A year after his great success, in July 1734, he published a second edition of the first Imitation along with a companion piece, *The Second Satire of the Second Book of Horace Paraphrased*. Horace's *Satire* II.ii. is a diatribe on the virtues of the simple life, ostensibly reporting the views of a peasant, Ofellus. This is an early Horatian work, vigorously, almost naively moral, and to the modern reader its poetry seems, perhaps, too simple and too didactic. How did Pope respond to this kind of Horatian moral simplicity? Was he able to make it relevant to his own time and his own life?

Again, Dacier's reading of the Horatian satire provides a useful introduction. As we might expect, he speaks warmly of this poem, praising its moral sentiments, but his comments on Ofellus are much more striking. For Dacier the important thing about Ofellus is that he is neither a pleasure-loving Epicurean nor a rigid Stoic but rather an independent and 'natural' thinker who has worked out his own philosophy between those two extremes. He sees the whole poem as a criticism of both selfish Epicurean excess in the pleasures of eating and excessive Stoic rigidity which excluded 'le plaisir de la bonne chere':

Elle tient le milieu entre les deux. Car elle n'exclut pas entierement le plaisir de la bonne chere. Elle l'admet, au contraire; mais elle enseigne les moyens de le ménager & de le dispenser sobrement. C'est précisément ce juste milieu qui estoit également inconnu à ces deux Philosophes, & c'est celuy que suivoit Ofellus. (VII, p. 85. See also his comment on line 82, p. 128)

Horace describes Ofellus as '*Rusticus*, abnormis *sapiens*, crassaque Minerva' ('a peasant, an independent sage of homespun wisdom') which Dacier translates: 'le Campagnard Ofellus, ce Philosophe sans Secte, cet homme libre & naturel' (VII, pp. 59–61), to stress both his independence and the 'natural' force of his thought as opposed to that of the strict philosophical schools. Thus, far from being a work with an obvious moral meaning, Dacier sees this satire as the celebration of independent moral thought: Ofellus' vision is powerful and his pleasures in hospitality are real very much because they are his own. Looked at from this point of view Horace's *Satire* II.ii. would seem to raise the question, what is the relationship between moral truth and the individual apprehension of it? Another version of that question could be, what is the relationship between philosophical truth and poetic vision?

When considering Pope's Imitation it is important to realize how he abbreviates and re-shapes Horace's text. Of the 135 lines which comprise the complete text of Horace's poem, roughly the first third is an aggressive attack on the extravagant and bizarre tastes of sophisticated Roman epicures that ends with a satiric portrait of the miserly Avidienus, an extreme contrast to the epicures. The next third broadens out the theme: it asserts the values of moderate living in terms of concern for health, old age, hospitality, fame, self-respect, public duty, and readiness for changes of fortune. In the final third Ofellus speaks in his own person, describing his life on his simple farm and expressing, in poetry which is at first warm and then immensely powerful, his individual vision of life.

Pope concentrates on the last two 'sections' of this poem: from the first third of the Latin poem, indeed, he neatly cuts twenty lines and thus creates a new shorter Latin text to work from.[1] He then gives full weight to the broader themes of the middle section. In these two sections Pope's Yorkshire friend Hugh Bethel takes the part of Ofellus.[2] But he makes the climax of his poem an evocation of his own life at Twickenham in a highly individual version of Horace's final section in which Pope himself becomes Ofellus. His overall treatment thus stresses the wider aspects of Horace's poem and suggests the continuing relevance of its moral vision. But at the same time it is clear that Pope must re-interpret that moral vision in his own way. His 'reading' of this moral Horace is by no means perfunctory nor unmediated by his own poetic personality.

One passage from the first section of the Imitation will suffice to illustrate how he treats Horace's moral attack on extravagant eating. After announcing his theme, '*Quae virtus & quanta, boni, sit vivere parvo*' (line 1 – '"The essence and value of simple living", gentlemen'), Horace insists that this talk ('Sermo') is not his but Ofellus'. Dacier interprets this disclaimer as implying that Horace knew that he was recognized as being an Epicurean in his tastes (VII, pp. 86–7). Ofellus begins by ridiculing the fastidious eating of Romans with their taste for peacocks and turbots, and in Pope's much abbreviated version this becomes:

> – ⁸*Leporem sectatus, equove Lassus –*
> *Cum labor extuderit fastidia, siccus, inanis,*
> *Sperne* cibum vilem. – ⁹*Foris est Promus, & atrum*
> *Defendens pisces hyemat mare: cum sale panis*
> *Latrantem stomachum bene leniet: unde? putas, aut*
> *Qui partum? Non in caro nidore Voluptas*
> *Summa, sed in* teipso *est* * **
> ¹⁰*Vix tamen eripiam, posito* pavone, *velis quin*
> *Hoc potius quam* gallina, *tergere palatum –*
> *Tanquam ad rem attineat quidquam: num vesceris ista*
> *Quam laudas, pluma?* – ¹¹*Laudas insane,* trilibrem
> Mullum, *in singula quem minuas pulmenta necesse est.*
> *Ducit te species video. Quo pertinet ergo*
> Proceros *odisse* lupos? *quia scilicet illis*
> *Majorem natura modum dedit, his breve pondus.*   (8–22)

(After you've been chasing a hare, when you are tired from your horse, when physical exercise has knocked the fastidiousness out of you, when you are dry and empty, then despise plain food. The steward is out, the blackened sea storms, safeguarding its fish: bread with a pinch of salt will assuage your barking belly. How, one wonders, is this achieved? The highest pleasure does not lie in costly aroma, but in yourself.

Even so, I shall never be able to stop you choosing to swab your palate with peacock, if it's served, rather than chicken – as though [its beauty] had anything to do with the matter. After all, do you eat those feathers which you praise? – Fool that you are, you praise a mullet for weighing three pounds which you have to cut up into individual portions. You're led by appearance, I see. So what's the point of disliking the pike which is long? Because, I suppose, nature has made the pike large and the mullet light.)

Horace's language here is deliberately aggressive and sarcastic, as befits the plain-speaking countryman, and in Pope's version the Latin has even more sharpness. Latin poetry characteristically gains force by adding up one example after another, and by cutting down Horace's examples here Pope gives that Latin an 'English' succinctness which he can then follow very closely. Fifteen lines from Ofellus become just fourteen from Bethel:

> ⁸Go work, hunt, exercise! (he thus began)
> Then scorn a homely dinner, if you can.
> ⁹Your wine lock'd up, your Butler stroll'd abroad,
> Or fish deny'd, (the River yet un-thaw'd)
> If then plain Bread and milk will do the feat,
> The pleasure lies in *you*, and not the meat.
> ¹⁰Preach as I please, I doubt our curious men
> Will chuse a *Pheasant* still before a *Hen*;

> Yet Hens of *Guinea* full as good I hold,
> Except you eat the feathers, green and gold.
> ¹¹Of *Carps* and *Mullets* why prefer the *great*,
> (Tho' cut in pieces e'er my Lord can eat)
> Yet for *small Turbots* such esteem profess?
> Because God made these large, the other less. (11–24)

This poetry is very much in the style of Ofellus' speech: '*Non in caro nidore Voluptas / Summa, sed in* teipso *est*' ('The highest pleasure does not lie in costly aroma, but in yourself'): 'The pleasure lies in *you*, and not the meat'; '*num vesceris ista / Quam laudas, pluma?*' ('Do you eat those feathers which you praise?'):

> Yet Hens of *Guinea* full as good I hold,
> Except you eat the feathers, green and gold. (19–20)

'*Laudas insane*, trilibrem / Mullum, *in singula quem minuas pulmenta necesse est*' ('Fool that you are, you praise a mullet for weighing three pounds which you have to cut up into individual portions'):

> Of *Carps* and *Mullets* why prefer the *great*,
> (Tho' cut in pieces e'er my Lord can eat) ... (21–2)

However, Pope's appeal to Horace as a moral authority is not always as simple as it might seem. We can see this, for example, when Pope uses the Horace for his own personal attacks on individuals. Horace's sketch of the miserly Avidienus allows Pope a devastating portrait of Wortley Montague and Lady Mary. Horace's portrait is made up of sharp details, conveyed with cutting sarcasm:

> ¹⁸*Sordidus a tenui victu distabit, Ofello*
> *Judice: nam frustra vitiam vitaveris istud,*
> *Si te alio pravum detorseris.* ¹⁹*Avidienus*
> ²⁰*(Cui* Canis *ex vero ductum cognomen adhaeret)*
> *Quinquennes oleas est, & sylvestria corna.*
> ²¹*Ac nisi* mutatum *parcit defundere* vinum, *&*
> *Cujus oderem olei nequeas perferre (licebit*
> *Ille* repotia, natales, *aliosque dierum*
> ²²*Festus albatus celebret) cornu ipse bilibri*
> *Caulibus instillat;* ²³*veteris non parcus aceti.* (35–44)

(There's all the difference between a squalid diet and a plain one, according to Ofellus: after all, there's no point avoiding one fault if you turn away into the opposite vice. Avidienus 'the Dog' (the nickname's stuck, because it's based on fact) eats olives five years old and wild cornels. He is too mean to open his wine until it's turned; and oil you couldn't stand the stench of (even though it's a wedding, a birthday or any other red-letter day he's celebrating in whitened garb) he secretes on the greens a drop at a time, from a two-pound horn, with his own hands; he's unstinting though with his old vinegar.)

Pope intensifies Horace's dry irony and turns this into a venomous personal attack:

> [18]'Tis yet in vain, I own, to keep a pother
> About one Vice, and fall into the other:
> Between Excess and Famine lies a mean,
> Plain, but not sordid, tho' not splendid, clean.
> [19]*Avidien* or his Wife (no matter which,
> For him you'll call a [20]dog, and her a bitch)
> Sell their presented Partridges, and Fruits,
> And humbly live on rabbits and on roots:
> [21]One half-pint bottle serves them both to dine,
> And is at once their vinegar and wine.
> But on some [22]lucky day (as when they found
> A lost Bank-bill, or heard their Son was drown'd)
> At such a feast [23]old vinegar to spare,
> Is what two souls so gen'rous cannot bear;
> Oyl, tho' it stink, they drop by drop impart,
> But sowse the Cabbidge with a bounteous heart.   (45–60)

'Canis' allows Pope his opening double edged jibe; while 'mutatum ... vinum' ('turned wine') becomes the sharper 'And is at once their vinegar and wine.' But Horace's list of family festive days ('repotia, natales, *aliosque dierum*' – 'a wedding, a birthday or any other red-letter day') produces Pope's most cruel thrust:

> But on some lucky day (as when they found
> A lost Bank-bill, or heard their Son was drown'd) ...   (55–6)

a cutting allusion to Lady Mary's awkward relationship with her son. The disturbing power of this is intensified by Dacier's comment on the significance of 'natales' here: 'Les Anciens celebroient avec beaucoup de joye non seulement le jour de leur Naissance, mais les jours de la Naissance de leurs Amis & de leurs Amies' (VII, p. 116). He mentions in this respect Horace's reference to Maecenas' birthday in *Ode* IV.xi. Pope's personal portrait cannot be confined within the bounds of 'moral satire'. Whereas Horace's type-portrait blends together satiric comedy and moral teaching, Pope's personal portrait and his own personal malice tear them apart. Indeed, for a moment we question whether this satirist can have moral standards if he is capable of such vicious attack, whatever the provocation. The striking contrast with the 'moral' Horace here drives that point home.[3]

And yet, for most of this Imitation Pope is even more moral and 'serious' than Horace, and imaginatively finds depth and resonance in Horace's poetry. We see this particularly in his treatment of the wider themes in the middle section of Horace's poem. At one point Horace speaks of the benefits of moderation as a preparation for eventual sickness and old age:

> [30] *Vides, ut pallidus omnis*
> *Cena desurgat dubia? quin corpus onustum*
> *Hesternis vitiis,* animum *quoque praegravat una,*
> *Atque affigit humo* divinae particulam aurae.
> [31] *Alter ubi dicto citius curata sopori*
> *membra dedit, vegetus praescripta ad munia surgit.*
> [32] *Hic tamen ad melius poterit transcurrere quondam:*
> *Sive diem festum rediens advexerit annus,*
> *Seu recreare volet tenuatum corpus: ubique*
> *Accedent anni,* & tractari mollius aetas
> Imbecilla *volet.* [33] *Tibi quidnam accedet ad istam*
> *Quam puer & validus prae-sumis mollitiem? seu*
> *Dura valetudo inciderit, seu tarda senectus?*   (58–70)

(Don't you see how pale everyone is when he rises from a 'puzzle feast'? When the body is laden with yesterday's excess, it weighs down the soul with it, and pins to the earth that particle of divine breath. His opposite, without ado, takes refreshment, surrenders to sleep, and then rises vigorous to his appointed tasks. Yet this same man will still be able to go over to better things from time to time, if the returning year brings round a feast day, or if he wants to build up his shrunken frame, and when his years advance, and his weak old age needs to be treated more indulgently. But you, what can you add to that indulgence which you have anticipated in your youth and manhood, if ill health befalls you, or slow old age?)

As Maresca points out (1966, pp. 28–9) Dacier explains 'divinae particulam aurae' in both Platonic and Judeo-Christian terms:

Une particule du souffle de la Divinité. C'est à-dire une partie de la Divinité même, qui n'est qu'un esprit, & que Platon appelle l'ame du monde. Cette idée du souffle de la Divinité, est venuë sans doute aux Anciens de l'Histoire de la Creation, qui leur estoit connuë. Dieu aprés avoir formé l'homme de la poussiere, luy inspira un souffle de vie: *inspiravit in faciem ejus spiraculum vitae.* Et c'est ce souffle de vie qu'ils ont appellé *particulam divinae aurae.*   (VII, pp. 126–7)

But Maresca here, as elsewhere, does not emphasize enough the difference between Pope and Dacier. What is striking is that Pope uses the details of this not for philosophical or religious purposes but for satiric attack, which brings him much closer to the Latin itself. Pope turns Horace's 'animum' ('soul') and 'divinae particulam aurae' ('that particle of divine breath') into sarcastic irony, but he takes the rest personally as a poet and discovers in it sudden depths:

[30]How pale, each Worshipful and rev'rend Guest
Rise from a Clergy, or a City, feast!
What life in all that ample Body, say,
What heav'nly Particle inspires the clay?
The Soul subsides; and wickedly inclines
To seem but mortal, ev'n in sound Divines.
[31]On morning wings how active springs the Mind,
That leaves the load of yesterday behind?
How easy ev'ry labour it pursues?
How coming to the Poet ev'ry Muse?
[32]Not but we may exceed, some Holy time,
Or tir'd in search of Truth, or search of Rhyme.
Ill Health some just indulgence may engage,
And more, the Sickness of long Life, Old-age:
[33]For fainting Age what cordial drop remains,
If our intemp'rate Youth the Vessel drains?   (75–90)

Horace's 'tenuatum corpus' ('shrunken frame') and 'tractari mollius aetas / Imbecilla *volet*' ('his weak old age needs to be treated more indulgently') are all too appropriate for Pope's physical condition. Horace's '*seu / Dura valetudo inciderit, seu tarda senectus*' ('if ill health befalls you, or slow old age') inspires him to allude to Terence's 'Senectus ipsa est morbus' ('Old age is itself sickness', *Phormio* IV.i.9):

Ill Health some just indulgence may engage,
And more, the Sickness of long Life, Old-age.   (87–8)

This sombre allusion to *Phormio* contrasts sharply with Horace's witty allusion to the same play in '*Cena ... dubia*' ('a puzzle feast') at the beginning of this passage (see Dacier, VII, pp. 125–6. For a fuller discussion of this Horatian passage see Lejay, 1911, pp. 320–1).

A little further on in the middle section Horace alludes very quickly, and sarcastically, to the despair that can follow from the disgrace caused by extravagance:

[36]*Das aliquid* Famae? *(quae* carmine gratior *aurem
Occupat humanam.) Grandes rhombi, patinaeque
Grande ferent una* [37]*cum* damno, dedecus. Adde*
[38]*Iratum patruum, vicinos, te tibi iniquum,
Et frustra mortis cupidum, cum deerit egenti*
[39]*As,* laquei *pretium.* –   (76–81)

(Do you take any account of Fame? (which captivates the ear of man more sweetly than any song). Great turbots and plate bring great disgrace, as well as expense. Add a scandalized uncle, the neighbours, you hating yourself, longing for death, but in vain since you lack in your poverty even a penny, the price of a noose.)

Pope catches these sarcastic jokes but brings out more fully the serious moral. For him the suggestion of financial loss ('damno'), public shame ('dedecus'), the personal despair are all too sobering:

> Unworthy He, the voice of Fame to hear,
> ([36]That sweetest Music to an honest ear;
> For 'faith Lord Fanny! you are in the wrong,
> The World's good word is better than a Song)
> Who has not learn'd, [37]fresh Sturgeon and Ham-pye
> Are no rewards for Want, and Infamy!
> When Luxury has lick'd up all thy pelf,
> Curs'd by thy [38]neighbours, thy Trustees, thy self,
> To friends, to fortune, to mankind a shame,
> Think how Posterity will treat thy name;
> And [39]buy a Rope, that future times may tell
> Thou hast at least bestow'd one penny well.   (99–110)

But perhaps the most striking passage in Pope's treatment of this middle section is his version of Horace's subsequent lines about the moral duty the rich have towards society. As Rudd points out this is a quite unique passage in Horatian satire which usually concentrates on the private self rather than public duty (1966, p. 172). Having warned the rich of the social rejection that can follow from extravagant living, Horace imagines a confident reply, to which he responds with some searching questions:

> – [40]*Jure, inquis, Thrasius istis*
> *Jurgatur verbis; ego vectigalia magna*
> *Divitiasque habeo tribus amplas regibus.* [41]*Ergo*
> *Quod* superat, *non est melius quo insumere possis?*
> *Cur eget indignus* quisquam *te divite? quare*
> [42]*Templa* ruunt *antiqua* Deum? *cur* improbe! *carae*
> *Non aliquid* patriae *tanto emetiris acervo?*   (81–7)

('It's right', you say, 'to rebuke Thrasius with words like that; but I have vast revenues and wealth enough for three kings.' Well then, is there no better object for you to spend your surplus on? Why should any man be undeservedly poor while you are rich? Why are the ancient temples of the Gods falling down? Why, you shameless man, when your heap is so huge, can you not spare a measure for your dear homeland?)

The Pope of the *Epistles to Burlington* and *Bathurst* finds here a short but powerful moral essay on the 'use of riches', and he drives home every detail of the Latin:

> [40]"Right, cries his Lordship, for a Rogue in need
> "To have a Taste, is Insolence indeed:
> "In me 'tis noble, suits my birth and state,
> "My wealth unwieldy, and my heap too great."
> Then, like the Sun, let [41]Bounty spread her ray,

> And shine that Superfluity away.
> Oh Impudence of wealth! with all thy store,
> How dar'st thou let one worthy man be poor?
> Shall half the [42]new-built Churches round thee fall?
> Make Keys, build Bridges, or repair White-hall:
> Or to thy Country let that heap be lent,
> As M**o's was, but not at five *per Cent.*　　　　(111–22)

Horace's '*Ergo / Quod* superat, *non est* melius quo *insumere possis?*' ('Well then, is there no better object for you to spend your surplus on?') now opens up into a new image:

> Then, like the Sun, let Bounty spread her ray,
> And shine that Superfluity away.　　　　(115–16)

'*Cur eget indignus* quisquam *te divite?*' ('Why should any man be undeservedly poor while you are rich?') strikes home to Pope:

> Oh impudence of wealth! with all thy store,
> How dar'st thou let one worthy man be poor?　　　　(117–18)

But then Pope finds in Horace topical advice: '*quare* / Templa *ruunt* antiqua *Deum?*' ('Why are the ancient temples of the Gods falling down?') What are these but the new London churches, built on marshy ground?

> Shall half the new-built Churches round thee fall?
> Make Keys, build Bridges, or repair White-hall ...　　　　(119–20)

Finally, he sees in Horace severe criticisms for the Duchess of Marlborough's stingy loans to the government: '*cur* improbe! carae / Non aliquid patriae *tanto emetiris acervo?*' ('Why, you shameless man, when your heap is so huge, can you not spare a measure for your dear homeland?'):

> Or to thy Country let that heap be lent,
> As M**o's was, but not at five *per Cent.*　　　　(121–2)

Pope's emphasis on public duty in this passage suggests the freshness of his response to the Latin: Dacier does not stress this at all in his commentary (VII, pp. 133–4).

The best of these passages are sharp and forceful, and they prepare for Pope's famous passage of self-characterization at the end of the poem, which in itself is a *tour de force*. To appreciate its full richness this passage must be compared in the closest detail with the Latin. Horace, having reported Ofellus' views in the first two parts of the satire, then explains how this Ofellus, who always lived frugally, lost his farm to the army veteran Umbrenus, but continued to live with his sons a life as rich in food and friendship as it had been when he himself had owned the land. After this short introduction, Ofellus then speaks in his own person, and his words form a memorable celebration of simplicity and moderation, bringing alive the warmth of hospitality and the strength of self-sufficiency, and rising to a highly imaginative passage on the idea of property and the strokes of fortune. Horace uses the speech to recapitulate all the main points of this satire and to underline and expand his moral:

[45]*Quo magis hoc credas, puer hunc ego parvus* Ofellum
Integris opibus novi non latius usum,
Quam nunc [46]accisis. *Videas,* metato *in agello,*
Non ego, narrantem, temere edi luce profesta
Quidquam praeter [47]olus, *fumosae cum pede pernae.*
At mihi seu [48]longum post tempus *venerat hospes,*
Sive operum vacuo, *&c. – bene erit, non* [49]piscibus
     urbe petitis,
Sed pullo *atque* haedo; *tum –*
          – [50]pensilis uva *secundas*
Et nux *ornabit* mensas, cum *duplice ficu.*
Posthac ludus erat [51]Cuppa potare Magistra,
Ac venerata Ceres, *ut culmo surgeret alto,*
Explicuit vino contractae seria frontis.
Saeviat atque novos moveat Fortuna tumultus!
Quantum hinc imminuet? quanto aut ego parcius, aut vos,
O pueri nituistis, ut huc [52]novus Incola *venit?*
[53]*Nam propriae telluris herum natura neque illum*
Nec me, aut quemquam statuit; nos expulit ille,
Illum aut [54]Nequities, *aut* [55]vafri inscitia juris,
Postremo expellit certe [56]vivacior haeres,
[57]*Nunc ager* Umbreni sub nomine, *nuper* Ofelli
Dictus, erit nulli proprius, sed cedet in usum
Nunc mihi, nunc alii. [58]*Quocirca vivite fortes!*
Fortiaque adversis opponite pectora rebus.   (94–116)

(To convince you of this, I know that in my childhood this same Ofellus was no more extravagant when his fortune was whole than now when it's been curtailed. You may see him on his small-holding, which he no longer owns, discoursing thus: 'On an ordinary day I have never, without a special reason, eaten anything except vegetables with a shank of smoked ham. But if after a long absence a guest arrived, or if I am free of work – then we shall make merry, not on fish fetched from the town, but on a chicken or a kid, after that, raisins and nuts and split figs will furnish a fitting dessert. After the meal it was our sport to quaff, with only the wine jar setting the limit; and our worship of Ceres, to ensure that her corn stalks would grow tall, smoothed away with wine the anxieties from the puckered brow. Let Fortune rage and stir up fresh tumults! What can she take from this? How much sleekness have either you or I lost, boys, since this new settler came? For Nature has established neither him, nor me, nor anyone as lord of his own land: he has dispossessed us, he will be dispossessed by villainy, or ignorance of the devious law, or at last, for sure, by an heir who outlives him. Today the land is called by Umbrenus' name, yesterday Ofellus'; it belongs to none, but will pass now into my use, now into another's. And so, live life with courage! Meet adversity with courageous hearts.)

What makes this speech so arresting are its charming details, the warmth of its tones, and the imaginative power of its final vision, as its language rises from Ofellus' simple discourse to eloquent rhetoric. Horace delights us with the richness of Ofellus' ordinary food: 'olus, *fumosae cum pede pernae*' ('vegetables with a shank of a smoked ham'), 'pullo *atque* haedo' ('a chicken or a kid'), '*tum* – / ... pensilis uva / ... nux ... *cum* duplice ficu' ('after that, raisins ... nuts ... and split figs'), which 'grace' ('*ornabit*') the dessert. The hospitality for long-absent friends is charmingly informal, shown by the drinking games at the end of the meal. Dacier remarks on the subtle blending of moderation and richness in Ofellus' entertainment and the 'veritable plaisir' that results: all too often, he says, the second course of a meal was followed by a debauched conclusion, but here it leads to pleasant drinking games and thankful libations to Ceres, goddess of the harvest (VII, pp. 138–42). But then this gives way to a strong and imaginative vision which suddenly challenges the whole idea of property and undercuts that great illusion, ownership:

> Nunc ager Umbreni sub nomine, *nuper* Ofelli
> Dictus, erit nulli proprius, sed cedet in usum
> Nunc mihi, nunc alii. (113–15)

(Today the land is called by Umbrenus' name, yesterday Ofellus'; it belongs to none, but will pass now into my use, now into another's.)

'Dominium', owning property, gives way to 'ususfructus', the right only of using and enjoying it; and we think for a moment of Lucretius' famous line 'vitaque mancipio nulli datur, omnibus usu' ('Life is granted to none freehold, to all on lease', *DRN.* iii.971). Dacier, rather impressively, thinks of Publius Syrus, Cicero, and Epictetus instead (VII, p. 145). The speech rises to its vigorous conclusion with a final, resounding 'golden line', '*Fortiaque adversis opponite pectora rebus*'. '*Fortiaque*' modifies '*pectora*' ('with brave hearts'), '*adversis*' goes with '*rebus*' ('the strokes of fate') and the verb '*opponite*' ('confront') stands dramatically in the centre.

From Horace's description of Ofellus Pope silently drops one line of Latin: 'cum pecore et gnatis fortem mercede colonum' ('with his cattle and his sons, a sturdy tenant-farmer'), line 115 in the full text. This makes a little easier his remarkable transformation of this passage into quite another world:

[45]Thus Bethel spoke, who always speaks his thought,
And always thinks the very thing he ought:
His equal mind I copy what I can,
And as I love, would imitate the Man.
In *South-sea* days not happier, when surmis'd
The Lord of thousands, than if now [46]*Excis'd*;
In Forest planted by a Father's hand,
Than in five acres now of rented land.
Content with little, I can piddle here
On [47]Broccoli and mutton, round the year;
But [48]ancient friends, (tho' poor, or out of play)
That touch my Bell, I cannot turn away.
'Tis true, no [49]Turbots dignify my boards,
But gudgeons, flounders, what my Thames affords.
To Hounslow-heath I point, and Bansted-down,
Thence comes your mutton, and these chicks my own:
[50]From yon old wallnut-tree a show'r shall fall;
And grapes, long-lingring on my only wall,
And figs, from standard and Espalier join;
The dev'l is in you if you cannot dine.
Then [51]chearful healths (your Mistress shall have place)
And, what's more rare, a Poet shall say *Grace*.
Fortune not much of humbling me can boast;
Tho' double-tax'd, how little have I lost?
My Life's amusements have been just the same,
Before, and after [52]Standing Armies came.
My lands are sold, my Father's house is gone;
I'll hire another's, is not that my own,
And yours my friends? thro' whose free-opening gate
None comes too early, none departs too late;
(For I, who hold sage Homer's rule the best,
Welcome the coming, speed the going guest.)   (129–60)

To make himself into Ofellus at this point is a fine move, but the
real master-stroke goes beyond that. Though all the details of this
passage come from the immediate Latin text, Pope actually switches
into a more mature Horatian style, speaking of his retreat at Twickenham more as if it were the Sabine farm of Horace's later poetry
than Ofellus' simple farm of *Satire* II.ii. The effect is utterly engaging,
for in terms of tone and nuance Pope brings together two Horaces
simultaneously, the simple moral Horace of this text and the more
subtle inward Horace of later works, towards which indeed this
Horatian passage finally came to point.[4] If, as Dacier suggests,
Ofellus offers one highly individual interpretation of moral truth,
here, alongside it, we have yet another. The words are the same, but
the meaning is different.

The changes in Ofellus' fortunes and the richness of Ofellus' life now become Pope's own, and English poetry glows with the warmth of Horatian Latin. The adaptations are wonderfully witty, and seem only to enhance Pope's portrait of his deep inner contentment as he contemplates his personal experience of self-sufficiency and moderation.[5] 'Integris *opibus*' ('when his fortune was whole') becomes 'In *South-sea* days not happier, when surmis'd / The Lord of thousands'; and '*Quam nunc* accisis' ('now, when it's been curtailed') produces a brilliant pun – 'than if now *Excis'd*'. '*Metato in agello*' ('small-holding which he no longer owns') has special meaning for Pope:

> In Forest planted by a Father's hand,
> Than in five acres now of rented land.   (135–6)

From the Horatian passage before this one, about changes of fortune, Pope takes the phrase '*contentus parvo*' ('content with little') and fuses it with Ofellus '*olus, fumosae cum pede pernae*' ('vegetables with a shank of smoked ham') to create the charming:

> Content with little, I can piddle here
> On Broccoli and mutton, round the year.   (137–8)

In the lines that follow he drops from the Latin text Horace's reference to neighbours ('gratus conviva per imbrem / vicinus' – 'or if in rainy weather a neighbour paid me a welcome visit') in order to concentrate on Ofellus' long-absent friends and his own. He neatly transfers 'operum vacuo' ('I am free of work') from Ofellus to the Tories now out of power – 'But ancient friends, (tho' poor or out of play).' Horace's '*non* piscibus *urbe*' ('not on fish fetched from the town') becomes

> 'Tis true, no Turbots dignify my boards,
> But gudgeons, flounders, what my Thames affords.   (141–2)

with its irresistible '*my* Thames'. He delights in the local 'mutton' from the nearby Hounslow-heath and Bansted-down, and 'these chicks my own'; and discovers all the ingredients of Ofellus' dessert growing quietly in his own walled garden:

> From yon old wallnut-tree a show'r shall fall;
> And grapes, long-lingring on my only wall,
> And figs, from standard and Espalier join ...   (145–7)

It is significant, also, that in his line 100 and line 102 of the Horace Pope silently changes the tenses of the verbs 'bene erat' to '*bene erit*', and 'ornabat' to '*ornabit*', to allow him to speak, in his Imitation, not of the past but of the present and the future, with the result that the whole passage becomes a generous *promise* of hospitality. (Writing to Cromwell on 25 June 1711 Pope had quoted these very lines and there also changed the verbs to the future tense to make them into a promise of hospitality, *Corr.* I, pp. 124–5.)

Furthermore, in line 103 of the Latin text Pope altered Heinsius' 'culpa' ('fault') to '*Cuppa*' ('wine-jar') to suggest 'with only the wine jar setting the limit'; but he remembered also Bentley's suggestion of 'cupa' ('wine-girl') which would mean 'with the wine-girl presiding over our revels.' This, and 'venerata Ceres' ('our worship of Ceres') join to produce an 'immoral'/'moral' fusion:

> Then chearful healths (your Mistress shall have place)
> And, what's more rare, a Poet shall say *Grace*.   (149–50)

Pope's index numbers indicate that Horace's 'novus Incola' ('new settler') from Octavian's army has inspired the witty allusion to the contemporary 'Standing Armies'; and from this point on Pope begins to explore Horace's ideas about the meanings of ownership. The 'ego' and 'vos' of Ofellus' address to his sons ('*quanto aut* ego *parcius, aut* vos, / O *pueri nituistis?*' – 'How much sleekness have either you or I lost, boys?') are turned nicely into an address to Pope's friends: we now hear, in the words of Homer himself, that Pope welcomes his friends, but also respects their freedom to depart, with the result that they, just like Ofellus' sons, truly 'possess' his house and joys:

> My lands are sold, my Father's house is gone;
> I'll hire another's, is not that my own,
> And yours my friends? thro' whose free-opening gate
> None comes too early, none departs too late;
> (For I, who hold sage Homer's rule the best,
> Welcome the coming, speed the going guest.)   (155–60)

Pope's allusion to his 'free-opening gate' and to his friends as travellers may well have been inspired by Dacier's quotation from Epictetus which he translates: '*Si celuy qui t'a donné la terre, te la laisse, uses – en comme d'une chose qui ne t'appartient point, & comme les Voyageurs usent des Hosteleries*' (VII, p. 145). There are also, however, allusions to Thomas à Kempis and Pope's own letters to Bethel (see Erskine-Hill, 1975, p. 315).

After this transformation of the centre of Ofellus' speech, Pope shifts again, and turns Horace's remaining lines into satire. He leads into this section by introducing Swift to offer a counter view:

> "Pray heav'n it last! (cries Swift) as you go on;
> "I wish to God this house had been your own:
> "Pity! to build, without a son or wife:
> "Why, you'll enjoy it only all your life." –
> Well, if the Use be mine, can it concern one

Whether the Name belong to Pope or Vernon?
What's [53]*Property*? dear Swift! you see it alter
From you to me, from me to [54]Peter Walter,
Or, in a mortgage, prove a Lawyer's share,
Or, in a jointure, vanish from the Heir,
Or in pure [55]Equity (the Case not clear)
The Chanc'ry takes your rents for twenty year:
At best, it falls to some [56]ungracious Son
Who cries, my father's damn'd, and all's my own.
[57]Shades, that to Bacon could retreat afford,
Become the portion of a booby Lord;
And Hemsley once proud Buckingham's delight,
Slides to a Scriv'ner or a City Knight.
[58]Let Lands and Houses have what Lords they will,
Let Us be fix'd, and our own Masters still.   (161–80)

For Horace's powerful assertion '*Nam* propriae telluris *herum natura neque illum / Nec me, aut quemquem statuit*' ('For Nature has established neither him, nor me, nor anyone as lord of his own land'), Pope asks:

What's *Property*? dear Swift! you see it alter
From you to me, from me to Peter Walter ...   (167–8)

Pope responds here not to the power of Horace's vision, as he will in the imitation of a comparable passage in *Epistle* II.ii., but rather to its possibilities for satire. The hints of Horace's ironic

... *nos expulit ille,*
Illum aut Nequities, *aut* vafri inscitia juris,
Postremo expellit certe vivacior haeres ...   (110–12)

(he has dispossessed us, he will be dispossessed by villainy, or ignorance of the devious law, or at last, for sure, by an heir who outlives him)

produce a whole list of legal wrangles. 'Nequities' ('villainy'), the index numbers inform us, is simply 'Peter Walter'. Pope's satiric ironies here could well have been suggested by Dacier's reading. On '*Illum aut* Nequities' he comments: 'Umbrenus m'a dépossedé, dit Ofellus & il sera luy-mesme dépossedé par son intemperance et par ses débauches. *Nequities* comprend tous les vices des prodigues, des luxurieux, & des débauchez' (VII, pp. 143–4). Horace's 'vafri inscitia juris' ('ignorance of the devious law') becomes 'Or in pure Equity (the case not clear)', while 'vivacior haeres' ('an heir who outlives him') emerges as 'some ungracious Son / Who cries, my father's damn'd, and all's my own.' Is it not better to have a true friend than such a son?

Finally, the names 'Ofellus' and 'Umbrenus' acquire symbolic power. At first Horace's '*Nunc ager* Umbreni sub nomine, *nuper* Ofelli / *Dictus*' ('Today the land is called by Umbrenus' name, yesterday Ofellus') produces:

> Well, if the Use be mine, can it concern one
> Whether the Name belong to Pope or Vernon?   (165–6)

But by the end 'Ofellus' emerges as a symbol of the great landowners of the past, 'Bacon' or 'Buckingham'; while 'Umbrenus' now turns out to be 'a booby Lord', 'a Scriv'ner or a City Knight'. If Horace's final line and a half urge us to resist the cruel blows of fortune, Pope's last couplet asks us to turn away with him from these more sordid strokes of fate. The contrast between Pope's conclusion and the Horace, however, may not have seemed as stark to eighteenth-century readers as seems to us. Although Dacier's translation brings out the idea of heroic resolve in the face of fortune, his final note emphasizes instead the need for acquiescence before the divinely ordained laws of change:

Cette consequence se tire naturellement des principes qu'il vient d'expliquer. Car puis qu'il est certain que toutes les choses du monde sont sujets au changement, & que le changement est la détermination de leur estre. C'est estre fou, de s'affliger, quand on voit qu'elles vont leur train. Il faut que nostre esprit acquiesce à cette Loy generale & universelle. Faire autrement, c'est gronder contre la Nature, & chercher plutost à corriger Dieu, qu'à se corriger soymesme.

(VII, pp. 145–7)

The conclusion to this Imitation is one of Pope's most imaginative transformations of Horace. At the centre is clearly the Horatian idea of the true inner self, what Horace, and indeed Cicero, often call the 'aequus animus'. This phrase, applied to Bethel in line 131, is used by Horace in *Epistles* I.xviii.112 and xi.30, and is often quoted by Pope in the letters (see, for example, *Corr.* I, p. 275). We have already seen in *Satire* II.i.70 the fine blending of 'equal' and 'partial' in 'aequus'; here the word gives depth to the ideal of the calmly balanced inner self.[6] The passage is also a celebration of friendship, which indeed, as the changes in the text show, is 'Horatian' rather than 'Ofellian'. And to this we must add the idea of independence: Dacier's whole interpretation of *Satire* II.ii., stressing that Ofellus is an independent thinker, has, I think, informed Pope's pride in his own individuality here, and in his own style of life.

But, as Erskine-Hill has so memorably shown, such Horatian traditions of the inner self are in England closely related to others: we also see here Pope using Horace to explore powerful public ideals, ideals which involve a relationship between private integrity and social responsibility, a deep commitment to 'use', and a profound concern for hospitality. These are indeed the ideals of this Imitation as a whole. Erskine-Hill has suggested that while Pope could not compete with Burlington and Bathurst, the great landowners, nevertheless 'the Horatian poem represented the extent to which he personally could fulfil the country house ethic which he admired' (1975, p. 317).

And yet, as Erskine-Hill himself fully recognizes, one can go further. The most subtle features of Pope's conclusion are first its questioning of the idea of property and second its own suggestions of the power of the poetic imagination. With Ofellus' rented land on the left-hand page and Horace's later poetry of the Sabine Farm in his head, Pope can assert that an entire life can be totally fulfilled on a tiny patch of rented land. Even more, with the help of Ofellus' powerful vision he can question the very concept of property and the accepted views of reality associated with it. The proud line of English country houses and their noble ancestries become, to the poet's eye, sordid legal wrangles and a depressing vision of social and moral degeneration masquerading as social mobility and economic growth.

We see here Pope responding to the most challenging and speculative aspects of Horace the moral teacher: this is indeed Dacier's and Dryden's Horace who instructs us how 'to Distinguish betwixt Truth and Falsehood, and betwixt our Conceptions of Things, and Things themselves'. The ideas of 'property' and 'ownership' are clearly two 'Notions, which they [men] have received from their Masters; and which they obstinately retain, without examining whether or no they are founded on right Reason'. The Horace of this whole Imitation is clearly the Horace who cultivates *true* self-knowledge and who, on that basis, 'labours to render us happy in relation to ourselves' and 'agreeable and faithful to our Friends' (Dryden, 'Discourse', pp. 74–5).

But the Horace of Ofellus' vision and Pope's conclusion is also Shaftesbury's poet of '*moral Magic*': a poet who draws images at once from real life and his own passions, and who discovers the true harmony of Nature in the love of proportion inherent in the workings of his own aesthetic imagination.

Of all other Beautys which *Virtuoso's* pursue, *Poets* celebrate, *Musicians* sing, and *Architects* or *Artists*, of whatever kind, describe or form; the most delightful, most engaging and pathetick, is that which is drawn from real *Life*, and from the *Passions*. Nothing affects the Heart like that which is purely *from it-self*, and *of its own nature*; such as *the Beauty of Sentiments*; *the Grace of Actions*; *the Turn of Characters*, and *the Proportions and Features of a human Mind*.

(Shaftesbury, 1714, I, pp. 135–6)

In our discussion of Pope's *Imitation of Epistle II.ii.* we shall discover how closely Shaftesbury identifies such a poet with the mature Horace, but it should be clear how this concern with the inner harmony of the self and the fusion of the aesthetic and the moral are relevant to Pope's poetry of self-portraiture here.

Relevant also is Shaftesbury's assertion here that the poet's act of aesthetic composition is not selfish, but social: 'For in the first place, the very Passion which inspires 'em, is itself *the Love of Numbers, Decency and Proportion*; and this too, not in a narrow sense, or after a *selfish* way (for Who of them composes for *himself?*) but in a friendly social View; for the Pleasure and Good of others; even down to Posterity, and future Ages' (1714, I, p. 136). In contrast to the images of inner chaos and intestine civil war in Horace's poem (lines 55–8) and his own (lines 69–72), Pope offers this final, calm image of himself. 'For', as Shaftesbury says, 'this is the Effect, and this the Beauty of their [the poets'] Art: "in vocal Measures of Syllables, and Sounds, to express the Harmony and Numbers of an inward kind; and represent the Beautys of a human Soul, by proper Foils, and Contrarietys, which serve as Graces in this Limning, and render this Musick of the Passions more powerful and enchanting"' (1714, I, pp. 136–7). For Shaftesbury this discovery of the fusion of moral and aesthetic truth is the discovery of the true self.

After the energetic and contradictory images of himself in the *Imitation of Satire II.i.*, Pope has, it seems, in this poem found that true self. For many eighteenth-century readers he would have found here the true Horace at the same time, the calm, powerful moral teacher. Yet Pope's ideal image of himself here, rich though it is, is also 'momentary'. In some sense, indeed, it is true because it is partial: a momentary glimpse of the real man, or, a true part of the whole, complex man. And if it is Horace who brings these harmonious visions, it is also Horace who, as we shall see in the next chapter, renders them illusions with the strident discords of *Satire* I.ii.

5

Horace, immoral:
The Imitation of Satire I.ii. (Sober Advice)

Here is a piece of poetry from Horace come out, which I warn you not
to take for mine, tho' some people are willing to fix it on me. In truth I
should think it a very indecent Sermon, after the *Essay on Man*.

Pope to Caryll, 31 December 1734

I hope he [Lord Duplin] will defend me from the imputation which all
the Town I hear lay upon me, of having writ that impudent satire.

Pope to Oxford, 30 December 1734

IN DECEMBER 1734 an obscene poem was printed in London,
Sober Advice from Horace, based on Horace's notorious *Satire* I.ii.
The work was anonymous, but, as the title-page stated, the author
had 'Imitated' the Horatian poem 'in the Manner of Mr. POPE'. In
fact, he warmly dedicated the work to 'ALEXANDER POPE, Esq.': 'Sir,
I have so great a Trust in your Indulgence toward me, as to believe
you cannot but Patronize this Imitation, so much in your own
Manner, and whose Birth I may truly say is owing to you' (*TE*, IV,
p. 73). It did, nevertheless, contain some sharp satiric remarks on
Pope and some of his close friends. The most shocking features of the
poem, however, were the Latin text and the footnotes. The Imitation
was printed '*Together with the* ORIGINAL TEXT, *as restored by the
Rev^{d.}* R. BENTLEY, *Doctor of Divinity. And some Remarks on the
VERSION*' (*TE*, IV, p. 71). The most obscene words in the Latin
poem stood out in large capitals, and 'the *Reverend Doctor*'
repeatedly complained in the footnotes that the Imitator had not
rendered them accurately enough, and, in the name of true scholarship, he indicated what they meant.[1]

But, although Pope repeatedly denied it, many contemporary
readers suspected the truth: this anonymous Imitation was in fact by
Pope himself. Having written two 'parodies' of Horace, he was now
writing a parody of himself. From every perspective *Sober Advice* is
an extraordinary work. Horace's *Satire* I.ii. is ostensibly about the
dangers of adultery: the poem urges that it is safer and more
enjoyable to have affairs with women of low rank ('meretrices') and
courtesans than with Roman wives ('matronae'). Though an early

78

work the poem is a triumph: lively, sensational, hard-hitting in the Lucilian manner, raised in its tone by some very sophisticated feats of language, but incorporating also frank sexual images and forthright Latin words. It abounds in satiric sketches and personal allusions, and weaves into its poetic texture individuals from Horace's time and the past, including Maecenas himself. In his Imitation Pope professes to offer this same 'Sober Advice' about adultery to the 'Young GENTLEMEN about Town', and to 'illustrate' his moral finds contemporary parallels for all Horace's scandalous characters and situations. He works into his poem every infamous adultery he can, attacks his usual enemies like Lady Mary and Lord Hervey, and even ridicules the sexual exploits and tendencies of his own friends Bolingbroke and Bathurst.

The contrast between this poem and the *Paraphrase of Satire II.ii.* could not be more striking. In the *Paraphrase* Pope is considering what, with enlarged consciousness, can perhaps be controlled and moderated: indulgence in eating, the use of riches, attitudes to possessions and property. In this poem he is confronting what cannot be so contained: sheer lust, sexual frustration, perversion, jealousy, aggression, and the very yearning for excitement and danger. How does Pope treat immorality in his own society, and how does he treat the 'obscenities' of Horace's poem? Are the footnotes simply 'pornographic' (Brower, 1959, p. 293)? Is Pope's poem merely a witty *jeu d'esprit* (Moskovit, 1965, p. 199); or is it, in fact, a moral work 'in a different key', 'neither perverse nor playful, as generally supposed, but rather ethical and satirical, in keeping with his recently assumed role of moral poet and imitator of Horace' (Aden, 1969, p. 47). Is the poem merely sensational personal abuse, or is it more seriously challenging and more substantially provocative?

There is no doubt that in the seventeenth and eighteenth centuries the 'immoral' sides of Horace's *Satire* I.ii. were notorious: its vulgar Latin words were recognized, at least by some, and to others the poem was evidence that Horace had himself been involved in adultery. Writing to Swift in early July 1734 Bolingbroke says: 'But it is impossible to talk so much of Philosophy, and forget to speak of Pope ... The Daemon of verse sticks close to him. He has been imitating the Satire of Horace which begins Ambubaiarum Collegia, Pharmacopolae, &c. and has chose rather to weaken the images than to hurt chaste ears overmuch.' (*Corr.* III, pp. 413–14). When referring to Augustus' adulteries and the law which forbade libellous poetry about such 'Villanies', Dryden notes: 'And our Poet [Horace] was not fit to represent them in an odious Character, because himself was dipt in the same Actions' ('Discourse', p. 69). Dryden is probably alluding, at least partly, to Horace's poetic description of 'himself' at the end of this satire, trying to escape from the scene of an adulterous affair.

Yet there were also attempts to moralize this work. Noting that it was written before Augustus' 'Loy *julia, De Adulteriis & Pudicitia*', Dacier asserts that Horace is attempting to advocate yet another middle way between two excesses: adultery on the one hand, and ruining oneself with courtesans on the other, the alternative to the latter being 'using' readily available servant-girls and boys. 'Le second excez qu'Horace blâme & qui est entierement opposé au premier, est de ceux qui ne bougeoient des vilains lieux, & qui se ruinoient avec les courtisanes' (VI, p. 107). He asserts that the poem shows there is a natural mean between these two extremes: 'Entre ces deux extremitez, ce Poëte établit un milieu, qui est celuy de la nature' (VI, p. 107). But he fully recognizes that Horace himself falls into the very faults he condemns, referring to Horace's warm praise for the beauty of courtesans, and to his 'own' adultery: 'Mais c'est une chose bien déplorable, qu'en voulant établir ce milieu, il tombe justement dans le defaut qu'il condamne' (VI, p. 107).

The most striking feature of Dacier's interpretation, however, is that on the basis of one line and a few suggestions, he makes the question of homosexuality a central issue. While approving Horace's condemnation of adultery, he strongly criticizes Horace's apparent acceptance of sexual relations with boys in line 117. He points out that 350 years before Plato had condemned 'l'amour infame des garçons' as 'un abominable peché contre la nature' (VI, pp. 109–10); and throughout his analysis, he uses Horace's poem against itself, commending highly the passages which describe, by contrast, 'natural' sexual desire and 'natural' moderation. At the same time he asserts that it is better for young people to learn the faults of their elders by reading such poetry than to be in ignorance, and he concludes that with all its faults, 'Cette Satire est d'ailleurs toute pleine de preceptes excellens' (VI, p. 110).

The way this satire begins is very significant. *Satire* II.ii. opens by clearly announcing its theme in the first line: '*Quae virtus & quanta, boni, sit vivere parvo.*' This work begins by completely disorientating the reader. At first it does not seem to be about adultery at all: it seems rather to be about the death of the singer Tigellius, then about the extremes of greed and avarice, and then about contradictions in human nature. Recognizing that the reader will be wondering what the point of all this is, Horace at last seems to announce his theme: 'Dum vitant stulti vitia, in contraria currunt' ('in avoiding one vice, fools run into its opposite'), but almost immediately this too evaporates. The examples of this moral dictum take over and finally lead to a new subject in line 37 – the disasters that befall adulterers – and this, at last, turns out to be what the satire is actually about. This play with ambiguity of the subject is extremely lively:

> Ambubajarum collegia, pharmacopolae,
> Mendici, mimae, balatrones; hoc genus omne
> Maestum ac sollicitum est cantoris morte Tigelli:
> Quippe Benignus erat –
>   – Contra hic, ne prodigus esse
> Dicatur, metuens, inopi dare nolit amico,
> Frigus quo duramque famem depellere possit.
> Hunc si percontteris, avi cur atque parentis
> Praeclaram ingrata stringat malus ingluvie rem,
> Omnia conductis coemens obsonia nummis:
> "Sordidus, atque animi quod parvi nolit haberi,"
> Respondent. laudatur ab his, culpatur ab illis.
>   Fufidius vappae famam timet ac nebulonis,
> Dives agris, dives positis in fenore nummis.
> Quinas hic capiti mercedes exsecat; atque
> Quanto perditior quisque est, tanto acrius urguet.
> Nomina sectatur, modo sumta veste virili
> Sub patribus duris, tironum. Maxime, quis non,
> Juppiter, exclamat, simul atque audivit? "At in se
> "Pro quaestu sumtum facit hic." Vix credere possis
> Quam sibi non sit amicus: ita ut Pater ille, Terenti
> Fabula quem miserum gnato vixisse fugato
> Inducit, non se pejus cruciaverit atque hic.
>   Si quis nunc quaerat, Quo res haec pertinet? Illuc:
> Dum vitant stulti vitia, in contraria currunt.   (1–24)

(The associations of performing flute girls, the salesmen of medicinal remedies, the beggars, actresses, clowns – they and all their kind are grief-stricken and distraught at the death of the singer Tigellius. He was such a generous man. In contrast, this man, afraid of being called spendthrift, refuses to give his poor friend the means to ward off cold and hunger's pains. Ask this other, who inherited a splendid fortune from his father, and his father before him, why he's scandalously stripping it away in his ruthless gluttony, buying up epicure's luxuries with borrowed cash: 'He doesn't want to be thought miserly and ungenerous', he'll answer. He's praised by some, condemned by others.

Fufidius fears being branded a simple Simon, an easy touch; he's rich in land, rich in cash lent out at interest. He extorts interest (five times the usual rate) on the principal; the more desperate the borrower, the more fiercely he harasses him. He hunts for IOUs from youths who are just of age and still subject to their fathers' rule. 'Ye Gods', everyone cries out on hearing this, 'But with those profits he must be spending a pile on himself'. You'd hardly believe how hard he is on himself: in fact the father in Terence's play who lived in misery after banishing his son did not torment himself as much as he does.

If anyone should now ask, where is all this taking us? Here: 'in avoiding one vice fools rush into its opposite'.)

What is so arresting here is Horace's sustained energy and exuberance. The first line is an astonishing feat of language, a hexameter of only three extraordinary words. '*Ambubajarum collegia, pharmacopolae*' ('The associations of performing flute girls, the salesmen of medicinal remedies'). The wild veering of the 'subject' only increases the energy and the feeling of improvisation as the sharp, contrasting portraits of the prodigal and Fufidius flash past. When a 'theme' is thrown in it seems to offer some point of orientation – 'Dum vitant stulti vitia, in contraria currunt' ('in avoiding one vice fools run into its opposite') – but as the poetry goes on it is in fact quickly forgotten. Dacier comments well on this opening: he sees that the real subject of the poem is adultery (VI, pp. 106–7), and for this discovery is complimented by Fraenkel (1957, p. 79, n. 4), but he says of the reader's bewilderment in line 24: 'Horace se rend justice: il a commencé cette Satire d'une maniere si bizarre, qu'il voyoit bien que naturellement quelqu'un luy devoit faire cette objection' (VI, p. 123).

Pope's imitation of this opening is very free, but in its own way it has all the life and hard-hitting force of the original, with one significant difference: Pope goes to his main subject at once. Horace writes first about men and money, exploring the moral and psychological perversities of prodigality and greed, and only gradually introduces sex and adultery. Pope focuses on the details of Horace's Latin but changes the men into women to produce a weird world of money and sexual frustration and aggression. After Pope's highly moral *Paraphrase of Satire II.ii.* we now have another view of wealth and property:

> The Tribe of Templars, Play'rs, Apothecaries,
> Pimps, Poets, Wits, Lord *Fanny*'s, Lady *Mary*'s,
> And all the Court in Tears, and half the Town,
> Lament dear charming *Oldfield*, dead and gone!
> Engaging *Oldfield!*, who, with Grace and Ease,
> Could joyn the Arts, to ruin, and to please.
>   Not so, who of Ten Thousand gull'd her Knight,
> Then ask'd Ten Thousand for a second Night:
> The Gallant too, to whom she pay'd it down,
> Liv'd to refuse that Mistress half a Crown.
>   *Con. Philips* cries, "A sneaking Dog I hate."
> That's all three Lovers have for their Estate!
> "Treat on, treat on," is her eternal Note,
> And Lands and Tenements go down her Throat.
> Some damn the Jade, and some the Cullies blame,
> But not Sir *H–t*, for he does the same.

> With all a Woman's Virtues but the P–x,
> *Fufidia* thrives in Money, Land, and Stocks:
> For Int'rest, ten *per Cent.* her constant Rate is;
> Her Body? hopeful Heirs may have it *gratis.*
> She turns her very Sister to a Job,
> And, in the Happy Minute, picks your Fob:
> Yet starves herself, so little her own Friend,
> And thirsts and hungers only at one End:
> A Self-Tormentor, worse than (in the Play)
> The Wretch, whose Av'rice drove his *Son* away.
> But why all this? I'll tell ye, 'tis my Theme:
> "Women and Fools are always 'in Extreme.   (1–28)

If Horace disorientates us with his veering subjects, Pope does the same with his extraordinary metaphors and his ambiguities of tone and subject. From one point of view, Pope is just writing scandalous personal satire directed against Anne Oldfield, Lady Castlemaine, the Duke of Marlborough (or Sir Edward Hungerford), Constantia Phillips, and Lady Mary (Horace's Fufidius). From another, Pope is using Horace's language about masculine avarice and prodigality to explore in challenging ways the strange relationship between the metaphors of sex and money: richness and barrenness, payment and repayment, yearning for wealth, contempt for bankruptcy, and loathing for impotence. In the first parody of Bentley's bad-tempered notes Pope draws attention to this overall reversal of the sexes throughout the opening of the poem: 'A Metaphrast had not turned *Tigellius*, and *Fufidius*, *Malchinus* and *Gargonius* (for I say *Malchinus*, not *Malthinus*, and *Gargonius*, not *Gorgonius*) into so many LADIES. *Benignus*, *hic*, *hunc* &c. all of the Masculine Gender: Every School-boy knows more than our Imitator' (*TE*, IV, p. 74). This note parodies Bentley's second and third notes on the spelling of '*Malchinus*' and '*Gargonius*' in lines 25 and 27 (1711, pp. 229–30).

Horace's '*Quippe* Benignus *erat*' ('He was such a generous man') becomes sharply ironic:

> Engaging *Oldfield!*, who, with Grace and Ease,
> Could joyn the Arts, to ruin, and to please.   (5–6)

Horace finds irony in the man who, fearing to be called a prodigal, grudges a poor friend enough money to banish the pangs of cold and hunger. Pope uses this as the final ironic twist to his own poetic version of the infamous stories surrounding Lady Castlemaine, who charged ten thousand a night:

> The Gallant too, to whom she pay'd it down,
> Liv'd to refuse that Mistress half a Crown.   (9–10)

Horace briefly tells of the man who in 'ruthless gluttony' (*'ingrata ... ingluvie'*) is scandalously stripping away a splendid fortune, inherited from his father, and his father before him (*'avi ... atque parentis / Praeclaram ... stringat malus ... rem'*), all because *'Sordidus, atque animi quod parvi nolit haberi'* ('He doesn't want to be thought miserly and ungenerous'). We now see whom he fears, and where all this land has gone, in an incredible fusion of the metaphors of land and sex:

> *Con. Philips* cries, "A sneaking Dog I hate."
> That's all three Lovers have for their Estate!
> "Treat on, treat on," is her eternal Note,
> And Lands and Tenements go down her Throat.   (11–14)

Pope takes the *'ingluvie'* ('crop') of *'ingrata ... ingluvie'* quite literally and sexually: 'down her Throat'. Dacier mentions the strange use of 'ingrata' here (VI, pp. 118–19).

Horace throws out a quick sketch of the rich Fufidius, who, fearing to be thought a worthless prodigal, charges five times the normal interest rate, and yet lives himself in poverty like Terence's 'Self-Tormentor'. This allows Pope to carry these metaphors further in a savage portrait of Lady Mary. Fufidius is 'rich in land, rich in cash lent out at interest' (*'Dives agris, dives positis in fenore nummis'*):

> With all a Woman's Virtues but the P–x,
> *Fufidia* thrives in Money, Land, and Stocks ...   (17–18)

He charges five times the usual interest rate (*'Quinas hic capiti mercedes exsecat'*):

> For Int'rest, ten *per Cent.* her constant Rate is;
> Her Body? hopeful Heirs may have it *gratis*.   (19–20)

That 'hopeful' is particularly bitter, given Lady Mary's unhappy relationship with her son. Fufidius' cruel treatment of his creditors Pope turns into soured family relations; and the *'Quam sibi non sit amicus'* ('how hard he is on himself') becomes:

> Yet starves herself, so little her own Friend,
> And thirsts and hungers only at one End ...   (23–4)

Horace's allusion to Terence's 'Self-Tormentor', the father who punished himself for cruelty to his son after he had banished him ('gnato ... fugato') becomes a cruel allusion to the real fate of Lady Mary's son:

> A Self-Tormentor, worse than (in the Play)
> The Wretch, whose Av'rice drove his *Son* away.   (25–6)

This leads directly to Pope's new interpretation of Horace's avowed theme 'Dum vitant stulti vitia, in contraria currunt' ('in avoiding one vice fools rush into its opposite'): ' "Women and Fools are always in Extreme.'

As Horace continues, nominally illustrating opposite extremes, the Latin suddenly becomes powerfully 'vulgar':

> *Malchinus tunicis demissis ambulat: est qui*
> Inguen *ad* obscaenum *subductis usque facetus:*
> *Pastillos Rufillus olet, Gargonius hircum.*
> *Nil medium est. sunt qui nolint tetigisse, nisi illas,*
> *Quarum subsuta talos tegat instita veste:*
> *Contra alius nullam, nisi olente in* fornice *stantem.*
>   *Quidam* notus homo *cum exiret fornice;* "Macte
> "*Virtute esto, inquit sententia dia Catonis,*
> "*Nam simul ac venas inflavit tetra libido,*
> "*Huc juvenes aequum est descendere, non alienas*
> "*Permolere uxores. –*
>   – *Nolim laudarier, inquit,*
> *Sic me, mirator* CUNNI CUPIENNIUS ALBI*
>   *Audire est operae pretium, procedere recte*
> *Qui moechos non voltis, ut omni parte laborent;*
> *Utque illis multo corrupta dolore voluptas,*
> *Atque haec rara, cadat dura inter saepe pericla.*   (25–40)

(Malchinus trails his tunic as he walks; another beau always keeps his hitched up indecently to his groin. Rufillus stinks of 'breath-fresheners', Gargonius like a goat. There's just no mean. Some men will touch no women except those whose ankles are covered by the long flounced skirt [i.e. married women]; whereas another, none unless she stands in a stinking brothel.

When a famous man was leaving a brothel, 'Bravely done, oh splendid man', was Cato's famous verdict; 'For as soon as foul lust has stiffened their veins, it's to this place that young men should come, and not screw other men's wives'. I would not wish to be praised in that way' says Cupiennius, connoisseur of a white cunt.

If you want adulterers' progress not to be smooth, it profits you to hear how on all sides they suffer, and how their pleasure is spoilt by great pain, and how pleasure itself is rare, and often is accompanied by harsh dangers.)

Cato refers to 'screwing other men's wives' ('*alienas / Permolere uxores*'); Cupiennius is a 'connoisseur of a white cunt' ('*mirator* CUNNI . . . ALBI') which, amazingly, stares at us in capital letters. The contrast with Dacier here is remarkable. Dacier notes that '*Vena* est un mot obscene', but refuses to translate '*Permolere*': 'C'est un terme trop libre pour estre traduit.' He mentions, however, that the word is used by Lucilius and Terence after the example of Theocritus' *Idyll* IV, adding helpfully that, in the Latin commentary on this Greek poem, 'le Scholiaste explique parfaitement ce mot.' He makes no comment at all on the force of 'cunni' (VI, pp. 131–3). (In Latin 'mirator' often suggests 'open-mouthed' amazement.) When Horace then finally announces his 'moral' theme it comes in a fantastic parody of Ennius:

> Audire est operae pretium procedere recte
> qui rem Romanam Latiumque augescere vultis. (*Annals*, 471–2)

(It profits you to hear, all you who wish the Roman state to progress successfully and Latium to increase.)

> *Audire est operae pretium, procedere recte*
> *Qui moechos non voltis, ut omni parte laborent . . .*   (37–8)

(It profits you to hear how adulterers do not progress easily and how on all sides they suffer.)

Here, as Fraenkel notes, 'The respectable verb *procedere* ['progress'] is degradingly joked with *moechos* ['adulterers']' (1957, p. 82; see also Dacier, VI, p. 133).

Pope's imitation focuses upon the most 'obscene' suggestions in this Latin, ostensibly merely illustrating his 'theme':

> *Rufa*'s at either end a Common-Shoar,
> Sweet *Moll* and *Jack* are Civet-Cat and Boar:
> Nothing in Nature is so lewd as *Peg*,
> Yet, for the World, she would not shew her Leg!
> While bashful *Jenny*, ev'n at Morning-Prayer,
> Spreads her Fore-Buttocks to the Navel bare.
> But diff'rent Taste in diff'rent Men prevails,
> And one is fired by Heads, and one by Tails;
> Some feel no Flames but at the *Court* or *Ball*,
> And others hunt white Aprons in the *Mall*.
>   My Lord of *L–n*, chancing to remark
> A *noted Dean* much busy'd in the Park,
> "Proceed (he cry'd) proceed, my Reverend Brother,
> " 'Tis *Fornicatio simplex*, and no other:
> "Better than lust for Boys, with *Pope* and *Turk*,
> "Or others Spouses, like my Lord of –
>   May no such Praise (cries *J–s*) e'er be mine!
> *J–s*, who bows at *Hi–sb–w*'s hoary Shrine.
>   All you, who think the *City* ne'er can thrive,
> Till ev'ry Cuckold-maker's flea'd alive;
> Attend, while I their Miseries explain,
> And pity Men of Pleasure still in Pain!   (29–50)

While Horace ridicules styles of dressing:

> *Malchinus tunicis demissis ambulat: est qui*
> Inguen *ad* obscaenum *subductis usque facetus . . .*   (25–6)

(Malchinus trails his tunic as he walks; another beau always keeps his hitched up indecently to his groin.)

Pope finds in his women sexual hypocrisy and bovine vulgarity:

> Nothing in Nature is so lewd as *Peg*,
> Yet, for the World, she would not show her Leg!
> While bashful *Jenny*, ev'n at Morning-Prayer,
> Spreads her Fore-Buttocks to the Navel bare.   (31–4)

In his adaptation of the story of Cato and the 'notus homo' ('a famous man'), all too appropriately transformed into one about the 'noted Dean', Thomas Sawbridge, indicted for rape (*TE*, IV, p. 384), Pope plays on Horace's 'notus homo' and '*juvenes*' (line 34) to produce neat allusion to homosexuality and himself: 'Better than lust for Boys, with *Pope* and *Turk*.' Finally, his use of large capital letters focuses attention on Horace's crudest words and image: '*mirator* CUNNI CUPIENNIUS ALBI' ('Cupiennius, connoisseur of a white cunt'). This allows him an obscene allusion to Viscountess Hillsborough's '*hoary Shrine*', playing on the metaphors of sex and religion, to which he adds a 'Bentley' note that underlines the powerful ambiguity of meaning in the Latin: 'Here the Imitator grievously errs, *Cunnus albus* by no means signifying a *white* or *gray Thing*, but a Thing under a *white* or *gray Garment*, which thing may be either black, brown, red, or particoloured' (*TE*, IV, p. 78). This note clearly parodies Dacier's weak reading of these words: 'Ce Cupiennius n'aimoit que les femmes de qualité qui portoient la robe blanche appelleé *stola*, car les Affranchies estoient habillées de noir, & les courtisanes avoient des habits de couleur' (VI, pp. 132–3).

These extracts hint at the most significant aspects of these two poems. As Horace's poem goes on it creates a veritable phantasmagoria of wild infatuations, daring adulteries, remorseless sexual energies, and cruel punishments. It portrays in satiric irony the overwhelming power of sexuality in human nature and Roman society, and shows how vicarious sexual activities satisfy in singular ways the human needs for conquest, secrecy, danger, self-destruction, and renown. Pope's central achievement in *Sober Advice* is to discover in the 'real' life of his own society perfect parallels for Horace's fantastic poetic vision of immorality, and to discover in them their passionate energies at the very moment he strikes them with his own fierce wit.

Far from simply condemning these people and events, such poetry seems to depend for its very life on their immorality, excess, and perverse energy. It becomes just as energetically immoral as they are.

Furthermore, far from being a simple 'truthful' work, the poem questions what 'truth' is. Pope delights to bring together poetic exaggeration and social rumour, the 'fictitious' people and events of Horace's poem and the truly notorious individuals and incidents of his own time. Concerned with those who have entered the true fiction of scandal, he asks whether this is poetic exaggeration or the real truth. In the metaphoric language of this extraordinary satiric fantasy Pope questions the validity of the ideals of 'Society', 'Nature', and 'Man' he had portrayed in works like the *Paraphrase of Satire II.ii.* and the *Essay on Man*. There he was concerned with moral passions and the metaphors of order. Here he is concerned with the confused metaphors of sex, money, religion, and politics: and he finds that the driving forces of his society, and its unifying agents, are the chaotic instincts of sheer lust, and the tangled powers of sexual frustration and sexual aggression.

All this involves yet another view of Horace and his poetic language. The Horace of *Satire* i.ii. is the poet who fuses together sophisticated literary parody with fierce personal invective and savage social criticism. This is the Horace of moral equivocation: by concentrating on endless sexual infatuations, he offers a salacious but damning view of his society. By honestly recognizing sexual needs and erotic pleasures, he half excuses, and even celebrates, the very actions he condemns. This is not Shaftesbury's Horace of Platonic moral idealism, but a poet parodying Aristotelian expediency. His poem boldly uses obscene Latin words to challenging effect, serving both his trenchant satire and his frank recognition of sexual realities.

It is clear that Pope fully endorses the non-moral reading of this Horatian satire. Indeed *Sober Advice* is, if anything, a parody of the interpretation of Horace as a moral teacher, and a parody of Pope's own moral teaching. The very title 'SOBER ADVICE from HORACE to the Young GENTLEMEN about Town. As deliver'd in his SECOND SERMON. Imitated in the Manner of Mr. POPE' suggests this; and, of course, the tone of the whole poem is mocking and ironical, including those passages which imitate what Dacier considered Horace's valuable moral teaching. At one point Horace urges:

> At quanto meliora monet, pugnantiaque istis
> Dives opis natura suae! tu si modo recte
> Dispensare velis, ac non fugienda petendis
> Inmiscere.
>   – Tuo vitio, rerumne labores,
> Nil referre putas? quare, ne poeniteat te,
> Desine matronas sectarier: unde laboris
> Plus haurire mali est, quam ex re decerpere fructus.   (73–9)

(How much better and how opposed to this is the teaching Nature offers, bountiful with her own wealth! – if only you are willing to manage life properly, and not confuse what you should shun with what you should seek. Do you think it makes no difference whether your trouble is due to your own fault or to circumstances? Therefore, that you may have no reason to repent, refrain from the pursuit of married women: in this undertaking, one is certain to drink the misfortune, unlikely to savour the fruit.)

Dacier sees this as true moral teaching, revealing the riches of nature and defining the genuine fulfilment that results from simply following her. On *'Dives opis natura suae'* he comments:

Ce passage est admirable: La Nature est assez riche de son propre fonds, sans qu'elle emprunte rien d'étranger. Les richesses de la Nature sont la beauté, la belle taille, l'embonpoinct: & c'est ce qu'elle demande. Les grands noms, la qualité, les honneurs, sont des biens de la Fortune: & c'est ce que la Nature ne demande point. Elle se contente de tout ce qui luy convient; tout le reste luy est à charge. (VI, p. 147)

But Pope offers a parody of this reading of the Horace, and a parody of his own moral thinking in the *Paraphrase of Satire II.ii.* and the *Essay on Man*:

> Hath not indulgent Nature spread a Feast,
> And giv'n enough for Man, enough for Beast?
> But Man corrupt, perverse in all his ways,
> In search of Vanities from Nature strays:
> Yea, tho' the Blessing's more than he can use,
> Shuns the permitted, the forbid pursues!
> Weigh well the Cause from whence these Evils spring,
> 'Tis in thyself, and not in God's good Thing:
> Then, lest Repentence punish such a Life,
> Never, ah, never! kiss thy Neighbour's Wife. (96–105)

This kind of parody brings out the equivocation and ironies of Horace's own language. Throughout his poem, Horace treads a very precarious line between 'genuinely' offering advice and using that as an excuse for personal satire and his own sophisticated ironies. Indeed, as we have seen, when Horace first adopts his tone of moral teacher he does so with a superbly bathetic parody of Ennius.

To see this allows us to look at the 'obscenity' of Pope's footnotes on the Latin text in a new way. It is perfectly clear that Pope wished to draw attention to the obscene language of Horace's poem, and we must realize that to do so was extremely daring. Although, as we have seen, some realized the meaning of these words, it was not acceptable to recognize them in print. No edition comments on them, and translators like Dacier and Watson (1760) invariably give modest versions of them, often stating that this is deliberate policy, which, of course, suggests that something is missing. Pope himself translates moderately, but then he uses 'Bentley's' notes to point to their real meanings. In doing this he parodies Bentley's style of close textual criticism, and hints at a link between textual pedantry and sexual obsession, both kinds of fetishism, and as Bentley's status suggests, both related to the religious obsession with purity. He also parodies Bentley's habit of focusing very closely on individual words. But, in addition, he also draws our attention to the real power of these obscene words in the Latin poem, and to the power of the genuinely uncensored text. Their force in the Latin derives from the clash of such words with the conventional 'literary' or 'political' words with which they are here scandalously involved. The final irony of these notes is that this sexually obsessed Bentley is actually right.

We have already seen how Pope singles out '*mirator* CUNNI CUPIENNIUS ALBI'. When Horace quotes the 'prick' itself, asking if when it swells with desire it really wants only a high-born woman, Pope brings out all the force of the Latin and all the 'political' and social implications of the passage:

> *Huic si, mutonis verbis, mala tanta videnti*
> *Diceret haec animus: Quid vis tibi? numquid ego a te*
> *Magno prognatum deposco consule* CUNNUM,*
> *Velatumque stola, mea cum conferbuit ira?*
> *Quid responderet? Magno patre nata puella est.*   (68–72)

(If a man's mind, when he beheld such suffering, were to say to him, speaking for his prick: 'What on earth do you want? Do *I* ever demand of you a cunt of illustrious consular stock, concealed in long skirts, when my passion is seething?' What would he reply? 'The girl's father is a famous man.')

> Suppose that honest Part that rules us all,
> Should rise, and say – "Sir *Robert!* or Sir *Paul!*
> "Did I demand, in my most vig'rous hour,
> "A Thing descended from the Conqueror?
> "Or when my pulse beat highest, ask for any
> "Such Nicety, as Lady or Lord *Fanny?* –
> What would you answer? Could you have the Face,
> When the poor Suff'rer humbly mourn'd his Case,
> To cry "You weep the Favours of her GRACE?   (87–95)

The placing of 'CUNNUM' ('cunt') right after '*consule*' in a line which is epic in style, rhythm, and alliteration is as powerful as it is bathetic. Pope has the witty 'A Thing descended from the Conqueror' picking up Horace's alliteration; but when he uses 'Bentley's' note to point to the force of the Latin, the metaphors of his 'textual' language get somewhat out of control: '*A Thing descended – why* Thing? *The*

Poet has it Cunnum; which, therefore, boldly place here' (*TE*, IV, p. 82). This note contrasts sharply with Dacier's comment on '*Magno prognatum deposco*' which makes no mention of 'cunnum' and attempts to find a moral meaning in the line: 'La Nature ne cherche qu'à se contenter: & dans ce dessein les grands noms, les richesses, la qualité, enfin tout ce qui ne vient pas d'elle, luy est étranger, & ne peut rien ajouter au plaisir & au soulagement qu'elle cherche' (VI, pp. 146–7). Significantly Pope translates 'muto' ('prick') as 'that honest Part that rules us all', and he has it rise to address its owners, the political leaders Walpole and Methuen, in the rhetoric of parliamentary debate. The refined upper classes here are basically sexual treats, and once again Pope plays on the theme of homosexuality, parodying the idea that it is unnatural: 'Such Nicety, as Lady or Lord *Fanny*.'

In the concluding section of his poem Horace asserts that sex with a young servant girl or a prostitute is much safer and more enjoyable than with other men's wives: '*Nec vereor, ne*, dum futuo, *vir rure recurrat*' (line 127 – 'I feel no fear, while I am fucking her, that her husband may come back from the country'). Pope 'translates' this

> Oh Love! be deep Tranquility my Luck!
> No Mistress H – *ysh* – *m* near, no Lady B – *ck*!   (175–6)

on which 'Bentley' comments:

Here the Imitator errs, the *Latin* has it *dum futuo*, a most necessary Circumstance! which ought to be *restored*; and may, by the change of a *single Word*, be the *same* with that of the Author, and one which wou'd marvelously agree with the Ladies in the second Line.   (*TE*, IV, p. 88)

This note is at once scandalous personal abuse, a satiric attack on Bentley, and true critical comment on the Horatian poetry. Dacier does not comment on any of these powerful Latin words and his own translation modestly turns 'cunnum' into 'les Dames' (VI, p. 89) or 'la fille' (VI, p. 95). Bolingbroke as we have seen, felt Pope had 'weakened the images'. Did Bolingbroke see the Imitation on its own before Pope had prepared the Latin text and added the footnotes to encourage this vigorous reading of the Horatian poem?[2]

Finally, given Dacier's heavy treatment of the hints of homosexuality in Horace's poem, it is important that Pope simply parodies that interpretation. All Pope's allusions to homosexuality in this poem are at once scandalous, high-spirited, and witty. At the end of the Imitation he turns into irony the very passage that so distressed Dacier (VI, pp. 172–4):

Nonne, cupidinibus statuat natura modum quem,
Quid latura, sibi quid sit dolitura negatum,
Quaerere plus prodest; & inane abscindere soldo?
Num, tibi cum faucis urit sitis, aurea quaeris
Pocula? num esuriens fastidis omnia praeter
*Pavonem, rhombumque? tument tibi cum inguina, num, si
Ancilla aut verna est praesto puer, impetus in quem
Continuo fiat, malis tentigine rumpi?
Non ego: namque parabilem amo venerem, facilemque.   (111–19)

(Wouldn't it be more use to enquire what limit nature has set to desires, which unfulfilled desires she will supply for herself and which will cause her pain, and to separate the hollow from the solid? When thirst parches your throat, do you demand golden goblets? When you're hungry do you disdain everything apart from peacock and turbot? When your member is swelling – if there's a serving girl or slave-boy available for immediate assault – would you rather stay erect till you're ruptured? Not I: I like sex which can be bought for cash without complications.)

> Has Nature set no bounds to wild Desire?
> No Sense to guide, no Reason to enquire,
> What solid Happiness, what empty Price?
> And what is best indulg'd, or best deny'd?
> If neither Gems adorn, nor Silver tip
> The flowing Bowl, will you not wet your Lip?
> When sharp with Hunger, scorn you to be fed,
> Except on *Pea-Chicks*, at the *Bedford-head*?
> Or, when a tight, neat Girl, will serve the Turn,
> In errant pride continue stiff, and burn?
> I'm a plain Man, whose Maxim is profest,
> "The Thing at hand is of all Things the *best*.   (143–54)

It is interesting here to see Pope return to the theme of plain eating from the *Paraphrase of Satire II.ii.*, but now in mockery. For Horace's '*Pavonem rhombumque*' ('peacock and turbot') Pope translates:

> When sharp with Hunger, scorn you to be fed,
> Except on *Pea-Chicks*, at the *Bedford-Head*?   (149–50)

and adds a note which shows 'Bentley's' profound knowledge of the classical world:

*PAVONEM, [Pea-Chicks] *Not ill-render'd, meaning a* young *or* soft Piece, *Anglice* a Tid-bit: *such as that Delicate Youth* Cerinthus, *whose Flesh, our* Horace *expressly says, was as* tender as a Lady's, *and our Imitator turn'd*
> Such Nicety, as Lady or Lord F —
not amiss truly; it agrees with My own Reading of tuo femore, *instead of* tuum femur, *and savours of the true Taste of Antiquity.*   (*TE*, IV, p. 86)

This note parodies Bentley's long discussion of the famous crux in line 81, in which he suggests a reading which implies Cerinthus is a homosexual (see also Fraenkel, 1957, pp. 84–6). It is clear that in the eighteenth century this witty treatment of homosexuality would have been daring. Dacier's full discussion of it was, in itself, bold, and it is significant that the Watson/Patrick edition of Horace, which as usual merely translates from Dacier's Preface and notes to the poem, makes no mention at all of this aspect of Dacier's interpretation (1760, II, pp. 26–9). To turn the Dacier into 'truthful' irony about the present age was even bolder.

As a totality *Sober Advice from Horace* is memorable not for its moral conviction, but for the lack of it. The poem is remarkable not for any 'corrective' personal satire, but for its ceaseless play of sharp wit and its exuberant delight in sheer scandal:

> And if the Dame says yes, the Dress says no. (132)

> What push'd poor *Ellis* on th' Imperial Whore?
> 'Twas but to be where CHARLES had been before. (81–2)

We see Pope here matching Horace's brilliant strokes of *personal* satire which, as Fraenkel says, 'come and go like lightning' (1957, p. 85):

> *Ut quondam Marsaeus amator Originis, ille*
> *Qui patrium mimae donat fundumque laremque ...* (55–6)

(As was once said by Marsaeus, Orgio's well-known lover, who gave his ancestral home and farm to an actress ...)

> To *Palmer*'s Bed no Actress comes amiss,
> He courts the whole *Personae Dramatis ...* (71–2)

> *Matronea, praeter faciem, nil cernere possis;*
> *Caetera, ni Catia est, demissa veste tegentis.* (94–5)

(You see only the face of a married woman, for unless she is Catia, her long robe conceals everything else.)

> A Lady's Face is all you see undress'd;
> (For none but Lady M – shows the Rest) ... (124–5)

The real challenge of *Sober Advice*, for modern readers at least, lies not in its sensational personal satire, but in the questioning of morality itself. The poem seems to suggest that moral accounts of human nature and human experience are both untruthful and inadequate. What we witness is the overwhelming force of sexuality which, though clearly exaggerated, rings all too true: the infamous adulteries Pope has woven into the poem, the vivid details of Mother

Needham's brothel, the ceaseless rain of personal allusions, create a world in which morality has little place and no force. The personalities include bishops, deans, politicians, aristocrats, actresses, judges, duchesses, ladies, one eminent textual critic, a rope-dancer, and a Reverend Doctor. They involve not only Pope's personal enemies, such as Lady Mary and Lord Hervey, but also Pope's friends, Bathurst and Bolingbroke ('Nothing so mean for which he can't run mad', line 64). But what Pope finds in his own society is only a mirror image of what Horace found in his.[3]

To see the full significance of this we must see *Sober Advice* in relation to Pope's other poems which confront the power of sexuality, sexual frustration, and, above all, the relationship between sexuality and identity in men and women. Pope had explored all these themes in the subtle ironies of *The Rape of the Lock* (1714) and considered them again from a tragic perspective in *Eloisa to Abelard* (1717). In the latter he suggested that a woman's very identity is bound to sexual passion, and that the contradictions in her nature tie her to the irreconcilable conflict between sexual desire and moral and religious conscience. In the *Epistle to Cobham* and *Epistle to a Lady*, contemporaneous with *Sober Advice*, we see Pope exploring the relationship between the 'ruling passion' and identity, and discovering that the passion which truly rules is rarely moral: rather it is ruthlessly egocentric, and often overtly sexual. Indeed, Pope's language shows that the 'ruling passion' is often subliminally sexual when it is apparently something else: the 'Lust of Praise', the 'Lust of Gold'. The portraits of men and women show again and again the force of sexuality, and, in particular, the acute 'crises of identity' it produces in women, manifested as utter contradictions in attitude, mood, and action:

> Now deep in Taylor and the Book of Martyrs,
> Now drinking citron with his Grace and Chartres.
> Now Conscience chills her, and now Passion burns:
> And Atheism and Religion take their turns;
> A very Heathen in the carnal part,
> Yet still a sad, good Christian at her heart.
>
> (*Epistle to A Lady*, 63-8)

What is impressive about *Sober Advice* is not, however, that it is serious in the manner of that poetry; but rather that it discovers, and re-creates the most challenging features of Horace's sexual jokes. The poem asks of itself, and Horace, questions which Freud was to ask in *Jokes And Their Relation to The Unconscious* (1905). Are jokes ever moral, or are they basically acts of either aggression or sexual exposure? Is a fierce attack on sexual excess in an individual

94

to some extent the response to unacknowledged aspects of the experience of a society, those aspects which are hidden and condemned precisely because they cannot be either understood or controlled? Is the power of the satiric attack, and the arousing of both indignation and delight in the reader, a testament to the latent power and importance of that which is condemned?

> From furious *Sappho* scarce a milder Fate,
> P–x'd by her Love, or libell'd by her Hate ...
> *(Imitation of Satire II.i.* 83–4)

In a vicious couplet like this we are puzzled by the power of the aggression, and the profound ambiguity of who is the victim and who the attacker.

Are both Pope's *Sober Advice* and Horace's *Satire* I.ii. ultimately attacks on the ruthless power of morality, and on the few who are rich and powerful enough to ignore it and live as they wish? We might remember a striking passage in Freud's study:

I will gladly renounce all the methods of satisfaction proscribed by society, but am I certain that society will reward this renunciation by offering me one of the permitted methods – even after a certain amount of postponement? What these jokes whisper may be said aloud: that the wishes and desires of men have a right to make themselves acceptable alongside of exacting and ruthless morality. And in our days it has been said in forceful and stirring sentences that this morality is only a selfish regulation laid down by the few who are rich and powerful and who can satisfy their wishes at any time without postponement. So long as the art of healing has not gone further in making our life safe and so long as social arrangements do no more to make it more enjoyable, so long will it be impossible to stifle the voice within us that rebels against the demands of morality. Every honest man will end by making this admission, at least to himself.

(trans. Strachey, 1976, p. 155)

In raising such questions *Sober Advice* underlines one recurring issue in Pope's Imitations of these three Horatian *Satires*, the whole relationship between satire and morality. The *Imitation of Satire II.i.* offers a highly paradoxical view of this question, despite its powerful assertions that the energy of satire is in fact moral. The *Paraphrase of Satire II.ii.* does all it can to blend together trenchant satire with imaginative moral teaching. *Sober Advice* questions whether satire ever can, or should, be a force for moral constraint. But in exploring those themes Pope had discovered so much else in Horace and in himself. Horatian satire had proved to be more varied, more surprising, more contradictory than one might have imagined. By December 1734 Pope appeared to have exhausted these subjects, and, perhaps, finished with 'Horace'. This, however, was not to be the case. All the subjects of these poems were still open, there was more Horace to explore, and more Pope to discover.

PART III
Mature Horace (1736–7)

6

Lyric Vision:
The Imitations of Odes IV.i. and IV.ix.

All hail! once pleasing, once inspiring Shade,
    Scene of my youthful Loves, and happier hours!
Where the kind Muses met me as I stray'd,
    And gently pressd my hand, and said, Be Ours.

Take all thou e're shalt have, a constant Muse:
    At Court thou may'st be lik'd, but nothing gain;
Stocks thou may'st buy & sell, but always lose;
    And love the brightest eyes, but love in vain!
          Pope to Teresa and Martha Blount, 13 September 1717

IN 1737, two years after *Sober Advice*, Pope published as a group three new Imitations of Horace. In March he brought out an Imitation of Horace's *Ode* IV.i., 'To Venus', in April an Imitation of *Epistle* II.ii., and in May an Imitation of *Epistle* II.i. These poems mark a whole new phase of Pope's relationship with Horace. There is a new seriousness in Pope's choice of Horatian models here, and a new depth in the Imitations themselves. After producing Imitations based on three early Horatian satires, he now presented Imitations modelled on Horace's very late poetry: the lyric which introduces Horace's last book of odes, and the two major works which together constitute Horace's last book of epistles.

We can account for this change partly in terms of the context in which the poems were written. It would seem that the period between 1736 and early 1737 was for Pope a time of contemplation and inward review. Between 1733 and 1735 Pope had published nine major poems, starting with the *Epistle to Bathurst* and ending with *Of the Characters of Women* and the second volume of his collected *Works*. During 1736 he published nothing new but worked on his own edition of his letters for publication in May 1737, and on these Imitations. If the letters involve an awareness of the past, so too do these poems. In addition, it would seem as if this was a period in which Pope became particularly aware of his age and of the loss of his friends and relations. Gay had died in December 1732, his mother in June 1733. Arbuthnot died in February 1735 and

Peterborough during that summer; in that same year Bolingbroke returned to France. In May 1736 Pope was forty-eight. In December 1736, as we shall see, Swift and Pope exchanged moving letters about increasing age and the loss of friends. Finally, this was a period of relative political calm. In the General Election of 1734 the Opposition had failed to defeat Walpole, and that struggle, temporarily at least, lost its momentum. The failure was marked, indeed, by Bolingbroke's decision to retire from the political struggle and return to France.

It is highly significant that all the Horatian poems Pope was drawn to at this time are retrospective poems, imbued with a strong sense of the past, and that two are specifically about age and loss. *Ode* IV.i., from one point of view at least, is concerned with the renewal of love in Horace as a man of fifty; and this is presented as an experience which painfully re-creates a lost past. *Epistle* II.ii. is an autobiographical poem in which Horace reviews his artistic work and the life it has involved; its poetry portrays a consciousness now deeply aware of time, loss, and death. In *Epistle* II.i., addressed to Augustus, Horace attempts to outline the development of Roman literary traditions, comments on contemporary taste, and pleads the cause of the new Augustan poetry in that context. At the same time Horace tries to define his own somewhat uneasy role as a poet in that world shaped by Augustus Caesar.

In these Imitations we will be exploring Pope's treatment of new Horatian themes: the writing of lyric poetry and the nature of poetic vision, time and loss, literary history and aesthetic judgement. At the same time, we will consider Pope's further development of subjects already raised: self-portraiture, the nature of property, the ideal of the Horatian mean. In Horace's late poetry the idea of art, and particularly the ideal of aesthetic perfection in lyric poetry, is never far away; and it is fascinating to see how Pope responds to this persistent preoccupation. We find here Pope exploring the Horace of the poetic imagination and the Horace of mature contemplation. This is the Horace who in the odes views life from the perspective of art, and who, in the epistles, views art from the perspective of life.

For our purposes it is convenient that the Imitations of 1737 include, indeed begin with, the imitation of an Horatian ode. Not only is the *Imitation of Ode IV.i.* impressive in itself, it also provides an opportunity to discuss briefly the nature of Horace's lyric poetry, and it is essential to know something about this in order to understand the late Horatian epistles. For these reasons I would like to consider this Imitation in some detail, and discuss along with it Pope's little poem based on four stanzas of *Ode* IV.ix. We do not know when this later piece was written; it was published for the first time posthumously by Warburton in his 1751 edition of Pope's works. But, as I hope to show, it relates very closely in theme and tone to this group of Imitations.

As J. B. Leishman (1956) has demonstrated, every serious translator or imitator of Horatian odes faces one virtually insuperable problem: the extreme complexity of their aesthetic forms and the elusive relationship between form and meaning. To begin with, these lyrics use extremely complex and intricate patterns in word order: Latin, being an inflected language, allows much greater freedom in the 'placing', or rather 'displacing', of words in poetry than is possible in English. We have already seen some of these effects in the satires, but in the odes Horace exploits this freedom to the full, and to a very large extent makes his poetry out of these subtle linguistic patterns. In addition, the odes exploit very strict, and sometimes elaborate, metrical forms. Latin quantity is more identifiable than English stress, and the various metres of Latin lyric poetry were more rigorously fixed than one is accustomed to in English verse. Horace's odes use a wide variety of such intricate metres, mostly based on archaic Greek models.

It is for this reason that when Horace in the *Epistles* speaks about writing lyric poetry, he talks about it, sometimes ironically, in terms of finding words that will fit the rhythms of the Latin lyre: '*Verba lyrae motura sonum conectere digner?*' ('Am I expected to weave together words which will move the lyre to give voice'?) as he puts it in *Epistle* II.ii.86. In English when words are displaced for the sake of rhythm or special effect the result is often extremely grating. One remembers Johnson's remark on Collins' *Odes*: 'He puts his words out of the common order, seeming to think with some later candidates for fame, that not to write prose is certainly to write poetry' (quoted by Leishman, 1956, p. 83). The best description of the general effect of an Horatian ode remains Nietzsche's enthusiastic testament:

Up to this day I have not had an artistic delight in any poet similar to that which from the beginning an Ode of Horace gave me. What is here achieved is in certain languages not even to be hoped for. This mosaic of words, in which every word, by sound, by placing, and by meaning, spreads its influence to the right, to the left, and over the whole; this minimum in extent and number of symbols, this maximum thereby achieved in the effectiveness of the symbols, all this is Roman, and believe me, elegant par excellence.   (Quoted by Commager, 1962, p. 50)

These features have always been recognized as forming the essence of Horace's lyric style.[1] Milton's famous translation of the Pyrrha ode, *Ode* I.v., is, indeed, precisely an attempt to translate these Latin qualities directly into English. Milton's Pyrrha ode, however, is the exception, not the rule: most seventeenth- and eighteenth-century translators simply despaired of re-creating these qualities, and attempted only to convey in quite different terms the paraphrasable meanings, tones, feelings of these poems, and their overall shapes.[2]

In addition, these aesthetic qualities present problems of interpretation which make translation and imitation of Horatian odes particularly challenging. What is the relationship between these distinctive aesthetic forms and 'meaning'? What kinds, and degrees, of emotion are expressed in such forms? How genuinely autobiographical are these lyrics, and how much are they stylized explorations of Greek, Alexandrian, and elegiac conventions?[3] How does one account for the strange 'veering' of the lines of thought in so many Horatian odes which often makes the isolation of a 'subject' difficult and, arguably, mistaken?

Questions of this kind confront us immediately when we approach Pope's *Imitation of Ode IV.i*. In one sense Horace's ode can be seen in terms of biography and the direct expression of emotion. At the opening Horace pleads with Venus not to subjugate him to love at his age, and in the middle he urges that a young and accomplished lawyer, Paulus Maximus, would be a more suitable person to inflame as a devotee. But at the end there is a dramatic reversal: Horace reveals that he is, in fact, passionately in love with a young man, Ligurinus, who seems cruelly out of reach and painfully hardhearted.

Most seventeenth- and eighteenth-century editions see the poem in such terms. Dacier, for example, stresses the autobiographical character of the opening and the fact that Horace was nearly fifty when he was 'touché de la beauté de Ligurinus' (Dacier, IV, pp. 12–13). He explains in great detail the rites which are being offered to Venus in the middle of the poem, showing that these were traditional Roman rituals. At the end, he stresses the beauty and tenderness of the emotions Horace expresses in his longing for Ligurinus. Commenting on Horace's final lines he asserts: 'Cette reprise d'Horace fait une des plus grandes beautez de cette Ode, & les huit derniers vers sont pleins d'une passion exprimée avec beaucoup de delicatesse' (Dacier, IV, p. 37).

But, as so often with the Horatian ode, the closer we look at it the more enigmatic it becomes. The opening of the poem is clearly about both the return of the experience of love and the return of Horace to the writing of lyric poetry: for a poet to speak of being in the power of Venus would mean he was going to write erotic poetry. Horace seems to be recounting an actual experience of love, and at the same time alluding to this elegiac convention in order to introduce this new fourth book of odes. What is the relationship between the emotion expressed and this poetic convention? Further, if the poem is about love and poetry why is the complimentary portrait of Paulus Maximus so extended? Finally, how do we interpret the ending of the poem? Does the poetic vision of the cruel, fleeing Ligurinus refer to a 'reality', or is it, indeed, a poetic fantasy?

Pope's Imitation of Horace's ode also seems to raise such questions. His Imitation seems to suggest that there are subtle relationships between the real and the imaginary, the past and the present, the person loved and the poetic image, the experience of loss and the experience of love, the world of emotion and the world of vision. How much did Pope draw this from Horace's ode, how much did he bring it to that poem?

> *Intermissa Venus diu*
> *Rursus bella moves? parce precor, precor!*
> *Non sum qualis eram, bonae*
> *Sub regno Cynarae: Desine, dulcium*
> *Mater saeva Cupidinum,*
> *Circa lustra decem flectere mollibus*
> *Jam durum imperiis: abi*
> *Quo blandae juvenum te revocant preces.* (1–8)

(Are you, Venus, stirring up again warfare long suspended? Show mercy, I beg and beseech you. I am not the man I was under the rule of good Cynara. Cease, fierce mother of sweet Desires, to drive with your soft commands one, near fifty, who is now hardened to them. Away, to where the wheedling prayers of youths are summoning you.)

This is what Nietzsche calls the mosaic of words. Adjectives are placed well before the nouns they modify, suspended to arouse interest in what it is they refer to and only 'completed' when their nouns are discovered: '*Intermissa ... bella*' ('suspended ... warfare'), '*bonae ... Cynarae*' ('good ... Cynara'), '*dulcium ... Cupidinum*' ('sweet ... desires'), '*mollibus ... imperiis*' ('soft ... commands'), '*blandae ... preces*' ('wheedling ... prayers'). Contrasting words are yoked together: '*dulcium ... saeva*' ('sweet ... fierce'), '*mollibus ... durum*' ('soft ... hardened'). The words '*imperiis*' ('commands') and '*durum*' ('hardened') are juxtaposed without syntactical connection in order to emphasize the paradox. But within this complex pattern how powerful is alliterative '*parce precor, precor*' ('Show mercy, I beg and beseech you'); and how simple and haunting is '*Non sum qualis, eram bonae / Sub regno Cynarae*' ('I am not the man I was under the rule of good Cynara'). Finally, how distinctive is the rhythm: the metre is the Second

Asclepiadean, a graceful metre used, significantly, in many of Horace's earlier love poems:

$$- \; - \; - \; \cup\cup \; - \; \cup \; \underset{\smile}{-}$$
$$- \; - \; - \; \cup\cup \; - \; \| \; - \; \cup\cup \; - \; \cup \; \underset{\smile}{-}$$

The heavy syllables at the beginning of every line tend to give strength and calm, the light syllables movement and grace.

This opening is in fact very sophisticated. '*Intermissa*' refers equally to the writing of lyric poetry and the experience of love. As Fraenkel (1957, pp. 410–14) points out, the traditional elegiac *recusatio* of the refusal to write about war is here turned upside down: here the poet claims he cannot write about the warfare of love. In addition, the poem seems an inversion of those hymns which invite a reluctant god to a celebration. At the same time the intensities of the feelings conveyed by '*parce precor, precor!*', and the poignant allusion to the self of the past, make us feel the force of a strange experience of love (see Dacier, IV, p. 13). Do the striking contradictions in language here allude to the pain of writing as well as the pain of love?

No English version of the poem could re-create all the subtle resonances which were available to Horace. By contrast Pope's opening seems much simpler. Using Horace's language and, in particular, his military metaphors, he imagines a similar experience of love:

> Again? new Tumults in my Breast?
> Ah spare me, Venus! let me, let me rest!
>   I am not now, alas! the man
> As in the gentle Reign of My Queen *Anne*.
>   Ah sound no more thy soft alarms,
> Nor circle sober fifty with thy Charms.
>   Mother too fierce of dear Desires!
> Turn, turn to willing Hearts your wanton fires.   (1–8)

Pope uses Horace's metaphors to convey his emotional confusion – 'new Tumults in my Breast', 'Ah sound no more thy soft alarms' – and Horace's conflicting adjectives to express his ambivalent attitude to that experience: 'Mother too fierce of dear Desires!' He expresses at once reluctance, 'Ah spare me ... Ah sound no more', and wistful regret: 'I am not now, alas!' Pope does not attempt to mirror Horace's complex word order; but he does attempt to convey something of the effect of Horace's rhythm, by counteracting the iambic movement of his lines with frequent trochees, and with nominally unstressed syllables which in fact carry the weight of stressed syllables: 'Ah spare me', 'Nor circle', 'Turn, turn to'. The effect is to re-create something of the weight of Horace's Asclepiadean metre. Perhaps the subtlest touch, however, is the transformation of '*bonae / Sub regno Cynarae*' ('under the rule of good Cynara') into 'As in the gentle Reign of My Queen *Anne*'. Is Pope alluding to his life at that time, or to the emotional world of his poetry at that period, in particular the intense *Eloisa to Abelard* and the early poems to Martha Blount?

> *Tempestivius in domo*
> Paulli, *purpureis ales oloribus,*
> *Comessabere* Maximi,
> *Si torrere jecur quaeris idoneum.*
> *Namque et nobilis & decens,*
> *Et pro solicitis non tacitus reis,*
> *Et centum puer artium,*
> *Latè signa feret militiae tuae.*
> *Et quandoque potentior*
> *Largis muneribus reserit aemuli,*
> *Albanos prope te lacus*
> *Ponet marmoream, sub trabe citrea.*
> *Illic plurima naribus*
> *Duces thura; lyraeque & Berecynthiae*
> *Delectabere tibiae*
> *Mistis carminibus, non sine fistulâ.*
> *Illic bis pueri die*
> *Numen cum teneris virginibus tuum*
> *Laudantes, pede candido*
> *In morem Salium ter quatient humum.* (9–28)

(It would be more seasonable for you, borne on the wings of gleaming swans, to hold your revels in the house of Paulus Maximus, if you are looking for a suitable liver to grill. After all, being well-born, good looking, eloquent on behalf of defendants under attack and a youth with a hundred skills, he will carry your forces' standard far and wide. And once he has triumphed and can mock his rival's lavish gifts, he will set you up by the Alban lake in marble form sheltered by a cedar roof. There you shall inhale clouds of incense, and you will delight in the lyre and the Phrygian flute with song accompanying, and pipes as well. There twice every day choirs of boys and delicate maidens shall hymn your divine power and with shining feet beat the earth in the triple time of the Salii dance.)

The panegyric begins with a touch of comic irony as Horace speaks of Venus, 'borne on the wings of gleaming swans' ('*purpureis ales oloribus*'), going to Paulus' house in order to find 'a suitable liver to grill', '*torrere jecur … idoneum*'. The praise of Paulus is what one might expect: '*nobilis*' ('well-born'), '*decens*' ('good-looking'), until we reach '*Et pro solicitis non tacitus reis*' ('and eloquent on behalf of defendants under attack'). This strange and daring detail, which would seem quite irrelevant to the world of Venus, is important just because of its oddness. Horace appears anxious to praise Paulus as being both a suitable follower of Venus and an exemplary Roman. If Roman elegiac poetry typically shows these worlds as being opposed, here Horace strikingly treats them as if they can be somehow brought together (see Fraenkel, 1957, pp. 413–14). Having presented Paulus in this way, he is then seen as a traditional elegiac lover, triumphing over the gifts of a lavish rival through sheer charm, and setting up a marble statue to Venus where religious ceremonies will be performed with music and dancing.

The details here are important for they blend together the real with the imaginary. As Dacier emphasizes, a specific and well-known place is mentioned, '*Albanos prope ... lacus*' ('by the Alban lake'), the fashionable spot where Paulus had a villa: 'Horace dit à Venus que Maximus luy fera un Temple prés de ce lac, parce qu'il avoit peut-estre là une maison' (Dacier, IV, p. 28). Having named this real place Horace then evokes imaginary, poetically conceived rituals which will take place 'there': '*Illic ... Illic*' ('there ... there'). He uses rich imagery of incense, music, and dance; and adds to the traditional Roman lyre ('*lyrae*') and pipe ('*fistula*') an exotic Eastern touch in the Phrygian flute ('*Berecynthiae | ... tibiae*'). Its music is juxtaposed with the much more traditionally Roman dancing 'in the Salian fashion' ('*morem Salium*'). Dacier explains here the many honours being offered to Venus: a statue, an expensive temple, many sacrifices, and finally the dancing which, he says, would be performed by children chosen from the best families, 'un certain nombre de jeunes garçons et de jeunes filles qui chantoient jusques à ce qu'on en choisist d'autres' (Dacier, IV, p. 33). What Dacier does not show is that this real world of a respectable Roman aristocrat blends, in the poetry, with the realm of the poetic imagination.

But this is precisely what Pope brings out. He notes Horace's initial touch of prosaic irony, and then attempts in his own way to explore the relationship between the real and the imaginary, now at Murray's house at the side of the Thames. That ordinary river reflects a 'visionary Scene' which is half a real social scene and half a poetic vision of grace and beauty:

> To *Number five* direct your Doves,
> There spread round MURRAY all your blooming Loves;
>   Noble and young, who strikes the heart
> With every sprightly, every decent part;
>   Equal, the injur'd to defend,
> To charm the Mistress, or to fix the Friend.
>   He, with a hundred Arts refin'd,
> Shall stretch thy Conquests over half the kind:

> To him each Rival shall submit,
> Make but his riches equal to his Wit.
>   Then shall thy Form the Marble grace,
> (Thy Graecian Form) and Chloe lend the Face:
>   His House, embosom'd in the Grove,
> Sacred to social Life and social Love,
>   Shall glitter o'er the pendent green,
> Where Thames reflects the visionary Scene.
>   Thither, the silver-sounding Lyres
> Shall call the smiling Loves, and young Desires;
>   There, every Grace and Muse shall throng,
> Exalt the Dance, or animate the Song;
>   There, Youths and Nymphs, in consort gay,
> Shall hail the rising, close the parting day.   (9–30)

The dry irony of 'To *Number five* direct your Doves' echoes the wit of Venus in all her array coming to find a 'fit heart' to inflame. Horace's striking line about Paulus' skill as a lawyer, however, becomes more directly attuned to the theme of love, and then extended in the direction of friendship.

> Equal, the injur'd to defend,
> To charm the Mistress, or to fix the Friend.   (13–14)

Murray's eloquence is here more idealistically imagined than in Horace. However, Horace's allusion to the traditional elegiac convention that the poet-lover can or should triumph over rich rivals by sheer quality, is turned by Pope into a sardonic aside:

> To him each Rival shall submit,
> Make but his riches equal to his Wit.   (17–18)

But the most interesting feature here is the way in which Pope interprets and develops the relationship between the real and the imaginary. While Dacier's commentary brings out the actuality of these rituals for Venus (see Dacier, IV, pp. 31–3), Pope blends with that the suggestions of 'vision' and aesthetic harmony in Horace's poetic description. The statue of Venus he sees amusingly in these terms:

> Then shall thy Form the Marble grace,
> (Thy Graecian Form) and Chloe lend the Face ...   (19–20)

But then Paulus' '*domus*' is fused with his villa by lake Albana to celebrate a place which is now 'Sacred to social Life and social Love'. Horace's religious rituals enacted by boys and tender maidens ('*pueri ... / cum teneris virginibus*') become the social gatherings of Murray and his young friends as viewed through the poetic imagination.

Horace's rich poetic language of ritual music and dance enables Pope to see in the society of his own time those visions of grace and harmony:

> There, every Grace and Muse shall throng,
> Exalt the Dance, or animate the Song;
> There, Youths and Nymphs, in consort gay,
> Shall hail the rising, close the parting day. (27–30)

Indeed, with Horace on the left-hand page, it is that poetically imagined place which is miraculously re-created at Murray's house: 'Where Thames reflects the visionary Scene.'

Horace follows his lines on Paulus with four lines which starkly contrast his own position with that of the young man. In the portrait of Paulus he used '*et*' five times to dwell on the youth's qualities; now, set against this, we find the word '*nec*' repeated five times:

> *Me nec femina, nec puer*
> *Jam, nec spes animi credula mutui,*
> *Nec certare juvat mero:*
> *Nec vincire novis tempora floribus.* (29–32)

(I now find no pleasure in woman or boy, nor in the fond hope of love returned, nor in joining lovers' drinking parties, nor in garlanding my brow with fresh flowers.)

Pope seems to have found these lines particularly powerful; every detail in Horace seems to make him conscious of some loss of experience or loss of hope as he contrasts his own position with that of Murray's:

> With me, alas! those joys are o'er;
> For me, the vernal Garlands bloom no more.
> Adieu! fond hope of mutual fire,
> The still-believing, still-renew'd desire;
> Adieu! the heart-expanding bowl,
> And all the kind Deceivers of the soul! (31–6)

Pope here brings out poignantly the many-sidedness of this lost 'love'. He takes Horace's last line about fresh blossoms first; and then turns Horace's '*nec spes animi credula mutui*' ('nor in the fond hope of love returned') into something very intense. Pope's metaphors touch on the continuation of the energy of the self and belief in the renewals of sexual desire:

> Adieu! fond hope of mutual fire,
> The still-believing, still-renew'd desire ... (33–4)

Horace's '*Nec certare juvat mero*' ('Nor in joining lovers' drinking parties') becomes a more solemn allusion, in which Horace's hint of competition between lovers is transformed into a celebration of comradeship: 'Adieu! the heart-expanding bowl'. Horace's *'puer'*, with its homosexual implications, is dropped; and Horace's simple *'femina'* produces a more complex and thoughtful climax: 'And all the kind Deceivers of the soul!' This arresting version of the Horace prepares for Pope's dramatic conclusion.

Horace's lines about his age could have been the end of the lyric, but at this point Horace, in a characteristic turn, contradicts what he has just said with lines poignantly addressed to another young man:

> *– Sed cur, heu! Ligurine, cur*
> *Manat rara meas lacryma per genas?*
> *Cur facunda parum decoro*
> *Inter verba cadit lingua silentio?*
> *Nocturnis te ego somniis*
> *Jam captum teneo: jam volucrem sequor*
> *Te, per gramina Martii*
> *Campi, te per aquas, dure, volubiles.* (33–40)

(But why, Oh Ligurinus, why is it that the odd tear trickles down my cheek? Why in the midst of eloquent speech does my tongue fall into humiliating silence? In my dreams at night it's you I see; now I've caught and held you, now I pursue you as you fly over the grass of the Campus Martius and the eddying waters, you callous boy.)

In his passion for Ligurinus Horace shows all the signs of the young lover, dramatically conveyed in this suddenly intense poetry: *'facunda'* ('eloquent') leads to *'silentio'* ('silence'); the contrast of *'Jam captum'* ('now I've caught and held you') *'jam volucrem'* ('now as you fly') is echoed in *'per gramina'* ('over the grass'), *'per aquas'* ('over the waters'); and the penultimate word, an apostrophe modifying the final 'te' ('you'), and forming an oxymoron with *'volubiles'* ('eddying'), is the painful *'dure'* ('callous'). The whole ending is a master-stroke, and this word *'dure'* gives it its real pathos: 'c'est un vocatif, qui fait une des grandes beautez de ce passage, parce qu'il marque la passion' (Dacier, IV, pp. 40–1).

Pope transforms this yearning for a young man into longing for a woman, Patty Blount, in the first printed version of the poem; and in doing so he seems to change the whole conception of the love:

> *– But why? ah tell me, ah too dear!*
> Steals down my cheek th'involuntary Tear?
> Why words so flowing, thoughts so free,
> Stop, or turn nonsense at one glance of Thee?
> Thee, drest in Fancy's airy beam,
> Absent I follow thro' th'extended Dream,
> Now, now I seize, I clasp thy charms,
> And now you burst, (ah cruel!) from my arms,

And swiftly shoot along the Mall,
Or softly glide by the Canal,
Now shown by Cynthia's silver Ray,
And now, on rolling Waters snatch'd away.   (37–48)

What Pope emphasizes here is the yearning of love as an imaginative experience as well as an emotional state. The key lies in Pope's elaboration of Horace's word-cluster '*Nocturnis te ego somniis*' ('Of the night, you, I, visions') in which he dramatically separates the '*te*' and the '*ego*' which Horace has artfully juxtaposed:

Thee, drest in Fancy's airy beam,
Absent I follow thro' th'extended Dream ...   (41–2)

The transformation is remarkable: if Horace's poetry shows him as the victim of his own cruel dreams of Ligurinus, Pope's poetry shows him indulging gently in this 'extended Dream' of poetic fancy:

And swiftly shoot along the Mall,
Or softly glide by the Canal,
Now shown by Cynthia's silver Ray,
And now, on rolling Waters snatch'd away.   (45–8)

What is impressive about this Imitation is the fact that it, like the original, can be read on many levels. In one sense it is a poignant study of the awareness of the loss of love kindled by the renewal of love itself. In this sense the poem should be seen in relation to *Eloisa to Abelard* and *To the Memory of an Unfortunate Lady* of 1717. In those poems Pope had shown himself a poet of the passions, exploring overwhelming intensities of feeling, deeply contradictory emotions and needs, and, through imaginative identification with others, a deep sense of loss and isolation brought about by unrequited or lost love. It is fascinating to see Pope eighteen years later return momentarily, and perhaps indeed reluctantly, to that emotional world in this Horatian ode:

Again? new Tumults in my Breast?
Ah spare me, Venus! let me, let me rest!
I am not now, alas! the man
As in the gentle Reign of My Queen *Anne*.   (1–4)

At the same time Pope's Imitation is an exploration of the ideal as it is present to the poetic imagination. Horace here is the poet of vision, and Pope at once discovers this aspect of Horace's ode and develops it further in his own Imitation. He internalizes in an individual way the 'visionary Scene' of Horace's ritual for Venus and Horace's dream of Ligurinus, and develops the conjunction between the dream and the actual place in Horace's poem. Indeed, it is the use of these contemporary names – 'the Canal', 'the Mall' – which helps to make this Imitation focus attention on the tension between the imaginary and the real. In this respect Pope's Imitation can be contrasted with Ben Jonson's translation, which shows that for a seventeenth-century English audience classical place-names are part of a 'poetic reality'.[4]

Putting these two approaches together one might say that in Pope's poem this imaginative experience becomes either a substitute for love, or a higher form of love. Whereas Horace's ode seems to end on a painful note of unrequited love and perhaps self-betrayal (see Commager, 1962, pp. 292–4), Pope's conclusion stresses a creative involvement in the experience of loss. Here we have yet another side of Horace that Pope found relevant to his own thought and poetry. Pope's *Pastorals, Windsor Forest*, the *Rape of the Lock*, show that Pope was concerned with the relationship between social reality and the poetic ideal, indeed between the world of time and timeless art, and the relationship between the emotions and the imagination. It is clear that Pope was interested in those Horatian odes which explore these issues.

A slight, but suggestive, example of this is found in a letter to Bolingbroke and his wife written on 9 April 1724, in which Pope affectionately imitates the opening of Horace's *Ode* III.iv., 'Descende caelo'. Having summoned Calliope, the muse of epic poetry, in the first stanza, Horace both questions the reality of the sounds he hears and asserts the reality of the imaginary world in which that 'experience' takes place:

> Descende caelo et dic age tibia
> regina longum Calliope melos,
>   seu voce nunc mavis acuta,
>   seu fidibus citharave Phoebi.
>
> auditis an me ludit amabilis
> insania? audire et videor pios
>   errare per lucos, amoenae
>   quos et aquae subeunt et aurae.   (*Odes*, III.iv. 1–8)

(Come down from heaven, Queen Calliope, and, I pray you, make much music, either with the flute, or, if you so choose, singing in your own clear voice, or with the strings of Phoebus' lyre.

Do you too hear, or is it I who am deluded by some delightful madness? I seem to hear her, and to wander in holy groves amidst sweet streams and breezes.)

In his letter Pope stresses the 'unreal' quality of this poetry, and relates it to both the absence of religious vision in Enlightenment France and to the power of his own poetic imagination:

Notwithstanding you tell me of the Oracles of our Lady of Lasource are ceas'd and that She returns no more answers, I shall expect the favour She promises to a poor Hermit on the banks of the Thames. In the mean time I see Visions of her and of Lasource.

> – An me ludit amabilis
> Insania, Audire et videor pios
>   Errare per lucos, amoenae
>   Quos et aquae subeunt et aurae.
> What pleasing Phrensy steals away my Soul?
>   Thro' thy blest Shades (La Source) I seem to rove
> I see thy fountains full, thy waters roll
>   And breath[e] the Zephyrs that refresh thy Grove
> I hear what ever can delight inspire
> Villete's soft Voice and St John's silver Lyre.
>   – Seu voce nunc mavis acuta
>   Seu fidibus, cytharave Phoebi.
>   I cannot subscribe my self better than as Horace did.
>   Vestris Amicum Fontibus et choris.

(Corr. II, p. 229)

The preoccupations with art, time, and loss are also evident in a very different poem, Pope's short Imitation based on four stanzas from Horace's *Ode* IV.ix. The Horatian stanzas Pope has imitated are concerned with the power of lyric poetry to immortalize the events of time which otherwise would perish utterly. The first three stanzas set the tone for the whole poem: written in the powerful Alcaic metre, they begin in a soaring rhetorical style which is, in fact, maintained to the very end of the poem, as seen in Horace's seventh stanza which Pope uses to make his fourth and final stanza:

> *Ne forte credas interitura, quae*
> *Longe sonantem natus ad Aufidum*
>   *Non ante vulgatas per artes*
>   *Verba loquor socianda chordis;*
>
> *Non, si priores Maeonius tenet*
> *Sedes Homerus, Pindaricae latent*
>   *Ceaeque, et Alcaei minaces*
>   *Stesichorique graves Camenae:*
>
> *Nec, si quid olim lusit Anacreon,*
> *Delevit aetas: [spirat adhuc amor,*
>   *Vivuntque commissi calores*
>   *Aeoliae fidibus puellae].*
>
> *Vixere fortes ante Agamemnona*
> *Multi; sed omnes illacrymabiles*
>   *Urgentur ignotique longa*
>   *Nocte, carent quia vate sacro.*

(Do not believe that these words will perish which I, born by the Aufidus which men hear from afar, utter for coupling with the strings of the lyre, using art not hitherto made public.

Even though Maeonian Homer occupies the first place, still Pindar's muse is not obscured nor the Cean's, nor the admonitions of Alcaeus, nor the weighty song of Stesichorus.

Nor has time destroyed the songs which Anacreon playfully composed an age ago; [the love is still breathing, the passions still living, which the Aeolian girl confided to her lyre].

There lived many heroes before Agamemnon, but all of them, unwept and unknown, are weighed down in unending night, because they lack a holy bard.)

The style of these opening lines is quite appropriate to their powerful assertions: four negative clauses sustain the high-sounding note – '*Ne forte credas*' ('Do not believe'), '*Non ante*' ('Not hitherto'), '*Non, si*' ('Even though'), '*Nec, si*' ('Nor'). In the second line of the first stanza Horace refers to himself in a confident periphrasis alluding to the river near his birthplace, '*Longe sonantem natus ad Aufidum*' ('[I] born by the Aufidus which men hear from afar'); and he speaks of the art of his poetry in the highest terms:

> *Non ante vulgatas per artes*
> *Verba loquor socianda chordis ...* (3–4)

(words I utter for coupling with the strings of the lyre, using art not hitherto made public)

Most impressively, the '*interitura*' ('they will perish') of line 1 stands alone until we find the '*Verba*' ('words') of line 4 which is its subject. In addition, the subordinate clause, '*quae / Longe*', and the descriptive phrase '*Non ante*', powerfully precede the words on which they depend. Finally, the whole stanza is welded together with the Alcaic metre which embraces all four lines, coming to a climax on its powerful third line, and flowing away in the fourth:

> *Nē fŏrtĕ crēdās īntĕrĭtūră, quāē*
> *Lōngē sŏnāntēm nātŭs ăd Āufĭdūm*
> *Nōn āntĕ vūlgātās pĕr ārtēs*
> *Vērbă lŏquōr sŏcĭāndă chōrdīs ...* (1–4)

In the second stanza Horace accepts that Homer stands supreme among Greek poets, but points to the lasting achievements of those Greek lyric poets who were his models. In the impressive rhythms Pindar, Simonides (from Ceos), Alcaeus himself, and Stesichorus, pass by. In the third stanza, Horace emphasizes that time has not destroyed even what Anacreon 'playfully composed' ('*si quid ... lusit*'); and he dramatizes with carefully placed verbs how the love and passions of Sappho still 'breathe' ('*spirat*') and 'live' ('*Vivunt-que*') in the music of her poetry.

The four stanzas which follow these in the whole poem, and omitted by Pope, assert that in the past there have been other Helens overwhelmed by passion, other Troys, other struggles between great heroes, other Hectors and Deiphobuses who suffered for their wives and children; but that all these have passed into oblivion because they had no poet to sing of them and their experiences. The climax to this line of thought comes in the powerful seventh stanza. The verb '*Vixere*' ('There lived') comes emphatically first, but then the whole stanza portrays the oblivion which has overcome them, unwept and unknown. '*Urgentur*' ('weighed down') has the suggestion of night pressing down on them like a tomb; and that third line has all the weight of the Alcaic metre centred upon it: '*Urgēntŭr īgnōtīquĕ lōngā*'. Only the '*vate sacro*' ('holy bard') could have saved them, '*sacro*' because possessing the power of bestowing the divine gift of immortality.

The claims that Horace is making here are more striking than they might appear. As Fraenkel has pointed out, 'The idea that lyric poetry can immortalize men's achievements is completely absent from the first three books of the *Odes*' (1957, p. 423). Only in this fourth book does Horace assert that his poetry will immortalize its subjects; and only here does he in fact write that type of public panegyric poetry on contemporary Romans which would make such claims appropriate. This ode, and the previous one, *Ode* IV.viii. with which it must be read, are notable for making such powerful and confident assertions.

From these four stanzas Pope has created a very distinctive lyric on the theme of art and loss:

> Lest you should think that Verse shall die,
>   Which sounds the Silver Thames along,
> Taught on the Wings of Truth, to fly
>   Above the reach of vulgar Song;
>
> Tho' daring Milton sits Sublime,
>   In Spencer native Muses play;
> Nor yet shall Waller yield to time,
>   Nor pensive Cowley's moral Lay.
>
> Sages and Chiefs long since had birth
>   E're Caesar was, or Newton nam'd,
> These rais'd new Empires o'er the Earth,
>   And Those new Heav'ns and Systems fram'd;
>
> Vain was the chief's and sage's pride
>   They had no Poet and they dyd!

In vain they schem'd, in vain they bled
They had no Poet and are dead!

Pope makes no attempt to re-create here the character of the Alcaic stanza nor to emulate the power of Horace's sweeping rhetoric. Rather he quietly explores and develops Horace's ideas as they seem applicable to his own poetry using a simpler, more aphoristic tetrameter metre. The most striking feature of the Imitation is Pope's emphasis on the 'Truth' of poetry. Horace, characteristically, claims immortality for his verse on the grounds of its artistic superiority; Pope sees his verse as lasting because it partakes of what he calls 'Truth':

Taught on the Wings of Truth, to fly
Above the reach of vulgar Song ...   (3–4)

Set against Horace's list of Greek lyric poets, Pope then explores the lasting quality of English poets, below the level of Milton: Horace's '*lusit*' for what Anacreon wrote playfully and '*Camenae*' (the Italian equivalent of the Greek Muses) produce a neat: 'In Spencer native Muses play'. The elegant poetry of Waller and the 'moral Lay' of 'pensive' Cowley may seem slight by comparison, but they have the power to endure, because they too embody what Pope calls 'Truth'.

It is because he has modified the Horace in this way that Pope can conclude with a very individual two stanza version of Horace's stanza 7: on the one hand, for Pope, the heroes are not just those engaged in heroic conflict, but those struggling to create new visions of society; on the other, he considers the fate of creative philosophical thinkers as well as generals. Next to the other 'Caesars' we have other 'Newtons':

These rais'd new Empires o'er the Earth,
And Those new Heav'ns and Systems fram'd ...   (11–12)

This makes the failure of their actions and their visions all the more poignant. But Pope counterpoints their loss with the potential power of the poet to immortalize those events and those philosophic visions. The poet of *The Essay on Man* recognizes the need for Horace's '*vates*': 'They had no Poet and are dead!'

7

The Horatian epistle:
The Imitation of Epistle II.ii.

The most melancholy effect of years is that you mention, the catalogue
of those we lov'd and have lost, perpetually increasing.
                                            Pope to Swift, 30 December 1736

HORACE'S *Epistle* II.ii., addressed to Julius Florus, is one of
Horace's most beautifully finished and richest verse epistles. Like its
companion piece, *Epistle* II.i. to Augustus, the poem is notable for
the complexity and subtlety of its form, the fine interweaving of its
various themes, and the calm maturity of its completed poetic vision.
Both are concerned with the art of poetry; but that to Augustus,
appropriately, treats the subject in public manner, raising questions
about culture, taste, and the public role of the poet, while this poem
is personal and inward, concerned with Horace and his own life. And
yet it has wider perspectives: at once private and universal, it brings
together, and distinguishes between, the demands of poetry which
concern the artist and the demands of life which affect everyone.

In approaching these two epistles we must realize that they raise
new and difficult questions about form and meaning. Whereas the
early satires, like *Satire* I.ii. and *Satire* II.ii., are relatively simple in
design, these late epistles are highly elusive. Indeed, it is difficult to
speak of either the 'subject' or the 'form' of a delicately orchestrated
work like *Epistle* II.ii.: both can be discussed only in relation to the
experience of reading, for in the mature Horatian epistle subjects and
form emerge only in the created time of imaginative involvement.
These epistles have been given the shape of casual conversation: they
are purposeful, but they seem to have no purpose. Related to this is
the notorious obliqueness of Horace's handling of the 'theme', and
the equally famous subtlety of his transitions. These characteristics,
evident in all Horace's poetry, are used with particular effect in the
epistle form of his maturity: it is as if one could not have a 'subject' or
a 'purpose' in writing to a friend.

The ostensible reason for *Epistle* II.ii. to Julius Florus is to explain
why Horace had not written to him before, and why, in particular, he
had not sent any new lyric poems. In Horace's hands this becomes a

fertile trope. It allows him to explore all his reasons for writing odes, and all his reasons for not writing them; to review his past and present life; to assess his achievements; to consider why one wants, or feels compelled to write; to think about the personal consequences of being of the tribe of poets; to enquire whether the anguish of writing has been worth the effort; to meditate on the poet's high, aesthetic, understanding of language; to consider if writing makes one happy or miserable; and to ask, at last, if it is time now to give up this 'folly' altogether in the name of true wisdom.

This accounts for something like the first half of the poem. Having arrived at that position, Horace can then explore the nature of wisdom in terms of the relationship between morality and experience, considering: the simplicity and the difficulty of moral demands; the relationship between physical and moral needs; the realities and illusions of possession; the human desire to build and create in the face of time, change, and death; the persistence of avarice despite the insubstantiality of all its desires; the mystery of individual human natures; the possibility and the impossibility of achieving self-possession; the value and undesirability of achieving self-satisfaction; and the idea that one might either live properly or give way to the young who can, at least, trifle with somewhat better grace.

The irony of the poem, and its wisdom, lies in the subtle juxtaposing of the various ideas, arguments, and sketches, which seem to comment silently on each other. The poem's line of argument, which appears to be so improvisational, so unpremeditated, is in fact, beautifully woven. But this argument does not give the work a clearly definable unity or focal point: its ironies are too elusive for that, its centre of gravity too much in motion, and its tones too fluid. With its 'structure' so exquisitely 'open' this poem positively invites many interpretations.[1]

TWO INTERPRETATIONS

Two eighteenth-century readings of this epistle present two very different 'Horaces' and, indeed, two very different 'poems'. André Dacier views this epistle in terms of Horace's dialogue with Julius Florus, and the Horace he sees in it is very much the moral teacher. Dacier explains that in the first part of the epistle Horace justifies himself to Julius Florus for not writing more poetry: 'Horace luy fait cette réponse pour se justifier, & pour luy faire voir l'injustice de ses plaintes' (Dacier, IX, p. 474). He argues that Horace offers five reasons for not writing poetry: he is lazy and runs away from work, like the boy in the opening story (lines 20 ff.); he is now getting too old to write (lines 55 ff.); he can't please the tastes of different readers (lines 58 ff.); it's impossible to write amid the noise of Rome (lines 65 ff.); trying to write lyric poetry leads to vanity or painful self-criticism (lines 87 ff.). The climax of the poem comes when Horace reveals that he is turning from the art of poetry to the art of life (lines 141 ff.).

Dacier then sees the second half of the poem as moral instruction about avarice and ambition which is directed very particularly at Julius Florus. Horace introduces this section by saying 'Quocirca mecum loquor haec' ('For this reason I utter these thoughts to myself', line 145); and Dacier comments: 'Horace fait semblant de ne parler qu'à soy-meme, pour faire mieux goûter ses raisons à son ami, pour le corriger plus facilement de l'avarice, de l'ambition, & de tous les autres vices ausquels il estoit sujet' (Dacier, IX, p. 516). Finally, at the end of the poem he sees the famous concluding questions as being addressed directly to Julius Florus who, as other poems reveal, is in need of such questioning. Dacier says of the key words in line 207: 'Ambitione, mortis formidine, & ira' ['ambition, fear of death, anger'] – Voilà le veritable caractere de Florus. Il estoit avare, ambitieux, emporté, superstitieux & timide. Voyez l'Ode XIV. du Livre II. & l'Epistre troisiéme' (Dacier, IX, p. 531). Dacier sees this epistle, therefore, in terms of argument, self-justification, and rather pointed moral teaching.

This approach can be contrasted with Shaftesbury's discussion of the nature of the Horatian epistle in general, and this epistle in particular. Shaftesbury sees the epistle form much more in terms of meditation and introspection, since, for him, Horace was pre-eminently a poet of inwardness and self-analysis. One of the central themes of his 'Advice to an Author' (1710) is the value of what he calls the 'Method of SOLILOQUY', or 'this self-examining Practice, and Method of inward Colloquy'. He asserts that this, which is his own method, is modelled specifically on Horace, 'the best Genius and most Gentleman-like of Roman Poets' (Shaftesbury, 1714, I, pp. 327–8). To make his point he quotes Horace's description of his debate with himself in Satire I.iv. 133–8, placing what for him are the key words in capitals:

> –Neque enim, cum lectulus, aut ME
> Porticus excepit, desum MIHI: "Rectius hoc est:
> "Hoc faciens, vivam melius: sic dulcis Amicis
> "Occurram." – Haec EGO MECUM
> Compressis agito labris.

(After all, when my couch or the colonnade gives me shelter, I don't desert myself: 'This is the more correct course; if I do this, I shall lead a better life; in this way I shall be agreeable to my friends.' These are the questions I debate with myself, though my lips are pressed together.)

He then quotes the very lines from *Epistle* II.ii. which Dacier says are really addressed to Julius Florus: '*Quocirca* MECUM *loquor haec . . .*' (line 145 – 'For this reason I utter these thoughts to myself'). Indeed, he quotes also the poem's final questions about avarice, ambition, and fear which, clearly, he saw as a model for universal self-examination: '*Non es avarus: abi, quid? caetera jam simul isto / Cum vitio fugêre?*' (205–6); ('You're not a miser? All well and good. But did all the other vices disappear along with avarice?' – Shaftesbury, 1714, I, p. 329).

The difference between teaching others and discovering oneself is, of course, rather fundamental, and it is not surprising that Dacier and Shaftesbury see such different poems here. This can be related to Shaftesbury's highly sophisticated approach to the epistle form, and again the contrast with Dacier is illuminating. Dacier sees very clearly that the connections between passages in this poem are often puzzling at first, and only in retrospect seem to acquire their full meaning as repetitions are noted and echoes heard: 'On n'a laissé la pluspart de ces Epistres dans la grande obscurité où elles sont, que pour n'avoir pas garde à ces liaisons & à ces reprises' (Dacier, IX, pp. 514–15). For Dacier the subtlety of these connections lies primarily in the way in which they constitute an argument in reply to Julius Florus: the applications of the opening stories underline Horace's own position; the passage on lyric poetry shows Julius Florus how hard it is to write such verse; the points that come to mind about property spring from Horace's inner debate with Julius Florus as Horace imagines what his friend might be thinking (see, for example, Dacier's comment on lines 170–1, IX, p. 522).

For Shaftesbury the art of the epistle involved a much subtler relationship between the writer and the recipient, and a much more complex attitude to 'art' itself. In the first 'Miscellany' of 'Miscellaneous Reflections' (1714), which ends with a chapter on the epistle form, he asserts: 'They who can read an *Epistle* or *Satir* of HORACE in a somewhat better than a mere Scholastic Relish, will comprehend that *The Concealment of Order* and *Method*, in this manner of Writing, makes the chief Beauty of the Work' (Shaftesbury, 1714, III, p. 21). Here Shaftesbury sees the idea in relation to Horace's blend of integrity and freedom in his approach to his recipients, the specific 'Courtiers, Ministers, and Great Men of the Times' (p. 21).

In 'Advice to An Author' he had explored this idea more in terms of the relationship between self-discovery and art. The '*Methodick*' manner, as Shaftesbury calls it, confesses its 'method', and because of that actually seems to analyse itself in a self-conscious way: 'Now tho every other Stile and genuine Manner of Composition has its Order and Method, as well as this which, in a peculiar sense, we call *the Methodick*; yet it is this Manner alone which professes Method, dissects it-self in Parts, and makes its own Anatomy' (Shaftesbury, 1714, I, p. 257). By contrast, because the author who writes in '*The Simple* Manner' wishes to express not simply 'himself' but actually the very order of Nature, he must conceal his art:

> *The Simple* Manner, which being the strictest Imitation of Nature, shou'd of right be the compleatest, in the Distribution of its Parts, and Symmetry of its Whole, is yet so far from making any ostentation of Method, that it conceals the Artifice as much as possible: endeavouring only to express the effect of Art, under the appearance of the greatest Ease and Negligence. And even when it assumes the censuring or reproving part, it does so in the most conceal'd and gentle way. (pp. 257–8)

But then, of course, those writers were anxious that their true skill and seriousness should be appreciated. To make this point Shaftesbury quotes from this epistle Horace's line on the final achievement of true poetry:

> When they had so polish'd their Piece, and render'd it so natural and easy, that it *seem'd* only a lucky Flight, a Hit of Thought, a flowing Vein of Humour; they were then chiefly concern'd lest it should *in reality* pass for such, and their Artifice remain undiscover'd. They were willing it shou'd be known how serious their Play was; and how elaborate their Freedom and Facility: that they might say as the agreeable and polite Poet, glancing on himself, *Ludentis speciem dabit & torquebitur.* (Shaftesbury, 1714, I, pp. 233–4)

For Shaftesbury, the Horace of the mature epistles is a highly self-conscious artist, at every point aware of his recipient, his art, and himself.

But his fundamental concern is himself, and Shaftesbury interprets this particular epistle in that light. As we saw in the 'Introduction' Shaftesbury interprets all Horace's late epistles as explorations of his need for independence from Maecenas and the 'Court' of Augustus. This poem is the assertion of his desire to give up poetry to find that true self. The whole poem is written to Florus as an uninvolved person to whom he could tell his true feelings: 'see Horace writing to a friend, not to Maecenas, nor under that heavy burden of a seeming obligation, but to an indifferent person, to whom, without offence, he could tell his griefs and positive resolution of retirement' (Shaftesbury, 1900, p. 362). The passage on Horace's time in Athens and involvement in the Civil War (lines 41–54) shows 'his better Condition and nobler Employments in earlier days, under the Favour and Friendship of *greater* and *better* Men [e.g. Brutus], whilst the *Roman* State and Liberty subsisted' (Shaftesbury, 1714, III, pp. 249–50). He hints at his own new position in the story of Lucullus' soldier '(which is honest Horace himself)' (lines 26–40); asserts it openly at the climax: ' "Nimirum sapere est abjectis utile nugis" [line 141 – 'I really must seek wisdom and put aside trifles']. For, as Lucullus' soldier has done with fighting, so Horace renounces writing' (Shaftesbury, 1900, p. 362). Significantly Shaftesbury imagines Horace's inner agitation as he thinks about this resolution: 'Horace is at ease. He has got his zona (his estate) again. Ah! many thanks to Maecenas. And will he leave Maecenas then? Will he retire and slight him? Is not this ungrateful?' (p. 362). But as a whole the poem portrays Horace's recognition of his true inner self, the self of what Shaftesbury calls Horace's *'returning, recovering state,* and his recourse to his first philosophy and principles' (p. 360). It is worth emphasizing at this point that for Shaftesbury the 'concealed art', the addressing of epistles to particular, named individuals, and the concern with self-exploration, went hand-in-hand with political freedom. He criticizes Seneca's letters to Lucilius from these points of view and clearly regards Horace's late satires and epistles as models of integrity (see Shaftesbury, 1714, III, pp. 20–5). This is a point we will explore further in considering Pope's *Imitation of Epistle II.i.*

These two interpretations enable us to define more clearly the character of Pope's *Imitation of Epistle II.ii.* From the very beginning Pope emphasizes the inward and meditative side of Horace's poem. He also fully recognizes the importance of the linking of themes, images, and metaphors that gives this mature Horatian poetry its distinctive character. But within these terms he creates from the Horatian epistle a very personal and individual poem, for throughout this Imitation he stresses loss, frustration, and failure, in his own life, and in the lives of others.

Pope makes this Horatian epistle into an elegy on time, defeat, and limited achievement, and in doing so brings out those very qualities in Horace's epistle. Whereas Dacier and Shaftesbury, each in their own ways, find in the epistle a confident Horace rich in new-found wisdom, Pope seems to discover a Horace rich in visions of failure. At least, this is the Horace with whom Pope most deeply identifies in his Imitation. And in doing so he discovers yet another side to the poetry, its emotional world. For Dacier and Shaftesbury this was not of primary importance; for Pope, identifying deeply with Horace as a fellow poet, this Horatian epistle aroused, it would seem, the whole range of feelings which attend examination of the self.[2]

Only sustained analysis of the complete poems could fully reveal how these two poems grow and develop next to each other; but let us try to gain some sense of this by considering Pope's treatment of five of the central themes in Horace's epistle: loss, the poet's public self, the art of poetry in the context of life, property, and the Horatian mean. Discussing each will show how in this mature Horatian poetry, consideration of any one theme involves almost every other. Taking these topics as they appear in the poems will give some idea of the living relationship between these two epistles.

LOSS

It is typical of Horace that he begins the epistle on a light note with two amusing stories, the sketch about the truant slave boy and the story of the soldier of Lucullus, which fit only obliquely into the poem they introduce. They seem to be told for their own sakes, as it were, and then, in retrospect, used ironically for Horace's argument about why he is not writing poetry. In contrast to Horace's light touches Pope introduces, right at the beginning, a note of resignation and defeat: 'You love a Verse, take such as I can send' (line 2). But the most striking feature of the opening sections of Pope's Imitation is that he quietly plays into the Horatian line of thought persistent allusions to theft and loss (see A. Williams, 1963, pp. 312–17). As we read the Pope next to the Horace we become gradually aware of a new 'order' carried out 'under the appearance of the greatest Ease and Negligence'. The fault of the slave boy in Horace's story is that he runs away:

> ... semel hic cessavit: &, ut fit,
> "In scalis latuit metuens pendentis habenae.
> "Des nummos, excepta nihil te si fuga laedat.   (14–16)

(... he did run off, once, and he hid (the way they do) under the stairs, afraid of the hanging strap. I've admitted his running away – that doesn't bother you at all, does it? – now you may give me the cash.)

Pope plays on that key word 'fuga' ('running away') and changes the fault to theft:

> "The Fault he has I fairly shall reveal,
> "(Cou'd you o'erlook but that) – it is, to steal.   (19–20)

But we notice, also, in this story a strange change: in the Horace a slave dealer is trying to sell a slave boy; but in Pope a Frenchman is trying to sell his own son; 'My only Son, I'd have him see the World' (line 6).

In commenting on this story Pope refers to another case of theft adjudicated by Sir Godfrey Kneller:

> Faith, in such case, if you should prosecute,
> I think Sir Godfrey should decide the Suit;
> Who sent the Thief that stole the Cash, away,
> And punish'd him that put it in his way. (23–6)

These arresting lines, which seem to question the whole idea of property, have no counterpart in Horace. In telling his own version of the story of Lucullus' soldier Pope presents yet another instance of theft, the example of a soldier, 'poor and old' driven frantic by the theft of his 'little purse of Gold':

> Tir'd with tedious March, one luckless night,
> He slept, poor Dog! and lost it, to a doit. (35–6)

When Horace applies the story of the soldier to his own life, explaining why he turned to poetry, he refers to the confiscation of his father's property after the battle of Philippi and this gives Pope yet another instance of the loss of property and, indeed, the loss of experience:

> ⁶*Romae nutriri mihi contigit, atque doceri,*
> *Iratus Graiis quantùm nocuisset Achilles.*
> *Adjecere bonae paulo plus artis Athenae:*
> *Scilicet ut possem* curvo *dignoscere* rectum,
> *Atque inter silvas Academi* quaerere *verum.*
> *Dura sed emovere loco me tempora grato;*
> *Civilisque rudem belli tulit aestus in arma,*
> *Caesaris Augusti non responsura lacertis.*
> *Unde simul primùm me dimisere Philippi,*
> *Decisis humilem pennis, inopemque* paterni
> *Et laris & fundi, paupertas impulit audax*
> *Ut versus facerem: sed, quod non desit, habentem,*
> *Quae poterunt unquam satìs expurgare* cicutae,
> *Ni melius dormire putem, quàm scribere versus?* (41–54)

(It was my fortune to be brought up in Rome, where I learned how much Achilles' wrath hurt the Achaeans. Kindly Athens added a little more refinement, taught me indeed to distinguish straight from crooked, and to seek after truth in the Academy's glades. But grim times evicted me from that sweet place: the tide of civil war bore me (no soldier) into an army that was to prove no match for Caesar's strength. As soon as Philippi demobilized me – crestfallen, wings clipped, lacking ancestral home and lands – shameless Poverty drove me to produce verse. But now that I have as much as I need, what hemlock could ever be adequate to purge my madness, if I did not think it better to sleep at nights than to scribble verses?)

To appreciate this important passage fully we must consider it in detail and note carefully the fine blending of different tones and feelings in what Fraenkel calls 'the only coherent piece of auto-biography which we possess from Horace's pen' (1957, p. 7). '*Romae*' stands impressively at its opening, as Horace alludes to his good fortune in having a father who brought him from the country to Rome so that he might have the best education possible. With warm irony he can now smile at his school's teaching of the *Iliad*: '*atque doceri, / Iratus Graiis quantùm nocuisset Achilles*' ('and learned how much Achilles' wrath hurt the Achaeans'). Do we think for a moment of the furious ('*iratus*') soldier of Lucullus? From Rome Horace went to Athens, to finish his education, and now he speaks of that experience with genuine warmth and affectionate irony: '*bonae ... Athenae*' ('Kindly Athens') added 'a little more refinement' ('*paulo plus artis*'). There, in the Academy's glades ('*inter silvas Academi*'), he pursued a more mature moral education, attempting '*curvo dignoscere* rectum' ('to distinguish straight from crooked'), and there he sought for truth ('quaerere *verum*'). The verbs in these lines momentarily take us into those inquiries, but the next line breaks in roughly upon them: '*Dura sed emovere loco me tempora grato*' ('But grim times evicted me from that sweet place'). The '*Dura*' and '*tempora*' ('grim ... times') are dramatically separated, and they cut across the '*loco ... grato*' ('that sweet ... place') with a chiasmic effect. Horace was, of course, on the Republican side in the civil war, and he remembers that momentous time of defeat as it affected him personally: he was a novice in war ('*rudem belli*'), humiliated at the battle of Philippi when he disgraced himself by running away ('*Decisis humilem pennis*' – 'crestfallen, wings clipped'), and was deprived of his father's home and estate, confiscated and given to Octavian's victorious soldiers ('*inopemque* paterni / Et laris & fundi*'). But if those words have solemn overtones Horace's attitude to his writing is amusingly reductive: '*paupertas ... audax*' ('shame-less Poverty') forced him ('*impulit*') to write. But now that he has sufficient store ('*satis*'), surely he'd be crazy to keep scribbling verses rather than just sleep. The '*dormire*' ('sleep') is set amusingly against '*scribere versus*', and the '*melius ... putem*' ('think it better'), with its careful subjunctive, presents the choice as one available to the mind.

Only close attention to every word and phrase can bring out the subtle tones and delicate ironies of this poetry. It is the language of a personality aware of itself, and which we feel could not be aware of itself without that language. This is Shaftesbury's 'Method of *inward Colloquy*' (1714, I, p. 328). Indeed, this thinking poetry actually creates thinking in us as we attempt to interpret the play of tone, and assess Horace's attitudes to his Republican past, his losses that resulted from the triumph of Augustus, and reasons that drew him to write poetry.

And, of course, interpretations vary: Dacier stresses the genuine pain of Horace's poverty, and yet his pleasure in being able now to celebrate Augustus' victory: 'Il fait icy un aveu sincere de son malheur, & de la misere qui l'avoit obligé à faire de vers; & il le fait d'autant plus volontiers que cet aveu tourne à la gloire d'Auguste' (Dacier, IX, p. 487). Carthy, in his translation of Horace's second book of epistles, simply translates Dacier's note to offer the same reading (1731, p. 74). But for Shaftesbury, as we have seen, all the weight of this passage rests upon Horace's yearning for his lost Republican past, and the allusion to Augustus would be neutral at best, if not very critical.

> ⁶Bred up at home, fully early I begun
> To read in Greek, the Wrath of Peleus' Son.
> Besides, my Father taught me from a Lad,
> The better Art to know the good from bad:
> (And little sure imported to remove,
> To hunt for Truth in *Maudlin*'s learned Grove.)
> But knottier Points we knew not half so well,
> Depriv'd us soon of our Paternal Cell;
> And certain Laws, by Suff'rers thought unjust,
> Deny'd all Posts of Profit or of Trust:
> Hopes after Hopes of pious Papists fail'd,
> While mighty WILLIAM's thundring Arm prevail'd.
> For Right Hereditary tax'd and fin'd,
> He stuck to Poverty with Peace of Mind;
> And me, the Muses help'd to undergo it;
> Convict a Papist He, and I a Poet.
> But (thanks to *Homer*) since I live and thrive,
> Indebted to no Prince or Peer alive,
> Sure I should want the Care of ten *Monroes*,
> If I would scribble, rather than repose. (52–71)

This recreation of Horace's meditative verse encourages us to enter into an activity of thought just as the original does; we watch Pope ingeniously turn the details of Horace's life into an account of his own. Horace's early education at Rome becomes Pope's education at home under the guidance of a father as concerned for his talented child as Horace's was. But Pope's father *himself* teaches his son 'The better Art to know the good from bad', 'curvo *dignoscere rectum*'. The groves of the Academy in Athens allow a compliment to Magdalen College which Pope could not attend because of his religion. The Roman civil war becomes the Glorious Revolution, and the confiscation of Horace's 'paterni / Et laris & fundi' has its counterpart in the loss of 'our Paternal Cell' because of anti-Catholic legislation. Pope clearly emphasizes the injustices of the law, the heroism of his father, and his own pride in now being self-sufficient, 'thanks to *Homer*' and 'Indebted to no Prince or Peer alive' – unlike Horace, he presumably implies. But Pope's 'critical' lines on 'mighty WILLIAM' are not as simple as they might seem: as Erskine-Hill (1981–2) has shown recently, they allude to a complex political situation, indeed, one just as complex as that to which Horace refers. This makes us aware how much these lines allow for questioning and speculation about those losses.

All these allusions to loss in the meditative verse of Pope's Imitation prepare for a remarkable moment. Horace's account of the main events of his life forms the first 'climax' of his epistle; after it he says briefly:

> [7]*Singula de nobis anni* praedantur *euntes,*
> *Eripuere* jocos, venerem, convivia, ludum;
> *Tendunt extorquere poemata, quid faciam vis?* (55–7)

(The years plunder us of our goods, one by one, as they pass. They've already snatched away merriment, sex, parties, play: now they're set on extorting poetry from me. What am I to do?)

These lines are a quick throw-away, leading to the '*quid faciam vis*' ('What am I to do?'). Horace does not dwell on the words, or in any way expand on the experiences they suggest. But this is precisely what Pope does, and in place of Horace's *brevitas* we have a short but powerful elegy on time, loss, and the self, and a climax that surprisingly follows Horace's climax:

> [7]Years foll'wing Years, steal something ev'ry day,
> At last they steal us from our selves away;
> In one our Frolicks, one Amusements end,
> In one a Mistress drops, in one a Friend:
> This subtle Thief of Life, this paltry Time,
> What will it leave me, if it snatch my Rhime?
> If ev'ry Wheel of that unweary'd Mill
> That turn'd ten thousand Verses, now stands still. (72–9)

These famous lines are not in themselves 'Horatian' – the pathos is held a little too long for that – but they suggest a profoundly Horatian awareness of the inner self. Horace's strong verbs 'praedantur' ('plunder'), '*Eripuere*' ('snatch'), '*extorquere*' ('extort') give way to the much more inward 'steal' and 'snatch'. Horace's 'jocos' and 'ludum' are put together to provide one contrast 'Frolicks', 'Amusements'; 'venerem', 'convivia', provide another 'Mistress', 'Friend'. The allusion to Milton's 'How soon hath Time the suttle theef of youth' deepens the tone (quoted *TE*, IV, p. 171); but it is Montaigne's reflection on the loss of self which gives Pope's poetry its true Horatian inwardness: 'What hereafter I shall be, will be but halfe a being, I shall be no more my selfe. I daily escape, and still steale my selfe from my selfe. *Singula de nobis anni praedantur euntes*' (*Essays*, trans. Florio, ed. Stewart 1931, II, p. 12). 'At last they steal us from our selves away', and 'What will it leave me, if it snatch my Rhime?' The fine reticent ambiguity of this last line makes us aware just how much the poet's identity is bound up with his craft. Throughout the Imitation 'Rhime' is Pope's apt equivalent for the elusive rhythms ('*numeros*') of Horace's lyric poetry; and this allows him to transform Horace's simple '*poemata*' ('poems') into a life-time's activity of turning out couplets: 'What will it leave me, if it snatch my Rhime?'

Coming as the climax to so many allusions to theft and loss, this poetry opens lines of thought rather than closing on a single subject. It asks what the relationships are between the 'self' and 'friends', 'experiences' and 'time'. On 2 December 1736 Swift wrote to Pope quoting these very lines of Horace:

I have too many vexations by my Station and the Impertinence of People, to be able to beare the Mortification of not hearing from a very few distant Friends that are left; and, considering how Time and Fortune hath ordered matters, I have hardly one friend left but your Self. What Horace says, Singula de nobis anni praedantur I feel every Month, at farthest; and by this computation, if I hold out two years, I Shall think it a Miracle. (*Corr.* IV, p. 44)

On 30 December Pope replied:

You ask me if I have got any supply of new Friends to make up for those that are gone? I think that impossible, for not our friends only, but so much of our selves is gone by the mere flux and course of years, that were the same Friends to be restored to us, we could not be restored to our selves, to enjoy them. (*Corr.* IV, p. 50)

It asks also how far the poet's true self is bound to his art; and, most profoundly, it explores the ways in which the idea of the self is bound to ideas about 'property'. As we have already seen in Chapter 4, and will see again in this chapter and in Chapter 10, the relationship between 'property' and the self is one of Horace's subtlest preoccupations. It is significant that Pope has introduced into Horace this metaphor of the theft of the self in those terms. We might remember, here, Locke's use of the word 'property' in the *Second Treatise of Government*. He uses it to mean that which is a personal possession in the ordinary sense, but also to refer to the three natural rights of man: 'Life, Liberty, and Estate': 'By *Property* I must be understood here, as in other places, to mean that Property which Men have in their Persons as well as Goods' (ed. Laslett, 1964, p. 401). Again, 'every Man has a *Property* in his own *Person*. This no Body has any Right to but himself' (p. 305). Indeed, we might remember that a father, Locke insists, '*cannot* by any *Compact* whatsoever, bind *his Children* or Posterity ... *the Father can no more give away the liberty of the Son*, than ... [he] can [give away the liberty] of any body else' (p. 364). We might also think back to the Frenchman trying to sell his own son: ' "Sir, he's your Slave, for twenty pounds a year' (line 8); ' "Tho faith, I fear 'twill break his Mother's heart' (line 16).

THE POET'S PUBLIC SELF

But, in fact, there is more to Horace's epistle than inward meditation: Horace also sees himself as a public figure, experiencing the strains of life in Rome as only a poet can. Admirers are only interested in when the next poem will be sent and yet all like different types of poems; he is expected to write amid the deafening noises and frantic activities of Rome; he has to endure the society of other poets and suffer both their compliments to him and their own need for flattery. Throughout these passages there are moments of self-consciousness, of exasperation and of disarming candour as Horace demands to be 'himself'.

In the Imitation it is fascinating to see how Pope responds to and uses these moments of self-awareness and irritation. We find him at once being himself and being Horace; but also, with Horace, struggling against the idea that he is merely a 'man of rhime'. If Horace says

> *quereris super hoc etiam, quod*
> *Exspectata tibi non mittam carmina mendax.* (24–5)

(You complain, over and above this, that I don't send you the verses you've been expecting, and I've broken my promise.)

Pope complains:

> Nay worse, to ask for Verse at such a time!
> D'ye think me good for nothing but to rhime? (31–2)

When Horace asks

> ⁹*Praeter caetera, me* Romaene *poemata censes*
> *Scribere posse, inter tot curas totque labores?* (65–6)

(Quite apart from everything else, do you think I can write poetry at Rome, in between so many anxieties and so many chores?)

Pope makes the question even more pointed and more searching:

> [9]But grant I may relapse, for want of Grace,
> Again to rhime, can *London* be the place?
> Who there his Muse, or Self, or Soul attends?
> In Crouds and Courts, Law, Business, Feasts and Friends? (88–91)

If Horace says,

> *Tu me inter strepitus nocturnos atque diurnos*
> *Vis canere, & contacta sequi vestigia vatum?* (79–80)

(And yet you want me, surrounded by constant din, night and day, to sing, and to trace the tracks trodden by the ancient bards?)

Pope makes this point but with a bit more self-dramatization:

> How shall I rhime in this eternal Roar?
> How match the Bards whom none e'er match'd before? (114–15)

But when Horace reminds us for a moment of the beauty of the Latin lyric:

> ... *hìc ego rerum*
> *Fluctibus in mediis, & tempestatibus Urbis,*
> *Verba lyrae motura sonum connectere digner?* (84–6)

(Here, beset by the tides of business, the storms of the city, am I expected to weave together words which will move the lyre to give voice?)

Pope turns this into something surprisingly sarcastic:

> Shall I, in *London*, act this idle part?
> Composing Songs, for Fools to get by heart? (125–6)

Pope's own personality, quite appropriately, emerges in these lines, demanding much more aggressively than Horace that he be recognized as being more than a poet. The strident, demanding 'I' of this poetry contrasts with the subtle 'ego' of Horace's introspective poetry, but contrasts even more, perhaps, with his own highly sensitive reflective consciousness. Indeed, Pope excels in characterising the social life of the poet and in finding witty equivalents for all that makes living and writing in Rome so impossible. For Horace's contractor with mules, a crane, a huge wagon, a mad dog and a mud-bespattered sow (lines 72–5) which make crossing Rome virtually impossible, he sees another vision of horrors in London:

> A Hackney-Coach may chance to spoil a Thought,
> And then a nodding Beam, or Pig of Lead,
> God knows, may hurt the very ablest Head.
> Have you not seen at Guild-hall's narrow Pass
> Two Aldermen dispute it with an Ass?
> And Peers give way, exalted as they are,
> Ev'n their own S–r–v– –nce in a Carr? (101–7)

Pope also responds fully to the ironies of Horace's sketch of the poets' mutual self-congratulations, and for a moment we are at once with Horace and in the world of the *Epistle to Arbuthnot*:

> [13]Carmina *compono, hic* elegos: "*mirabile visu*!
> "*Caelatumque novem Musis opus*!" (91–2)

(I compose odes, he writes elegies: 'What a marvellous sight! A masterpiece, engraved by the nine Muses themselves!')

produces more biting satire:

> [13]Thus we dispose of all poetic Merit,
> Yours *Milton*'s Genius, and mine *Homer*'s Spirit.
> Call *Tibbald Shakespear*, and he'll swear the Nine
> Dear *Cibber*! never match'd one Ode of thine. (135–8)

Horace's references to the famous temple of Apollo on the Palatine now open, he says, to Roman bards ('vacuam Romanis vatibus aedem', line 94) is turned into sardonic ridicule of '*Merlin*'s Cave':

> Lord! how we strut thro' *Merlin*'s Cave, to see
> No Poets there, but *Stephen*, you, and me.
> Walk with respect behind, while we at ease
> Weave Laurel Crowns, and take what Names we please. (139–42)

Horace and his contemporaries take the names of the their Greek masters, Alcaeus, Callimachus, Mimnermus; Pope and his associates wish, of course, to be Roman:

> "My dear *Tibullus*!" if that will not do,
> "Let me be *Horace*, and be *Ovid* you.
> "Or, I'm content, allow me *Dryden*'s strains,
> "And you shall rise up *Otway* for your pains." (143–6)

Horace's comments on his own involvement in this kind of thing are amusing:

> *Multa fero, ut placem* genus irritabile vatum,
> *Cùm scribo, & supplex populi suffragia capto:*
> *Idem, finitis studiis, & mente receptâ,*
> *Obturem patulas* impunè legentibus *aures*. (102–5)

(While I'm still writing, and humbly canvassing for public support, I put up with a lot to placate the peevish race of poets; but once I've finished such studies, and recovered my senses, I shall without compunction close my gaping ears to their recitals.)

But Pope is much more sarcastic, and much more aggressive. Horace's '*Multa fero*' and the 'genus irritabile vatum' bring out frustration and hostility in a very different personality:

Much do I suffer, much, to keep in peace
This jealous, waspish, wrong-head, rhiming Race;
And much must flatter, if the Whim should bite
To court applause by printing what I write:
But let the Fit pass o'er, I'm wise enough,
To stop my ears to their confounded stuff.

(147–52)

THE ART OF POETRY IN THE CONTEXT OF LIFE

These views of the poets and their poetry give rise to three passages on the art of poetry and the art of life that form the 'centre' of Horace's epistle. In order to appreciate their full effect we must take them together, and only then compare them with Pope's Imitation. The first Horatian passage is, in itself, many-sided although seemingly effortless. With indulgent irony Horace smiles at the self-satisfaction of poets who write bad verse; he leads them from this to a magnificent passage on the true poet's attitude to poetic language and the language of his culture; and he then claims that, in fact, he would rather be a bad writer whose failings escaped him, than a good writer who through self-knowledge and self-criticism is irritable and unhappy. The changes of viewpoint here are quite astonishing, and the control of tone remarkable:

> [14]*Ridentur mala qui componunt carmina: verùm*
> *Gaudent scribentes, & se venerantur, & ultro,*
> *Si taceas, laudant quidquid scripsere, beati.*
> *At qui* legitimum *cupiet fecisse poema,*
> *Cum tabulis animum censoris sumet honesti:*
> *Audebit quaecunque* parum splendoris *habebunt,*
> *Et sine pondere* erunt, & honore indigna *ferentur,*
> *Verba movere loco; quamvis* invita *recedant,*
> *Et versentur adhuc intra penetralia Vestae:*
> [15]*Obscurata* diu populo *bonus* eruet, *atque*
> *Proferet in lucem speciosa vocabula rerum,*
> *Quae priscis memorata Catonibus atque Cethegis,*
> *Nunc situs informis premit & deserta vetustas:*
> *Adsciscet* nova, *quae* genitor produxerit usus:
> *Vehemens &* liquidus, *puroque simillimus amni,*
> *Fundet* opes, *Latiumque beabit divite linguâ:*
> *Luxuriantia compescet: nimis aspera sano*
> *Levabit cultu, virtute carentia tollet.*
> *Ludentis* speciem dabit, & *torquebitur; ut qui*
> *Nunc Satyrum, nunc agrestem Cyclopa movetur:*
> [16]*Praetulerim scriptor delirus inersque videri,*
> *Dum mea* delectent *mala me, vel denique* fallant,
> *Quàm sapere, & ringi.*

(106–28)

(People who compose bad poems are laughed at: but they enjoy writing them, hold themselves in awe, take the lead, if you hold back, in praising what they've written, and they are happy. But the man whose ambition is to create a poem that satisfies the laws will assume, along with his writing tablets, the attitudes of a scrupulous censor. Without hesitation, if any words are too shabby, lack substance, or do not deserve their position, he will expel them, however much they protest and shrink back, even if they frequent Vesta's innermost shrine. Vivid expressions which have languished remote from public notice he will charitably search out and bring into the light: they were used by men like Cato and Cethegus in olden times, but now are depressed by unsightly mould and years of neglect. He will grant recognition to new words, if usage, which sired them, will vouch for their worth. Forceful and crystal clear, just like an unsullied stream, he will pour out his resources and bless Latium with richness of language. He will prune back luxuriant growth; by careful cultivation he will make the rough smooth; he'll weed out what is worthless; he'll make it look like child's play, although he's in agony, like a dancer who performs as a satyr one moment, as the savage Cyclops the next. I'd rather be taken for a raving, incompetent scribbler, as long as I enjoyed my faults, or at least wasn't aware of them, than know, and wince.)

The ironic lines on the self-satisfaction of the poor poet, and indeed the whole previous passage on poets' mutual self-congratulation, are juxtaposed remarkably with this passage on poetic language. Here, more powerfully than anywhere else in his work, Horace celebrates the art of poetry, and he does so specifically in terms of attitudes to language itself. The only comparable passage is the corresponding passage on poetry at the centre of *Epistle* II.i. (lines 125–38), and there, as we shall see, he concentrates on the moral and religious value of the poet's work.

Throughout this passage Horace insists that the true poet must have an imaginative but critical approach to his own language and the language of his time. When he wishes to write a poem that satisfies the laws ('legitimum') he will take up, with his tablets, the 'attitudes of a scrupulous censor' ('*animum censoris ... honesti*'); and he will remove words from their place if they are 'too shabby' ('parum splendoris *habebunt*'), lack substance ('sine pondere') or 'do not deserve their position' ('honore indigna *ferentur*'). But if this seems only negative, Horace writes energetically of the poet's imaginative interest in old words, lost in the past, and new words which current use has brought to life. His own metaphors are colourful as he expresses these imaginative ideas: words lost for so long ('Obscurata *diu*') the poet searches out ('*eruet*') and brings into the light, terms which though once spoken by great men which now lie low through 'unsightly mould' ('*situs informis*') and 'years of neglect' ('*deserta vetustas*'). In addition to these words, which Horace imaginatively sees as the dead ancestors of the people, the true poet will 'grant recognition to'('*Adsciscet*') fresh words which use has 'sired' and brought forth: '*Adsciscet* nova, *quae* genitor produxerit usus' ('He will grant recognition to new words, if usage, which sired them, will vouch for their worth.')

In these lines the nation's vocabulary is seen as being intimately connected to its origins, its past and present life. Horace now imagines the poet as pouring forth this language in a rich crystal river which is 'forceful and crystal clear' ('Vehemens & liquidus') and blessing Latium with what he calls, wonderfully, 'richness of language' ('*divite linguâ*'). These metaphors of the river then give way to metaphors of farming: the poet will 'prune back luxuriant growth' ('*Luxuriantia compescet*'); smooth what is too rough with what Horace calls 'careful cultivation' ('*sano ... cultu*'); and weed out what is worthless ('*virtute carentia tollet*' – '*virtute*' here blending moral and physical power). But while the poet performs these great feats he will in his finished work give what Shaftesbury calls 'the appearance of the greatest Ease and Negligence' (1714, I, p. 257):

> Ludentis *speciem dabit*, & torquebitur; *ut qui*
> Nunc Satyrum, nunc agrestem Cyclopa movetur ...   (124–5)

(... he'll make it look like child's play, although he's in agony, like a dancer who performs as a satyr one moment, as the savage Cyclops the next.)

This passage on the nature of the poet's language shows in what high esteem Horace held the art of poetry in general and his own poetry in particular. If in the passage in the *Epistle to Augustus* he praises Virgil's epic poetry and his own religious *Carmen Saeculare*, here he is surely celebrating the achievement of his own lyric poetry – its perfection of form, its use of Greek models, and possibly its rediscovery of the power of ordinary words through their use in lyric contexts. He sees poetry as being what his own odes perhaps are – a unique aesthetic and moral achievement in the context of the Graeco-Roman tradition.

It is only because this passage is so powerful that Horace can so brilliantly undercut it, saying that really the self-delusion of the bad poet is much better than the unhappiness of the good poet who 'knows and winces' ('*sapere, & ringi*'). But if we are inclined to reject this as mere irony, Horace at once underlines the point with one of his most memorable stories:

> Fuit haud ignobilis *Argis*,
> Qui se credebat miros audire tragoedos,
> In vacuo laetus sessor plausorque theatro:
> Caetera qui vitae servaret munia recto
> More; bonus sanè vicinus, amabilis hospes,

Comes *in uxorem;* posset *qui ignoscere servis,*
Et signo laeso non insanire *lagenae:*
Posset *qui rupem, & puteum vitare patentem.*
Hic ubi cognatorum opibus curisque refectus
Expulit elleboro morbum bilemque meraco,
Et redit ad sese: "Pol me occidistis, amici,
Non servastis, ait; cui sic extorta voluptas,
Et demtus per vim mentis gratissimus error. (128–40)

(There was a nobleman from Argos who used to believe he was watching marvellous actors as he sat, blissfully, and applauded in an empty theatre. He coped with all the other business of life quite normally – he was a decent neighbour, a genial host, nice to his wife, indulgent to his slaves (he wouldn't lose his head if one had swigged from a bottle), he could steer a course past stumbling-blocks and uncovered wells. When with his family's help he'd been given treatment, and rid himself of the disorder with draughts of neat hellebore, on coming to himself, 'But friends,' he said 'you've killed me, not cured me: you've robbed me of my pleasure, you've deprived me by force of an illusion that gave me huge enjoyment.')

This amusing and touching defence of folly and delusion has been a *locus classicus* for great praisers of folly like Erasmus and Montaigne. The details of the sketch are so engaging: the tragic actors are of the highest quality (*'miros'* – 'marvellous'); he not only sits happily but applauds (*'plausorque'*) in the empty theatre. How ironically rare are all his normal qualities: *'bonus sanè vicinus'* ('a decent neighbour'), 'Comes *in uxorem*' ('nice to his wife'), '*Et signo laeso* non insanire *lagenae*' ('he wouldn't lose his head if one [a slave] had swigged from a bottle'). How tragic is the cry *'me occidistis, amici, / Non servastis'* ('But friends, you've killed me, not cured me'), how poignant the *'voluptas'* ('pleasure') lost, and how infinitely moving the superlative *'gratissimus'* in *'mentis gratissimus error'* ('an illusion that gave me huge enjoyment'), now forever lost.

Only Horace could follow this passage on the high demands of lyric poetry and this story on the need for folly with some lines which seem to contradict both and yet subtly depend upon them in order to express what is arguably the central point of the entire epistle:

[17]*Nimirum sapere est abjectis utile nugis,*
Et tempestivum pueris *concedere ludum;*
[18]*Ac non verba sequi fidibus modulanda Latinis,*
Sed verae numerosque modosque *ediscere* vitae.
Quocirca mecum *loquor haec, tacitusque recordor ...* (141–5)

(I really must seek wisdom and put aside trifles, leave such sport to boys, whose age it suits, not search out words to fit to Latin strings, but learn the notes and tunes of life itself. For this reason I utter these thoughts to myself, and reflect on them in silence.)

This is wonderfully understated: it is simply appropriate to seek wisdom ('*sapere*'), to throw away trifles ('*nugis*'), and to leave sport ('*ludum*') to the young whose age it suits. For Horace this means not searching out words that will fit the music of the Latin lyre (the '*verba . . . modulanda*' is finely interwoven in the line with '*fidibus . . . Latinis*'), but rather to learn ('*ediscere*') the notes and tunes ('numerosque modosque') of what Horace calls simply 'verae . . . vitae' ('life itself'). The rhythms of these two lines are perfectly calm, and 'verae' prepares for a wonderful final cadence on 'vitae'. What is needed now is not writing poetry but speaking with the inner self ('mecum *loquor*') and silent reflection ('*tacitusque recordor*'); but only the experience of poetry could enable him to say this to himself in just this way. If the art of poetry must give way to the art of life, it must not do so before it has illumined as nothing else can what that greater art might be.

It is fascinating, however, to see how differently Dacier and Shaftesbury interpret these lines. Dacier, emphasizing the moral side of this epistle, sees in '*Sed* verae numerosque modosque *ediscere* vitae' the idea of choosing appropriate actions: 'Cette expression est fort belle. Comme tous les sons ne font pas une harmonie agreable, mais seulement certains sons: ainsi toutes les actions ne rendent pas une vie heureuse & tranquille, mais seulement certaines actions suivies, & qui n'ont rien de discordant' (Dacier, IX, p. 515). But for Shaftesbury, these lines represent Horace's supreme moment of discovery: the discovery of the private inner self as its own harmony: '*Sed verae numerosque modosque ediscere vitae* . . . This is character. But if for outward ears only and the judgements abroad, what difference between this labour and that other – *Verba sequi fidibus modulanda Latinis?*' (Shaftesbury, 1900, p. 204). For Shaftesbury the difference between the discovery of true self, which is 'character', and the writing of lyric poetry lies in the recognition of the profound privacy of the inner self which contrasts sharply with the poet's public self: 'Continue, therefore, and keep the harmony, if possible, uninterrupted; if not, restore it again as soon as possible, and dwell not on the miscarriage' (p. 204).

However we interpret these lines their full effect comes from their position in the epistle: after Horace has treated aspects of the writing of poetry so scornfully, but also after he has shown what a high art it is; after he has shown that there is a need for delusion, but also after he has urged the need for wisdom. This is the turning point and 'centre' of the poem, which comes somewhat past its centre.[3] And no sooner have we read these lines than they appear to have been merely a transition: they take us immediately to some of those important moral demands which, indeed, seem to make life an art and all forms of experience a challenge to consciousness.

Pope treats the whole central section of Horace's epistle in a very individual way. He gives a 'faithful' rendering of Horace's passage about poetry and language, but then gives a different turn to Horace's Man of Argos story and to Horace's climax, changing the line of thought, the tones, and the emotions expressed. He begins with a fresh and lively translation of Horace's passage about language which catches both the ironies about 'bad Rhimers' and the eloquence and power of Horace's compelling assertions:

> [14]In vain, bad Rhimers all mankind reject,
> They treat themselves with most profound respect;
> 'Tis to small purpose that you hold your tongue,
> Each prais'd within, is happy all day long.
> But how severely with themselves proceed
> The Men, who write such Verse as we can read?
> Their own strict Judges, not a word they spare
> That wants or Force, or Light, or Weight, or Care,
> Howe'er unwillingly it quits its place,
> Nay tho' at Court (perhaps) it may find grace:
> Such they'll degrade; and sometimes, in its stead,
> [15]In downright Charity revive the dead;
> Mark where a bold expressive Phrase appears,
> Bright thro' the rubbish of some hundred years;
> Command old words that long have slept, to wake,
> Words, that wise *Bacon*, or brave *Raleigh* spake;
> Or bid the new be *English*, Ages hence,
> (For Use will father what's begot by Sense)
> Pour the full Tide of Eloquence along,
> Serenely pure, and yet divinely strong,
> Rich with the Treasures of each foreign Tongue;
> Prune the luxuriant, the uncouth refine,
> But show no mercy to an empty line;
> Then polish all, with so much life and ease,
> You think 'tis Nature, and a knack to please:
> "But Ease in writing flows from Art, not Chance,
> "As those move easiest who have learn'd to dance.
> [16]If such the Plague and pains to write by rule,
> Better (say I) be pleas'd, and play the fool;
> Call, if you will, bad Rhiming a disease,
> It gives men happiness, or leaves them ease.   (153–83)

One could hardly imagine a better imitation of this Horatian passage. Pope has caught the warmth of Horace's tolerant ironies about the happy bad poet at the beginning of the passage; and at the end almost convinces us that he too would rather be a deluded if happy poet. But above all he warms deeply to the idea that writing involves moral rigour and courage, a vigorous and imaginative apprehension of the past, a concern for the words of the present and future. He explores Horace's central convictions here, and conveys powerfully what he understands the Latin to mean. Horace's 'legitimum ... *poema*' ('poem that satisfies the laws') is seen with a touch of irony, 'such Verse as we can read'; while his aesthetic criteria, 'parum splendoris *habebunt*' ('are too shabby'), 'sine pondere' ('lack substance') are translated straight, 'That wants or Force, or Light, or Weight, or Care'. Horace's 'honore indigna' ('do not deserve their position'), and the 'invita' of words unwilling to leave their places, are given strong and deeply felt political overtones, drawing upon the political metaphors of the Horatian passage:

> Howe'er unwillingly it quits its place,
> Nay tho' at Court (perhaps) it may find grace:
> Such they'll degrade; and sometimes, in its stead,
> In downright Charity revive the dead ...   (161-4)

Horace uses vivid metaphors to convey how the poet unearths the language of the past; Pope, characteristically, uses the power of rhetorical verbs to convey that creative strength: 'Mark', 'Command', 'bid', 'Pour'. Horace's '*quae* genitor produxerit usus' ('if usage, which sired them') is neatly turned in another direction '(For Use will father what's begot by Sense)'. The *divite linguâ* ('richness of language') with which Latium is blessed becomes rather neatly, 'Rich with the Treasures of each foreign Tongue.' At the end Pope fuses the idea of imitating Nature with the ideal of Horatian ease, as seen through his own eyes in the *Essay on Criticism*. Here he stresses in Horace's 'Ludentis *speciem dabit, &* torquebitur' just what Shaftesbury emphasizes, that the poet wants not only his 'Ease' to be appreciated but the 'Art' that gave rise to it. He refines, however, Horace's image of the dance: in place of the contrasting movements of the dancing Satyr and the rough Cyclops Pope imagines an elegant dance that one must learn.

But from this point on Pope emphasizes not success but failure. His version of the Man of Argos story has a completely different character which stresses not the need for illusion but the failure of a 'cure'. He gives the passage a political context, and shows how a worthy 'Patriot' Lord is reduced to a mere statistical vote:

> There liv'd, *in primo Georgii* (they record)
> A worthy Member, no small Fool, a Lord;
> Who, tho' the House was up, delighted sate,
> Heard, noted, answer'd, as in full Debate:
> In all but this, a man of sober Life,

Fond of his Friend, and civil to his Wife,
Not quite a Mad-man, tho' a Pasty fell,
And much too wise to walk into a Well:
Him, the damn'd Doctors and his Friends immur'd,
They bled, they cupp'd, they purg'd; in short, they cur'd:
Whereat the Gentleman began to stare—
My Friends? he cry'd, p–x take you for your care!
That from a Patriot of distinguish'd note,
Have bled and purg'd me to a simple *Vote*.   (184–97)

And then, so movingly, Pope considers his own failure. Next to Horace's remarkable lines which suggest his achieved calm, Pope places sardonic and self-deprecating reflections on himself:

[17]Well, on the whole, *plain* Prose must be my fate:
Wisdom (curse on it) will come soon or late.
There is a time when Poets will grow dull:
I'll e'en leave Verses to the Boys at school:
To Rules of Poetry no more confin'd,
I learn to smooth and harmonize my Mind,
Teach ev'ry Thought within its bounds to roll,
And keep the equal Measure of the Soul.   (198–205)

Nowhere in the *Imitations* is it clearer that Pope is not attempting to compete with Horace, and yet many critics assume he is and comment on the 'weakness' of Pope's version (see, for example, Brower, 1959, p. 303). Only if we see that he is *responding to* Horace's inimitable achievement do we appreciate this moment of gentle self-mockery.[4]

And yet at once the tone becomes deeper, in an expansion of Horace's '*Quocirca* mecum *loquor haec, tacitusque recordor*', which is in accord with Shaftesbury's 'inward' interpretation of that line:

[18]Soon as I enter at my Country door,
My Mind resumes the thread it dropt before;
Thoughts, which at Hyde-Park-Corner I forgot,
Meet and rejoin me, in the pensive Grott.
There all alone, and Compliments apart,
I ask these sober questions of my Heart.   (206–11)

For a moment Pope seems to leave Horace for Boileau:

Tantôt, cherchant la fin d'un vers que je construi,
Je trouve au coin d'un bois le mot qui m'avait fui.
(*Epistle*, vi. 27–8; quoted *TE*, IV, p. 179)

but, in fact, he enters into a very Horatian retreat. Indeed, he brings into Horace's poem Horace's own retreat where the self can return to itself once more: 'Vilice silvarum et mihi me reddentis agelli' ('Bailiff of my woods and of the little farm which restores me to my self again') (*Epistle* I.xiv. I). Here Pope sees his Horatian self in terms of 'my Mind' and 'my Heart'. If Pope has played down the quiet intensity of Horace's 'climactic' lines, he has here produced their equivalent; and his emphasis is not on achievement but on the need for further effort.

PROPERTY

In the final part of this epistle Horace concentrates on the kind of wisdom one might attempt to acquire in life. If we approach the poem in a moralistic way we would agree with Dacier that he offers teaching on 'avarice' and 'ambition'. If we think of that wisdom in terms of the development of consciousness we would say he explores the idea of possession, the difficulties of moderation, and the nature of self-satisfaction. Moral achievement then becomes a way of thinking and feeling. Nowhere is this clearer than in the passage on property:

> [21]*Si* proprium *est, quod quid librâ mercatur & aere est,*
> *Quaedam (Si credis* consultis) *manicipat* usus;
> *Qui te pascit ager, tuus est; & villicus Orbi,*
> *Cùm segetes occat, tibi mox frumenta daturus,*
> *Te dominum sentit–*
> [22]*–das nummos; accipis uvam,*
> *Pullos, ova, cadum temeti: nempe modo isto*
> *Paulatim mercaris agrum, fortasse trecentis,*
> *Aut etiam supra nummorum milibus emtum.*
> *Quid refert vivas* numerato nuper, *an* olim?
> *Emtor Aricini quondam, Veientis & arvi,*
> [23]*Emtum coenat olus, quamvis aliter putat; emtis*
> *Sub noctem gelidam lignis calefactat ahenum.*
> *Sed* vocat *usque* suum, *quà populus adsita certis*
> *Limitibus vicina refugit jurgia: tanquam*
> [24]*Sit* proprium *quidquam, puncto quod mobilis horae,*
> *Nunc prece, nunc pretio, nunc vi, nunc sorte supremâ*
> *Permutet dominos, & cedat in altera jura.*
> *Sic, quia* perpetuus *nulli datur* usus, *& haeres*
> *Haeredem alterius, velut unda supervenit undam:*
> *Quid* vici prosunt, *aut* horrea? *quidve Calabris*
> *Saltibus adjecti Lucani; si metit Orcus*
> *Grandia cum parvis, non exorabilis auro?* (158–79)

(What you buy 'by balance and bronze', becomes your property certainly; but there are also cases (so the lawyers tell us) where use confers ownership. The farm that feeds you is yours; and Orbius' bailiff, when he plants seed in order to give you corn by and by is acknowledging you as his landlord. You hand over cash: in exchange you receive grapes, chickens, eggs, a cask of liquor; surely, by this procedure you are purchasing, by instalments, the farm that would cost maybe three hundred thousand, or even more, if bought outright. What difference does it make to you whether you paid for what you live off just now or years ago? The purchaser, some time ago, of lands at Aricia and Veii has had to buy the vegetables he's dining off (however much he prefers to think otherwise); he's had to buy the firewood that warms his pot in the chill of night; and yet he calls it all his own, right up to the line of poplars he planted to mark his boundaries and avert disputes with his neighbours; as if anything can be one's own that, in a moment of fickle time, by prayer or by purchase, by force or (definitively) by death, can exchange owners, and pass into another's possession. And so, since 'enjoyment in perpetuity' is granted to no man, and heir follows another's heir like wave succeeding wave, what's the profit of estates and granaries? Why add tracts in Lucania to your ranches in Calabria, when Death mows down the great with the small, and no gold will buy him off?)

Horace here explores with much greater maturity and subtlety the ideas he had expounded in Ofellus' speech in *Satire* II.ii.; playing on the two types of ownership in law *'usucapio'* (possession by use) and *'dominium'* (ownership), Horace insists that it is use rather than money that gives real ownership ('proprium'). This is argued at first with charming wit: *'Qui te pascit ager, tuus est'* ('the farm that feeds you is yours'); *'das nummos; accipis uvam, / Pullos, ova, cadum temeti'* ('You hand over cash; in exchange you receive grapes, chickens, eggs, a cask of liquor'). Horace's paradoxes here are quite irresistible: you are buying 'by instalments' (*'paulatim'*) an estate worth three hundred thousand sesterces, while the owner is buying for an incredible amount, greens for his dinner (*'olus'*) and firewood for his fire (*'lignis'*), although, of course, he *thinks* otherwise (*'quamvis aliter putat'*).

Horace's language then intensifies as he contemplates the consequences of these subversive ironies: nothing can be one's own which 'in a moment of fickle time' (*'puncto quod mobilis horae'*),

> Nunc prece, nunc pretio, nunc vi, nunc sorte supremâ
> Permutet dominos, & cedat in altera jura.   (173–4)

(by prayer or by purchase, by force or (definitively) by death, can exchange owners, and pass into another's possession)

As in Ofellus' speech 'property' is simply an illusion: it is the possessions which do the changing here, not the owners; 'perpetuus usus' ('enjoyment in perpetuity') is granted to none; heir follows heir like the waves of the sea; and Death (*'Orcus'*) who can never be bought off with gold (*'non exorabilis auro'*) reaps everything, however great or small the estates or granaries. The subdued power of this language creates not terror or despair but a calm vision of futility.

Pope's imitation of the second half of Horace's epistle moves back and forth between the 'Horatian' and the 'non-Horatian'. At times he turns Horace's speculative ironies into simpler satiric attack, as in the powerful passage on 'servile Chaplains' (lines 220–5); but in other places he enters completely into the spirit of Horace's poetry. The climax of this section is certainly his version of this passage on property. Pope begins by re-creating all Horace's relaxed but subversive ironies, and ends by transforming the hints of grandeur in Horace's language into an intense but thoughtful rhetoric:

> [21]If there be truth in Law, and *Use* can give
> A *Property*, that's yours on which you live.
> Delightful *Abs-court*, if its Fields afford
> Their Fruits to you, confesses you its Lord:
> All [22]Worldly's Hens, nay Partridge, sold to town,
> His Ven'son too, a Guinea makes your own;
> He bought at thousands, what with better wit
> You purchase as you want, and bit by bit;
> Now, or long since, what diff'rence will be found?
> You pay a Penny, and he paid a Pound.
> [23]Heathcote himself, and such large-acred Men,
> Lords of fat *E'sham*, or of Lincoln Fen,
> Buy every stick of Wood that lends them heat,
> Buy every Pullet they afford to eat.
> Yet these are Wights, who fondly call their own
> Half that the Dev'l o'erlooks from Lincoln Town.
> The Laws of God, as well as of the Land,
> Abhor, a *Perpetuity* should stand:
> Estates have wings, and hang in Fortune's pow'r
> [24]Loose on the point of ev'ry wav'ring Hour;
> Ready, by force, or of your own accord,
> By sale, at least by death, to change their Lord.
> *Man?* and *for ever?* Wretch! what wou'dst thou have?
> Heir urges Heir, like Wave impelling Wave:
> All vast Possessions (just the same the case
> Whether you call them Villa, Park, or Chace)
> Alas, my BATHURST! what will they avail?
> Join *Cotswold* Hills to *Saperton*'s fair Dale,
> Let rising Granaries and Temples here,
> There mingled Farms and Pyramids appear,
> Link Towns to Towns with Avenues of Oak,
> Enclose whole Downs in Walls, 'tis all a joke!
> Inexorable Death shall level all,
> And Trees, and Stones, and Farms, and Farmer fall.   (230–63)

Again, as with the passage on poetic language, one could hardly imagine a finer imitation, alive to all the tones and ironies of the Horace, and yet making of them something individual and memorable. We hear once more the conversational charm of Horace's language, its calm wisdom, and its sharp pointedness:

> He bought at thousands, what with better wit
> You purchase as you want, and bit by bit ...   (236–7)

Horace's delight in simple details is beautifully re-created: 'All Worldly's Hens', 'every stick of Wood', and 'every Pullet'. And Pope's language comes alive with Horace's fine ironies: the sticks of the rich merely 'lend them heat'; pullets are what the great 'afford to eat'; land is what they 'fondly call their own' ('vocat *usque* suum'); and it is estates which 'change their Lord' ('*Permutet dominos*'). Indeed, as far as Pope is concerned

> The Laws of God, as well as of the Land,
> Abhor, a *Perpetuity* should stand ...   (246–7)

and Horace's '*puncto quod mobilis horae*' ('which in a moment of fickle time') inspires a stroke of genius:

> Estates have wings, and hang in Fortune's pow'r
> Loose on the point of ev'ry wav'ring Hour ...   (248–9)

But from here on Pope utterly transforms every detail of his Latin text: 'perpetuus' now is '*Man? and for ever?* Wretch! what wou'dst thou have?' (line 252). '*Quid* vici *prosunt, aut* horrea?' ('what's the profit of estates and granaries?') provokes a poignant cry:

> All vast Possessions (just the same the case
> Whether you call them Villa, Park, or Chace)
> Alas, my BATHURST! What will they avail?   (254–6)

(What a superb touch the possessive 'my BATHURST' is.) '*quidve Calabris / Saltibus adjecti Lucani*?' ('Why add tracts in Lucania to your ranches in Calabria?') allows Pope to see the whole landscape gardening movement so dear to himself, and the whole process of enclosure, as being grandly but profoundly absurd:

> Join *Cotswold* Hills to *Saperton*'s fair Dale,
> Let rising Granaries and Temples here,
> There mingled Farms and Pyramids appear,
> Link Towns to Towns with Avenues of Oak,
> Enclose whole Downs in Walls, 'tis all a joke!   (257–61)

And finally Horace's awesome '*Orcus ... non exorabilis auro*' ('Death ... whom no gold will buy off') looms into the imagination once again:

> Inexorable Death shall level all,
> And Trees, and Stones, and Farms, and Farmer fall.   (262–3)

Once again Pope emphasizes the loss and failure implicit in Horace's epistle, and, in fact, reveals his personal involvement in it. Indeed, this passage offers a striking contrast to his imitation of the comparable passage at the end of the *Paraphrase of Satire II.ii.* There Pope celebrates his personal success in achieving his own self-sufficiency on what land he has; here he involves himself in an all-embracing vision of futility.

THE 'HORATIAN MEAN'

If Horace's lines on property are at once consoling and disconcerting in their wisdom, then so too is the whole ending of Horace's epistle; and again, as in the treatment of the art of poetry, it is the subtle shifting of attitudes that makes the poetry so challenging. Horace begins by dwelling on the mystery of contradictory human natures and yearnings; he then attempts to define his own ideas of how he will approach life in terms of a balance between such extremes. But just when we imagine we finally know what Horatian 'wisdom' is, he asks his most disturbing and provocative questions, making them the note on which this whole epistle ends.

To introduce the conclusion Horace describes two brothers, one who can do nothing but work, the other who does nothing but trifle (lines 182–6). These contradictory extremes raise questions about human nature, motivation, and the search for fulfilment. But rather than moralize, Horace acknowledges that no one can explain such contradictions except that 'Genius' who is the 'NATURAE DEUS HUMANAE' ('the God of Human birth') who, although divine, lives in each individual person and gives to them their nature and their goals:

> *Scit* Genius, *natale comes qui temperat astrum:*
> NATURAE DEUS HUMANAE, *mortalis in unum—*
> *Quodque caput, voltu mutabilis, albus & ater.*　　　(187–9)

(Only the *genius* knows, who goes with us and moderates our natal star, that god of human birth, who dies with each of us, though his face may vary, white or black.)

Horace's mature poetry is given much of its depth by the recognition of this haunting deity, who clearly demands that we acknowledge the importance of human individuality.[5]

In the lines which follow Horace outlines what he presents as ideas for the conduct of his own life. He will attempt to live moderately, steering between extremes, and trying to be content with a modest degree of success:

[27]*Utar, & ex modico, quantum res poscit, acervo*
Tollam; nec metuam, quid de me judicet haeres,
Quod non plura datis invenerit. & tamen idem
Scire volam, quantùm simplex hilarisque nepoti
Discrepet, & quantum discordet parcus avaro;
Distat enim, spargas tua prodigus, an neque sumtum
Invitus facias, neque plura parare labores;
An potiùs, puer ut festis Quinquatribus olim,
Exiguo gratoque fruaris tempore raptim.
[28]*Pauperies immunda domûs procul absit. ego, utrûm*
Nave ferar magnà an parvâ; ferar unus & idem.
Non agimur tumidis velis Aquilone secundo:
Non tamen adversis aetatem ducimus Austris.
Viribus, ingenio, specie, virtute, loco, re,
Extremi primorum, extremis usque priores.　　　　　　　(190–204)

(I shall make use of what I have, and from my modest heap I'll take whatever my needs demand; nor shall I fear the verdict my heir passes on me when he fails to find more than I've left him. Nevertheless I shall still want to remember the distinction between straightforward cheerfulness and prodigality, and the gap that separates the thrifty man from the miser. For there is all the difference between scattering one's wealth wastefully and being prepared to spend it without toiling to get still more, but instead, as when one was a schoolboy in the spring holiday, enjoying one's time, so short and so sweet, before it's gone. May filthy poverty stay far from my house. It makes no difference to me as passenger whether the ship is big or small; I'm still the same man, unchanged. I'm not always borne along, sails unfurled, with a north wind behind me; but nor do I have to battle all my life against the sirocco. In strength, in wit, in looks, in worth, in rank, in wealth, I stand behind the first, but still before the last.)

In this memorable expression of the 'Horatian mean' there is a fine blend of what Horace is and what he might be. Horace's language here is carefully contrived to prevent this ideal from seeming too simple or too easy. The lines begin with the future tense, '*Utar*' ('I shall make use of'), include an important subjunctive, '*absit*' ('may filthy poverty stay far from my house'), and move gradually into a present passive, '*Non agimur*' ('I'm not always borne along'). The distinctions between the giver and the spendthrift, the frugal and the miserly are seen as things he 'shall still want to remember' ('*Scire volam*'). Lovely linguistic touches show that he will remain the same no matter what the size of the vessel of his life, which Pope stresses with his Roman type:

> *ego, utrûm*
> *Nave ferar magnà an parvâ; ferar unus & idem.*　　　(199–200)

(It makes no difference to me as passenger whether the ship is big or small; I'm still the same man, unchanged.)

That repetition of *'ferar'* ('I am carried') is very neat; and the negative passive verb, *'Non agimur'* ('I'm not borne') and a negative active verb, *'Non ... ducimus'* ('I do not battle') emphasize the contrasts between good and bad fortune. And only after all this do we find a line of six crucial nouns, and a perfectly balanced conclusion:

> *Viribus, ingenio, specie, virtute, loco, re,*
> *Extremi primorum, extremis usque priores.* (203–4)

(In strength, in wit, in looks, in worth, in rank, in wealth, I stand behind the first, but still before the last.)

But lest this appear too complacent, and lest we feel for too long the warm glow of self-satisfaction, Horace breaks off to give us, as it were, another ending. He imagines that Julius Florus replies that he is not avaricious:

> ²⁹*Non es avarus: abi. quid? caetera jam simul isto*
> *Cum vitio fugere? caret tibi pectus inani*
> *Ambitione? caret mortis formidine & irâ?*
> *Somnia, terrores magicos, miracula, sagas,*
> *Nocturnos lemures, portentaque Thessala rides?*
> *Natales gratè numeras? ignoscis amicis?*
> *Lenior & melior fis accedente senectâ?*
> *Quid te exempta juvat spinis de pluribus una?*
> * Vivere si rectè nescis, decede peritis.*
> *Lusisti satìs, edisti satìs, atque bibisti:*
> *Tempus abire tibi est: ne potum largiùs aeque*
> *Rideat, & pulset lasciva decentiùs aetas.* (205–16)

(You're not a miser? – All well and good. But did all the other vices disappear along with avarice? Is your heart free from pointless ambition? Is it free of fear and resentment at death? Dreams, the terrors of the occult, sorcery, witches, haunting ghosts, outlandish monsters – can you laugh at them? Do you count your birthdays, and feel thankful? Do you forgive your friends? Are you becoming a milder and a better man as old age comes on? What good does it do you to pull out one thorn, and leave so many in? If you don't know how to live life well, make way for those who do. You've had your fill of sport, of food, of drink: it's time for you to leave; if not, because you've drunk more than you should, you'll be jeered at and pushed aside by the young: merrymaking suits them better.)

It would seem that the purpose of *this* ending is to completely disorientate Julius Florus, and the reader. Nowhere, in a poetry of subtle questions, has Horace compiled a list of such utterly unnerving inquiries: *'caret mortis formidine & irâ?'* ('Is [your heart] free of fear and resentment at death?'); *'Natalis gratè numeras?'* ('Do you count your birthdays, and feel thankful?'); *'ignoscis amicis'* ('Do you forgive your friends?' – especially those who don't write letters);

'*Lenior & melior fis accedente senectâ?*' ('Are you becoming a milder and a better man as old age comes on?')

Horace ends this epistle by making us feel that we do not know how to live or how to cope with experience, and probably never will. But with beautiful irony he hints that we might remember that we have in fact had quite sufficient ('*satìs*') from life, even if we have never learned how to live or how to appreciate the experience: '*Lusisti satìs, edisti satìs, atque bibisti*' ('You've had your fill of sport, of food, of drink'). Our unfulfilled life having been so rich in fulfilment, we might at least have the grace to leave when the meal is over.

Pope gives the whole ending to his Imitation a very different character. Whereas Horace stresses the mystery of human nature, Pope asserts not only that its contradictions are explicable to God but also that in themselves they actually suggest His divine purpose. In his portrait of himself he stresses not the difficulties of attaining the Horatian mean, but rather the instrinsic value of such moderation, and, indeed, his *right* to live in this self-sufficient manner. He turns Horace's haunting questions into meditative moral rhetoric tinged with elegiac melancholy, and ends on a note of sharper irony. At the cnd of this Imitation we find, in its *own* terms, an impressive variety of tones and an individual version of Horace's shifting positions.

Horace's brief sketch of the two brothers, one given to play, the other to wealth and endless work, clearly struck chords in Pope, always alive to such inconsistencies:

> Why, of two Brothers, rich and restless one
> Ploughs, burns, manures, and toils from Sun to Sun;
> The other slights, for Women, Sports, and Wines,
> All *Townshend*'s Turnips, and all *Grovenor*'s Mines ...   (270–3)

But Pope actually produces a clear solution to Horace's mystery: above Horace's 'Genius' is a 'Directing Pow'r' who actually 'forms the Genius', and resolves all contradictions in His own 'great End'. Why individuals are different, Pope asserts,

> Is known alone to that Directing Pow'r,
> Who forms the Genius in the natal Hour;
> That God of Nature, who, within us still,
> Inclines our Action, not constrains our Will;
> Various of Temper, as of Face or Frame,
> Each Individual: His great End the same.   (278–83)

We must note, however, that while these important lines seem so different from the Horace, it is difficult to say quite how much, since Horace's religious ideas were interpreted in the eighteenth century in various, indeed contradictory, ways. On these lines Warburton comments: 'Here our Poet had an opportunity of illustrating his own Philosophy; and thereby giving a much better sense to his Original; and correcting both the *naturalism* and the *fate* of Horace' (Pope, *Works*, ed. Warburton, 1751, IV, pp. 238–9). But Shaftesbury insists that the ancients thought of the genius in religious terms. Criticizing Dacier's reading of *Ode* IV.xi he asserts that 'without regard to any exterior or superior demon, the soul or genius itself (the true demon) committed to every man at his birth, was by the ancients esteemed sacred of itself, as so committed and entrusted by nature, or the supreme universal divinity' (Shaftesbury, 1900, p. 357). It would seem likely that Pope thought that in Horace's 'NATURAE DEUS HUMANAE' he had found confirmation of his theory of the Ruling Passion. We will explore this subject further in Part IV.

After this powerful assertion of divine wisdom Pope offers a final view of himself. But if before in the poem he had seemed speculative, uncertain, or threatened, now he appears very confident. Whereas Horace formulates the mean so cautiously, Pope becomes very assertive:

> [27]Yes, Sir, how small soever be my heap,
> A part I will enjoy, as well as keep.
> My Heir may sigh, and think it want of Grace
> A man so poor wou'd live without a *Place*:
> But sure no Statute in his favour says,
> How free, or frugal, I shall pass my days:
> I, who at some times spend, at others spare,
> Divided between Carelesness and Care.
> 'Tis one thing madly to disperse my store,
> Another, not to heed to treasure more;
> Glad, like a Boy, to snatch the first good day,
> And pleas'd, if sordid Want be far away.
> [28]What is't to me (a Passenger God wot)
> Whether my Vessel be first-rate or not?
> The Ship it self may make a better figure,
> But I that sail, am neither less nor bigger.
> I neither strut with ev'ry fav'ring breath,
> Nor strive with all the Tempest in my teeth.
> In pow'r, Wit, Figure, Virtue, Fortune, plac'd
> Behind the foremost, and before the last.   (284–303)

And this leads to a conclusion which, although based entirely on Horace's final questions, gives them a quite distinct character. Whereas Dacier saw Horace's lines as moral inquiry directed particularly at Julius Florus, and Shaftesbury read them as inner self-examination, Pope transforms them into the rhetoric of moral reflection:

[29]"But why all this of Av'rice? I have none."
I wish you joy, Sir, of a Tyrant gone;
But does no other lord it at this hour,
As wild and mad? the Avarice of Pow'r?
Does neither Rage inflame, nor Fear appall?
Nor the black Fear of Death, that saddens all?
With Terrors round can Reason hold her throne,
Despise the known, nor tremble at th' unknown?
Survey both Worlds, intrepid and entire,
In spight of Witches, Devils, Dreams, and Fire?
Pleas'd to look forward, pleas'd to look behind,
And count each Birth-day with a grateful mind?
Has Life no sourness, drawn so near its end?
Can'st thou endure a Foe, forgive a Friend?
Has Age but melted the rough parts away,
As Winter-fruits grow mild e'er they decay?
Or will you think, my Friend, your business done,
When, of a hundred thorns, you pull out one?
[30]Learn to live well, or fairly make your Will;
You've play'd, and lov'd, and eat, and drank your fill:
Walk sober off; before a sprightlier Age
Comes titt'ring on, and shoves you from the stage:
Leave such to trifle with more grace and ease,
Whom Folly pleases, and whose Follies please.   (304–27)

Horace's questions are simple and conversational: *'caret mortis formidine & ira?'* ('Is [your heart] free of fear and resentment at death?'). Pope is so grand:

> Does neither Rage inflame, nor Fear appall?
> Nor the black Fear of Death, that saddens all?   (308–9)

We find in Pope's lines a surprising mixture of tones, but it is, significantly, the continued elegiac note which makes the poetry so different from Horace's, the feeling of age, of potential bitterness, and of continued emotional strain: 'Has Life no sourness, drawn so near its end?' Horace's simple *'ignoscis amicis?'* ('Do you forgive your friends?') produces a double-edged question: 'Can'st thou endure a Foe, forgive a Friend?' *'Lenior & melior fis accedente senectâ?'* ('Are you becoming a milder and a better man as old age comes on?') acquires a haunting image, probably from Sanadon's note on the line:[6]

> Has Age but melted the rough parts away,
> As Winter-fruits grow mild e'er they decay?   (318–19)

Yet again Pope emphasizes limitation and failure now drawing on Horace's own dry ironies: *'Quid te exemta juvat spinis de pluribus una?'* ('What good does it do you to pull out one thorn, and leave so many in?') can be translated 'straight':

> Or will you think, my Friend, your business done,
> When, of a hundred thorns, you pull out one?   (320–1)

Pope's final stanza is sharp and cryptic, and underlines the potential bluntness of the Horace. Horace says sardonically, '*Vivere si rectè nescis, decede peritis*' ('If you don't know how to live life well, make way for those who do'); Pope is more direct: 'Learn to live well, or fairly make your Will'. He emphasizes the potential embarrassment of age ('Walk sober off'), the casual cruelty of youth ('shoves you from the stage'), and the sharp contrast between the follies of the young which are so pleasing, and those of the old which are merely distasteful:

> Leave such to trifle with more grace and ease,
> Whom Folly pleases, and whose Follies please.   (326–7)

As a totality Pope's Imitation of this Horatian epistle is distinguished for the openness of Pope's response to the Horatian text. His involvement with each of Horace's themes is intense, and yet his own movement from one 'subject' to another is fluid. Furthermore Pope's own poetic voice is neither simply introspective nor merely public: his poetry rises to rhetoric and falls to conversation, sharpens in irritation, and becomes still in the resonances of meditation. As such it represents an impressive internalization of both the themes and the form of one of Horace's most challenging epistles. Indeed the many-sidedness of Pope's Imitation, and its own interweaving of themes, draws attention to the openness of this Horatian poem. If Dacier's 'moralistic' interpretation and Shaftesbury's 'political' readings tend to close the Horatian work, this Imitation, by virtue of its poetic engagement with poetry, brings the Horatian epistle to life in this essential respect. Together these poems suggest that the art of poetry is never to rest in one position, never to close on its subject. Is this perhaps the hardest thing to achieve in every form of discourse and every form of life? 'Ludentis *speciem dabit, & torquebitur*'.

8

Poetry and politics:
The Imitation of Epistle II.i. ('To Augustus')

I am as you guess'd, returned from one Journey, & now I must add I am going on another: But to the quietest place I can go to, where I never yet pass'd a fortnight, but by a fatality, I think, I fall to writing verses. I wrote there my last Epistle; & began an Imitation of the finest in Horace this spring; which I propose to finish there this autumn. I mean Lord Peterborow's at Southampton, where I am to put the last hand too to the Garden he begun, & lived not to finish. It is a place that always made me Contemplative, & now Melancholy; but tis a Melancholy of that sort which becomes a Rational Creature, & an Immortal Soul. Pope to Fortescue, 21 September 1736

THE POEM Pope was hoping to finish at Southampton in the autumn of 1736 was almost certainly his Imitation of *Epistle* II.i., Horace's most elaborate and most eloquent discussion of the nature of Augustan poetry and of the role of the poet in society. It is clear that Pope took great pains with this Imitation: his 'Advertisement' suggests a fresh and stimulating reading of Horace's poem, his Imitation has an impressive inner unity which is imaginatively modelled on that aspect of Horace's poem, and Pope's language possesses throughout its own subtle eloquence. If the Horatian epistle is 'the finest in Horace' Pope's Imitation of it is, unquestionably, the climax of his engagement with the mature Horace.

In interpreting and evaluating this Imitation I want to stress the richness of Pope's response to the whole of this Horatian epistle. Comparison with the *Imitation of Epistle II.ii.* here underlines the point. The one thing Pope did not attempt, or achieve if he did attempt it, was to find his own equivalent for the seamless web of moving thought that gives Horace's *Epistle* II.ii. both its ineffable calm and its extraordinary strength. But this is precisely what he has achieved in this Imitation of *Epistle* II.i.

To begin to appreciate this we must approach Horace's poem bearing in mind all that we said about the nature of the Horatian epistle in the previous chapter, particularly Shaftesbury's interpretation of the form, which stresses the relationship between this poetic form and political independence. Looked at from this point of view

Horace's epistle is indeed about both poetry and politics, and the art of the whole poem is to weave these two themes together. We must try to see the inner relationships between: Horace's polite but cautious attitude to Augustus, constructed in his carefully controlled poetic language; his finely judged and urbanely expressed comments on contemporary taste in poetry and drama; his assessment of the important developments in the traditions of Roman literature and culture; and his exploration of the role of the poet in society as exemplified by the newest Augustan poetry which is seen as the culmination of all that was best in the growth of a genuinely Latin literature. As in the case of the *Epistle* II.ii. to Julius Florus, it is the subtle interweaving of all these themes which gives Horace's thought its richness and depth.

It seems to me that Pope took such a view of Horace's poem and that this accounts for the nature of his Imitation. Pope makes Horace's poem an opportunity to assess the strengths and weaknesses of the English poetic tradition, to comment satirically on the state of English drama in his own time, to explore the development of an English Augustan tradition under the influence of French Neo-Classicism, and to consider, with these traditions and Horace's ideals in mind, the role of the poet and artist in the England of his own time. But in doing this his ultimate aim was to make his poem a sustained exploration of the relationship between poetry and politics. The famous political ironies of this Imitation, however we interpret them, should not, therefore, be isolated from the poem's whole pattern of thought. To follow that line of thought next to the Horatian original is to appreciate Pope's most considered and successful attempt to re-create in English the full complexities of a mature Horatian epistle.

Preeminent among the strengths that make this Imitation so impressive is the control of tone: we might even say it gives the poem its essential unity. This is a purely Horatian achievement, to make us feel that the same voice is speaking now about Augustus, now about poetry, now about himself, now about cultural patterns, now about public fame, now about poetic achievement. What distinguishes Horace's epistle is the control of these various tones as he moves from polite compliment to dry irony, from warm involvement to cool detachment, from high eloquence to sharp sarcasm. The work is memorable for this singular fusion of irony, urbanity, and eloquence; and in the poetry of his Imitation, written in 'Contemplative' Southampton, Pope has created his own version of that confident Horatian persona which reflects on everything with cool urbanity and speaks only in the eloquence of irony.

Pope's *Epistle to Augustus* is, however, by no means unproblematical; indeed it raises three quite fundamental issues. The first concerns the image of Augustus Caesar in Horace's poem and Pope's own Imitation, and the attitudes to the relationship between Horace and Augustus as portrayed in Horace's poem and as 'mirrored' in Pope's. As several studies have recently shown, the evaluation of the Roman Augustus, and the use of Augustus as a symbolic figure in 'Augustan' England, were contradictory (see headnote to this chapter on p. 293). On the one hand he was regarded as the essence of the civilized and cultivated ruler who had created the great 'Pax Romana' out of the chaos of civil war; on the other hand, he was considered the ruthless, immoral tyrant who had destroyed the Roman republic and deprived her people of their liberty. The Opposition generally focused on this latter image in order to attack Augustus/George II who had, they argued, in his own way given up England's liberty. How did this affect the interpretation of Horace's *Epistle to Augustus* and the image of *Horace* in that poem?

Dacier's reading of the poem in this respect is somewhat more ambiguous than is usually recognized. He begins by noting Suetonius' famous remarks that Augustus had to request Horace to address an epistle to him, and that, in doing so, Augustus asked rather pointedly whether Horace was afraid to be seen as his friend. He then argues that the whole epistle is a very positive and elegant response to that reproach, indeed all the more elegant for correcting that fault: 'Sur quoy Horace luy écrivit cette belle Lettre, où il repare admirablement la faute qu'Auguste avoit bien voulu luy reprocher' (Dacier, IX, p. 308). In arguing this Dacier sees Horace as portraying Augustus in the most positive terms, as a civilized ruler controlling the state with fear of arms, and improving Roman morals with laws and, indeed, with his own high moral standards (Dacier, IX, pp. 267 and 311). But as he goes on, Dacier introduces other perspectives: he argues that Horace compliments Augustus on his taste in poetry by contrasting it with that of Alexander the Great, but he notes also that Horace is openly critical of his taste in theatre (Dacier, IX, pp. 432–3, and 419–21). And towards the conclusion of his commentary Dacier introduces the idea that the main subject of the letter is, in fact, what emerges only at the end: Horace's personal excuse to Augustus for not writing the kind of poetry Augustus actually wanted. Commenting on Horace's *recusatio* in line 249 he states rather surprisingly: 'Horace continuë de s'excuser; ce qui est le principal sujet de cette Lettre' (Dacier, IX, p. 433). These remain, however, only minor points in an interpretation which gives a positive account of Augustus and a relatively unproblematical view of Horace's relationship with him.

Shaftesbury, however, takes a quite different view of the poem. Anxious to condemn Augustus but also to exonerate Horace, he sees the epistle as a subtle criticism of Augustus' taste: 'Whoever has a thorow *Taste* of the Wit and Manner of HORACE, if he only compares his Epistle to AUGUSTUS (*lib.* 2) with the secret Character of that Prince from SUETONIUS and other Authors, will easily find what Judgement that Poet made of the *Roman Taste*, even in the Person of this sovereign and admir'd *Roman Prince*; whose natural Love of Amphitheatrical Spectacles, and other Entertainments (little accommodated to the Interest of the *Muses*) is there sufficiently insinuated' (Shaftesbury, 1714, I, p. 269, footnote; see also Shaftesbury, 1900, pp. 396–8). Shaftesbury saw the work as an exploration of the relationship between taste and politics, and, indeed, an attempt to correct Augustus' poor taste and crass manners: 'That Prince indeed was ... oblig'd in the highest degree to his poetical and witty Friends [Horace and Maecenas], for guiding his Taste, and forming his Manners; as they really did, with good effect, and great advantage to his Interest' (Shaftesbury, 1714, I, pp. 269–70, footnote). How do these two interpretations relate to Pope's Imitation?

The second issue concerns Pope's interpretation of Horace's related arguments about aesthetic judgement, the development of Roman literature, and the social value of poetry. As Fraenkel has emphasized, this epistle is not about poetry in general, but rather a defence of, and in a sense, a historical justification for, the new Augustan poetry, with its high aesthetic ideals matched by serious moral and political concerns. As Fraenkel puts it: 'In this epistle it is Horace's primary object to outline the character and scope of that new poetry and to allot to it its proper place in the body politic' (1957, p. 388). The literary judgements which Pope makes in his Imitation have been much discussed, and praised; but what has not been fully considered is how far, and in what ways, Pope has redefined Horace's aesthetic criteria, and how far he has attempted to re-evaluate the development of English poetry and drama according to any similar coherent historical pattern.

The third issue concerns Pope's approach to the overall style, tone, and structure of this epistle. Even Dryden, so critical of Horace's low style, makes this poem an exception, because there is 'so much Dignity in the Words, and ... so much Elegancy in the Numbers' ('Discourse', p. 64). How far does Pope's Imitation recognize this dignity of style, and how much does it 'recognize' what we would now regard as other challenging features of Horace's poem: its ambiguities of tone, its provocative lines of thought, its shifting of positions? As we will see, interpretations of the tone of crucial passages varied considerably: what Dacier regards as carefully restrained praise Bolingbroke denounced as patent flattery. Finally, does Pope agree with Shaftesbury when he asserts so clearly what is so flatly denied by others, that there is a profound relationship between this mature Horatian style and deep commitment to political and personal freedom?

Pope's 'Advertisement' to his Imitation clearly alludes to some of these issues and provides important guides as to how Pope read this Horatian epistle. It shows, first of all, that Pope was well aware of the double view of Augustus as civilized ruler and as tyrant. With dry irony he speaks of the changes he has made to Horace's poem in this respect: he notes that Horace *paints [His Prince] with all the great and good qualities of a Monarch, upon whom the* Romans *depended for the Encrease of an* Absolute Empire. *But to make the poem entirely English, I was willing to add one or two of those Virtues which contribute to the Happiness of a* Free People, *and are more consistent with the Welfare of* our Neighbours' (*TE*, IV, p. 191).

He also notes particularly that it was a mistake to think that Augustus was 'a Patron of Poets in general', and that this epistle was 'a general Discourse of Poetry'. He sees the poem very much in its local time, emphasizing that Augustus *'prohibited all but the Best Writers to name him'*, and asserting that the epistle was *'an* Apology for the Poets, *in order to render* Augustus *more their Patron.'* He goes on to stress that Horace was specifically attempting to plead *'the Cause of his Contemporaries'*, showing that aesthetically and morally, they were superior to earlier writers, and were in those terms *'useful to the State'* (*TE*, IV, pp. 191–2).

Finally, Pope argues very directly against the view that Horace was the base flatterer of Augustus or anyone else. Indeed, he goes out of his way to stress Horace's essential independence, emphasizing that Horace's plea for contemporary poets in the Epistle was argued against *'the Taste of the Town'*, *'the Court and Nobility'*, and *'lastly against the Emperor himself, who had conceived them of little use to the Government'* (*TE*, IV, 191–2). He concludes with a strong and clear assertion of Horace's fundamental integrity: *'We may farther learn from this Epistle, that* Horace *made Court to this Great Prince, by writing with a decent Freedom toward him, with a just Contempt of his low Flatterers, and with a manly Regard to his own Character'* (*TE*, IV, p. 192).

How can these issues be related to our reading of the openings of these two poems? The problems are posed at once at Horace's extremely cautious beginning:

> Cum tot ¹sustineas & tanta negotia, solus:
> Res Italas armis tuteris, moribus ornes,
> Legibus emendes; in ²publica commoda peccem,
> Si longo sermone morer tua tempora, Caesar.   (1–4)

(When so many and so great are the responsibilities which you shoulder alone, defending the Italian state with your arms, embellishing it with your morals, reforming it with your laws, I would be offending against the public good if I were to waste your time in lengthy talk.)

These lines seem to be impeccably respectful, if rather low-keyed. Let us consider Dacier's very 'positive' account of them. According to Dacier Horace sees Augustus as the supreme example of a civilized ruler, not only protecting the state with fear of arms and improving her morals with laws, but actually setting himself the example of those high moral standards: Dacier translates '*moribus ornes*', 'vous l'embellissez par les bonnes moeurs dont vous donnez vous-mesme l'exemple' (Dacier, IX, p. 267; see also pp. 310–11). Dacier notes particularly the force of '*solus*' ('alone'), emphasizing how much all this depends on one man, a powerful allusion to Augustus' '*absoluë Monarchie*' (p. 310).

Horace follows his quiet opening with a very impressive passage which would perhaps have made a more striking beginning: the tone is raised and we are suddenly involved imaginatively in the world of myth. The '*Caesar*' at the end of the first stanza leads powerfully to the '*Romulus, & Liber pater*' of the first line of the next, but the reason for the passage is at first arrestingly unclear:

> ³Romulus, & Liber pater, & cum Castore Pollux,
> Post ingentia facta, ⁴Deorum in templa recepti,
> Dum terras hominumque colunt genus, aspera bella
> Componunt, agros adsignant, oppida condunt;
> ⁵Ploravere suis non respondere favorem
> Speratum meritis. Diram qui contudit Hydram,
> Notaque fatali portenta labore subegit,
> Comperit ⁶Invidiam supremo fine domari.
> ⁷Urit enim fulgore suo qui praegravat artes
> Infra se positas: extinctus amabitur idem.   (5–14)

(Romulus, father Bacchus, Castor and Pollux, after their heroic achievements, were admitted to the temples as gods, but while they lived on earth among mortal men, ending fierce wars, settling men on the land, founding cities, they complained that their popularity failed to come up to their deserts. Hercules, who crushed the loathsome Hydra, who subdued with enforced labour those notorious monsters, discovered that Envy can be overcome only by dying. With his own white heat the hero scorches the talents he subdues; once extinguished, he will be loved.)

The actions of the legendary leaders of Rome, and of Hercules, seem to parallel the deeds of Augustus himself, but their fates, if so, are somewhat disconcerting: great merit is only appreciated after death. The language is memorably succinct in the manner of the odes: '*Comperit Invidiam supremo fine domari*' ('discovered that Envy can be overcome only by dying'), '*Urit enim fulgore suo*' ('With his own white heat the hero scorches'), '*extinctus amabitur idem*' ('once extinguished, he will be loved'). The fresh treatment of these myths, the challenging suggestions, the eloquence, and the disconcerting moral realism, are the Horatian qualities here.

Dacier, however, does not emphasize these disturbing implications. Rather he concentrates on the deification of Augustus, which he presents in positive terms, and on what he takes to be Horace's implication that true heroism, like that of Augustus, lies not in making war but in concluding it. Commenting on '*aspera bella / Componunt*' he states: 'Le veritable heroïsme ne consiste pas moins à terminer les guerres qu'à les continuer. Horace n'employe icy que des expressions qui ne conviennent pas moins à Auguste qu'aux Heros qu'il vient de nommer, & il y a là beaucoup de politesse & d'adresse' (Dacier, IX, p. 313; Carthy in his note on the passage stresses this even more, 1731, p. 36).

Only after Horace has implied that Caesar's fate might be the same as those of his illustrious predecessors, does he reveal that he was really trying to say the opposite. And only afterwards does he reveal that, in fact, all this was merely an introduction to his subject: he really wants to talk about attitudes to old and new poetry. This is Horatian modulation at its best, either elegantly complimentary, or just on the edge of contradiction and irony:

> [8]*Praesenti Tibi* maturos *largimur honores:*
> [9]*Jurandasque tuum per nomen ponimus aras,*
> [10]Nil oriturum *aliàs,* nil ortum tale *fatentes.*
>   Sed tuus hoc populus sapiens & justus in uno,
> Te nostris Ducibus, Te Graiis *anteferendo,*
> Caetera nequaquam simili ratione modoque
> Aestimat; &, nisi quae terris semota, suisque
> Temporibus defuncta videt, fastidit & odit.   (15–22)

(But on you, while you are still in our midst, we lavish timely honours, we build altars at which we swear by your name, declaring that none such as you has ever arisen or ever will arise again.

But this your people wise and just in this one respect, in placing you above our Roman leaders, above the Greeks, values all else according to a very different scale, and despises and rejects eveything except what it sees has passed on from this world and has had its day.)

The play of tone here is extremely ambiguous and can be interpreted in many ways. Dacier attempts to define the tone of 'Nil oriturum *aliàs*, nil ortum tale *fatentes*' by comparing it with *Ode* IV.ii. 37–40; he suggests that Horace has raised the tone to compliment Augustus with his living deification, but has still kept it within the appropriate bounds of the epistle style:

Il dit icy en un seul vers ce qu'il dit en quatre dans l'Ode II. du Livre IV.

> *Quo nihil majus, meliusque terris*
> *Fata donavêre, bonique Divi:*
> *Nec dabunt, quamvis redeant in aurum*
> *Tempora priscum.*
>> [(a ruler) greater and better than any the fates and gracious gods have given the world, or ever will give, even if the years return to the age of gold.]

Et sur cela on peut remarquer en passant la différence qu'il y a entre la simplicité du stile de l'Epistre ou de la Satire, & la majesté & la magnificence de celuy de l'Ode.   (Dacier, IX, pp. 319–20)

Bolingbroke, and others, however, saw this famous line as patent flattery. When trying to formulate his idea of a great 'patriot King', he referred to it very sarcastically:

We are willing to indulge this pleasing expectation [the emergence of a great 'Patriot King'], and there is nothing we desire more ardently than to be able to hold of a British prince, without flattery, the same language that was held of a Roman emperor, with a great deal.

Nil oriturum aliàs, nil ortum tale fatentes.   (1754, III, p. 40)

And yet Horace's line of thought after this compliment seems wryly amused: the people are *Augustus'* people ('*tuus hoc populus*'); '*sapiens & justus in uno*' ('wise and just in this one respect') seems marginally ironic; and the '*fastidit & odit*' ('despises and rejects') amusingly excessive.

Pope's imitation of this whole opening is quite brilliant, not only because of the way it sets George II 'with' and 'against' Augustus, but also because these ironies in Pope's own text can either be a criticism of Horace as the flatterer of Augustus or a tribute to the fine detachment and ironic astringency which are so evident in Horace's text if one wishes to see them. From the very beginning Pope goes far beyond Dacier's interpretation of this poem, and raises fundamental questions about the potential ironies of the Horatian text.

While You, great Patron of Mankind, [1]sustain
The balanc'd World, and open all the Main;
Your Country, chief, in Arms abroad defend,
At home, with Morals, Arts, and Laws amend;
[2]How shall the Muse, from such a Monarch, steal
An hour, and not defraud the Publick Weal?　　　　　(1–6)

As every commentator has recognized, the surface here is perfectly 'Horatian', its ironies utterly devastating. But this poetry is working on at least three levels. On the one hand Pope is clearly using the positive image of Augustus as found in Dacier to more or less annihilate George II. The phrase 'great Patron of Mankind' is patently absurd, and the 'Main' was open chiefly to Spanish raiders. Horace's *'Res Italas armis tueris'* ('defending the Italian state with your arms') produces a rapier-like allusion to the king's protracted visit to Hanover where he was, presumably, in the arms of his mistress Madame Walmadon: 'Your country, chief, in Arms abroad defend.' To the 'Morals' and 'Laws' of Augustus' regime Pope adds the one thing in which George II had no interest at all, 'Arts'. He plays brilliantly on Horace's *'peccem'*, taking it to mean 'sin' rather than 'offend', and imagines that the seductive Muse of poetry might 'steal / An hour' with the King and somehow 'defraud the Publick Weal.'[1]

On the other hand, Pope's ironies directed at George II clearly can point ironically at the image of Augustus as presented by Dacier and others. Pope's 'great Patron of Mankind' would fit Dacier's Augustus but not that shown in Suetonius and Tacitus (see Weinbrot, 1978, Chapters 1 and 2). Dryden, using Suetonius, argued forcefully that Augustus' personal morals were quite monstrous; they were certainly much worse than those of George II ('Discourse', pp. 66–9); and, as we have seen, Shaftesbury and even Dacier himself, questioned Augustus' taste in 'Arts'. Together these two perspectives raise a third: how far is Pope actually questioning Dacier's interpretation of the Horatian poetic text? How far does he actually see another Horatian text here, one much more reserved in tone, much more critical in its ironies, much more challenging in its turns of thought?

After the cutting ironies and ambiguities of his opening, Pope surprises us with what looks like a 'straight' translation of Horace's second paragraph:

[3]Edward and Henry, now the Boast of Fame,
And virtuous Alfred, a more [4]sacred Name,
After a Life of gen'rous Toils endur'd,
The Gaul subdu'd, or Property secur'd,

Ambition humbled, mighty Cities storm'd,
Or Laws establish'd, and the World reform'd;
5Clos'd their long Glories with a sigh, to find
Th'unwilling Gratitude of base mankind!
All human Virtue to its latest breath
6Finds Envy never conquer'd, but by Death.
The great Alcides, ev'ry Labour past,
Had still this Monster to subdue at last.
7Sure fate of all, beneath whose rising ray
Each Star of meaner merit fades away;
Oppress'd we feel the Beam directly beat,
Those Suns of Glory please not till they set.   (7–22)

But Edward III, Henry V, and Alfred – Pope's equivalents for
Romulus, father Liber, and Castor and Pollux – had strong political
overtones in the 1730s. For the Opposition they, more than any
other English kings, were both conquerors and champions of
English liberty (see Levine, 1967, pp. 434–41, and Schonhorn,
1968, 432–8). These lines implicitly criticize George II, and either
praise Augustus if we assume Dacier's and Carthy's reading, or
criticize Augustus if we adopt the 'Opposition' view. Furthermore,
the deification of Augustus during his lifetime, although mentioned
positively by Dacier, was strongly criticized by Bolingbroke and
others (see Levine, 1967, p. 437). And yet these ironies are contained in a verse paragraph which is a re-creation of the Horatian
qualities we noted above: the eloquence, the *brevitas*, and the
challenging coolness in tone – 'Those Suns of Glory please not till
they set.' Pope's own language makes us aware of that firm detachment in the Horatian text in a way that Dacier's commentary does
not.

In the next two paragraphs Pope moves into patent parody and
then to cool Horatian astringency:

To Thee, the World its present homage pays,
The Harvest early, 8but mature the Praise:
Great Friends of LIBERTY! in *Kings* a Name
Above all Greek, above all Roman Fame:
Whose Word is Truth, as sacred and rever'd,
9As Heav'n's own Oracles from Altars heard.
Wonder of Kings! like whom, to mortal eyes
10None e'er has risen, and none e'er shall rise.
    Just in one instance, be it yet confest
Your People, Sir, are partial in the rest.
Foes to all living worth except your own,
And Advocates for Folly dead and gone.
Authors, like Coins, grow dear as they grow old;
It is the rust we value, not the gold.   (23–36)

What Dacier considered Horace's carefully observed poetic decorums are here thrown to the wind: 'Great Friend of LIBERTY!', 'Wonder of Kings!' The 'Te nostris Ducibus, Te Graiis' is snatched from Horace's second paragraph to provide the extravagant 'Above all Greek, above all Roman Fame'; 'maturos' ('timely') provides a lovely irony, 'The Harvest early, but mature the Praise'; and the climactic 'Nil oriturum *aliàs*, nil ortum tale *fatentes*' becomes pure sarcasm: 'None e'er has risen, and none e'er shall rise.'[2] But if this is in part a criticism of Augustus the Roman tyrant and Horace his flatterer, Pope switches at once into Horatian detachment with a superb change of tone:

> Just in one instance, be it yet confest
> Your People, Sir, are partial in the rest. (31–2)

With a fine pun on 'dear' and eloquent Horatian *brevitas* he tells us:

> Authors, like Coins, grow dear as they grow old;
> It is the rust we value, not the gold. (35–6)

In these opening lines we begin to see the complexity of Pope's attitudes to the Roman Augustus, George II, and the Horatian text. The main point I want to make at this stage is that by criticizing the Roman Augustus Pope is not by that account disparaging Horace, as Weinbrot, for example, has argued (1978, Chapter 6). The ironies of Pope's text certainly raise this as a possibility, and they give us, as it were, two Roman Augustuses and two Horaces. But as the Imitation goes on the ironies of Pope's text draw particular attention to, and are a tribute to, the astringency of Horace's text and the detachment implicit in its finer and more challenging turns of thought. Indeed Pope's Imitation seems an attempt to emulate the moral and intellectual independence Horace achieved in poetic eloquence.

In the next section of his epistle Horace concentrates on the Roman taste for its older literature, and here Horace's tone becomes much more openly ironical and critical. The tenor of his argument is perfectly clear: the Roman public prefer old poetry and drama, however obscure and faulty, to what is modern; they love to repeat conventional and banal opinions about the old writers rather than think about them afresh; they take it as a personal insult if anyone dares to criticize them; and they reject out of hand anything that is contemporary simply because it is new and written by the living. This satire is amusing and instructive in itself, but it is also designed to overcome the blind prejudices which, it would seem, stood in the way of a fair appreciation of the new Augustan poetry. The poor reception of Horace's own first three books of Odes were an example of just this, and Horace's feelings perhaps sharpen this attack on the Roman public. With wit and irony, and a sharp eye for the absurdities of conventionality, Horace appeals for a more vigorous and critical attitude to the past and a fairer and more appreciative attitude to the present. Characteristically he does this with explicit or implicit questions that challenge the basis of conventional assumption. Do we always have to, indeed can we always, compare Rome with Greece? What *is* 'a classic'? Have the old works *no* faults? When does the old stop and the new begin? With persistent irony this Horatian text deconstructs the whole time-honoured activity of judging classics by the measure of time.

Pope very ingeniously turns this section of Horace into an assessment of English taste and the English classics. The overall argument is very similar to Horace's, but the Imitation is arresting primarily because of the examples Pope has chosen, his own challenging critical stance, and his fresh re-creation of Horace's urbane ironies and calmly shifting tones. We might expect another *Dunciad*, but, thanks to Horace, we get an open and genuinely speculative type of criticism – a new battle of ancients and moderns, fought in favour of the moderns along Horatian lines. For all the strengths of the *Essay on Criticism* and the *Epistle to Arbuthnot*, there is something appealing in what is for Pope a new style of literary criticism – judicious but tolerant, historically sophisticated, fresh and lively in its approach to the relationship between the literature of the past and the taste of the present.

Throughout this section of the Imitation Pope's adaptations of Horace's examples are not merely clever; it is clear that imitating Horace has allowed Pope to think afresh about the significance of individual English poets, both 'major' writers like Shakespeare, Spenser, and Milton, and 'minor' figures like Cowley, Rowe, and the Restoration 'Miscellanists'. Equally important are the criteria of artistic evaluation which emerge from Pope's judgements, and the distinctive tones of his criticism. Horace here is concerned primarily with perfection of form and finish, which he says is generally lacking in the work of older writers; Pope, however, explores the achievements of writers more fully, and hints at other issues. In particular he considers the taste for the bawdy, criticizing here Chaucer and Skelton; the portrayal of the passions, praising Cowley, Southern, and Rowe; the power of individual poetic languages; and affectation in poetic style, criticising Spenser, Sidney, and Milton.

The significance of Pope's criteria only emerges as the Imitation grows, but let us consider several passages to show how he applies them within the English tradition. Sometimes Pope imaginatively stretches his Horatian text in order to introduce his English poets, as he does at the very beginning of this section, when Horace first speaks about the Roman taste for all things ancient:

> [11]*Sic fautor* Veterum, *ut tabulas peccare vetantes,*
> *Quas bis quinque viri sanxerunt, foedera regum,*
> *Vel Gabiis, vel cum rigidis aequata Sabinis,*
> *Pontificum libros, annosa volumina vatum,*
> [12]*Dictitet Albano* Musas *in monte locutas.* (23–7)

(So much do they prefer the ancients that the Tablets forbidding vice ordained by the Ten Men, the treaties of the Kings established with Gabii or with the dour Sabines, the priestly books, the hoary bardic rolls – these they insist were uttered by the very Muses on the Alban Mount.)

For these obscure, moral, and non-literary texts Pope finds some witty and challenging literary classics:

> [11]Chaucer's worst ribaldry is learn'd by rote,
> And beastly Skelton Heads of Houses quote:
> One likes no language but the Faery Queen;
> A Scot will fight for Christ's Kirk o' the Green;
> And each true Briton is to Ben so civil,
> [12]He swears the Muses met him at the Devil. (37–42)

Horace claims ironically that the Romans love the venerable moral Tablets 'forbidding vice' ('*tabulas peccare vetantes*'); Pope reverses this to make a witty comment on the contemporary taste for 'Chaucer's worst ribaldry' and 'beastly Skelton'. The obscurity of ancient Roman law provides a fine allusion to Spencer's bizarre language, 'One likes no language but the Faery Queen'; and Horace's references to the treaties made with the 'dour Sabines' and to 'the priestly books' fuse to produce the witty: 'A Scot will fight for Christ's Kirk o' the Green.' True British taste for *classic* writing is, of course, different from such barbarity; playing on Horace's '*Albano* Musas *in monte locutas*' ('uttered by the very Muses on the Alban Mount') Pope says sardonically:

> And each true Briton is to Ben so civil,
> He swears the Muses met him at the Devil. (41–2)

An important feature of this type of criticism is that these literary texts are seen in a social, national, indeed nationalistic context. Both Horace and Pope are aware of the way in which literary classics which form the school curriculum are part of the national heritage, and become inseparable from the conventional opinions that grow up around them. The dangers of these platitudes are amusingly portrayed by both Horace and Pope:

"[28]*Adeo sanctum est vetus omne poema!*
"*Ambigitur* [29]*quoties, uter utro sit prior; aufert*
"*Pacuvius docti famam senis, Accius alti:*
"*Dicitur Afrani toga convenisse Menandro;*
"*Plautus ad exemplar Siculi properare Epicharmi;*
"*Vincere Caecilius gravitate, Terentius arte.*
"*Hos ediscit, & hos arcto stipata theatro*
"*Spectat Roma potens;* [30]*habet hos numeratque poetas*
"*Ad nostrum tempus, Livî scriptoris ab aevo.*   (54–62)

(Such is the sanctity of any poem that's old! Whenever people dispute which is better than the other, Pacuvius is awarded the prize for learning among the ancients, Accius for sublimity. It is said Afranius' Roman dress suits Menander; Plautus goes at a gallop like his Sicilian model Epicharmus; Caecilius is the winner for weightiness, Terence for artistry. These are the authors mighty Rome reads at school, these she watches in the packed theatre; these are the poets she has cherished and counted as her own from the days of Livius to our time.)

Pope's note on this paragraph is very acute: 'the whole Paragraph has a mixture of Irony, and must not altogether be taken for Horace's own Judgement, only the common Chatt of the pretenders to Criticism; in some things right, in others wrong: as he tells us in his answer, *Interdum vulgus rectum videt, est ubi peccat* ['Sometimes the crowd sees straight, but sometimes it's mistaken']' (*TE*, IV, p. 201). With this in mind Pope produces just the same show:

"Yet surely, [28]surely, these were famous men!
"What Boy but hears the sayings of old Ben?
"In all [29]debates where CRiticks bear a part,
"Not one but nods, and talks of Johnson's Art,
"Of Shakespear's Nature, and of Cowley's Wit;
"How Beaumont's Judgment check'd what Fletcher writ;
"How Shadwell hasty, Wycherly was slow;
"But, for the Passions, Southern sure and Rowe.
"These, [30]only these, support the crouded stage,
"From eldest Heywood down to Cibber's age.   (79–88)

The traditional debating points of the English present are here seen as but echoes of, or variations on, the debating points of the Latin past: the choice is between the learned ('*docti*') Pacuvius or the sublime ('*alti*') Accius:

"Not one but nods, and talks of Johnson's Art,
"Of Shakespear's Nature, and of Cowley's Wit ...   (82–3)

Plautus wrote quickly, like his model Epicharmus: 'How Shadwell hasty, Wycherly was slow.' Pope treats such conventional judgements with a fine blend of tolerance and irony. When banality has such ancient precedent what else can one do? But in doing so, he fundamentally questions, as Horace does, what it is that truly makes these writers great.

But the real triumph here is Pope's expression of his own fresh and vigorous literary judgements in his own strong, urbane style, which was made possible only by Horace. The finest passage in this respect is appropriately Pope's imitation of Horace's central passage on the need for balanced judgement in assessing the achievements of the past, Horace's own answer to conventional literary opinions of his time:

> [31]*Interdum vulgus rectum videt: est ubi peccat.*
> *Si* [32]*veteres ita miratur laudatque poetas,*
> *Ut nihil anteferat, nihil illis comparet: errat:*
> *Si quaedam nimis* [33]antiquè, *si pleraque* [34]durè
> *Dicere credit eos,* [35]ignavè *multa; fatetur;*
> *Et sapit, & mecum facit, & Jove judicat aequo.*
> [36]*Non equidem insector,* delendaque carmina *Livî*
> *Esse reor, memini quae* [37]plagosum, [38]mihi parvo,
> *Orbilium* dictare. –
>   *Sed emendata videri*
> *Pulchraque, & exactis minimum distantia, miror:*
> *Inter quae* [39] verbum emicuit *si forte* decorum, &
> *Si* [40]*versus paulo concinnior unus & alter;*
> *Injuste* totum *ducit venditque poema.*   (63–75)

(Sometimes the crowd sees straight, but sometimes it's mistaken. If it so admires and praises the ancient poets that it allows nothing to surpass or approach them, it's wrong. If it thinks their writing is occasionally too archaic, sometimes unsophisticated, often plain dull, then it shows taste, it agrees with me, and delivers a sane and balanced judgement worthy of Jove himself. I am certainly not condemning or proposing the destruction of those rhymes of Livius that I remember Orbilius drumming into me with blows when I was a child. But when they are regarded as flawless, unblemished, virtual masterpieces, I am amazed. In those old books if there is a chance flash of a neat phrase, or if a line or two sounds a bit better than the rest, that undeservedly carries the whole poem and sells it.)

Pope's imitation is a perfect fusion of Pope and Horace: the ideas are half from the Latin poet, half from the English, the urbanity of the ironies and the confident balancing of attitudes are now equally Horatian and Popean, and the control of tone is masterful:

> [31]All this may be; the People's Voice is odd,
> It is, and it is not, the voice of God.
> To [32]Gammer Gurton if it gives the bays,
> And yet deny the Careless Husband praise,
> Or say our fathers never broke a rule;
> Why then I say, the Publick is a fool.

But let them own, that greater faults than we
They had, and greater Virtues, I'll agree.
Spencer himself affects the [33]obsolete,
And Sydney's verse halts ill on [34]Roman feet:
Milton's strong pinion now not Heav'n can bound;
Now serpent-like, in [35]prose he sweeps the ground,
In Quibbles, Angel and Archangel join,
And God the Father turns a School-Divine.
[36]Not that I'd lop the Beauties from his book,
Like [37]slashing Bentley with his desp'rate Hook;
Or damn all Shakespear, like th'affected fool
At Court, who hates whate'er he [38]read at School.
   But for the Wits of either Charles's days,
The Mob of Gentlemen who wrote with Ease;
Sprat, Carew, Sedley, and a hundred more,
(Like twinkling Stars the Miscellanies o'er)
One Simile, that [39]solitary shines
In the dry Desert of a thousand lines,
Or [40]lengthen'd Thought that gleams thro' many a page,
Has sanctify'd whole Poems for an age.   (89–114)

This is at once an imaginative transformation of Horace and a demonstration of the kind of balanced judgement that is needed in approaching the past. It makes Horace's distinctive kind of literary criticism wholly alive. Even the challenging contradiction of Pope's first couplet draws on what Horace says some lines later: '*& Jove judicat aequo*' ('and delivers a sane and balanced judgement worthy of Jove himself'). The single key words in Horace blossom into compelling judgements on the English classics:

'antiquè' ('archaic'): 'Spencer himself affects the obsolete' ... (97)
'durè' ('unsophisticated'): 'And Sydney's verse halts ill on Roman feet' ... (98)
'ignavè' ('plain dull'):

> Now serpent-like, in prose he sweeps the ground,
> In Quibbles, Angel and Archangel join,
> And God the Father turns a School-Divine.   (100–2)

The first half of Horace's point about the poems of Livius becomes sharp contemporary allusion, as his old teacher Orbilius with his blows ('plagosum ... Orbilium'), Horace as a child ('mihi parvo'), and the verses of Livius ('delendaque carmina *Livî*'), take new forms:

> Not that I'd lop the Beauties from his book,
> Like slashing Bentley with his desp'rate hook;
> Or damn all Shakespear, like th'affected fool
> At Court, who hates whate'er he read at School.   (103–6)

The rest of the lines become a shrewd assessment of the distinctive kind of limited achievement which one finds in the poetry of 'Sprat, Carew, Sedley, and a hundred more.' Horace's 'verbum emicuit ... decorum' ('there is a chance flash of a neat phrase') and 'versus ... concinnior' ('a line or two sounds a bit better') are all too apt:

> Sprat, Carew, Sedley, and a hundred more,
> (Like twinkling Stars the Miscellanies o'er)
> One Simile, that solitary shines
> In the dry Desert of a thousand lines,
> Or lengthen'd Thought that gleams thro' many a page ...   (109–13)

Horace ends this whole section of his poem with some outspoken lines, which concentrate on the contemporary dramatic performance of older plays, and attempts to expose the real motives that lie behind this adulation of everything ancient and scorn for everything new. Horace reveals that in this disparagement of the new there is a deep conflict of the generations, the stifling hate and envy the old feel for the vigour of the young. This kind of forcefulness in Horace clearly appealed to Pope – here is the *'manly'* Horace of Pope's 'Advertisement' – and it inspires in Pope equal directness. Indeed Pope intensifies Horace's view that the struggle of taste can be seen in terms of the struggle between fathers and sons. Working with the 'patres' ('elders') in Horace (line 81) he emphasizes just how much this is a generation conflict, and how much the fathers, and those who support them, are motivated by envy of youthful creativity:

> How will our Fathers rise up in a rage ...   (125)

> You'd think [44]no Fools disgrac'd the former Reign,
> Did not some grave Examples yet remain,
> Who scorn a Lad should teach his Father skill
> And, having once been wrong, will be so still.   (127–30)

> ... he envies, not admires,
> And to debase the Sons, exalts the Sires.   (133–4)

As we see in some of the portraits in the *Epistles to Burlington* and *Bathurst* Pope was fascinated by such conflicts. It is interesting here to see him following Horace in so clearly taking the side of youth: '*Nostra sed impugnat, nos, nostraque lividus odit*' (line 89 – 'he attacks our genius, and in his envy hates us and everything we do'). It would seem likely, furthermore, that Pope was alluding to the struggle between the King and the Prince of Wales (see Schonhorn, 1968, pp. 436–42). Whether this is the case or not, it is clear again that literary questions are seen as being bound up with issues that are social and, indeed, political. This, of course, leads to the next theme.

Having ridiculed the Roman taste for everything antique, Horace changes tack and begins to explore another issue relevant to his main subject, the attitudes of different societies at different times to their artists. The pictures he draws are deliberately exaggerated: the most complex is the portrait of Greece in a time of peace trifling in idleness and raving over its artists; by contrast he offers a short sketch of early Rome where life is quite distressingly industrious and moral, and in which there is no place for art at all. These passages are extremely important because they gradually lead Horace to the central section of his poem and his assertions about the moral, political, and religious value of the new Augustan poetry. It is typical of Horace, of course, that he approaches this subject obliquely, dealing with it, as it were, before he actually does; but this only gives depth to the central passage when it comes. Characteristically, also, this prelude to Horace's powerful assertion of the public value of the poet and his poetry contains wry scorn for art as a serious activity and ridicule for the poet as a social figure.

Pope's handling of this aspect of Horace's epistle, and these passages in particular, is very impressive. A fascinating feature of the Imitation as a whole is Pope's attempt to chart the development of an English Augustan tradition from Ben Jonson and Dryden in the seventeenth century, through the Restoration and the influence of French classicism, to the Augustan literature of his own time. In his interpretation of this development, Pope concentrates on what he sees as its fundamental qualities: its growing moral seriousness which is ironically contrasted so often with the moral laxity of the Court and aristocracy, its increasing concern for 'correctness', and its growing political consciousness. He uses Horace's aesthetic criteria to praise what he regards as the strong features of literature in his own time, and Horace's *'Progress of Learning'* to show how these features developed out of the best writing of the seventeenth century. But he blends with them his own moral, stylistic, and social criteria outlined above. Pope's 'Advertisement' makes clear how with all this in mind he interprets this general aspect of Horace's poem:

He shews (by a view of the Progress of Learning, and the Change of Taste among the Romans) *that the Introduction of the Polite Arts of* Greece *had given the Writers of his Time great advantages over their Predecessors, that their* Morals *were much improved, and the Licence of those ancient Poets restrained: that* Satire *and* Comedy *were become more just and useful; that whatever extrava-*

*gancies were left on the Stage, were owing to the Ill Taste of the Nobility; that
Poets, under due Regulations were in many respects useful to the* State; *and
concludes, that it was upon them the Emperor himself must depend, for his Fame
with Posterity.* (*TE*, IV, p. 192)

It is from this perspective that we should look at Pope's imitations
of Horace's passage on Greece, Rome, and contemporary Rome.
Horace's lines on the Greek passion for art after the Persian wars are
as provocative as they are unforgettable:

> [47]*Ut primum positis nugari Graecia bellis
> Coepit, & in* Vitium fortuna labier aequa;
> *Nunc Athletarum studiis, nunc arsit* [48]*equorum;*
> [49]*Marmoris, aut eboris fabros, aut aeris amavit;
> Suspendit* [50]*picta vultum mentemque tabella;
> Nunc* [51]*tibicinibus, nunc est gavisa tragoedis:*
> [52]*Sub nutrice puella velut si luderet infans,
> Quod cupide petiit, mature plena reliquit.
> Quid placet, aut odio est, quod non mutabile credas?
> Hoc Paces habuere bonae, ventique secundi.* (93–102)

(When first Greece laid warfare aside and began to trifle, to drift in the current of
prosperity into degeneracy, she would be ablaze with enthusiasm, now for
athletes, now for horses; she would fall in love with craftsmen in marble, ivory,
or bronze; she would stand, eyes and mind transfixed, before a painting; at one
moment it was flute-music she enjoyed, at another tragedy. She was like a little
baby with her toys: what she had sought so passionately, she soon tired of and
abandoned. Does *anything* give pleasure or loathing which you're sure won't
change? This is the effect of unbroken wholesome peace and following winds.)

This poetry is at once warmly appreciative and coolly damning.
The negative overtones are persistent: '*nugari*' ('to trifle'); the ironical '*in* Vitium fortuna labier aequa' ('to drift in the current of
prosperity into degeneracy'); the ironical contrast of '*Nunc tibicini-
bus, nunc est gavisa tragoedis*' ('at one moment it was flute-music she
enjoyed, at another tragedy'); the reference to childish impetuosity
and impatience; and the sardonic conclusion, '*Hoc Paces habuere
bonae, ventique secundi*' ('This is the effect of unbroken wholesome
peace and following winds'). At the same time, the poetry itself
warms to the aesthetic delights and the fine artistic creations it
dismisses as mere folly: '*arsit*' ('ablaze with enthusiasm'); '*amavit*'
('fall in love with') are set beautifully against the workers in '*Marmoris ... eboris ... aeris*', warming, indeed, that marble, ivory, or
bronze; and the eyes and mind ('*vultum mentemque*') hang on the
painted tablet. As we condemn we too wonder.

For Pope this could only mean the captivating decadence of the
Restoration, and one could imagine no finer imitation than this:

[47]In Days of Ease, when now the weary Sword
Was sheath'd, and *Luxury* with *Charles* restor'd;
In every Taste of foreign Courts improv'd,
"All, by the King's Example, liv'd and lov'd."
Then Peers grew proud in [48]Horsemanship t'excell,
New-market's Glory rose, as Britain's fell;
The Soldier breath'd the Gallantries of France,
And ev'ry flow'ry Courtier writ Romance.
Then [49]Marble soften'd into life grew warm,
And yielding Metal flow'd to human form:
Lely on [50]animated Canvas stole
The sleepy Eye, that spoke the melting soul.
No wonder then, when all was Love and Sport,
The willing Muses were debauch'd at Court;
On each [51]enervate string they taught the Note
To pant, or tremble thro' an Eunuch's throat.
But [52]Britain, changeful as a Child at play,
Now calls in Princes, and now turns away.
Now Whig, now Tory, what we lov'd we hate;
Now all for Pleasure, now for Church and State;
Now for Prerogative, and now for Laws;
Effects unhappy! from a Noble Cause.   (139–60)

There is here just that Horatian ambiguity between disapproval and fascination, and so much comes from Horace to make this possible: 'equorum' ('horses') takes one to 'New-market's Glory rose, as Britain's fell'; '*Marmoris, aut eboris fabros, aut aeris amavit*' ('she would fall in love with craftsmen in marble, ivory, or bronze') produces the even more haunting

> Then Marble soften'd into life grew warm,
> And yielding Metal flow'd to human form ...   (147–8)

The eyes and mind ('*vultum mentemque*') hung on painted tablets produces the brilliant

> Lely on animated Canvas stole
> The sleepy Eye, that spoke the melting soul.   (149–50)

And flautists and tragedians become the beginnings of that great corruption, opera.

But Pope goes further than this by giving his whole passage a distinctly political character, attempting to explore the relationship between these particular forms of aesthetic beauty and the fluid moral and political sensibilities of an immature, irresponsible, and yet strangely 'noble' attempt to restore England to its proper traditions of Monarchy. Pope's individual lines and the whole drift of his argument are wonderfully enigmatic:

> In every Taste of foreign Courts improv'd,
> "All, by the King's Example, liv'd and lov'd." (141–2)

The Court follows suit ('Then Peers grew proud in Horsemanship t'excell'); and the Muses, so able to serve them, see their place:

> No wonder then, when all was Love and Sport,
> The willing Muses were debauch'd at Court. (151–2)

Significantly the nation as a whole can provide no alternative to this aristocratic loss of inner identity and moral strength:

> But Britain, changeful as a Child at play,
> Now calls in Princes, and now turns away.
> Now Whig, now Tory, what we lov'd we hate ... (155–7)
>
> Now for Prerogative, and now for Laws ... (159)

It is fascinating to see Horace's final sardonic lines given this new, and appropriate, political character, concluding with a neat pun on 'noble': 'Effects unhappy! from a Noble Cause.' By doing this Pope prepares for his central passage even more subtly than Horace himself.

Clearly Pope sees the Horatian lines as an opportunity to explore the relationship between excessive refinement in art and the loss of political vigour in the Restoration. In these terms we can relate this passage to Shaftesbury's exploration of the relationship between true art and liberty in 'Advice to An Author' which uses Rome as the example. We shall see soon how Shaftesbury interprets Horace's lines on Roman tragedy in this context; but here we must note how Shaftesbury argues that Rome lost its new-found artistic strength and language, which he sees as being intimately bound up with liberty:

'Twas the Fate of ROME to have scarce an intermediate Age, or single Period of Time, between the Rise of Arts and Fall of Liberty. No sooner had that Nation begun to lose the Roughness and Barbarity of their Manners, and learn of GREECE to form their *Heroes*, their *Orators* and *Poets* on a right Model, than by their unjust Attempt upon the Liberty of the World, they justly lost their own. With their Liberty they lost not only their Force of Eloquence, but even their Stile and Language it-self. (Shaftesbury, 1714, I, p. 219)

Horace's lines on life in early Rome provide a contrast with this portrait of Greece; they are much simpler, and drily tongue-in-cheek, and reveal that the early Romans had no interest in art whatsoever. They were sturdy, reliable, and moral people, and mostly interested in money:

> [53]*Romae dulce diu fuit & solenne, reclusa*
> *Mane domo vigilare, clienti promere jura,*
> *Cautos* [55]*nominibus certis expendere nummos,*
> [54]*Majores audire, minori dicere, per quae*
> *Crescere res posset, minui damnosa libido.*　　　(103–7)

(In Rome for many a long year it was a daily duty and joy to be up at dawn, open the house, give counsel to clients, lend out money with adequate security to credit-worthy borrowers, to seek advice from one's elders, and to give it to one's son on how to make wealth grow, and reduce costly consumption.)

Pope, fortunately, caught Horace's irony here, and gives a refreshingly sardonic vision of the good old days of paternalism and moral rectitude in which there was no place whatsoever for any form of art:

> [53]Time was, a sober Englishman wou'd knock
> His servants up, and rise by five a clock,
> Instruct his Family in ev'ry rule,
> And send his Wife to Church, his Son to school.
> To [54]worship like his Fathers was his care;
> To teach their frugal Virtues to his Heir;
> To prove, that Luxury could never hold;
> And place, on good [55]Security, his Gold.　　　(161–8)

But these views lead to yet another contrast: Horace reveals that now Rome is in grip of a craze for scribbling verses which has spread through society like wildfire to include everyone from the reasonably competent to the utterly hopeless. He himself, he confesses ironically, is in its power. Horace's little sketch of this modern craze for poetry and his own folly is charm itself:

> *Mutavit mentem populus levis,* [56]*& calet uno*
> *Scribendi studio; pueri, patresque severi*
> *Fronde comas vincti coerant, & carmina dictant.*
> *Ipse ego, qui nullos me affirmo scribere versus,*
> *Invenior* [57]*Parthis mendacior, & prius orto*
> *Sole, vigil calamum, & chartas, & scrinia posco.*　　　(108–13)

(The fickle people has had a change of heart and now is afire with one obsessive passion for writing: youths and stern fathers alike tie the poet's garlands in their hair, and declaim their verses while they dine.

I myself, though I swear I never write a line, am shown up as more deceptive than the Parthians, because I'm awake before sunrise, calling for pen, paper, and books.)

Pope's imitation is satirical and self-mocking, a perfect re-creation of this wry Horatian self-depreciation:

> Now Times are chang'd, and one [56]Poetick Itch
> Has seiz'd the Court and City, Poor and Rich:
> Sons, Sires, and Grandsires, all will wear the Bays,

Our Wives read Milton, and our Daughters Plays,
To Theatres, and to Rehearsals throng,
And all our Grace at Table is a Song.
I, who so oft renounce the Muses, [57]lye,
Not – 's selfe e'er tells more *Fibs* than I;
When, sick of Muse, our follies we deplore,
And promise our best Friends to ryme no more;
We wake next morning in a raging Fit,
And call for Pen and Ink to show our Wit.   (169–80)

These delightful ironies take Horace into a passage about the public value of the poet and his poetry which is at the centre of the whole epistle. Characteristically, Horace begins what Pope calls 'an intermixture of Irony', but then the poetry grows in intensity and finally rises in tone to an imaginative climax:

[61]*Hic error tamen & levis haec insania, quantas*
Virtutes habeat, sic collige; Vatis [62]*avarus*
Non temere est animus: [63]*versus amat, hoc studet unum;*
Detrimenta, [64]*fugas servorum,* incendia *ridet;*
Non [65]*fraudem Socio, puerove incognitat ullam*
Pupillo: Vivit siliquis, & pane secundo.[66]
[67]*Militiae quanquam piger & malus,* utilis urbi,
Si das hoc, parvis quoque rebus magna juvari,
[68]*Os tenerum pueri balbumque poeta figurat:*
Torquet [69]*ab* obscaenis *jam nunc sermonibus aurem;*
Mox etiam pectus praeceptis format amicis,
Asperitatis, & invidiae corrector, & irae.
Recte facta refert; [70]*orientia tempora notis*
Instruit exemplis: [71]inopem *solatur, &* aegrum.
Castis cum [72]*pueris ignara puella mariti*
Disceret unde [73]*preces, vatem ni Musa dedisset?*
Poscit opem Chorus, & praesentia numina *sentit;*
Coelestes implorat aquas docta prece blandus;
Avertit morbos, [74]metuenda pericula *pellit;*
Impetrat & Pacem, & *locupletem frugibus annum;*
[75]*Carmina Dì superi placantur, carmine Manes.*   (118–38)

(This failing, though, this slight touch of madness, has a host of virtues; hear what they are. A poet's mind doesn't readily turn to avarice. It's his verse that he loves; *that* is his only concern. Loss of fortune, flight of slaves, fires – he laughs at them all. He never plots to defraud his partner or his ward. He lives on pulse and inferior bread. On the battlefield, it's true, he's no use – a liability in fact: nevertheless, he's an asset to his country, if you'll allow that great causes can be served by lowly means. It's the poet who shapes the child's lisping speech, who yanks the schoolboy's ear away from dirty talk; later he instructs the youth's heart with friendly precepts, checking all harshness, envy, and hot temper; to the man in his prime he relates noble deeds, instructs him with accepted models; and he consoles the misery and illness of age. How would the chaste youths and unwed maidens learn their prayers, if the muse hadn't provided a bard to teach them? With persuasive appeals (because the poet taught them the litany) their choirs implore the gods' aid, feel the gods' own presence, beseech heaven for rain, ward off disease, repel frightful dangers, obtain by their prayers both peace and a year rich in crops. It's with poems that the gods above, with poems that the spirits below are placated.)

The key phrase is 'utilis urbi' ('an asset to his country'): Horace is asserting here that the works of this harmless innocent have in fact important moral, social, and religious value. These lines parallel the section on poetic language in *Epistle* II.ii., but whereas there the concentration was on aesthetic purity within the context of the historical development of the language, here Horace emphasizes the profound moral effect of poetic language on the growing mind and heart.

> *Torquet ab* obscaenis *jam nunc sermonibus aurem;*
> *Mox etiam pectus praeceptis format amicis,*
> Asperitatis, & invidiae corrector, & irae.   (127–9)

(He yanks the schoolboy's ear away from dirty talk; later he instructs the youth's heart with friendly precepts, checking all harshness, envy, and hot temper.)

The poet actually moulds and gives form to the heart (*'pectus … format'*), correcting and calming its passions. *'Recte facta refert'* ('he relates noble deeds') refers to epic poetry; and the lines on the suppliant hymn clearly refer to Horace's own *Carmen Saeculare* sung by a chorus of boys and girls in 17 B.C. In these lines Horace imagines that the children feel the presence of the gods as they sing the poet's prayer, and actually bring about the health (*'Avertit morbos'*), the peace (*'Pacem'*), and the richness of which they sing (*'locupletem frugibus annum'*). Horace affects for a moment here a touching and profound *naiveté*, a simple faith. The final magnificent line brings together the gods of eternity with the gods of the political state and puts them momentarily under the sway of lyric poetry: *'Carmina Dì superi placantur, carmine Manes'* ('It's with poems that the gods above, with poems that the spirits below are placated').

Pope's note on this central passage shows that he sees very clearly both the personal character of Horace's lines and its striking modulations in tone. Referring to Horace's point about the poet being a poor soldier he comments:

Horace had not acquitted himself much to his credit in this capacity; (*non bene relicta parmula*, [*Od.*II vii 10]) in the battle of Philippi. It is manifest he alludes to himself in this whole account of a Poet's character; but with an intermixture of Irony: *Vivit siliquis & pane secundo* has a relation to his Epicurism; *Os tenerum pueri*, is ridicule: The nobler office of a Poet follows, *Torquet ab obscaenis – Mox* *etiam pectus – Rectè facta refert, &c.* which the Imitator has apply'd where he thinks it more due than to himself. He hopes to be pardoned, if, as he is sincerely inclined to praise what deserves to be praised, he arraigns what deserves to be arraigned, in the 210, 211, and 212th Verses. (*TE*, IV, p. 211)

Pope's imitation is an astonishing re-orchestration of all this poetry: he too begins by presenting himself as an innocent naive, but intermixes this with sharp allusions to his power as an Opposition satirist; he then openly attacks the corruption of the court of this new 'Augustus'; he turns Horace's lines on the moral value of poetry into a fine compliment to Addison and reaches his own climax by turning the lines on the epic into a magnificent tribute to Swift; then, in a bold stroke, he turns Horace's climax into wonderful bathos, satirizing the absurd metrical versions of the Psalms by Hopkins and Sternhold, written in the sixteenth century, but still immensely popular in the eighteenth. Although the passage is long, one needs the whole of it to appreciate Pope's play of tone and irony, and to feel the force of the great off-centred climax in praise of Swift. He begins with delightful irony:

> Yet Sir, [61]reflect, the mischief is not great;
> These Madmen never hurt the Church or State:
> Sometimes the Folly benefits mankind;
> And rarely [62]Av'rice taints the tuneful mind.
> Allow him but his [63]Play-thing of a Pen,
> He ne'er rebels, or plots, like other men:
> [64]Flight of Cashiers, or Mobs, he'll never mind;
> And knows no losses while the Muse is kind.
> To [65]cheat a friend, or Ward, he leaves to Peter;
> The good man heaps up nothing but mere metre,
> Enjoys his Garden and his Book in quiet;
> And then – a perfect Hermit in his Diet.
> Of little use the Man you may suppose,
> Who says in verse what others say in prose;
> Yet let me show, a Poet's of some weight,
> And ([67]tho' no Soldier) useful to the State.
> [68]What will a Child learn sooner than a song?
> What better teach a Foreigner the tongue?
> What's long or short, each accent where to place,
> And speak in publick with some sort of grace.
> I scarce can think him such a worthless thing,
> Unless he praise some monster of a King,
> Or Virtue, or Religion turn to sport,
> To please a lewd, or un-believing Court.
> Unhappy Dryden! – In all Charles's days,
> Roscommon only boasts unspotted Bays ...   (189–214)

Pope recreates Horace's self-deprecating irony in those opening lines on his quiet withdrawal to the Garden at Twickenham. But

within this self-portrait, Pope blends together two apparently irreconcilable roles: the inward Horatian, privately cultivating his art
and himself which Horace himself ironically presents (*'versus amat,
hoc studet unum'* – 'It's his verse that he loves; *that* is his only
concern'), and the dangerous and subversive Opposition poet writing
from the safety of that apparent retirement. Pope, in fact, brings
together here two ideas about retreat, the 'Horatian' which emphasizes the cultivation of the inner self, and the Stoic which, as we saw in
Chapter 3, emphasizes active involvement in the public and political
arena despite what was often enforced retirement or exile. The Horatian text provides unexpected opportunities to a mind alert to every
possible hint for such social and political satire: 'avarus' ('avarice') –
'And rarely Av'rice taints the tuneful mind'; 'fugas *servorum*' ('flight
of slaves') – 'Flight of Cashiers'; 'fraudem Socio' ('to defraud his
partner') – 'To cheat a Friend, or Ward, he leaves to Peter.' Horace's
amusing *'Os tenerum pueri balbumque poeta figurat'* ('It's the poet
who shapes the child's lisping speech') becomes a superb jibe at the
inability of the new German kings of England to speak English,
helpful advice for the recipient of this epistle:

> What will a Child learn sooner than a song?
> What better teach a Foreigner the tongue?
> What's long or short, each accent where to place,
> And speak in publick with some sort of grace.　　(205–8)

After such subtle ironies Pope makes his position crystal clear in
some blunt and daring lines:

> I scarce can think him such a worthless thing,
> Unless he praise some monster of a King,
> Or Virtue, or Religion turn to Sport,
> To please a lewd, or un-believing Court.　　(209–12)

Again he looks back to the Restoration, and now finds even its
greatest poet sadly tainted by the uncertain moral and political
character of the monarch and that time:

> Unhappy Dryden! – In all Charles's days,
> Roscommon only boasts unspotted Bays ...　　(113–14)

This takes us to the heart of Pope's whole Imitation: as far as Pope
is concerned, the Augustan poet of his time must be at every level
concerned with the moral and political life of the country, and so
must be everywhere in opposition to the King, the Court, the
government, and the moneyed interests of the city.[3] In his portrait of
himself Pope uses every detail in the Latin to convey this idea in
almost invisible irony:

> Yet Sir, reflect, the mischief is not great;
> These Madmen never hurt the Church or State ...   (189–90)

> Allow him but his Play-thing of a Pen,
> He ne'er rebels, or plots, like other men ...   .   (193–4)

> The good man heaps up nothing but mere metre,
> Enjoys his Garden and his Book in quiet ...   (198–9)

> Of little use the Man you may suppose,
> Who says in verse what others say in prose ...   (201–2)

William Empson suggests that the ultimate insult of this poem lies in the implication: 'I am safe in saying this, though you would persecute me if you could understand it, because you can't' (1935, p. 232).

The climax of Pope's Imitation, however, comes with the unexpected praise of Addison as the gentlest moral writer of the age, and of Swift as its most heroic. Horace's three lines on the power of the poet to form and cultivate the heart, inspire in Pope sympathetic and understanding lines on Addison's achievement in the *Spectator*:

> And in our own (excuse some Courtly stains)
> No whiter page than Addison remains.
> He, [69]from the taste obscene reclaims our Youth,
> And sets the Passions on the side of Truth;
> Forms the soft bosom with the gentlest art,
> And pours each human Virtue in the heart.   (215–20)

We might remember now Cowley: 'But still I love the language of his Heart' (line 78). But Horace's mere two lines on the moral idealism of great epic poetry, which inspires 'the man in his prime' ('*orientia tempora*') with famous examples ('*notis ... exemplis*') and brings comfort to the helpless and sick at heart ('inopem *solatur, &* aegrum'), are expanded to portray, in those very terms, the supreme moral and political achievements of Swift's life and work:

> Let Ireland tell, how Wit upheld her cause,
> Her Trade supported, and supply'd her Laws;
> And leave on SWIFT this grateful verse ingrav'd,
> The Rights a Court attack'd, a Poet sav'd.
> Behold the hand that wrought a Nation's cure,
> Stretch'd to [71]relieve the Idiot and the Poor,
> Proud Vice to brand, or injur'd Worth adorn,
> And [70]stretch the Ray to ages yet unborn.   (221–8)

After this, how daring is Pope's patent parody of Horace's climax in the ridicule of the psalms of Hopkins and Sternhold; and yet Pope carries it off with supreme Horatian assurance. Again, as in the 'Days of Ease' passage, we are aware of a perfect ambiguity of tone: as

Hazlitt would say, we hardly know whether to laugh or cry at these 'pathetic strains', this vision of needy absurdity:

> Not but there are, who merit other palms;
> Hopkins and Sternhold glad the heart with Psalms;
> The [72]Boys and Girls whom Charity maintains,
> Implore your help in these pathetic strains:
> How could Devotion [73]touch the country pews,
> Unless the Gods bestow'd a proper Muse?
> Verse chears their leisure, Verse assists their work,
> Verse prays for Peace, or sings down [74]Pope and Turk.
> The silenc'd Preacher yields to potent strain,
> And feels that grace his pray'r besought in vain,
> The blessing thrills thro' all the lab'ring throng,
> And [75]Heav'n is won by violence of Song.   (229–40)

It is just possible that Pope saw hints of irony in the Horace, but whether he did or not, Pope's poetry here is utterly subversive of Horace's impressive text. Never have the outpourings of the English Sunday hymnal, the earnest strains of the 'proper Muse', and the ceremonies of the Roman state religion been so calmly annihilated.

Pope's imitation of this central passage is impressive not only for its fine satiric ironies and its praise of Addison and Swift, but because it shows Pope presenting his convictions to himself and his readers in a uniquely Horatian manner. It is clear that what he finds most compelling in Horace's defence of Augustan poetry is its insistence on the moral seriousness and the political and social commitment of that type of poetry. Pope's Horace here is similar to Shaftesbury's Horace, a poet profoundly aware of the relationships between poetry, morality and liberty, and deeply concerned with the expression of his own inner freedom and independence in the language of poetry. But Pope's thinking on these topics is not static or rigid, and in a most Horatian manner he can half celebrate the moral laxity of the Resoration, while he utterly condemns the morals of the 'unbelieving' Court of his own time; both ridicule and enjoy the absurdity of moral earnestness and conventional religion; praise Swift for the hand 'Stretch'd to relieve the Idiot and the Poor', but smile at the songs sung by 'The Boys and Girls whom Charity maintains', just as he satirizes both the moral earnestness of 'sober' Englishmen of the past and the literary frivolities of the present. This is an extraordinary achievement: clear convictions and strong certainties emerge from this poetry, but there is always a certain detachment and distance felt in the quality of the irony, and felt in those distinctively Horatian moves of thought which invite the poet to recognise in the contradictions of his own position opportunities for continued reflection. Pope's ironical treatment of moral seriousness in this satire on religious poetry intensifies rather than detracts from the Horatian character of his epistle, and asks us to speculate further on what might indeed be the moral and spiritual value of public poetry.

After this central passage Horace makes a new start and considers some important new themes which eventually allow him to look afresh at some of the issues he has considered in the first half of the epistle. The sequence of topics here is very interesting, and the ways in which they are interwoven more impressive, I think, than is often seen. Horace now, for the first time in the poem, speaks of Latin satire, charting its growth from its origins in the rustic Fescennine verses. He explores both its freedoms and its dangerous power, and speaks of the creation of the law in the Twelve Tables which forbade harmful libel, the very law, in fact, which he refers to at the end of *Satire* ii.i. After this he considers the seminal influence of Greece on Italy's far less sophisticated culture, and appropriately leads from this to a section on the difficulty of writing comic drama, touching briefly on the limitations of the well-loved Plautus. This brings him back to the present and the problems of contemporary taste again: he ridicules the emphasis on mere spectacle in the contemporary theatre, and does so knowing presumably, Augustus' passion for this kind of entertainment. Horace here chooses to stand on somewhat dangerous ground, but he dispels anxiety by confessing with amusing irony that he understands full well why Augustus is so wary of poets, portraying with charming wit the problems and strains that poets create in their relations with other people, particularly with the great and powerful, who could be such helpful patrons. This leads Horace to a very complex conclusion in which he on the one hand praises Augustus' treatment of those poets who have been of political service to the *princeps* and his state, Virgil and Varius, but on the other disclaims completely the value of his own work. In a witty and daring *rescusatio*, he excuses himself from writing the very poetry he has been advocating throughout the epistle on the grounds that his own weak efforts to write such poetry might have the effect only of inadvertent satire, ridiculing and disgracing both Augustus and himself. Having begun this second half of the poem by talking about the dangers of satire, Horace concludes by saying one should certainly not write it without intending to.

In imitating the second half of this epistle Pope explores further the social and political aspects of Horace's text, which is on one level obviously about literature, taste, and the artist. We see this in his discussion of the growth of English satire, the nature of 'correctness', tragedy and comedy, the contemporary theatre, and finally in his own version of Horace's personal address to Augustus and his brilliant study of Horace's concluding *recusatio*. It is extremely interesting here to compare Shaftesbury's interpretations of individual passages of the Horatian text with Pope's imitations. Both Shaftesbury and Pope see Horace as blending aesthetics with politics at virtually every point, and yet they seem to do so in different ways. Shaftesbury, imaginatively, sees Horace's latent Republicanism coming to the surface in these final passages. Does Pope, the Opposition poet, see something similar or something more complex?

Perhaps the most interesting feature of Horace's accounts of the growth of Roman satire and the development of Roman tragedy is his recognition of native energy in those literary forms and at the same time his sense that restraint upon that vigour was to some extent necessary and desirable. As Horace presents it this energy and its control can be seen as raising questions which are either political or artistic, or both. We can see this in his passage on the growth of Latin satire out of the Fescennine verses, which he imagines to have been an innocent type of friendly abuse enjoyed as part of the celebrations after the harvest. Horace's account of this development is to some extent allegorical rather than historical: satire beginning in innocent jest, becoming later cruel and malicious, causing fear throughout society, and eventually leading to a law against libel which finally, through 'fear of a beating' ('*formidine fustis*'), led poets again to 'eulogize and give pleasure' ('benedicendum, delectandumque'):

> [76]*Agricolae prisci, fortes, parvoque beati,*
> *Condita post frumenta, levantes tempore festo*
> *Corpus, & ipsum animum spe finis dura ferentem,*
> *Cum sociis operum, & pueris & conjuge fida,*
> *Tellurem porco, Silvanum lacte piabant,*
> *Floribus & vino Genium memorem brevis aevi.*
> *Fescennina per hunc inventa licentia morem*
> [77]*Versibus alternis opprobria rustica fudit;*
> *Libertasque recurrentes accepta per annos*
> *Lusit amabiliter:* [78]*donec jam saevus apertam*
> *In rabiem verti coepit jocus, & per honestas*
> *Ire domos impune minax. Doluere cruento*
> *Dente lacessiti: fuit intactis quoque cura*
> *Conditione super communi:* [79]*quin etiam lex*
> *Poenaque lata, malo quae nollet carmine quemquam*
> *Describi. Vertere modum, formidine fustis*
> *Ad* [80]*benedicendum, delectandumque redacti.*   (139–55)

(The yeomen of old, sturdy and content with little, after the crops were gathered in would make a holiday, and relax both body and the spirit which had endured hardships in the hope of respite; with their sons and loyal wife who'd shared their labours, they would appease the Earth with the offering of a pig, Silvanus with milk, and their Genius, reminder of life's brevity, with garlands and wine. It was in this setting that Fescennine licence was devised, and in alternating verses poured forth a stream of unsophisticated badinage. This free speech, welcomed with the yearly round, made for friendly sport: until the joking became savage, and began to turn into undisguised madness and ran amok threatening respectable households, unchecked. The bleeding victims of its bite screamed in pain, and even the unscathed felt anxious for the public good. So much so that a law was made, with fixed penalties, forbidding the writing of malicious poems against anyone. Out of fear of a beating, the poets changed their style and were forced to eulogize and give pleasure.)

Dacier gives a positive account of these lines, emphasizing that the last two lines are specifically about the creation of satire in which a proper balance between honest criticism and pleasant wit was achieved: 'Ce changement produisit la *Satire*, qui estoit une espece de Poëme plus châtié, & rempli de railleries plaisantes, qui n'avoient rien ni de deshonneste, ni de trop piquant' (Dacier, IX, p. 387). In discussing the important 'benedicendum, delectandumque' Dacier stresses particularly that this did not involve flattery, which came in only with new comedy: 'Mais j'ay de la peine à le croire, parce qu'il est certain que la Satire, qui succeda aux vers Fescennins, n'étoit nullement flateuse, la flaterie ne s'insinua que longtemps après dans la nouvelle Comedie' (Dacier, IX, p. 389).

Shaftesbury too takes a positive view of these lines, but he sees them in social and political terms, and defends this control as an expression of the early Roman concern for liberty. He argues that this restraint on wit was a natural development within the community itself and not the result of 'Foreign Power' or 'Home Tyranny'; and therefore 'Instead of any Abridgement, 'twas in reality an Increase of *Liberty*' (Shaftesbury, 1714, I, pp. 250–1). Stressing Horace's lines 151–2, '*fuit intactis quoque* Cura / CONDITIONE *super* COMMUNI' ('even the unscathed felt anxious for the public good') he argues that this kind of restraint was in fact necessary for liberty: 'Their FESCENNIN, and ATELLAN way of Wit, was in early days prohibited, and *Laws* made against it, *for the Publick's sake*, and in regard to the Welfare of the *Community*: Such *Licentiousness* having been found in reality contrary to the just *Liberty* of the People' (Shaftesbury, 1714, I, p. 251).

Pope offers a very different view of the growth of English satire. He is, of course, interested in the myth that satire was originally a harmless social activity in which 'Taunts alternate innocently flew' ('*Versibus alternis*') as part of healthy and vigorous rural celebrations. And he is also interested in the partly natural corruption of this into 'the point that left a sting behind' which was deeply damaging to society itself: 'Triumphant Malice rag'd thro' private life.' But Pope extends his portrait in one significant direction: he suggests that most poets became flatterers as a result of what were, from the social point of view, healthy restrictions, and only a few learnt the fine art of satire:

> Our [76]rural Ancestors, with little blest,
> Patient of labour when the end was rest,
> Indulg'd the day that hous'd their annual grain,
> With feasts, and off'rings, and a thankful strain:
> The joy their wives, their sons, and servants share,
> Ease of the toil, and part'ners of their care:
> The laugh, the jest, attendants on the bowl,
> Smooth'd ev'ry brow, and open'd ev'ry soul:
> With growing years the pleasing Licence grew,
> And [77]Taunts alternate innocently flew.
> But Times corrupt, and [78]Nature, ill-inclin'd,
> Produc'd the point that left a sting behind;
> Till friend with friend, and families at strife,
> Triumphant Malice rag'd thro' private life.
> Who felt the wrong, or fear'd it, took th' alarm,
> Appeal'd to Law, and Justice lent her arm.
> At length, by wholesom [79]dread of statutes bound,
> The Poets learn'd to please, and not to wound:
> Most warp'd to [80]Flatt'ry's side; but some, more nice,
> Preserv'd the freedom, and forbore the vice.
> Hence Satire rose, that just the medium hit,
> And heals with Morals what it hurts with Wit.   (241–62)

With Dacier's reading of Horace clearly in mind Pope decries the fact that in England, 'Most warp'd to Flatt'ry's side'. He implies that Horace's 'benedicendum, delectandumque' could be taken either ironically as 'Flatt'ry', or as the new refined form, satire, which can both heal and hurt, is both cutting and moral. This account of both the growth and the nature of satire is, in fact, much more complex and provocative than Horace's is, and highly relevant to Pope's conception of his own art and to the state of poetry in his own time, so marred by patent flattery.

After showing the natural vigour of early Roman society in itself and its early satiric verse, Horace then explores the cultivating influence of Greece on Latin art, an influence which culminated, of course, in the new Augustan poetry. Horace speaks of this cultivation, however, not in contemporary but in historical terms. Having so delicately damned the Greeks for their passion for art in his first view of their society, he now, characteristically, gives exactly the other side of that picture, in the warmest possible tones:

[81]*Graecia capta, ferum victorem cepit, & Artes*
Intulit agresti Latio, sic horridus ille
Defluxit [82]*numerus Saturnius, & grave virus*
Munditiae pepulere: sed in longum tamen aevum
Manserunt, hodieque manent, [83]*vestigia ruris.*
Serus enim Graecis admovit acumina chartis;
Et post [84]*Punica bella quietus, quaerere coepit,*
Quid [85]*Sophocles, & Thespis, & Aeschylus utile ferrent:*
Tentavit quoque rem si digne vertere posset;
Et placuit sibi, natura sublimis, & acer:
Nam [86]*spirat tragicum satis, & feliciter audet:*
Sed [87]*turpem putat in scriptis, metuitque* lituram.   (156–67)

(Captured Greece captivated her savage conqueror, and introduced culture into uncivilized Latium. And thus that uncouth old Saturnian metre ebbed away, and elegance drove out its loathsome infection; yet traces of rusticity lingered on for many a long year, and linger still today. The Roman poet was late in focusing his attention on Greek books; not until the peace after the Punic Wars did he start to ask what Sophocles and Thespis and Aeschylus had to offer. He even experimented to see if he could imitate them worthily. Being by nature sublime and vigorous, he liked his efforts; he has the tragic spirit well enough; his bold flights are successful; but because he feels it disgraceful, he dreads to use his eraser.)

Yet again we have different interpretations: Dacier stresses what is most evident, the gradual aesthetic refinement of Roman poetry and drama, but commenting on the growth of Greek tragedy and noting that the early Roman imitators had a natural talent for this form (Dacier, IX, pp. 395–9). Shaftesbury seizes on this later point and sees the whole passage in terms of Horace's latent Republicanism. He argues that there is a relationship between Rome's natural talent for tragedy and its early love of free democracy and hatred for tyrants: ''Twas no wonder indeed that the Roman people should soon come to the taste of tragedy; for they were free and popular, and had the true foundation of a taste in this kind, which is a relish of the afflictions and misfortunes of those who make the world unfortunate and afflict the people' (Shaftesbury, 1900, p. 397). For Shaftesbury the energy of Roman tragedy was the energy of freedom.[4]

For Pope the crucial question was the dynamic relationship between energy and correctness:

[81]We conquer'd France, but felt our captive's charms;
Her Arts victorious triumph'd o'er our Arms:
Britain to soft refinements less a foe,
Wit grew polite, and [82]Numbers learn'd to flow.
Waller was smooth; but Dryden taught to join
The varying verse, the full resounding line,
The long majestic march, and energy divine.
Tho' still some traces of our [83]rustic vein

> And splay-foot verse, remain'd, and will remain.
> Late, very late, correctness grew our care,
> When the tir'd nation [84]breath'd from civil war.
> Exact [85]Racine, and Corneille's noble fire
> Show'd us that France had something to admire.
> Not but the [86]Tragic spirit was our own,
> And full in Shakespear, fair in Otway shone:
> But Otway fail'd to polish or refine,
> And [87]fluent Shakespear scarce effac'd a line.
> Ev'n copious Dryden, wanted, or forgot,
> The last and greatest Art, the Art to blot. (263–81)

Pope is concerned with the energy of English poetic language seen in relation to native vigour, the influence of French Neo-Classicism, and England's own 'late' concern for 'correctness' and 'polish'. Pope's imitation is not as political as Shaftesbury's interpretation, and yet he is as deeply concerned to underline the strengths of English energy and daring as Horace was to note the values of native Roman spirit. It is fascinating to see this worked out not overtly in terms of politics but in terms of poetic language and artistic ideals. The little section on metre is indicative. Horace talks about the decline of the ancient Saturnian accentual measure in the wake of the development of quantitative metres based on Greek models:

> Defluxit numerus Saturnius, & grave virus
> Munditiae *pepulere* ... (158–9)

(And thus that uncouth old Saturnian metre ebbed away, and elegance drove out its loathsome infection.)

For Pope, this is the development of 'correctness' in seventeenth-century verse; but he goes beyond Horace's simple contrast to discover momentarily a great fusion:

> ... but Dryden taught to join
> The varying verse, the full resounding line,
> The long majestic march, and energy divine. (267–9)

Energy and vigour here are more valuable than Horace's 'Munditiae' ('elegance'). After this, Horace's 'vestigia ruris' ('traces of rusticity') becomes a neat allusion to 'splay-foot verse'; and then Horace's '*Serus*' ('late') and '*Et post* Punica bella *quietus*' ('the peace after the Punic Wars'), allow Pope to make his main point:

> Late, very late, correctness grew our care,
> When the tir'd nation breath'd from civil war. (272–3)

Again, however, there are complexities, for Pope's language recognizes qualities that go beyond mere correctness: 'Corneille's noble fire' set against 'Exact Racine', and the 'Tragic spirit', 'full in

Shakespear, fair in Otway'. Here Pope is emphasizing something seen by Horace himself, who stresses how much the native Latin writer was 'by nature sublime and vigorous' (*'natura sublimis, & acer'*) so that 'his bold flights are successful' (*'feliciter audet'*). But to balance this, both Horace and Pope forcefully set the limits of such achievements: *'metuitque* lituram' ('he dreads to use his eraser') –

> Ev'n copious Dryden, wanted, or forgot,
> The last and greatest Art, the Art to blot. (280–1)

If Shaftesbury finds Horace's republican spirit in these lines on tragedy, we find in Pope a concentration on English energy and vigour. But Pope's view is more complex than Shaftesbury's: the careful balancing of the strengths and weaknesses of both vigour and polish underline the importance of both values in Pope's re-assessment of what true Augustan poetry might be.

Pope's imitation of Horace's section on comedy and the contemporary Roman taste for mere spectacle in the theatre is striking in several ways. First, both Horace and Pope present the absurdities in the theatres of their times as the supreme indication of the level to which taste and culture had dropped in their respective societies. Horace here is bold in his criticisms of Plautus, suggesting that he relied too much on stock comic characters and merely wrote for money (lines 171–6); and he is openly scathing in his contempt of the use of spectacular scenery, costumes, and diversions which in contemporary productions overwhelm the play itself and, in fact, are the only things that interest the audience (lines 182–207). Pope turns these passages into pointed criticism on Restoration and contemporary comedy (lines 287–95), and into a satiric attack on the contemporary taste for operas and pantomimes and for the elaborate and absurd scenery and costumes of theatrical productions (lines 304–37). Second, however, Horace and Pope offer contrasts to this in short passages which stress the emotional power of great drama which, though merely feigned, seems to transport the spectator from one place to another through genuine emotional involvement (Horace, lines 208–13, Pope, lines 338–47). In general terms, both contrast the inward, emotional realities of the true poet's airy nothings with the superficial illusions of public spectacle.

Two passages will illustrate the nature of this satire. First, Horace's bold criticism of comic dramatists:

> *Creditur, ex* [88]medio *quia res arcessit, habere*
> *Sudoris minimum; sed habet* comoedia *tanto*
> *Plus oneris, quanto veniae minus.* [89]*Adspice Plautus*
> *Quo pacto* [90]partes tutetur *amantis ephebi,*
> *Ut patris attenti, lenonis ut insidiosi?*

Quantus sit Dorsennus [91]edacibus in parasitis!
Quam [92]non astricto *percurrat pulpita* socco!
Gestit enim [93]nummum in loculos demittere, post hoc
Securus, cadat, an recto stet fabula talo.   (168–76)

(People think that because it takes its material from ordinary life, comedy involves less effort: in fact, it involves a heavier load, because fewer allowances are made. Consider how Plautus serves up the roles of the young lover, the stingy father, the treacherous pimp, how he outdoes Dorsennus with his gluttonous parasites! How sloppy are the comedian's shoes in which he runs across the stage! Because he's only eager to drop the cash into his purse: after that, he doesn't care if the play stands or falls.)

Dacier asserts that these lines are about both Plautus and Dorsennus, the latter assumed to be a writer of primitive Atellan farce (for the sources of this interpretation see Brink, 1982, p. 213). He emphasizes that for Horace these writers illustrate how hard it is to write good comedy: Plautus excelled in plot and intrigue, but was weak in characterization and falls back on stock types. Dorsennus lacked originality and was artistically crude, as casual as the 'sloppy shoe' ('non astricto ... socco') of the comic actor. Each is all too typical of the comic dramatist who, in fact, writes merely for money (Dacier, IX, pp. 400–3).

All this was too inviting for Pope. The lines on Plautus allow him some shrewd comments on Restoration dramatists, those on Dorsennus some jibes at the contemporary theatre:

Some doubt, if equal pains or equal fire
The [88]humbler Muse of Comedy require?
But in known Images of life I guess
The labour greater, as th'Indulgence less.[89]
Observe how seldom ev'n the best succeed:
Tell me if [90]Congreve's Fools are Fools indeed?
What pert low Dialogue has Farqu'ar writ!
How Van wants grace, who never wanted wit!
The stage how [92]loosely does Astraea tread,
Who fairly puts all Characters to bed:
And idle Cibber, how he breaks the laws,
To make poor Pinky [91]eat with vast applause!
But fill their [93]purse, our Poet's work is done,
Alike to them, by Pathos or by Pun.   (282–95)

Horace's '*Quam* non astricto *percurrat pulpita* socco!' ('How sloppy are the comedian's shoes in which he runs across the stage!') becomes a wonderful jibe at Aphra Behn's notoriously licentious plays:

The stage how loosely does Astraea tread,
Who fairly puts all Characters to bed.   (290–1)

And his '*Quantus sit Dorsennus* edacibus in parasitis!' ('how he outdoes Dorsennus with his gluttonous parasites!') is the apt hint for ridicule of the famous moment in Cibber's *Love Makes a Man* when Penkethman has to eat a cold chicken on stage as fast as he possibly can:

> And idle Cibber, how he breaks the laws,
> To make poor Pinky eat with vast applause! (292–3)

This is hardly what 'Augustan' literature is supposed to be.

The second passage is Horace's attack on spectacle in the theatre which in essence becomes an attack on the society which demands it. As Horace asserts in his final thrust it is the people ('populum') (line 197) in the audience who are the real spectacle ('*spectacula*')(line 198):

> [96]*Saepe etiam audacem fugat hoc terretque poetam;*
> *Quod numero plures, virtute & honore minores,*
> *Indocti, stolidique, &* [97]*depugnare parati*
> *Si discordet eques, media inter carmina poscunt*
> *Aut* [98]*ursum aut* pugiles: *his nam plebecula gaudet.*
> *Verum* [99]*Equitis quoque jam migravit ab* aure *voluptas*
> *Omnis, ad incertos oculos, & gaudia vana.*
> *Quattuor aut plures aulaea premuntur in horas;*
> *Dum fugiunt* [100]*equitum turmae, peditumque catervae:*
> *Mox trahitur manibus* Regum *fortuna retortis;*
> *Esseda festinant, pilenta, petorrita, naves,*
> *Captivum portatur ebur, captiva Corinthus.*
> [101]*Si foret in terris, rideret Democritus; seu*
> *Diversum confusa genus panthera camelo,*
> *Sive* [102]*elephas albus vulgi converteret ora:*
> *Spectaret* populum *ludis attentius ipsis,*
> *Ut sibi praebentem mimo spectacula plura* ... (182–98)

(Often even a brave poet takes fright and flees because of the public. As great in numbers as they are devoid of quality and worth, not only are they ignorant and mindless, they're ready to start a fight if a gentleman disputes their judgment. In the middle of the play they call for a bear, or boxers: those are what the common herd enjoys. But even with the gentry, pleasure has moved altogether from the ear to the fickle eyes and their illusory pleasures. For four hours or more the theatre-curtain is down, while troops of cavalry and hordes of infantry stage a retreat. Next, dethroned kings are dragged along, hands tied behind their backs; chariots speed past, then carriages, coaches, ships; loads of captured ivory are displayed, and captured bronze. If he were alive, Democritus would laugh at the crowds as they stare at some weird cross between a panther and a camel, or gawp at an albino elephant. He would watch the audience with keener interest than the actual show, because they offer a finer spectacle than any actor.)

Dacier comments particularly on the force of Horace's joke that the people are the spectacle (Dacier, IX, p. 413); but for Shaftesbury this passage was Horace's ultimate condemnation of Roman society because of this movement in taste from the ear to the eye. Quoting lines 187–8, '*migravit ab* aure *voluptas / Omnis, ad* incertos oculos, *& gaudia vana*' ('pleasure has moved altogether from the ear to the fickle eyes and their illusory pleasures') he asserts that poets destroyed both tragedy and opera because they 'ran all into the *eye*' by turning to 'the machine and decorations of the theatre': 'For this is vulgar, miserable, barbarous, and is directly that which corrupted the Roman stage, or rather, made it impossible for them to succeed in their tragedy or opera' (Shaftesbury, 1900, pp. 396–7). Again he associates this with Rome's loss of liberty; indeed, he asserts that this point about spectacle belonged more properly to the passage about the Roman talent for 'Republican' tragedy. Commenting on those lines on tragedy he states: 'But here Horace is forced to be a little lame. He shuffles off from his subject and gets to comedy, though it is plain he had his thought elsewhere; and the machines he afterwards speaks of as the corruption of the stage were far more applicable here than there' (Shaftesbury, 1900, pp. 397–8).

It is notable that Pope, like Shaftesbury, again stresses the social and political overtones of Horace's poetry here.[5] Horace mentions that the taste for spectacle has moved from the ordinary people to the knights, and in his summary of the argument of Horace's poem Pope stresses this: Horace shows '*that whatever extravagancies were left on the Stage, were owing to the Ill Taste of the Nobility*' (TE, IV, p. 192). With powerful irony Pope dwells on the view of society these changes in taste reveal:

> [96]There still remains to mortify a Wit,
> The many-headed Monster of the Pit:
> A sense-less, worth-less, and unhonour'd crowd;
> Who [97]to disturb their betters mighty proud,
> Clatt'ring their sticks, before ten lines are spoke,
> Call for the Farce, the [98]Bear, or the Black-joke.
> What dear delight to Britons Farce affords!
> Farce once the taste of Mobs, but now of [99]Lords;
> (For Taste, eternal wanderer, now flies
> From heads to ears, and now from ears to eyes.)
> The Play stands still; damn action and discourse,
> Back fly the scenes, and enter foot [100]and horse;
> Pageants on pageants, in long order drawn,
> Peers, Heralds, Bishops, Ermin, Gold, and Lawn;
> The Champion too! and, to complete the jest,
> Old Edward's Armour beams on Cibber's breast!
> With [101]laughter sure Democritus had dy'd,
> Had he beheld an Audience gape so wide.
> Let Bear or [102]Elephant be e'er so white,
> The people, sure, the people are the sight!   (304–23)

Pope castigates every level of his society just as Horace had done, and finds in its theatrical taste something of the essence of the nation itself:

> What dear delight to Britons Farce affords!
> Farce once the taste of Mobs, but now of Lords ...　　(310–11)

Indeed Pope finds in Horace an opportunity to show that his society sees royalty as a mere theatrical spectacle. Horace's '*Mox trahitur manibus* Regum *fortuna retortis*' ('Next, dethroned kings are dragged along, hands tied behind their backs') allows Pope an allusion to the competition between the contemporary theatres in representing the coronation of Henry the Eighth and Anne Boleyn: for one of these, Pope tells us, 'the Armour of one of the Kings of England was borrowed from the Tower, to dress the Champion' (*TE*, IV, p. 222, footnote):

> The Champion too! and, to complete the jest,
> Old Edward's Armour beams on Cibber's breast!　　(318–19)

In contrast to all this absurdity the true poetic dramatist, Horace insists, is one who imaginatively transforms the spectator himself with the power of feigned emotion, and actually seems to transport him from one place to another:

> *Ac ne forte putes, me, quae facere ipse recusem,*
> *Cum recte tractent alii, laudare maligne;*
> *Ille per extentum funem mihi posse videtur*
> *Ire Poeta,* [110]*meum qui pectus* inaniter *angit,*
> *Irritat, mulcet, falsis terroribus implet,*
> *Ut magus, & modo me Thebis, modo ponit Athenis.*　　(208–13)

(But just in case you suspect that I'm stingy with praise for other poets who succeed in an enterprise which I decline to attempt, in my view that poet is capable of walking the tightrope, and can, like a wizard, conjure up in my heart anxiety without a cause, agitate me, soothe me, fill me with fictitious terrors, and put me in Thebes one moment, and in Athens the next.)

Dacier stresses the importance of this short passage, and argues that Horace is again talking about tragedy, and in particular about the tragic emotions of pity and fear (Dacier, IX, pp. 416–19). Shaftesbury quoting lines 211–13 in 'An Essay on the Freedom of Wit and Humour' sees this as Horace's own study of the '*moral Magic*' of the poetic visionary (1714, I, p. 136). Pope, who in the 'Preface' to his edition saw Shakespeare as the great poet of the passions, seems to bring both these interpretations together: he emphasizes the emotional realities of the poet's 'airy nothings' ('inaniter') which contrast so powerfully with all forms of mere show:

Yet lest you think I railly more than you teach,
Or praise malignly Arts I cannot reach,
Let me for once presume t'instruct the times,
To know the poet from the Man of Rymes:
'Tis He, [110]who gives my breast a thousand pains,
Can make me feel each Passion that he feigns,
Inrage, compose, with more than magic Art,
With Pity, and with Terror, tear my heart;
And snatch me, o'er the earth, or thro' the air,
To Thebes, to Athens, when he will, and where.   (338–47)

Pope must have known that Augustus was, as Suetonius records, very partial to the kind of theatrical spectacle Horace satirizes; and therefore realized how daring this passage was, and also, how delicately Horace handles his 'approach' to Augustus in the lines which follow. As we have seen, Shaftesbury in 'Advice to an Author' saw this whole section as being directed towards Augustus. In the letter to Pierre Coste of 1709 he spells this out more fully:

Read but the passage of Horace to Augustus in the exquisite satire, for it was more than a critique upon the Roman stage – and those sort of spectacles in which (as we know by Suetonius) the monarch, as polite as he pretended to be, had a popular taste. So that Horace had a delicate string to touch in this affair, as delicate almost as if he had been to write to him upon his own *Ajax*, [in] which he had wittily said he *had fallen upon his sword*, and was self-murdered. But perhaps the subtle wit of his friend Horace helped to guide his hand. And here in this epistle to him, though he attacks him not in person, it is more than likely he attacks his relish.   (Shaftesbury, 1900, p. 396)

Dacier, too, fully recognizes the delicacy of Horace's position. He notes that Augustus was extremely fond of comedy and spectacle: 'Auguste aimoit fort la Comedie & il estoit attaché à ces sortes de divertissemens plus qu'un Prince ne le doit estre, jusques là qu'il avoit tâché de faire luy-mesme des Pieces; mais il avoit eu le bonheur de n'y pas réüssir' (Dacier, IX, p. 419). But he sees also how Horace overcomes his problem: having criticized Augustus he now criticizes the very poets he is attempting to commend to Augustus' attention:

Il ne veut pas accuser absolument le goût d'Auguste, de peu de protection qu'il donnoit aux Poëtes dont il parle; il aime mieux rejetter cela sur les Poëtes mesmes, qui rebutoient ce Prince par leurs defauts & par leurs manieres grossieres & chagrines. Il y a là beaucoup de bienseance & de politesse.
                              (Dacier, IX, p. 421)

This, indeed, produces one of the finest moments in the poem: Horace, in a letter to Augustus in support of the new 'Augustan' poets, now confesses the exasperating qualities of just these poets:

[113]*Multa quidem nobis facimus mala saepe poetae,*
(Ut vineta egomet caedam mea) cum tibi librum
[114]*Sollicito* damus aut fesso: *cum laedimur,* [115]*unum*
Si quis amicorum *est ausus reprendere* versum:
Cum loca iam [116]*recitata revolvimus* irrevocati:
Cum [117]*lamentamur non* apparere *labores*
Nostros, & tenui *deducta poemata* filo:
Cum [118]*speramus eo rem venturam, ut simul atque*
Carmina rescieris nos fingere, commodus ultro
Arcessas, & *egere vetes,* & scribere cogas.   (219–28)

(Admittedly, we poets often do ourselves many a bad turn (if I may damage my
own vineyard) when we offer you a book while you're busy, or tired; when we
take offence if a friend dares to find fault with a single line; when, uninvited, we
unroll yet again a passage we've recited before; when we lament that people
don't notice our craftsmanship, or the gossamer thread our poems are spun
from; when we go so far as to expect that the moment you hear we're composing
poetry, you'll rush to take the initiative by sending for us, banish our poverty,
and compel us to write.)

These urbane ironies might be aimed at all poets, but they are
particularly applicable to the Augustan poets the whole epistle is
supporting, with their new devotion to high aesthetic ideals, their
concern for the perfection of every line, and their worthy commit
ment to public themes. This is Horace at his most sophisticated,
warning Augustus about the dangers of the very artistic ideals he has
been advocating throughout the poem, and arresting the attention he
desires with the irresistible charm of that irony.

Pope's imitation seems to me to be one of the most engaging
passages in his whole poem, a moment when he speaks straight to
George II in an irony that transcends irony:

My Liege! why Writers little claim your thought,
I guess; and, with their leave, will tell the fault:
We [113]Poets are (upon a Poet's word)
Of all mankind, the creatures most absurd:
The [114]season, when to come, and when to go,
To sing, or cease to sing, we never know;
And if we will recite nine hours in ten,
You lose your patience, just like other men.
Then too we hurt our selves, when we defend
A [115]single verse, we quarrel with a friend;
Repeat [116]unask'd; lament, the [117]Wit's too fine
For vulgar eyes, and point out ev'ry line.
But most, when straining with too weak a wing,
We needs will write Epistles to the King;
And [118]from the moment we oblige the town,
Expect a Place, or Pension from the Crown;
Or dubb'd Historians by express command,

> T'enroll your triumphs o'er the seas and land;
> Be call'd to Court, to plan some work divine,
> As once for LOUIS, Boileau and Racine.   (356–75)

Pope was clearly fascinated by Horace's treat for the connoisseur; and, with the help of no less than thirteen key words in the Latin, he actually creates in the pure language of poetry the impossible moment of rapport: 'My Liege! why Writers little claim your thought, / I guess'. To our amazement, Pope of the *Epistle to Arbuthnot* and the ignorant king are happily in accord:

> And if we will recite nine hours in ten,
> You lose your patience, just like other men.   (362–3)

All the faults of poets are honestly confessed to the king himself: 'irrevocati' ('uninvited') becomes 'Repeat unask'd'; Horace's 'unum ... versum' ('a single line') is prominently placed: 'when to defend / A single verse, we quarrel with a friend'.

> *Cum lamentamur non* apparere *labores*
> *Nostros, &* tenui *deducta poemata* filo ...   (224–5)

(when we lament that people don't notice our craftsmanship, or the gossamer thread our poems are spun from)

becomes: 'lament, the Wit's too fine / For vulgar eyes, and point out ev'ry line'. Only at the end does Pope openly turn the satire around the other way:

> But Most, when straining with too weak a wing,
> We needs will write Epistles to the King ...   (368–9)

For this, Horace's 'Carmina' is neatly transformed into 'history':

> Or dubb'd Historians by express command,
> T'enroll your Triumphs o'er the seas and land ...   (372–3)

The full effect of Pope's passage only comes from seeing these strident ironies out of his own more delicate nuances, and seeing that movement itself next to Horace's challenging play of wit.[6]

But if we imagine that Horace follows this address to Augustus with a straightforward conclusion to the poem we are very much mistaken. The ending of this epistle is one of Horace's finest *recusatio* passages. He begins by saying openly to Augustus that the task of celebrating his qualities in verse deserves careful thought:

> *Sed tamen est* [119]*operae pretium* cognoscere, *quales*
> Aedituos *habeat belli spectata domique*
> *Virtus,* [120]*indigno non committenda* poetae.   (229–31)

(Nevertheless, it's worth your while to find out the qualities of the priests who tend the shrine of your greatness, proven in peace and war, that should not be entrusted to an unworthy poet.)

To underline his point Horace quotes the example of Alexander the Great, who showed true judgement in allowing only Apelles to paint him and only Lysippus to make bronze statues of him, but erred so disastrously, so Horace claims, in allowing Choerilus to write a poem about him. This passage is important because having ridiculed the taste of his subjects, Horace is now reminding Augustus that he, at least, has a particular need for good taste. The way Horace sets out Alexander's error is designed to amuse but also to speak home to the recipient of this letter:

> [112]*Gratus Alexandro regi Magno fuit ille*
> *Choerilus, incultis qui versibus & male natis*
> *Rettulit acceptos, regale numisma, Philippos.*
> *[Sed veluti tractata notam labemque remittunt*
> *Atramenta, fere scriptores carmine foedo*
> *Splendida facta linunt. idem rex ille, poema]*
> *Qui tamen ridiculum tam carè prodigus emit,*
> *Edicto vetuit, ne quis se, praeter Apellem,*
> Pingeret, *aut alius Lysippo duceret* aera
> Fortis [122]Alexandri vultum simulantia: *quod si*
> *Judicium subtile videndis artibus illud*
> *Ad libros, & ad haec Musarum dona vocares,*
> [123]*Boeotum in crasso jurares aere natum.*   (232 44)

(King Alexander the Great's favour shone on the notorious Choerilus, who traded his uncouth and ill-conceived verses for the kingly coinage bearing Philip's head. But just as ink stains and spoils anything it touches, so can writers besmirch heroic achievements in repellent poetry. That same great king, who with poetry paid so dear and bought so badly, forbade by decree that anyone other than Apelles should paint his portrait, or anyone besides Lysippus carve in bronze the likeness of mighty Alexander's features. But if you were to summon that judgement, so fine in the visual arts, to books and literature, you'd swear it was born in the sluggish air of Boeotia.)

But Horace has no sooner quoted the example of Alexander as a good-humoured warning to Augustus, than he turns around and makes it into an open compliment to Augustus for his discernment in choosing to patronize Virgil and Varius. The lines are elegantly articulated to emphasize Augustus' judgement and generosity; the poets themselves, subjects of the verb 'neque dedecorant' ('bring no discredit') come only, though strongly, at the end:

> [At neque dedecorant tua de se judicia, atque
> Munera quae, multa dantis cum laude, tulerunt
> Dilecti tibi Virgilius Variusque poetae:]   (245–7)

(But the poets you love, Virgil and Varius, bring no discredit on your judgements of their worth or on the gifts they receive, which bring much praise to the giver.)

These are important lines because they show to the Roman public, and to Augustus himself, that the princeps appreciates what, in Horace's view at least, is the great poetry of his time. Pope, we note, puts every word in Roman type, brackets the lot, and sets next to them a large blank space in his own text, which says better than words all that needs to be said.

Horace's lines on Augustus' recognition of Virgil and Varius, however, should not really be isolated like this, for they lead by means of three negatives into the *recusatio*, which is itself, of course, couched throughout in negative terms. 'At neque dedecorant' ('bring no discredit') takes Horace to this superb series of manoeuvres:

> *Nec magis expressi* [124]*vultus per ahenea signa,*
> *Quam per vatis opus mores, animique virorum*
> *Clarorum apparent. Nec sermones ego mallem*
> *Repentes per humum,* [125]*quam res componere gestas,*
> *Terrarumque* [126]*situs, & flumina decere, & arces*
> *Montibus impositas; &* [127]barbara regna, *tuisque*
> *Auspiciis totum* [128]confecta duella *per orbem,*
> *Claustraque* [128]*Custodem* Pacis cohibentia Janum,
> *Et* [129]*formidatam* Parthis, te Principe, Romam.
> *Si quantum cuperem, possem quoque: sed neque parvum*
> [130]*Carmen* Majestas *recipit* tua, *nec meus audet*
> *Rem tentare pudor, quam vires ferre recusant.*
> *Sedulitas autem* [131]stultè *quem* diligit, urget,
> *Praecipuè cum se* numeris commendat & arte.
> *Discit enim citius, meminitque libentius illud,*
> *Quod quis* [132]deridet, *quam quod probat & veneratur.*
> *Nil moror* [133]*officium quod me gravat; ac neque* ficto
> *In* [134]pejus *voltu proponi cereus usquam,*
> *Nec pravè factis decorari versibus, opto:*
> *Ne* [135]*rubeam* pingui *donatus* munere; *& una*
> *Cum* [136]*scriptore meo, capsa porrectus aperta,*
> *Deferar in vicum vendentem thus & odores,*
> *Et piper, & quicquid chartis amicitur ineptis.*   (248–70)

(Nor are physical features represented in bronze statues more effectively than the character and mind of great men are revealed by the poet's craft. For my own part, I wouldn't choose to compose pedestrian 'conversations' rather than declaim epic themes – the far-flung lands, the rivers, the mountain fortresses, the foreign realms you've conquered, the wars you've waged and won over all the world, 'the bolts that confine Janus in his temple to guard our peace', 'Parthia trembles at Rome under your leadership' – if only my desire were matched by my abilities! But your greatness does not admit of a feeble poem, and my sense of shame dares not attempt a task my strength refuses to bear. It is foolish to overwhelm with officious praise a man you admire, especially when your chosen medium is poetic art; for people learn more quickly and remember more gleefully what they laugh at than what they approve and revere. I have no time for a favour that oppresses me; I have no desire to have a waxwork caricature of my face put on show, nor to be eulogized in badly made verse, for fear I'd have to blush at receiving such flabby homage and be dispatched along with my poet, laid out in an open casket, to the street where they sell incense, spices, pepper, and whatever else is wrapped in scrap paper.)

Horace ends his poem with this daring apology, indicating to Augustus that he himself cannot write the kind of Augustan poetry he has been advocating in this very poem. He has the strength only to write his pedestrian 'conversations' (*'sermones ... Repentes per humum'*), and this is hardly what is required. Of course, there are ironies here as, in typical *recusatio* style, Horace's language actually soars into the high rhetoric he says he cannot write, with vigorous alliteration and a fine syntactic climax enclosing the crucial *'te Principe'* ('under your leadership'):

> *Claustraque Custodem* Pacis *cohibentia Janum,*
> *Et formidatam* Parthis, *te Principe, Romam.*   (255–6)

('the bolts that confine Janus in his temple to guard our peace', 'Parthia trembles at Rome under your leadership.')

But that language is carefully contained between the undercutting ironies of Horace's disclaimers, *'Nec ... ego mallem'* ('I wouldn't choose') before, and after, *'Si quantum cuperem, possem quoque'* ('if only my desire were matched by my abilities!').

Horace's subtlest move however is to allude to the fact that Augustus was known to be sensitive about being praised in poor verse, as is recorded by Suetonius. Horace says clearly *'sed neque parvum / Carmen* Majestas *recipit* tua' ('But your greatness does not admit of a feeble poem'), and he uses this as an opportunity to explore the dangers of weak eulogy. Nothing is more dangerous than praise in numbers and art ('numeris ... *& arte'*) when it does not work:

> *Discit enim citius, meminitque libentius illud,*
> *Quod* quis deridet, *quam quod* probat *& veneratur.*   (262–3)

(for people who learn more quickly and remember more gleefully what they laugh at than what they approve and revere.)

In a master-stroke Horace puts himself into Augustus' position, and makes clear that he would not like to see himself anywhere in wax with his features so misshapen. In a brilliant fantasy, Augustus and his poet (*'Cum scriptore meo'*) are carried out together in one coffin (*'una ... capsa ... aperta'*), down to a street of grocers' shops (*'vicum vendentem'*) where perfumes (*'odores'*) and pepper (*'piper'*) are sold, and everything else that is wrapped in sheets of useless paper (*'chartis*

... *ineptis*').[7] One could hardly ask for a more daring conclusion to this epistle to Augustus advocating the values of Augustan poetry.

To understand the extraordinary moves of Horace's conclusion helps us, I think, to appreciate the distinctive quality of Pope's famous last lines. Pope begins by turning into scornful satire Horace's suggestion that Augustus must think carefully about suitable poets to record his merit:

> Yet [119]think great Sir! (so many Virtues shown)
> Ah think, what Poet best may make them known?
> Or chuse at least some Minister of Grace,
> Fit to bestow the [120]Laureat's weighty place.   (376–9)

Horace's 'indigno ... poetae' ('unworthy poet') becomes very neatly 'the Laureat's weighty place'. Then Pope, leaving for a moment the lines about the ink that stains, gives a forceful version of Horace's lines about Alexander, first bringing out in his own language the suggestions of Horace's '*duceret* aera / Fortis Alexandri vultum simulantia' ('carve in bronze the likeness of mighty Alexander's features'), before then following Horace into bathos:

> [121]Charles, to late times to be transmitted fair,
> Assign'd his figure to Bernini's care;
> And great [122]Nassau to Kneller's hand decreed
> To fix him graceful on the bounding Steed:
> So well in paint and stone they judg'd of merit:
> But Kings in Wit may want discerning spirit.
> The Hero William, and the Martyr Charles,
> One knighted Blackmore, and one pension'd Quarles;
> Which made old Ben, and surly Dennis swear,
> "No Lord's anointed, but a [123]Russian Bear."   (380–9)

But the climax comes after the blank space next to Horace's lines about Virgil and Varius in his own version of Horace's *recusatio* passage. Pope begins with Horace's high rhetoric, turned, of course, into pure irony, and ends by assserting boldly his inability to write praise and his refusal to write flattery. If the subtlety of the Horace lies in the play of tone in his approach to Augustus, the subtlety of Pope lies in echoing all that rich language and finding within it every possible aggressive irony:

> Not with such [124]Majesty, such bold relief,
> The Forms august of King, or conqu'ring Chief,
> E'er swell'd on Marble; as in Verse have shin'd
> (In polish'd Verse) the Manners and the Mind.
> Oh! could I mount on the Maeonian wing,
> Your [125]Arms, your Actions, your Repose to sing!
> What [126]seas you travers'd! and what fields you fought!

Your Country's Peace, how oft, how dearly bought!
How [127]barb'rous rage subsided at your word,
And Nations wonder'd while they dropp'd the sword!
How, when you nodded, o'er the land and deep,
[128]Peace stole her wing, and wrapt the world in sleep;
Till Earth's extremes your mediation own,
And [129]Asia's Tyrants tremble at your Throne –
But [130]Verse alas! your Majesty disdains;
And I'm not us'd to Panegyric strains:
The Zeal of [131]Fools offends at any time,
But most of all, the Zeal of Fools in ryme.
Besides, a fate attends on all I write,
That when I aim at praise, they say [132]I bite.
A vile [133]Encomium doubly ridicules;
There's nothing blackens like the ink of fools;
If true, a [134]woful likeness, and if lyes,
"Praise undeserv'd is scandal in disguise:"
Well may he [135]blush, who gives it, or receives;
And when I flatter, let my dirty leaves
(Like [136]Journals, Odes, and such forgotten things
As Eusden, Philips, Settle, writ of Kings)
Cloath spice, line trunks, or flutt'ring in a row,
Befringe the rails of Bedlam and Sohoe.   (390–419)

The details of the satiric irony here are superb: '*quam* res com-
ponere gestas' ('declaim epic themes') – 'Your Arms, your Actions,
your Repose to sing!'; '*Pacis*' ('peace') – 'Your Country's Peace, how
oft, how dearly bought!'; '*barbara regna*' ('foreign realms') – 'How
barb'rous rage subsided at your word'; '*tuisque / Auspiciis* totum
confecta duella *per* orbem' ('the wars you've waged and won over all
the world') –

> How, when you nodded, o'er the land and deep,
> Peace stole her wing, and wrapt the world in sleep ...   (400–1)

Horace's '*sed neque parvum / Carmen* Majestas *recipit* tua' ('but
your greatness does not admit of a feeble poem') is brilliantly
mistranslated: 'But Verse alas! your Majesty disdains', throwing into
sharp ambiguity the subject and object. The warning about the
danger of foolish zeal ('*Sedulitas ... stultè*') in verse is translated with
distressing accuracy:

> The Zeal of Fools offends at any time,
> But most of all, the Zeal of Fools in ryme.   (406–7)

The ironical remark about men learning what they deride more
quickly than what they approve and esteem ('*Quod* quis deridet,
quam quod probat & veneratur') Pope takes personally:

> Besides, a fate attends on all I write,
> That when I aim at praise, they say I bite.   (408–9)

In order to underline the point about a 'vile Encomium' Pope leaps back to Horace's remark about Choerilus' uncouth and misbegotten verses for Alexander, saved up in brackets:

> [*Sed veluti tractata notam labemque remittunt*
> *Atramenta, fere scriptores carmine foedo*
> *Splendida facta linunt.*]   (235–7)

(But just as ink stains and spoils anything it touches, so can writers besmirch heroic achievements with repellent poetry.)

> A vile Encomium doubly ridicules;
> There's nothing blackens like the ink of fools ...   (410–11)

Horace's 'ficto / In pejus *voltu proponi cereus*' ('a waxwork caricature of my face put on show') becomes the motto to Pope's whole satiric address to George as a new Augustus:

> If true, a woful likeness, and if lyes,
> "Praise undeserv'd is scandal in disguise" ...   (412–13)

Horace ends by identifying himself with Augustus, blushing at what might be the result of inept poetic praise; Pope sets himself resolutely apart from this Augustus and his mob of flatterers, and openly invites contemptuous neglect should he ever join their ranks:

> Well may he blush, who gives it, or receives;
> And when I flatter, let my dirty leaves
> (Like Journals, Odes, and such forgotten things
> As Eusden, Philips, Settle, writ of Kings)
> Cloath spice, line trunks, or flutt'ring in a row,
> Befringe the rails of Bedlam and Sohoe.   (414–19)

It would be nice to think that it was after 'receiving' this *Epistle* that George II made his only recorded comment on Pope: 'Who is this Pope that I hear so much about? I cannot discover what is his merit. Why will not my subjects write in prose?' (*TE*, IV, p. 362).

PART IV

The time of tension (1738)

9

Idealism and scepticism:
The Imitation of Epistle I.vi.

Every valuable, every pleasant thing is sunk in an ocean of avarice and
corruption. The son of a first minister is a proper match for a daughter
of late South Sea director, – so money upon money increases, copu-
lates, and multiplies, and guineas beget guineas in *saecula saeculorum*.

> O cives, cives! quaerenda pecunia primum est
> Virtus post nummos.

My body is sick, my soul is troubled, my pockets are empty, my time
is lost, my trees are withered, my grass is burned! So ends my history.
Pope to Broome, 14 July 1723

AFTER THE MASTERFUL ACHIEVEMENT of the *Epistle to
Augustus* we move into a very different world for Pope's last two
complete Imitations of Horace which came out in the winter of 1738
– the *Imitations of Epistle I.vi.* and *Epistle I.i.* If the *Epistle to
Augustus* shows what richness of thought can be achieved in the
calm of retreat, these poems reveal what powerful tensions are
produced by vigorous involvement in the world. We find in these
Imitations new stresses in attitude and commitment, a darker view of
society, a deeper scepticism, and a much more disturbed and
troubled poetry of self-portraiture.

These changes are certainly due partly to the political climate of
the winter of 1737–8. With the death of Queen Caroline in the
autumn of 1737, and growing dissatisfaction with the government's
peace policies, Walpole's position was weaker than it had ever been.
The Opposition saw its chance and rallied itself for a concerted
attack on him in Parliament, led by Carteret, Pulteney, Wyndham
and Barnard. The drive gained momentum throughout the winter
and then failed disastrously in May. Pope's two Imitations were
published in the midst of these events when the outcome was still
uncertain, the *Imitation of Epistle I.vi.* in January 1738, the *Imitation of Epistle I.i.* in March. If the two 'Dialogues' of the *Epilogue
to the Satires* (originally boldly called *One Thousand Seven Hundred
and Thirty Eight*) which came out in May and July reflect Pope's first
disappointment at the failure, these Imitations, published in the

midst of the struggle, seem to express the strain of uncertainty, the hope of success, and the fear of failure.

These two Imitations certainly show a view of Pope's society very different from what we have so far seen, one most akin to the dark visions of the *Epistle to Bathurst* and the *Dunciad*. Pope's concerns are now money, corruption, and power, and in Pope's exploration of these we find disturbing uncertainties about human emotions and aspirations, and about the aims of life for both the individual and the society. The Horatian poems to which Pope is drawn are now *Epistle* I.vi., with both its powerful idealism and its haunting expression of scepticism, and *Epistle* I.i., in which Horace attempts to explore the relationship between his personal views of life and those of his contemporaries who are so deeply motivated by materialism. In these Horatian poems Pope finds new forms and new languages, to be shaped for his own purposes. In the Imitation of the first, addressed to William Murray, a young member of the Opposition, Pope explores what involvement in the world of his time might mean; in the second, addressed to Bolingbroke, Pope is drawn into vigorous political attack, although he claims he now yearns for retirement. In this final Imitation Pope presents a disturbed and tormented image of the inner contradictions that seem at once to rend and constitute both himself and his society.

In analysing these two Imitations it is valuable also to study Pope's two completions to Swift's Imitations of *Satire* II.vi. and *Epistle* I.vii. Pope's completed version of the former in fact was published in March 1738, and was presented there for the first time in Pope's manner with the Latin poem. The date of composition of the latter is uncertain, but its themes of 'Maecenas', moral independence, and retreat relate it, like *Satire* II.vi. closely to the two major Imitations of this year. Discussing these 'Swiftian' works will also allow us to consider Shaftesbury's highly original interpretations of the Horatian poems which he regarded as Horace's own most intense works, written at what he saw as Horace's own time of tension and uncertainty.

PROBLEMS OF INTERPRETATION

Pope's *Imitation of Horace's Epistle I.vi.*, the famous *Nil admirari*, raises extremely interesting questions about emotions and ideals in the context of both philosophic conviction and philosophic scepticism. To most modern critics this Horatian epistle has seemed a memorable expression of sustained scepticism in persistent irony (see Brower, 1963, pp. 179–80, for example). Horace begins by suggesting that perhaps only calm indifference to all things can keep us happy in life; but then, assuming we might disagree, runs rapidly through the common ways of living, urging us to pursue them if we like them, but at the same time undercutting every one. He does all this with remarkable brevity and speed, and at the end throws off a friendly good-bye ('*Vive, vale!*'), asking us, if we have any better ideas, to pass them on. If not, he suggests we follow his. The total effect of this bright, driving irony is quite disconcerting, for Horace seems to hint at an emptiness at the centre of every kind of experience and every type of activity. Admiring great works of art, following the path of Virtue, struggling against competitors to succeed in business, making money, being an influential person in society, enjoying fine food, trifling with love and frivolities – the epistle sees them all as equally good, and equally pointless.

It is very striking, however, that while modern critics discover sustained scepticism in this epistle, eighteenth-century interpreters saw it as an expression of high moral idealism. Dacier sees the epistle not just as presenting moral teaching but as offering genuine spiritual wisdom concerned with the proper attitude to the things of this world. This interpretation, however, is composed of several strands. In one sense he gives a strongly Stoic reading of the poem: Horace is essentially attacking the desires and fears that are involved in the 'admiration' of riches and honours, and is throughout advocating the 'apathy' implicit in the phrase 'Nil admirari'. Those emotional entanglements are 'entierement opposée à la vertu, qui consiste à avoir son esprit dans une assiete ferme & tranquille, sans qu'il puisse estre surpris, ému, ni étonné de quoy que ce foit' (Dacier, VIII, p. 291).

But Dacier also attempts to fuse this Stoicism with a proper religious faith which in fact makes true 'admiration' possible. He stresses that the Epicureans abused the idea of indifference by taking it to excess: 'Car les Epicuriens le poussoient à un excés tres-pernicieux; & le raisonnement mesme qu'Horace tire de leurs principes, pourroit estre fort nuisible, si on ne le corrigeoit par les lumieres de la verité & de la raison' (Dacier, VIII, p. 291). He argues that in this epistle Horace is attacking 'l'admiration vicieuse & folle qui naist de l'ignorance, & qui porte les hommes à desirer ou à craindre les objets ausquels elle s'attache'; but actually advocating another kind of admiration, 'une admiration raisonnable & intelligente, qui porte les hommes à la vertu, & que Platon appelle, par cette raison, *la Mere de la Sagesse*' (Dacier, VIII, p. 291). Dacier seems to feel that, in this sense, Horace's epistle is an attempt to raise consciousness to this higher level of awareness which he describes very carefully as a faith in God that transcends the concepts of 'happiness' and 'unhappiness':

Pour estre exempt de cette derniere admiration [of material objects], il faut avoir une ame grande & genereuse, s'estre acquis par son travail une connoissance exacte des choses du monde, & de leurs principes, & avoir toûjours presens les exemples que nous fournissent les siecles passez, pour nous apprendre que hors la vertu, tout nous doit estre indifferent dans cette vie, & qu'il n'y a rien qui puisse nous faire ni bien ni mal: car Dieu, par son infinie sagesse, n'a pas mis entre les mains d'un autre le pouvoir de nous rendre ni heureux, ni malheureux.

(Dacier, VIII, pp. 291–2)

Dacier emphasizes that at the heart of this philosophy is the belief that the soul is in itself more 'admirable' than anything it can behold, and this, clearly, could be the source of a profound inner calm. He stresses that this is essentially a Socratic conviction which was espoused also by Democritus and Seneca:

Democrite & les autres Philosophes avoient tiré ce sentiment de l'Echole de Socrate, qui enseignoit qu'il n'y avoit rien d'admirable pour nous que nostre ame. Et c'est ce que Seneque a fort bien employé dans sa Lettre VIII. *Cogita in te praeter animum nihil esse mirabile, cui magno nihil magnum est. Pensez qu'il n'y a rien d'admirable en vous que vostre ame; si elle est grande, elle ne trouve rien de grand.* On vera dans la suite que l'admiration dont il s'agit icy, embrasse le desire & la crainte. (Dacier, VIII, pp. 292–3)

As we would expect, Shaftesbury interprets *Epistle* I.vi. in a very similar way, and recognizes some of the tensions that Dacier's interpretation suggests. In the letter to Pierre Coste of 1706 he sees it as embodying the essence of Horace's 'third period' in which Horace was struggling 'to get clear of the Court pleasures'; and yet he too sees that the treatment of 'admiration' in this epistle is at first very puzzling:

And if the word pleasures surprise you, see how thoroughly, and as one may say revengefully and spitefully he treats pleasure (even love and mirth) in his bitter irony at the end of Ep. VI. of Bk. I, which is one of the most puzzling as to philosophy, because it seems in the beginning to favour the anti-theistical sort, by speaking against amazement and astonishment about the order of the heavens, as if it were after the Lucretian or Epicurean kind. But it is strongly of the other sort, and means quite another thing, as I could show you at leisure out of Cicero, Seneca, and those copies of ancient Socratic philosophy, from the originals of which Horace drew his, when he was either in or towards this his third period.

(Shaftesbury, 1900, p. 365)

In the 'Miscellaneous Reflections' of 1714 Shaftesbury pursues this further when discussing the important idea that in the search for true self-knowledge, 'we are to begin rather by the *averse*, than by the *prone* and *forward* Disposition' (Shaftesbury, 1714, III, p. 202). For

Shaftesbury the path to self-knowledge and genuine religious enthusiasm involves initially the *via negativa* and that is why Horace begins this epistle with this negative gesture, 'Nil admirari'. Quoting Epictetus he asserts: 'This subdu'd or moderated *Admiration* or *Zeal* in the highest Subjects of *Virtue* and *Divinity*, the Philosopher calls symmetron kai kathistēmenēn tēn orexin ['the harmonious and regulated desires']; the contrary Disposition to alogon kai ōstikon ['the illogical and impetuous element']' (p. 202, footnote). Referring to Epictetus' repeated injunctions against 'this over-forward Ardour and Pursuit of high Subjects which runs naturally into Enthusiasm and Disorder', he asserts:

To this HORACE, in one of his latest Epistles of the deeply philosophical kind, alludes.

> Insani sapiens nomen ferat, aequus iniqui,
> Ultra quam satis est Virtutem si petat ipsam.   Ep. 6. lib. 1.

[Even the wise man would be labelled madman, the stable unbalanced, if he were to pursue Virtue itself to excess.]

And in the beginning of the Epistle,

> Nil admirari propè res est una, Numici,
> Solaque quae posset facere & servare beatum.   Ibid.

[To marvel at nothing is perhaps the one and only thing which can make and keep us happy.]

For tho these first Lines (as many other of HORACE's on the Subject of Philosophy) have the Air of the EPICUREAN *Discipline* and LUCRETIAN *Stile*; yet, by the whole taken together, it appears evidently on what System of ancient Philosophy this Epistle was form'd. Nor was this Prohibition of the *wondering* or *admiring* Habit, in early Students, peculiar to *one* kind of Philosophy alone. It was common to many; however the Reason and Account of it might differ, in one Sect from the other.   (Shaftesbury, 1714, III, pp. 202–3, footnote)

Shaftesbury emphasizes, in fact, a growth in admiration achieved through this negation: although admiration 'may be justly call'd the inclining Principle or first Motive to PHILOSOPHY; yet this Mistress, when once espous'd, teaches us *to admire*, after a different manner from what we did before' (Shaftesbury, 1714, III, p. 203, footnote).

These eighteenth-century interpretations of Horace's *Epistle* I.vi. pose very difficult questions about the interpretation of Pope's Imitation. How far did Pope share these views of Horace's poem? If so, how much is his poem an attempt to re-create that vision, or how much is it, on the contrary, an attempt to express a belief in more conventional moral values, as J. W. Tupper (1900, pp. 212–13) suggested, or a belief in active political involvement as John M. Aden (1969, Chapter 4) argues? These critics have attempted to contrast the ironic detachment of Horace's poem with the Juvenalian intensities of Pope's rhetoric.

All these issues point to an even more fundamental one: if Pope has responded to the idealism of this poem as interpreted in the eighteenth century, has he also responded to the scepticism modern critics have detected? And if he has, what is the relationship between that idealism and that scepticism: what is the relationship in poetic language between philosophical indifference to 'good' and 'evil' and the questioning of those very categories? Is Pope's poem a condemnation of emotional attachments, or an attempt to understand the nature of their power? Is his ironic stance one which expresses firm belief or allows detached speculation?

Most writers have said that Pope's poem is really very different from Horace's, and that, in particular, the circumstances in which it was written have given the work a quite different rationale. Addressed to William Murray, one of Pope's new young friends and a rising member of the Opposition, it was published when the new move against Walpole was in full force. Murray, in fact, was about to gain fame for his eloquent speech before the House of Commons in support of the merchantmen's petition against Spanish raids. Whereas Horace's epistle is either an expression of spiritual or sceptical detachment, Pope's poem has been seen as a work of moral and political commitment, written to a member of the Opposition and quite explicitly supporting the Opposition's position.

There is no doubt that Pope's Imitation has these important political overtones: Murray is heralded as potentially a great orator, and Lord Cornbury is praised for rejecting the Government's attempt to buy his support; there are allusions to election corruption and scorn for moneyed interests, which in the 1730s had powerful political implications beyond Horace's scorn for materialism. But Pope's poem cannot be reduced to a simple political or moral position. The political commitments of a poet are usually bound up with a nexus of attitudes, emotions, and 'beliefs'. Political allusions in Pope's poetry are rarely straightforward, and his own moral positions can be extremely ambiguous. The tensions of this Imitation arise, I think, because, in writing a political poem, Pope responds deeply to Horace's scepticism, at times blending it with other convictions, at times transforming it into his own thought, and at times wholly embracing Horace's sardonic views of 'truth'. What makes the poem interesting, I think, is the shifting relationship between Pope's political commitments and Horace's intense idealism and intense doubt. Both these epistles are about the desires, emotional involvements, and activities people might 'use', or avoid, in the attempt to give their meaningless lives point and direction.

'NIL ADMIRARI'

Nil Admirari, *prope res est una, Numici!*
Solaque, quae possit facere & servare beatum.
   ²*Hunc Solem, & Stellas, & decedentia certis*
Tempora momentis, sunt qui ³*formidine nulla*
Imbuti, spectent. –
   – ⁴*Quid censes munera Terrae?*
Quid Maris, extremos Arabas ⁵*ditantis, & Indos?*
Ludicra quid, ⁶*plausus, & amici dona Quiritis,*
Quo spectanda modo, ⁷*quo sensu credis, & ore?*
   ⁸*Qui* timet *his adversa, fere miratur eodem*
Quo cupiens pacto: pavor est *utrique* molestus;
Improvisa simul species exterret utrumque.
⁹*Gaudeat, an doleat, cupiat, metuatve, quid ad rem?*
Si, quicquid vidit melius, pejusve sua spe,
Defixis oculis, animoque & corpore torpet?
¹⁰*Insani sapiens nomen ferat, aequus iniqui,*
Ultra quam satis est, virtutem si petat ipsam.   (1–16)

(To marvel at nothing is perhaps the one and only thing which can make and keep us happy.

This sun, the stars, the seasons passing in their unalterable motions – these some men can contemplate and feel no fear. What's your attitude to the riches of the earth, or of the sea, which enrich far-off Arabs and Indians; to such trifles as the applause and favours of the citizens when they like you – how do you think these should be contemplated, with what feelings and expression?

The man who fears the reverse of these baubles 'marvels' in almost the same way as the man who desires them: each is beset by agitation, and any unexpected apparition immediately terrifies each of them. Whether he feels joy or grief, desire or fear, what's the difference if, whenever he sees anything better or worse than he expected, his eyes are glazed, and he is dumbstruck and paralysed? Even the wise man would be labelled madman, the stable unbalanced, if he were to pursue Virtue itself to excess.)

'Admirari' means not just 'to admire' but 'to be astonished at, to wonder', and it has associations of hoping ('optare') and desiring and striving after. Horace plays on all the meanings of this rich word in his opening lines. His neat phrase 'Nil admirari' suggests the *ataraxia* of the Epicureans or the *apatheia* of the Stoics, a calm equanimity of mind, an absence of intense emotion. What matters is both how we see things (*'spectent', 'Quo spectanda modo'*), and how we feel about them (*'quo* sensu ... *& ore'*, 'with what feelings and expression'). And he who fears ('timet') marvels ('*miratur*') just as much as the man who desires ('cupiens'). Excitement ('*pavor*') startles ('*exterret*') the man who feels joy or grief ('*Gaudeat, an doleat*'), who desires or fears ('*cupiat, metuatve*'). Then, ironically, 'his eyes are glazed, and he is dumbstruck and paralysed' ('*Defixis oculis, animoque & corpore torpet*'). The wise man ('*sapiens*') should even be careful, Horace says dryly, not to be excessive in the pursuit of Virtue for fear that he too may become unbalanced ('*Insani*').

In these lines Pope saw possibilities for exploring the emptiness of the show of the great, and the power of emotions which unbalance the mind and 'snatch the man away'. His approach is at once highly idealistic and deeply questioning, and his tones move from the confident to the sardonic with disorientating swiftness:

> "Not to Admire, is all the Art I know,
> "To make men happy, and to keep them so."
> [Plain Truth, dear MURRAY, needs no flow'rs of speech,
> So take it in the very words of *Creech*.]
> ²This Vault of Air, this congregated Ball,
> Self-centred Sun, and Stars that rise and fall,
> There are, my Friend! whose philosophic eyes
> Look thro', and trust the Ruler with his Skies,
> To him commit the hour, the day, the year,
> And view ³this dreadful All without fear.
> Admire we then what ⁴Earth's low entrails hold,
> Arabian shores, or Indian seas infold?
> All the mad trade of ⁵Fools and Slaves for Gold?
> Or ⁶Popularity, or Stars and Strings?
> The Mob's applauses, or the gifts of Kings?
> Say with what ⁷eyes we ought at Courts to gaze,
> And pay the Great our homage of Amaze?
> If weak the ⁸pleasure that from these can spring,
> The fear to want them is as weak a thing:
> Whether we dread, or whether we desire,
> In either case, believe me, we admire;
> Whether we ⁹joy or grieve, the same the curse,
> Surpriz'd at better, or surpriz'd at worse.
> Thus good, or bad, to one extreme betray
> Th' unbalanc'd Mind, and snatch the Man away;
> For ¹⁰Vertue's self may too much Zeal be had;
> The worst of Madmen is a Saint run mad.   (1–27)

After the impressive first couplet Pope's throw-away '[Plain Truth, dear MURRAY, needs no flow'rs of speech, / So take it in the very words of *Creech*]' is actually very Horatian – '(*Nec meus hic* Sermo, *sed quem praecepit Ofellus*)', *Satire* II.ii.1. Yet at once Pope offers a majestic version of Horace's own rhetorical '*Hunc Solem, & Stellas, & decedentia certis / Tempora momentis.*' Pope asserts that a calm religious philosopher can actually 'trust the Ruler with his Skies' and 'To him commit the hour, the day, the year.' This is quite clearly based upon Dacier's Stoic/Christian reading of the poem, and indeed his religious interpretation of these particular lines: 'Il est certain que dans l'Univers nous ne voyons rien qui merite par luy-mesme nostre admiration. Les cieux, le Soleil, les étoiles, les saisons, &c. obeïssent comme nous aux ordres du Maistre Souverain qui a tout créé par sa parole' (Dacier, VIII, p. 259).

But Pope's tone in speaking of this man of faith is somewhat detached – he, like Horace, is not directly speaking for himself. Yet Horace's challenging questions ('*censes?*', '*credis?*' – 'what's your attitude?', 'how do you think?') Pope turns into a higher rhetoric, 'Admire we then what Earth's low entrails hold?'; and, after this, he neatly turns Horace's '*amici dona Quiritis*' ('favours of the citizens when they like you') into 'the gifts of Kings', so that he can transform Horace's 'sensu ... ore' into a sarcastic jibe at the Court:

> Say with what eyes we ought at Courts to gaze,
> And pay the Great our homage of Amaze? (16–17)

But Pope is just as alarmed as Horace at the equally disturbing effect of contradictory emotions. He emphasizes the 'timet' ('fears'), the 'cupiens' ('desires') and the 'utrique', 'utrumque' ('whether ... whether') in the Latin text, and brings this out in his own imitation:

> Whether we dread, or whether we desire
> In either case, believe me, we admire;
> Whether we joy or grieve, the same the curse,
> Surpriz'd at better, or surpriz'd at worse. (20–3)

Horace's questions become assertions in Pope, but the ironies are the same. Horace's paradoxical '*aequus iniqui*' ('stable, unbalanced') becomes 'betray / Th'unbalanc'd Mind, and snatch the Man away'; and Horace's tense '*Insani sapiens*' ('mad/wise') Pope couples with 'virtutem' to give it a religious edge:

> For Vertue's self may too much Zeal be had;
> The worst of Madmen is a Saint run mad. (26–7)

In these opening lines we begin to see the characteristic tensions of Pope's Imitation of this Horatian poem. Dacier and Shaftesbury approach the Horatian epistle from the position of their own Stoic/Christian beliefs, and so they find in it, finally, the fixed position from which it was written. Pope is much more actively engaged with the ironic details of the language and its shifting positions, with the result that he undermines the idea that Horace's poem is written from any fixed point of view. In addition, whereas Dacier and Shaftesbury use Horace's poem to advocate moral and spiritual detachment, Pope uses it to explore the meaning of commitment and attachment to worldly activities. By doing this Pope underlines the real challenge of Horace's searching satirical ironies. Stoic idealism or Christian vision can in themselves question the value of human desires and activities; but Pope, with those perspectives clearly in mind, pursues his questioning in a much more concrete way. He questions the aspirations and activities of his own time not by advocating detachment but involvement. The most searching ironies of Horace's poem come from its use of the ironical imperative, and this is what Pope focuses upon.

RICHES AND REPUTATION

Horace moves directly from his opening speculations to his ironic imperatives, and here we see the distinctive irony of *Epistle* i.vi. for the first time in all its brilliance:

> [11]*I nunc, argentum & marmor* [12]*vetus, aeraque & artes*
> *Suspice; cum gemmis* [13]*Tyrios mirare colores:*
> *Gaude, quod spectant oculi te mille loquentem:*
> *Gnavus* [15]*mane forum, & vespertinus pete tectum:*
> [16]*Ne plus frumenti dotalibus emetat agris*
> *Mucius. Indignum, quod sit pejoribus ortus!*
> [17]*Hic tibi sit potius, quam tu mirabilis illi?*
> [18]*Quicquid sub terra est, in apricum proferet Aetas,*
> *Defodiet, condetque nitentia.* [19]*Quum bene notum*
> *Porticus Agrippae, & via te conspexerit Appi,*
> *Ire tamen restat* Numa [20]*quo devenit & Ancus.*   (17–27)

(Go on, then, gaze on silver and antique marble, bronze and works of art, marvel at jewels and Tyrian dyes; rejoice that a thousand eyes behold you as you speak; work hard, go early to the forum, come late home; don't let Mucius, from the fields that came as a dowry, reap more corn than you. It's not right, when he's of lower birth! Is he to be marvellous in your eyes, rather than you in his? Whatever now lies beneath the earth, time will bring forth into sunlight, and bury and hide today's splendour. In Agrippa's arcade and the Appian Way they may know you and take notice of you: still the journey remains to where Numa and Ancus have gone.)

Still drawing on the word 'Admirari', Horace urges us to gaze with rapture ('*Suspice*') on silver plate, to marvel ('*mirare*') at Tyrian dyes, to rejoice ('*Gaude*') in social esteem, to rush ('*pete*') to the Forum. And then he calmly reminds us that when Agrippa's colonnade and the Appian Way have looked ('*conspexerit*') on us, so well known ('*bene notum*'), we still have to go where Numa and Ancus have already gone ('*devenit*'). The passage relies upon this host of verbs which lead so quickly to the death. The sheer absurdity of this frantic activity is evident in the competition with Mucius, on which Horace dryly remarks: '*Hic tibi sit potius, quam tu mirabilis illi?*' ('Is he to be marvellous in your eyes, rather than you in his?').

Pope's vision of these lines at once echoes Horace's detached ironies and blends them with other thoughts and feelings. The key to his passage is the fact that, after the first few lines, Pope addresses it directly to Murray himself:

> [11]Go then, and if you can, admire the state
> Of beaming diamonds, and reflected plate;
> Procure a *Taste* to double the surprize,
> And gaze on [12]Parian Charms with learned eyes:
> Be struck with bright [13]Brocade, or Tyrian Dye,
> Our Birth-day Nobles splendid Livery:
> If not so pleas'd, at [14]Council-board rejoyce,
> To see their Judgments hang upon thy Voice;
> From [15]morn to night, at Senate, Rolls, and Hall,
> Plead much, read more, dine late, or not at all.
> But wherefore all this labour, all this strife?
> For [16]Fame, for Riches, for a noble Wife?
> Shall [17]One whom Nature, Learning, Birth, conspir'd
> To form, not to admire, but be admir'd,
> Sigh, while his Chloë, blind to Wit and Worth,
> Weds the rich Dulness of some Son of earth?
> Yet [18]Time ennobles, or degrades each Line;
> It brighten'd CRAGS's, and may darken thine:
> And what is Fame? the Meanest have their day,
> The Greatest can but blaze, and pass away.
> Grac'd as thou art, [19]with all the Pow'r of Words,
> So known, so honour'd, at the House of Lords;
> Conspicuous Scene! another yet is nigh,
> (More silent far) where Kings and Poets lye;
> Where MURRAY (long enough his Country's pride)
> Shall be no more than TULLY, or than HYDE!   (28–53)

What is interesting here is the way in which Pope uses Horace's ironies to at once enhance and question his own compliment to Murray. Horace's cryptic reference to Mucius' wife's dowry Pope turns into consolation to Murray over an unsuccessful address to a lady. More importantly, Horace's ironic line '*Hic tibi sit potius, quam tu mirabilis illi*' is made into a very positive compliment to Murray:

> Shall One whom Nature, Learning, Birth, conspir'd
> To form, not to admire, but be admir'd ...   (40–1)

But the other lines seem much more enigmatic, at once complimenting Murray for his talent and energy and at the same time questioning the value of such committed activity:

> If not so pleas'd, at Council-board rejoyce,
> To see their Judgments hang upon thy Voice;
> From morn to night, at Senate, Rolls, and Hall,
> Plead much, read more, dine late, or not at all.
> But wherefore all this labour, all this strife?
> For Fame, for Riches, for a noble Wife?   (34–9)

Horace's quick adage '*Quicquid sub terra est, in apricum proferet
Aetas, / Defodiet, condetque nitentia*' ('Whatever now lies beneath
the earth, time will bring forth into sunlight, and bury and hide
today's splendour') becomes ominously personal:

> Yet Time ennobles, or degrades each Line;
> It brighten'd CRAGS's, and may darken thine ...   (44–5)

And Horace's lines about the colonnades are turned into moralizing
which, while praising Murray, remind him of his death:

> Where MURRAY (long enough his Country's pride)
> Shall be no more than TULLY, or than HYDE!   (52–3)

VIRTUE

The above lines are a strange fusion of personal compliment,
eighteenth-century moralizing, and Horatian scepticism, as the
rhetoric of poetry reminds an orator of the ultimate silence. But it is
this mixture of tones that gives them their individual character. We
find another fusion in the next passage. Horace throws together his
favourite comparison of physical and moral disease, in order to
recommend, in a mere line and a half, the pursuit of Virtue:[1]

> [21]*Si latus, aut renes morbo tententur acuto,*
> *Quaere fugam morbi –*
> – [22]*Vis recte vivere? quis non?*
> *Si Virtus hoc* una *potest dare, fortis* omissis
> *Hoc age* deliciis –   (28–31)

(If you're afflicted by agonizing pain in the lungs or kidneys, then seek a cure for
the pain. Do you desire the good life? Who does not? If Virtue alone has it in her
gift, be brave, shun comforts, set to.)

Pope turns this into satire and praise for a single notable individual:

> [21]Rack'd with Sciatics, martyr'd with the Stone,
> Will any mortal let himself alone?
> See Ward by batter'd Beaus invited over,

And desp'rate Misery lays hold on Dover.
The case is easier in the Mind's disease;
There, all Men may be cur'd, whene'er they please.
Would ye be [22]blest? despise low Joys, low Gains;
Disdain whatever CORNBURY disdains;
Be Virtuous, and be happy for your pains.   (54–62)

Pope both intensifies Horace's satiric irony and warms to his brief optimism. The 'morbo ... acuto' ('agonizing pain') becomes 'Rack'd ... martyr'd', and 'Quaere fugam morbi' ('seek a cure for the pain') becomes sarcastic jibes at the dubious doctors Ward and Dover. His tone is actually much more sarcastic than Horace's; we can hardly take straight

The case is easier in the Mind's disease;
There, all Men may be cur'd, whene'er they please.   (58–9)

In Horace such lines would be only gently ironic; in Pope there is often the possibility of intense pessimism. But the lines in praise of Cornbury are much more idealistic than Horace's quick encouragement to Virtue. Horace's 'Virtus ... una' ('Virtue alone') very brilliantly becomes Cornbury himself, and the 'omissis ... deliciis' ('shun comforts') refers to the government pension Cornbury rejected: 'despise low Joys, low Gains; / Disdain whatever CORNBURY disdains'. The move from 'una' to 'CORNBURY' is typical of the type of imaginative leap which for its full effect at once transgresses and respects Horace's text.

MONEY

Horace turns immediately from those who think Virtue means something to those who do not, and here, in a passage on the worship of money, we hear his most sarcastic tones:

– [23]Virtutem verba putas, ut
Lucum ligna? [24]cave ne portus occupet alter,
Ne Cybiratica, ne Bithyna negotia perdas.
[25]Mille talenta rotundentur, totidem altera: porro
Tertia succedant, & quae pars quadret acervum.
Scilicet [26]Uxorem cum dote, fidemque, & [27]Amicos,
Et genus & formam regina [28]Pecunia donat:
Ac bene nummatum decorat Suadela, Venusque.
Mancipiis locuples, eget aeris [29]Cappadocum rex;
Ne fueris hic tu –   (31–40)

(Perhaps you think Virtue mere verbiage, and a sacred grove just timber? Then make sure your competitor doesn't beat you to harbour, and you lose your trade with Cibyra or Bithynia. Let a thousand talents be rounded off, then another; let a third join them, and one to square the heap. No doubt a wife (with dowry), credit, friends, birth, beauty, are presents of our sovereign lady, Money; and the man with plenty of cash is graced by Persuasion and Venus. The king of Cappadocia, though rich in slaves, is short of ready money; be not like unto him.)

This kind of driving sarcasm clearly appealed to Pope:

> [23]But art thou one, whom new opinions sway,
> One, who believes as Tindal leads the way,
> Who Virtue and a Church alike disowns,
> Thinks that but words, and this but brick and stones?
> Fly [24]then, on all the wings of wild desire!
> Admire whate'er the maddest can admire.
> Is Wealth thy passion? Hence! from Pole to Pole,
> Where winds can carry, or where waves can roll,
> For Indian spices, for Peruvian gold,
> Prevent the greedy, and out-bid the bold:
> [25]Advance thy golden Mountain to the skies;
> On the broad base of fifty thousand rise,
> Add one round hundred, and (if that's not fair)
> Add fifty more, and bring it to a square.
> For, mark th'advantage; just so many score
> Will gain a [26]Wife with half as many more,
> Procure her beauty, make that beauty chaste,
> And then such [27]Friends – as cannot fail to last.
> A [28]Man of wealth is dubb'd a Man of worth,
> Venus shall give him Form, and Anstis Birth.
> (Believe me, many a [29]German Prince is worse,
> Who proud of Pedigree, is poor of Purse) ...   (63–84)

Horace's cryptic allusion to the destruction of sacred groves, '*Virtutem verba putas, ut / Lucum ligna?*' ('Perhaps you think Virtue mere verbiage, and a sacred grove just timber?'), allows Pope a quick jibe at Tindal's free thinking, and the hint of some kind of materialism at its centre. Pope emphasizes the energetic activity of this money-making, using ironic imperatives here more than Horace does. This allows Pope to suggest that the wild attempt to gain fulfilment in the pursuit of money is some kind of intense emotional experience:

> Fly then, on all the wings of wild desire!
> Admire whate'er the maddest can admire.
> Is Wealth thy passion? Hence! from Pole to Pole ...   (67–9)

The question 'Is Wealth thy passion?' is not as simple as it looks. Horace's image of rounding off the thousand talents ('rotundentur') and then squaring the heap ('quadret') becomes in Pope a sinister 'golden Mountain'. Horace imagines ironically that the money is a goddess, '*Pecunia*', who provides a wife, credit and friends to the

wealthy: '*Uxorem* cum dote, fidemque, & Amicos.' Pope sub-
ordinates 'fidem' ('credit') to '*Uxorem*' and 'Amicos': the cash
miraculously 'gains' a wife and 'Procures her beauty', and, so sarcastically, provides 'such Friends – as cannot fail to last'. Horace's
'*nummatum*' ('the man with plenty of cash') becomes a City
Knight: 'Venus shall give him Form' ('Formam') 'and Anstis Birth'
('genus'). Horace's brief allusion to the 'Cappadocum rex' who
lacks cash ('*eget aeris*') becomes a witty allusion to the Prince of
Wales' mean income from his parents:

> (Believe me, many a German Prince is worse,
> Who proud of Pedigree, is poor of Purse) ...   (83–4)

In their respective lines here both Horace and Pope focus on the
essential emptiness of the pursuit of money. From this point
onward both emphasize the absurdity of a host of other human
activities, desires, and ways of living, caught and portrayed in
lively little sketches. We see here Horace's talent for throwing
together a string of brief satiric stories, conveyed in snatches of
conversations and enlivened with personal allusions. Pope's imitations of them are superb, and in these bizarre situations both
poets discover the quintessential absurdity of human attitudes to
money:

> – [30]*Chlamydes Lucullus (ut aiunt)*
> *Si posset centum Scenae praebere rogatus,*
> *Qui possum tot? ait: tamen & quaeram, & quot habebo*
> *Mittam. Post paulo scribit, sibi millia quinque*
> *Esse domi chlamydum: partem, vel tolleret omnes.*
> [31]*Exilis domus est, ubi non & multa* supersunt,
> *Et dominum fallunt, & prosunt furibus.* [32]*Ergo,*
> *Si res sola potest facere & servare beatum,*
> *Hoc primus repetas opus, hoc postremus omittas.*   (40–8)

(Lucullus, they say, was once asked if he could lend a hundred cloaks for the
stage. 'How can I lend so many?' he said; 'but I'll look and send what I have.'
A little later he wrote, 'I have five thousand cloaks at home; take some, or all.'
It's a poor house where there is not plenty to spare, which escapes the master
and benefits the thieves. Therefore if wealth is the only thing that can make
and keep you happy, be the first at this work, and last to leave.)

This cryptic sketch speaks for itself, and Horace adds only his
sardonic comment '*Exilis domus est, ubi non et multa* supersunt'
('It's a poor house where there is not plenty to spare'). Pope uses
these lines on Lucullus to allude to his own Timon figure, and
playing on Horace's 'supersunt' ('there is to spare'), he looks
through sceptical Horatian eyes at the spectacle of excess:

> His Wealth brave [30]Timon gloriously confounds;
> Ask'd for a groat, he gives a hundred pounds;
> Or if three Ladies like a luckless Play,
> Takes the whole House upon the Poet's day.
> [31]Now, in such exigencies not to need,
> Upon my word, you must be rich indeed;
> A noble superfluity it craves,
> Not for your self, but for your Fools and Knaves;
> Something, which for your Honour they may cheat,
> And which it much becomes you to forget.
> [32]If Wealth alone then make and keep us blest,
> Still, still be getting, never, never rest.   (85–96)

In the *Epistle to Burlington* Pope had satirized excessive wealth but, to some extent, justified its social benefits. Now, inspired by Horace's '*Et* dominum fallunt, & prosunt furibus' ('which escapes the master and benefits the thieves'), he takes a grimmer view:

> Not for your self, but for your Fools and Knaves;
> Something, which for your Honour they may cheat,
> And which it much becomes you to forget.   (92–4)

His version of Horace's insistent '*Hoc primus repetas opus, hoc postremus omittas*' ('be the first at this work, the last to leave') emphasizes in its own language the obsessiveness of the Latin: 'Still, still be getting, never, never rest'.

POLITICS

If money making does not appeal to us Horace urges us to enter public life, and his sketch shows us what this means:

> [33]*Si Fortunatum species & gratia praestat,*
> [34]Mercemur *servum, qui dictet nomina, laevum*
> *Qui fodiat latus, & cogat trans pondera dextram*
> *Porrigere,* [36]*Hic multum in* Fabia *valet, ille* Velina:
> *Cuilibet hic fasces dabit, eripietque curule*
> *Cui volet* importunus *ebur.* [37]*Frater, pater, adde:*
> *Ut cuique est aetas, ita quemque* [38]facetus *adopta.*   (49–55)

(If pomp and power bring a man happiness, let's buy a slave to prompt us with names, to nudge our left side and make us reach out the right hand across the street: 'This one counts for much in the Fabian, and this in the Veline tribe; this one can bestow the rods on the man of his choice, or, if displeased, snatch the ivory throne from whomsoever he will.' Don't forget a 'brother' or 'father': be affable, and according to his age, adapt the greeting to adopt the man.)

Pope picks up the absurdity of Roman politics, and, in this poem with political overtones, adopts the passage to his own time all too easily:

[33]But if to Pow'r and Place your Passion lye,
If in the Pomp of Life consist the Joy;
Then [34]hire a Slave, (or if you will, a Lord)
To do the Honours, and to give the Word;
Tell at your Levee, as the Crouds approach,
To whom [35]to nod, whom take into your Coach,
Whom honour with your hand: to make remarks,
Who [36]rules in Cornwall, or who rules in Berks;
"This may be troublesome, is near the Chair;
"That makes three Members, this can chuse a May'r."
Instructed thus, you bow, embrace, protest,
Adopt him [37]Son, or Cozen at the least,
Then turn about, and [38]laugh at your own Jest.   (97–109)

Horace's 'Mercemur *servum*' ('let's buy a slave') becomes the sarcastic 'Then hire a Slave, (or if you will, a Lord)'; the Roman tribes 'Fabia' and 'Velina' are now the politically dubious 'Cornwall' and 'Berks' (see *TE*, IV, p. 243). Horace's 'importunus' ('if displeased') inspires a witty 'This may be troublesome, is near the Chair.' But, most imaginatively, Pope translates 'facetus' not as 'eloquent' which is the normal translation, but as 'facetiously', to give his imitation the most cynical conclusion possible: 'Then turn about, and laugh at your own Jest.'

FOOD, VICE, LOVE

Dropping the idea of public life as quickly as it was taken up, Horace switches to the epicure, and produces another bizarre sketch:

Si, [39]bene qui caenat, bene vivit, "lucet, eamus
"Quo ducit gula: piscemur, venemur:" ut [40]olim
Gargilius, qui mane plagas, venabula, servos,
Differtum transire forum populumque jubebat,
Unus ut e multis populo spectante referret
Emptum mulus aprum.   (56–61)

(If living well means eating well, then 'at first light let's follow where our gullets lead; let's fish, and hunt', like Gargilius used to. In the morning he would order his nets, spears, slaves across the packed forum, through the crowds; later, a single mule out of the many, before the people's gaze, would carry home a boar he'd bought.)

The comedy of the '*Emptum ... aprum*' ('bought ... boar') on the '*Unus ... mulus*' ('*a single ... mule*') is wonderfully absurd, conveyed in words that crisscross over each other. Pope remembers at once a Lord Russell who, according to Spence, lived so luxuriously he had to hunt to find an appetite, crying out, when he did, 'Oh, I have found it'. This is the man who once called a famished beggar 'a happy dog!' for being hungry (*TE*, IV, p. 244):

> Or if your life be one continu'd Treat,
> If [39]to live well means nothing but to eat;
> Up, up! cries Gluttony, 'tis break of day,
> Go drive the Deer, and drag the finny-prey;
> With hounds and horns go hunt an Appetite –
> So [40]Russel did, but could not eat at night,
> Call'd happy Dog! the Beggar at his door,
> And envy'd Thirst and Hunger to the Poor. (110–17)

The contradictions of Horace's story inspire in Pope a much more scathing comment on the disparities between luxury and poverty, and on the lunacy of his own time. Horace can suggest the comedy of hunting a bought boar with 'hunting-nets' ('*plagas*') and 'spears' ('*venabula*'), but hunting 'an Appetite' takes us into quite another world.

Alluding more and more rapidly to ways of living as he nears the end of his poem, Horace refers sharply to the viciousness of the wicked crew of Odysseus who ate the sacred cattle of the sun, throws off a mere two lines on love and jesting which linguistically simply repeat themselves, and ends with a disconcertingly ironic stroke addressed straight to the reader:

> – [41]*Crudi, tumidique lavemur,*
> *Quid deceat, quid non, obliti: Cerite cera*
> *Digni,* [42]*remigium vitiosum Ithacensis Ulyssei,*
> *Cui potior* [43]*patria fuit interdicta voluptas.*
> [44]*Si (Mimnermus uti censet) sine amore, jocisque,*
> *Nil est jucundum; vivas in amore, jocisque.*
> [45]*Vive, vale! si quid novisti rectius istis,*
> *Candidus imperti: si non, his utere mecum.* (61–8)

(Bloated with undigested food, let's go to the baths, forgetful of what's decent or indecent, fit to be classed as men of Caere, like Ithacan Ulysses' wicked crew, for whom forbidden pleasure meant more than fatherland.

If, as Mimnermus thinks, 'without love, without sport, there is no sweetness', then – live for love and sport.

Live long, farewell! If you know anything better than what I've told you, be generous, share it with me; if not, make do with this, as I do.)

Pope expands Horace's first lines into an open attack on the profligates of his own time:

> Or shall we [41]ev'ry Decency confound,
> Thro' Taverns, Stews, and Bagnio's take our round,
> Go dine with Chartres, in each Vice out-do
> [41]K–l's lewd Cargo, or Ty–y's Crew,
> From Latian Syrens, French Circaean Feasts,

> Return well travell'd, and transform'd to Beasts,
> Or for a Titled Punk, or Foreign Flame,
> Renounce our [43]Country, and degrade our Name? (118–25)

Horace's 'remigium vitiosum' ('wicked crew') becomes 'K[innoul]l's lewd Cargo, or Ty[rawle]y's Crew', ambassadors at Constantinople and Lisbon and well-known rakes. They stand for all those aristocrats of the eighteenth century to whom '*interdicta voluptas*' ('forbidden pleasure') 'meant more than fatherland' ('*potior patria*'). Picking up those repeated Latin words about love and pleasure, Pope finds a bit of Mimnermus in both Rochester and Swift:

> If, after all, we must with [44]Wilmot own,
> The Cordial Drop of Life is Love alone,
> And Swift cry wisely, "Vive la Bagatelle!"
> The Man that loves and laughs, must sure do well. (126–9)

But even here there are tensions. Mimnermus represents a lively '*joie de vivre*', but Rochester and Swift speak for more disturbed attitudes to pleasure and frivolity. Pope alludes to Rochester's bitter lines about love:

> The Cordial-drop Heav'n in our cup has thrown,
> To make the nauseous Draught of Life go down.
> (quoted *TE*, IV, p. 245)

and Swift's favourite saying is much at variance with his own intensities. And Pope finishes on a darker but more personal note:

> [45]Adieu – if this advice appear the worst,
> E'en take the Counsel which I gave you first:
> Or better Precepts if you can impart,
> Why do, I'll follow them with all my heart. (130–3)

The relationship between these two poems is complex because each work is in itself so enigmatic. Horace's epistle begins by advocating calm indifference, but as it goes on it seems both to endorse and to contradict that wisdom in terms of its own irony and its own language: the sustained irony of the poem is at once calmly aloof from, and intensely involved with, the subjects of its satire. This language is supremely dismissive in its rapidity and brevity, and energetically alive in the quick turns of its thought and in the very succinctness of its sharp sketches and flashing ironies. The poem's famous ironic imperatives involve us imaginatively in both action and scorn for action, in purpose and pointlessness. The calm we feel at the end of reading this Horatian epistle is the calm of superior knowledge gained by imaginatively passing through the very commitments we look at with such scorn. The poem distils for us the essential absurdity of passions and attitudes that we still find partly meaningful; and we are finally left without the cool indifference Horace seems to advocate, half-tangled in our pointless human yearnings.

Pope's Imitation seems to me similarly enigmatic. It is certainly not a straightforward political work; the political overtones are there, but as part of a complex vision. If the compliment to Cornbury is unequivocal, the 'advice' to Murray is extremely paradoxical; if Pope is scornful of the force of money in his society, he is also cynical about political life. If Pope suggests the possibility of passionate commitment to the ideals of the inner life amid public corruption, then he seems also to doubt the validity of such a stance in its own terms and in terms of political commitment. Indeed Pope's poem seems to doubt itself in just the same way, for it is at once more passionately committed and more cynical than the original. As Martin Price puts it, 'Pope darkens Horace at every point' (1965, p. 170). This is a poem involved in intense political activity, but it also looks through that activity, and perhaps even, in a strange way, prophesies its failure. Its distinctive poetry seems born from the interrelationship between idealism and scepticism, confidence and doubt.

In one sense the passion of this Imitation is indeed 'Juvenalian', powerful in its language and scathing in its contempt for absurdity and corruption in high places. But to call this poetry Juvenalian is not to account fully for Pope's achievement, because those qualities are blended with the cool Horatian detachment, the intensity of Horace's own irony, Horace's delight in the absurd, and a most Horatian scorn for ceaseless activity. If the passion of this verse is akin to that of Juvenal, then the self-awareness and self-questioning in which that passion is entangled is, in profound and unusual ways, Horatian. If Horace's famous *brevitas* inspires Pope's typical concentrated intensity, then, at the same time, Pope's characteristic satiric vigour and moral fervour have been touched by Horace's compelling scepticism.[2]

This Imitation and the *Imitation of Epistle I.i.*, indeed, take us into the very darkest areas of Horace's scepticism and of Pope's, as we see in so many human desires, activities and ideals an essential absurdity. It is this that makes such satire more than just satire. Significantly, in these poems both Horace and Pope take a darker view of human inconsistencies and contradictions than we have seen before. Deep inconsistencies in desires and actions, and the perennial human inability for people to know, or be happy with, who they are, or what they are, or what they are doing, provoke both Pope and Horace into some of their most haunting poetry. Both discover a driving inner emptiness at the heart of yearnings for fulfilment, yearnings which manifest themselves in strange desires or bizarre actions. In the *Epistle to Cobham* and *Sober Advice* Pope saw these desires as the motivating forces of existence, and the fact that in some sense they can never be fulfilled as providing life with both its tragic absurdity and its endlessly sustained energy. The perpetual failures of society, indeed, provide the satirist with his own sources of poetic energy. These perpetually fulfilled and unfulfilled passions, tinged with the force of sexuality, seem to sustain experience itself. It is no accident that Pope speaks of his ruling passions as the 'Lust of Gold' or the 'Lust of Praise'. What else could give life its strange, distorted energies?

10

Fables of the self:
The Imitations of Satire II.vi. and Epistle I.vii.

Horace, pour faire sa cour à Mecenas, témoigne dans cette Satire [II.vi.],
qu'il est content de sa fortune, & que les graces qu'il a receuës de luy,
l'ont mis en estat de ne pouvoir rien souhaiter.
(Dacier, VII, p. 452)

Hoc erat in votis, modus agri, &c., and *concha salis puri*. Off, off with
these masks. (Shaftesbury, 1900, p. 109)

ON 1 MARCH 1738, just one week before he brought out his last
Imitation of Horace, the *Imitation of Epistle I.i.*, Pope published a
reprint of Swift's Imitation of Horace's *Satire* II.vi. with a conclusion
done by himself. Swift's Imitation of the main section of Horace's
satire had been written in August 1714, and been printed for the first
time in the 'last' volume of the Pope/Swift *Miscellanies* of 1727,
without the Latin text. Now Pope printed it alongside the whole of the
Latin poem with index numbers which he, presumably, introduced
himself. His version of the end of the satire, the story of the town
mouse and the country mouse, is done in octosyllabic couplets. As
such it is not only an 'Imitation of Horace', but also an Imitation of
Swift.

In 1739 he included in his collected works an addition to another of
Swift's Imitations. Swift had published in 1713 an Imitation of the
famous story of Philippus and Volteius which ends Horace's *Epistle*
I.vii., adapted to portray ironically the relationship between himself
and Harley. Pope's poem is an Imitation, again in the Swiftian mode,
of the first part of this Horatian epistle, and, though in fact 'complete' in itself, it ends by suggesting one should read the rest of the
poem in Swift's version. It is difficult to date Pope's two 'Swiftian'
Imitations, although it would appear from Bathurst's letter to Swift
of 5 October 1737, that the addition to the *Imitation of Satire II.vi.*
was done by the autumn of 1737 (quoted *TE*, IV, p. 248). Pope's
Imitation of the opening of *Epistle* I.vii. may have been done at the
same time, or may have been done early in 1738 (see Aden, 1969,
pp. 85–91).

It is convenient to take these two poems together, however,

because as a pair they form a special aspect of Pope's treatment of Horace. To begin with, it is valuable to compare not only how Pope and Swift approach different sections of the same poem, but how Swift's whole way of imitating Horace compares with Pope's. Their two styles are very different, as Pope's 'Advertisement' to the Imitation of *Satire* II.vi. made clear:

> The World may be assured, this Publication is [in] no way meant to interfere with the *Imitations of Horace* by Mr. *Pope*: His Manner, and that of Dr. *Swift* are so entirely different, that they can admit of no Invidious Comparison. The Design of the one being to sharpen the Satire, and open the Sense of the Poet; of the other to render his native *Ease* and *Familiarity* yet more easy and familiar.
>
> (*TE*, IV, p. 249)

But these distinctions, in fact, only begin to account for the different views of Horace which these imitations offer to the reader of Pope's *Imitations*. It is particularly illuminating to compare these Swift/ Pope Imitations with both Dacier's and Shaftesbury's readings of, and comments on, these poems. Dacier offers a very conventional reading of each of these poems; but Shaftesbury's allusions to Horace's *Satire* II.vi. constitute his most original and provocative reading of any Horatian poem, and his comments on *Epistle* I.vii. represent his most intense evocation of what were, for him, supreme Horatian/Stoic ideals, expressed in Horace's most agonizing poetry. Why is it that for Swift these poems were models of 'Ease and Familiarity' whereas for Shaftesbury they were Horace's most tormented works? How do Pope's Swiftian Imitations relate to these sharply contrasting interpretations, and how do they relate to Pope's whole reinterpretation of Horace in 1738?

SWIFT, DACIER, SHAFTESBURY

These two Horatian poems are concerned, in different ways, with Horace's relationship with Maecenas, and, put together, they form a striking diptych. *Satire* II.vi. is a celebration of Horace's life of retreat at his Sabine farm, seen in dramatic contrast to the hectic life of Rome. It is a poem of diminutives, revealing the richness of Horace's modest desires amply fulfilled by his 'little' farm, and concluding with the charming story of the town mouse and the country mouse, itself a moral tale told in miniature. Central to the poem, however, and subtly woven into it, is Horace's intimate relationship with Maecenas, finely acknowledged, it would seem, in Horace's warm allusions to his patron. Crucial in this respect is the fact that Horace's cherished farm was a gift from Maecenas. *Epistle* I.vii., however, looks at this relationship from another point of view. Imagining that Maecenas has reproached Horace for staying away from him in the country longer than he said he would, Horace replies by boldly asserting his need to maintain his independence. In controlled and dignified tones he points out to Maecenas their mutual obligations, and reminds him of the respect they have been accustomed to show each other. While fully acknowledging the magnitude of Maecenas' gifts, Horace courageously offers to return the whole lot, if their relationship is to entail slavish obedience and attention from Horace. The epistle ends with the story of Philippus and Volteius, an account of catastrophic 'patronage' in which the gift of a farm destroys the contentment of the easy-going man to whom it was given. If *Satire* I.vi. records Horace's depth of gratitude to Maecenas, celebrating the life he has made possible for Horace, the later epistle explores the dangers that such generous appreciation might involve.

Swift's Imitations of these two poems are about his relationship with Harley at the time of the Tory ministry, when Harley was a patron to Swift, then the Tories' chief pamphleteer. In 1713 Swift, at the age of forty-six, was rewarded for his work by being made Dean of St Patrick's in Ireland, very much at Harley's instigation. In the first of his two Imitations, the rendering of the story of Philippus and Volteius from *Epistle* I.vii., Swift portrays himself as Volteius taken up by Harley as Philippus. With sardonic irony he presents Harley's interest in him as being merely a 'Jest', and shows the gift of the Dublin Deanship as being a crushing financial disaster. The tone is light-hearted, but the ironies possess the characteristic Swiftian astringency. In the Imitation of the first part of *Satire* II.vi. Swift expresses in warmer ironies the pleasure of his intimate relationship with Harley, in lines closely modelled on Horace's characterization of his relationship with Maecenas. From the point of view of Pope's *Imitations*, Swift's relationship with Harley as presented in these poems is important for the comparison it offers with Pope's relationship with Bolingbroke, in the *Imitation of Epistle I.vii.*, and again in the *Imitation of Epistle I.i.* Some of the points that emerge in this chapter will be explored further when we consider that final Imitation, addressed to Bolingbroke in yet another of Maecenas' roles as created by Horace.

Both of Swift's Imitations would seem to assume a fairly conventional reading of these two Horatian poems such as we find in Dacier. In his commentary on *Satire* I.vi. Dacier stresses Horace's inner contentment on his Sabine farm and the warmth of his intimate relationship with Maecenas (Dacier, VII, p. 452). In his commentary on *Epistle* I.vii. he emphasizes the moral value of Horace's assertion

of his independence and the delicacy of Horace's manner of convey-
ing his position to Maecenas:

C'est une des plus belles Epistres d'Horace. Elle enseigne de quelle maniere on
doit vivre avec les Grands. Il faut avoir pour eux toute l'assiduité & tous les égards
qu'exigent l'amitié, le devoir & la reconnoissance, selon l'âge & l'état où l'on est.
Mais un honneste homme ne reconnoist jamais des bienfaits par la perte de sa
liberté. On cesse d'être vertueux quand on cesse d'estre libre.
(Dacier, VIII, p. 361)

He stresses the pleasant, if firm, tone of the epistle, and argues that
the wit and grace of the story of Philippus and Volteius would have
amused rather than offended Maecenas: 'Mecenas ne le lut pas sans
rire de la justesse & de la naïveté de la comparaison' (Dacier, VIII,
p. 384).

It is fascinating to move from these interpretations to Shaftesbury's reading of these poems. Shaftesbury turns to the famous
opening lines of *Satire* I.vi. three times in the 'Philosophical
Regimen': '*Hoc erat in votis*' ('This is what I used to pray for'). But
whereas most readers of Horace have seen them as an expression of
deep contentment, Shaftesbury sees in them anxiety, strain, and
self-questioning. We see here Horace the idealist struggling against
his own wishes for moderation, contentment, and charm. This is a
Horace aware of the subtle dangers of 'small possessions': 'ktēseidion' ('a small property'), 'oikarion' ('a small house'), 'doularion' ('a
little slave'):

Mask of the first (viz., ktēseidion, doularion) ['a small property', 'a little slave'].
Duty: a part, a character.
    Mask of the second (viz., oikarion) ['a small house']. Philosophical: a way of
living, neatness, nature, husbandry, garden. *Hoc erat in votis, modus agri*, &,
and *concha salis puri* [This used to be my wish, a little piece of land and a small
shell of pure salt]. Off, off with these masks.   (Shaftesbury, 1900, p. 109)

These are 'diminutives indeed!': 'O subtle enemies! more dangerous
than all open ones ... whose sting goes deepest, and is never felt'
(p. 109).

For Shaftesbury these lines represent Horace's first expression of
his self-questioning which begins his 'third period' (Shaftesbury,
1900, p. 361). Shaftesbury takes the '*erat*' in the first line to be a real
past tense. The lines show Horace now aware of what used to be his
desires, and now testing what were his own wishes and apparently
deepest yearnings:

Watch strictly when the fancy runs out upon any notable design or outward piece
of work. *Hoc erat in votis; modus agri*, &c ... and *paulum silvae* ... and merely
concha salis puri ... How rotten is all this. And yet how covered over ... But

endeavour, notwithstanding, to bring it forth into the light, examine the idea, bring it to the test ... Is it virtue, or has it anything in common with virtue?

(Shaftesbury, 1900, p. 122)

Thus Horace tries to distinguish between his true self and his 'artificial self' of the past. In doing so he explores the involvement of self in property, and now we have powerful meditation on that word 'propria' ('one's own') related, of course, to 'proprium' ('property'). Speaking scornfully of the 'recommendation of country life, agreeableness of a place, seat alterations, gardens, groves', Shaftesbury continues:

Now see what thou hast got by thy success in this way. Hoc erat in votis [this was what I used to pray for], and so now auctius atque di melius fecere: bene est [the gods have granted me these, and more; I am content]. But is it so? Propria haec mihi munera [are these gifts really mine]? Are these *propria*? are they thine? honestly thine? thy own very true and certain possessions properly belonging to thee and naturally thine?   (Shaftesbury, 1900, p. 126. Translation changed)[1]

This inwardly agonized Stoic Horace is, of course, struggling to escape from the court of Augustus and from Maecenas himself. Shaftesbury asserts that this is the meaning of what he sees as the repeated 'fables' in late Horatian poetry:

Here it is that by my fables I pretend to discover Horace, and lay open his secret. As soon as ever Horace comes to fables he is dipt. He dares only tell his mind in fables. All his fable-pieces are of the third period. They are in all seven ... All mean that same thing. If you have the moral of one, you have it all. One key serves to all the locks.   (Shaftesbury, 1900, pp. 361–2)

The first fable to reveal Horace's profound yearning for independence and freedom from Maecenas is the story of the town mouse and the country mouse: 'The first, which is that of the mice in Sat. VI., Bk. II., you have read, I dare say, often enough in your life. But now I pray you read once again. For when formerly you read it you little thought perhaps that even Maecenas should have been meant by the city mouse and Horace by the poor frighted country one' (Shaftesbury, 1900, p. 362).

The second is the story of the soldier of Lucullus in *Epistle* II.ii.26–40; and the third and fourth are in *Epistle* I.vii. which Shaftesbury regards as Horace's most profound assertion of his essential independence and integrity. His interpretative paraphrase of this epistle is the climax of his very personal reading of Horace:

And now, therefore, if you please, go to the third and fourth apologue, and read with wondrous care (for this is the most wondrous, nice, and artful piece that perhaps was ever written in the world) the seventh epistle of Book I. Here the apologue of the fox and weasel is first related, and is put with all the force imaginable for Maecenas against Horace. But by that following story of Vulteius, he sets all right, and shows Maecenas that the effect (as I told you) ceases from another cause. His mind is no longer the same that it was. Had he ever so little estate he would now retire and philosophise. Though not a word of philosophy all this while to Maecenas. It is a paw-word, as they say, and though he asserts the thing itself thus plainly, yet he uses other names of liberty and rest, for philosophy was too shocking, too harsh an idea for the soft Maecenas. Yet does not Horace abate one tittle of his right. 'If you upbraid me', says he; 'Maecenas, if you reproach me for ingratitude take back your gifts'. 'Cuncta resigno', v.34. 'Magis apta tibi tua dona relinquam', v.43, apt indeed for you a great man, an Atridas, not apt for poor Ithaca, such a mind as mine, naturally mean and simple, and now at last returned into so homely and rough a philosophy, out of which and a tolerable contented state of poverty, you, Maecenas, debauched me, as that orator Philip did Vulteius. For it was not out of mere hunger that I got cunningly and fox-like into your granaries. I was enticed, corrupted, and drawn. Nor is it at this time a bellyful and plenty merely that keeps me from making court to you, as having got what I wanted. It is not this makes me desire to be at liberty, as if I only meant a life of indolence through a kind of surfeit of pleasure, but no real dislike rest and liberty above either pleasures or riches, or all that the Indies and Arabia can afford one. If you believe it not, try me, I beseech you, once again in honest poverty. Leave me but where you found me. Let me be empty again, lean and hungry as I was, when out of Court, and see if you can catch me there by the same baits a second time.'

(Shaftesbury, 1900, pp. 362–3)

HORATIAN CONTENTMENT

Horace begins *Satire* ii.vi. with what has generally been seen as an expression of deep contentment as he meditates on the nature of his Sabine farm and on the quality of life it seems to offer, or perhaps, to demand of him:

> *Hoc erat in votis; modus agri non ita magnus,*
> *Hortus ubi, & tecto vicinus jugis aquae fons,*
> *Et paulum sylvae super his foret: auctius atque*
> [2]*Dii melius fecere: bene est: nil amplius oro,*
> *Maia nate, nisi ut* [3]*propria haec mihi munera faxis.*
> [4]*Si neque majorem feci ratione mala rem,*
> *Nec sum facturus vitio culpave minorem;*
> *Si veneror stultus nihil horum; "O si angulus ille*
> *"Proximus accedat, qui nunc denormat agellum!*
> *"O si urnam argenti fors quae mihi monstret, ut illi,*
> *"Thesauro invento qui mercenarius agrum*
> *"Illum ipsum mercatus aravit, dives amico*
> *"Hercule! si quod adest, gratum juvat; hac prece te oro*
> *Pingue pecus domino facias,* [5]*& caetera, praeter*
> *Ingenium;* [6]*utque soles, custos mihi maximus adsis!*
> *Ergo ubi me in montes & in arcem ex urbe removi,*
> [7]*Quid prius illustrem Satiris, Musaque pedestri?*

Nec mala me ⁸Ambitio perdit, nec plumbeus Auster,
Autumnusque gravis, Libitinae quaestus acerbae. (1–19)

(This is what I used to pray for: a piece of land, not too big, with a garden, and, near to the house, a constant spring of water and a bit of woodland as well. The gods have granted me these, and more. I am content. I ask for nothing more, Mercury, except that you confirm these gifts as my own. Since I have not increased my fortune by dishonest means, and do not intend to fritter it away by neglect or misdeed; since I utter no such foolish prayer as these: 'Oh, that I might acquire that corner of my neighbour's land, that now spoils my little plot', 'Oh, that luck might show me a pot of money – like that man who with the treasure he found bought and farmed the very fields where he'd worked as a hireling, a rich man now, thanks to Hercules' kindness'; since what I have makes me happy and contented, this is the prayer I address to you: 'Make my sheep fat, and all that's mine (except my wits), and, as you are and have been, be my strong guardian still'. So, now I've moved from the city to the hills, to my stronghold, there is no other subject I'd sooner celebrate in these satires (where my muse keeps her feet on the ground). Here accursed ambition cannot destroy me, nor the leaden South wind and autumn's oppressiveness, profitable only to the sour undertakers.)

From one point of view we might say these words express a feeling of contentment and serenity: what Horace longed for has now been given to him, indeed he has been given more than he desired. From another we might say they explore the relationship between desire and possession. In contrast to the frantic desires of *Nil Admirari*, we see here the inner peace of one who desired little and has, perhaps for that very reason, been given much. The modesty and simplicity of Horace's desires are charmingly expressed: '*modus agri*' ('a piece of land') '*non ita magnus*' ('not too big'); '*paulum sylvae*' ('a bit of woodland'); '*Hortus*' ('a garden') and '*fons*' ('a spring of water') where the water is so richly '*jugis*' ('constant'). Now that he has been given all this and more, he can say simply, '*bene est*' ('I am content'). What was wished for is present ('*Hoc erat in votis*' – 'This is what I used to pray for'), and what is present is all that could be wished for – '*quod adest, gratum juvat*' ('what I have makes me happy and contented'). But Horace makes clear that this contentment is dependent on his own willingness to accept it, and not give in to longings that are all too natural: '*Si neque ... feci*' ('Since I have not increased'), '*Si veneror ... nihil*' ('Since I utter no prayer'), '*si quod adest*' ('since what I have'). These conditional clauses express the factual reason why the god should grant the speaker's prayer.

The Imitation offers a very distinctive version of this. In place of Horace's deep feelings and meditative voice, we have a more conversational tone and a little less contentment:

228

I've often wish'd that I had clear
For life, six hundred pounds a year,
A handsome House to lodge a Friend,
A River at my garden's end,
A Terras-walk, and half a Rood
Of Land, set out to plant a Wood.
    [2]Well, now I have all this and more,
I ask not to increase my store;
But here a Grievance seems to lie,
[3]All this is mine but till I die;
I can't but think 'twould sound more clever,
To me and to my Heirs for ever.
    [4]If I ne'er got, or lost a groat,
By any *Trick*, or any *Fault*;
And if I pray by Reason's rules,
And not like forty other Fools:
As thus, "Vouchsafe, oh gracious Maker!
"To grant me this and t'other Acre:
"Or if it be thy Will and Pleasure
"Direct my Plow to find a Treasure:"
But only what my Station fits,
[5]And to be kept in my right wits.
Preserve, Almighty Providence!
[6]Just what you gave me, Competence:
And let me in these Shades compose
Something in [7]Verse as true as Prose;
[8]Remov'd from all th'ambitious Scene,
Nor puff'd by Pride, nor sunk by Spleen.
    In short, I'm perfectly content,
Let me but live on this side *Trent*:
Nor cross the Channel twice a year,
To spend six months with Statesmen here.   (1–32)

It is uncertain whether lines 9–28 which appeared for the first time
in this complete version are by Pope or Swift (Butt argues they are by
Pope, but notes disagreements, *TE*, IV, p. 248). If Pope did add them
he introduced into Swift's Imitation a very significant note of discontent. The most striking change in them is the play on the word
'propria' ('one's own'), the only word in the whole Latin poem
singled out in different type. Pope picked this word out in the Latin
either because of what Swift had made of it, or, more likely I think,
because he wanted to attribute this sentiment to Swift in these extra
lines which he added himself. Whichever is the case, the concentration on that word gives a new character to the opening of the
Imitation, introducing a note of self-conscious irony. Horace says
'*nil amplius oro, / Maia nate, nisi ut* propria *haec mihi numera faxis*'
('I ask for nothing more, Mercury, except that you confirm these gifts
as my own'):

> But here a Grievance seems to lie,
> All this is mine but till I die;
> I can't but think 'twould sound more clever,
> To me and to my Heirs for ever. (9–12)

These lines are clearly playing ironically on what Shaftesbury at least considered the central issue of the Horatian opening.

And yet this opening is not characteristic of Swift's approach to *Satire* II.vi. The rest of the Imitation only shows how different Swift's Horatian style is from Pope's: in Swift's Imitation there is little depth of feeling, no passionate rhetoric, no emotional intensity. There is indeed little sense of close involvement with Horace's language, with his subtleties of tone and feeling, and with his complexities of form. For the Swift of these Imitations Horace is much more a poet of dramatic situations, of conversation, of human relationships, a poet of men's attitudes to themselves and others' attitudes to them. Swift's Imitation of the central part of *Satire* II.vi. is an attempt to re-create the light ironies that are an essential part of what was generally considered the warm and intimate relationship between Horace and Maecenas. One passage will show how successfully Swift succeeds in this attempt. In the Horatian poem two casual references to Maecenas finally bring Horace to his famous lines on his relationship with his patron. With a fresh start, Horace, relaxed and confident, remembers how long he has known Maecenas, and portrays with warm irony the chit-chat that is the sign of their intimacy and affection:

> [15]*Septimus octavo proprior jam fugerit annus,*
> *Ex quo Maecenas me coepit habere suorum*
> *In numero, dumtaxat ad hoc, quem tollere rheda*
> *Vellet, iter faciens, & cui concredere nugas*
> *Hoc genus; Hora quota est? Threx est Gallina Syro par?*
> *Matutina parum cautos jam frigora mordent:*
> *Et quae rimosa bene deponuntur in aure.* (40–6)

(Seven years, nearly eight, have now passed, since Maecenas began to number me among his friends, at least to the extent of being prepared to take me in his carriage when he went on a journey, and of sharing with me such trifles as 'What time is it?', 'Is the Thracian Chicken a match for Syrus?' 'These cold mornings catch you if you're not careful' – the sort of thing that it's safe to entrust to an indiscreet ear.)

Swift catches Horace's tone here to perfection, and transforms this into a charming celebration of his relationship with Harley, with all Horace's wit:

> [15]'Tis (let me see) three years and more,
> (October next it will be four)

Since HARLEY bid me first attend,
And chose me for an humble friend;
Wou'd take me in his Coach to chat,
And question me of this and that;
As, "What's o'clock?" And, "How's the Wind?"
"Who's Chariot's that we left behind?
Or gravely try to read the lines
Writ underneath the Country Signs;
Or, "Have you nothing new to-day
"From Pope, from Parnel, or from Gay?
Such tattle often entertains
My Lord and me as far as Stains,
As once a week we travel down
To Windsor, and again to Town,
Where all that passes, *inter nos*,
Might be proclaim'd at Charing-Cross.   (83–100)

In no sense does this poetry attempt to re-create the tones and feelings of the Horace, its rhythms, and its moral and psychological implications. Rather it seems a very self-conscious parody of the original, its jaunty rhythms and lilting rhymes underlining the sense of pastiche. The contrast to this style, and to Swift's image of the 'Horace–Maecenas' relationship portrayed here, will come in Pope's *Imitation of Epistle I. vii.*

DIMINUTIVES

It would seem virtually impossible to square Shaftesbury's agonized reading of the opening of *Satire* II.vi. with Swift's general approach to this poem despite some of the tensions in the Swift/Pope opening of the Imitation. But how does Pope approach the final fable? What is his attitude to Horace's diminutives, and to the possibility that this is a story about personal liberty?

Horace's story of the town mouse and the country mouse expands on the poem's basic country–city contrast, but does so in captivating miniature. The first half takes us into the most charming vision of country life on the smallest scale, and culminates in the city mouse's sophisticated response to it which itself can be measured only in millimetres:

[24]*Olim*
Rusticus urbanum murem mus paupere fertur
Accepisse cavo, veterem vetus hospes amicum;
Asper, & attentus quaesitis, ut tamen arctum
Solveret hospitiis animum: quid multa? neque ille
Sepositi ciceris, nec longae invidit avenae:
Aridum & ore ferens acinum, semesaque lardi

Frustra dedit, cupiens varia fastidia coena
Vincere tangentis male singula dente superbo:
Cum pater ipse domus palea porrectus in horna
Esset ador loliumque, dapis meliora relinquens.
Tandem urbanus ad hunc, Quid te juvat, inquit, amice,
Praerupti nemoris patientem vivere dorso?
Vis tu homines urbemque feris praeponere sylvis?
Carpe viam (mihi crede) comes, terrestria quando
Mortales animas vivunt sortita, neque ulla est
Aut magno aut parvo leti fuga: quo bone circa,
Dum licet, in rebus jucundis vive beatus:
Vive memor quam sis aevi brevis.　　　　　　　　　　　(79–97)

(Once upon a time, the story goes, a country-dweller welcomed a guest from town to his poor hole, a mouse like himself, and a friend of long standing. Normally austere and cautious with his stores, yet he could relax his stinginess when entertaining. In fact, such was his generosity, he didn't even begrudge his friend the chickpea he'd been saving, or his long oat; he brought out, in his own mouth, a shrivelled berry, and some half-eaten scraps of bacon, eagerly seeking with this variety of fare to overcome his friend's fastidiousness. But he would no more than touch one dainty after another with a disdainful tooth, while the lord and master, stretched out on fresh chaff, was eating spelt and darnels, forgoing the choicer morsels of the banquet. Finally, the city-dweller turned to his host, and said, 'What's the point of a life of privation on a dizzy ridge in the forest? Wouldn't you rather have human beings and town than these uncivilized woods? Don't waste time, but take my advice and come along with me. In as much as all earthly creatures are given souls that die, and there is not, for great or for small, any escape from the grave; therefore, my good fellow, while you may, enjoy life's pleasures in comfort; and all your life remember how short your time must be.')

So much of the charm of this lies in the elegant word play which shows Horace's Latin at its most precise:

> *Rusticus urbanum murem mus paupere fertur*
> *Accepisse cavo, veterem vetus hospes amicum ...*　　　　(80–1)

(a country-dweller welcomed a guest from the town to his poor hole, a mouse like himself, and a friend of long standing)

The words in different cases echo each other in sound and meaning (*'murem mus'*, *'veterem vetus'* – 'mouse, mouse', 'old, old') and fall exquisitely into place – *'Rusticus urbanum'* ('country city'), *'hospes amicum'* ('host, friend'). To the poet of the *Rape of the Lock* such verbal dexterity was clearly a delight:

> [23]Our Friend Dan *Prior* told, (you know)
> A Tale extreamly *a propos*:
> Name a Town Life, and in a trice,
> He had a Story of *two Mice*.

[24]Once on a time (so runs the Fable)
A Country Mouse, right hospitable,
Receiv'd a Town Mouse at his Board,
Just as a Farmer might a Lord.
A frugal Mouse upon the whole,
Yet lov'd his Friend, and had a Soul;
Knew what was handsome, and wou'd do't,
On just occasion, *coute qui coute.*
He brought him Bacon (nothing lean)
Pudding, that might have pleas'd a Dean;
Cheese, such as men in Suffolk make,
But wish'd it Stilton for his sake;
Yet to his Guest tho' no way sparing,
He eat himself the Rind and paring.
Our Courtier scarce could touch a bit,
But show'd his Breeding, and his Wit,
He did his best to seem to eat,
And cry'd, 'I vow you're mighty neat.
"As sweet a Cave as one shall see!
"A most Romantic hollow Tree!
"A pretty kind of savage Scene!
"But come, for God's sake, live with Men:
"Consider, Mice, like Men, must die,
"Both small and great, both you and I:
"Then spend your life in Joy and Sport,
"(This doctrine, Friend, I learnt at Court.)   (153–82)

From the minutiae of Horace's text Pope has created a tiny world of equal charm. Horace's country mouse though so poor 'yet he could relax his stinginess when entertaining' – '*ut tamen arctum / Solveret hospitiis animum*':

A frugal Mouse upon the whole,
Yet lov'd his Friend, and had a Soul;
Knew what was handsome, and wou'd do't,
On just occasion, *coute qui coute.*   (161–4)

The '*rusticus mus*', trying so hard to be the perfect host, brings 'in his own mouth, a shrivelled berry, and some half-eaten scraps of bacon' ('*Aridum & ore ferens acinum, semesaque lardi / Frustra dedit*'):

He brought him Bacon (nothing lean)
Pudding, that might have pleas'd a Dean;
Cheese, such as men in Suffolk make,
But wished it Stilton for his sake ...   (165–8)

Horace's *urbanus mus* behaves very badly but quite disarms the criticism we feel for his rudeness, by talking like an Epicurean philosopher and quoting Horatian odes. In the language of philosophy he announces:

> ... *terrestria quando*
> *Mortales animas vivunt sortita* ...　　　　　　　(93–4)

(In as much as all earthly creatures are given souls that die ...)

'*Carpe viam (mihi crede) comes*' ('Don't waste time, but take my advice and come along with me') reminds us of Horace's famous 'Carpe diem' ('Snatch the day'); and '*Vive memor quam sis aevi brevis*' ('all your life remember how short your time must be') is pure Horatian wisdom. Pope's city mouse is just as cultivated, but he shows it by being *au fait* with the very latest taste in 'Romantic' landscape:

> "As sweet a Cave as one shall see!
> "A most Romantic hollow Tree!　　　　　　　(175–6)

He is also, however, equally aware of the eternal truths:

> "Consider, Mice, like Men, must die,
> "Both small and great, both you and I ...　　　　　　　(179–80)

At the end, however, Pope introduces a sardonic aside which, so significantly, relates this thinking to the Court. This mouse is indeed a 'Courtier':

> "Then spend your life in Joy and Sport,
> "(This doctrine, Friend, I learnt at Court.)　　　　　　　(181–2)

A mouse propounding the Epicurean theory of the mortality of the soul will, of course, make an impression upon a simple country creature. A witty parody of epic poetry takes him to a sumptuous palace and the lavish remains of a city feast (lines 100–11). Pope echoes the epic parody with an allusion to the moon in *Romeo and Juliet* 'That tips with silver all these frute tree tops' (II.ii. 107–8), neatly parodies the mixture of styles in the architecture of the great house, and offers a lovely view of the Courtly epicure and his convert (lines 187–209). Then the catastrophe in Horace falls, with all the noise and confusion of epic poetry, comparable to the parody at the end of *Satire* I.ii.:

> 　　　　　　　... *cum subito ingens*
> *Valvarum strepitus lectis excussit utrumque;*
> *Currere per totum pavidi conclave, magisque*
> *Exanimes trepidare, simul domus alta Molossis*
> *Personuit canibus. Tum rusticus, Haud mihi vita*
> *Est opus hac, ait, & valeas: me sylva cavusque*
> *Tutus ab insidiis tenui solabitur ervo.*　　　　　　　(111–17)

(... when suddenly the tremendous banging of the doors hurled both of them off their couches. They ran the length of the room in terror: but greater fear still shook them, scared out of their wits, once the great mansion was filled with the barking of mastiffs. Then the country mouse said, '*I* have no need of this way of life. I wish you joy of it: *I'll* find *my* consolation in my hole in the forest: it's safe from attack, even if my vetch is poor'.)

This inspires in Pope a miniature *tour-de-force*, full of invention and lively wit which concludes with the crucial word:

> No sooner said, but from the Hall
> Rush Chaplain, Butler, Dogs and all:
> "A Rat, a Rat! clap to the door –
> The Cat comes bouncing on the floor.
> O for the Heart of Homer's Mice,
> Or Gods to save them in a trice!
> (It was by Providence, they think,
> For your damn'd Stucco has no chink)
> "An't please your Honour, quoth the Peasant,
> "This same Dessert is not so pleasant:
> "Give me again my hollow Tree!
> "A Crust of Bread, and Liberty.   (212–23)

How do we assess the significance of Horace's famous story and Pope's imitation of it? Horace's story is in one sense simply a delightful act of imagination and perception which charms us with the known world seen from another perspective. We are captivated with this tiny world, enchanted by its play of wit and irony, delighted with the precision and aptness of its language. Within this, however, Horace shows the most winning kind of self-criticism in which he satirizes himself, his poetry, and his characteristic moral vision. So much of the charm of this story comes from Horace's parody of his own Epicureanism and his own philosophy in the words of the 'urbanus mus'; he parodies here the moral themes of the first part of this very poem with its deep celebration of country life and the hospitality and friendship that it makes possible. The story does more than enforce its obvious moral; at a more sophisticated level it makes us amused with what Horace characteristically approves of and charms us with what he characteristically condemns. Unless we take the severe Shaftesburian line on these issues, we can only say this is a poetry of self-delighting self-parody.

The complexity of attitudes we find in such poetry is very Popean indeed: one thinks particularly of Pope's self-parody in the language of the *Rape of the Lock* and the *Epistle to Burlington*. Pope's imitation of the story has, I think, something of the standing in his work that Horace's story has in his: it is significant because it presents in miniature concerns that are more passionately treated in other works. The contrast in tone between this and the *Imitations of*

Epistle I.vi. and *Epistle I.i.* could not be greater. Published between these two intense, complex, and enigmatic works, its major importance lies in treating so lightly themes which are much more seriously considered in other works – retreat, wealth, influence, liberty. In the two full Imitations of 1738, each of these themes is the cause of concern and anxiety; here they are the sources of sophisticated self-parody blending together, delight in miniature with a not very strenuous concern for 'Liberty'.

Read in 1738 Swift's Imitation of Horace's poem of deep longing and deep contentment with this new conclusion must have been for many very nostalgic. If Swift's part of the poem brings alive his relationship with Harley in 1714, the poetry of Pope's conclusion takes us back to the *Rape of the Lock* of the same year. The Tories had been out of power since that very year; Harley had died in 1724; Swift had not been in England since 1727; and Pope had not written in this carefree style for twenty years. To many in March 1738 the publication of this Imitation must have had the effect of returning to a lost world.

INDEPENDENCE

If *Satire* II.vi. could be the source of such nostalgia, Horace's *Epistle* I.vii., a more astringent poem, could not be. As mentioned above, Swift's imitation of the concluding fable was a witty portrayal of his early relationship with Harley. The Horatian story on which Swift's poem is based is a shrewd study of the relationship between an energetic and successful figure and a less ambitious, more easy-going man he decides to patronize and reward with the gift of a farm. The gift means nothing but hard work, ill luck, and failure for Volteius, and in the end, the exhausted and distraught man pleads for what would then seem the impossible – to be returned to his former state of easy contentment.

Pope's Imitation, based on the opening 42 lines of the original, is a study of Horace's assertion of his essential independence in his relationship either with an imaginary 'patron' he didn't have, or with Bolingbroke. But does Pope take Dacier's or Shaftesbury's view of Horace's relationship with Maecenas? Does he stress independence within a relationship which involves mutual understanding, or independence from a figure who can no longer understand his former friend?

> *Quinque dies tibi pollicitus me rure futurum,*
> *Sextilem totum mendax desideror. Atqui*
> *Si me vivere vis sanum recteque valentem,*

> *Quam mihi das aegro, dabis aegrotare timenti,*
> *Maecenas, veniam; dum ficus prima calorque*
> *Designatorem decorat lictoribus atris;*
> *Dum pueris omnis pater & matercula pallet;*
> *Officiosaque sedulitas, & opella forensis*
> *Adducit febres, & testamenta resignat.*
> *Quod si bruma nives Albanis illinet agris,*
> *Ad mare descendet vates tuus, & sibi parcet,*
> *Contractusque leget; te, dulcis amice, reviset*
> *Cum Zephyris, si concedes, & hirundine prima.* (1–13)

(I promised I'd be in the country for just five days; but I broke my word, and you've been missing me all August. But, Maecenas, you do wish me health and strength; you'd excuse me if I were ill: excuse me too when I'm afraid of illness. This is the season of early figs, and sultry heat, and the undertakers with their retinues in black, when every mother and father blanches with fear for their youngsters, when social duties and business chores bring on fevers, and unseal wills.

When winter covers the Alban countryside with layers of snow, your own poet will go down to the sea, take care of himself, wrap up warm, and read. He'll visit you again, dear friend – if you don't mind – with the west winds and the first swallow.)

Horace imagines that he has not kept his promise to join Maecenas in Rome and that Maecenas has complained about this. Horace fully admits his fault – '*mendax*' ('I broke my word') – but rather than give reasons, he asks for indulgence of his fears of illness, which are expressed in terms of engagingly overstated fantasy:

> *... dum ficus prima calorque*
> *Designatorem decorat lictoribus atris ...* (5–6)

(this is the season of early figs, and sultry heat, and the undertakers with their retinues in black)

The hyperboles end with an amusing '*et testamenta resignat*' ('and unseal wills'). After such comic exaggeration the next line looks more promising: '*Quod si bruma nives Albanis illinet agris*' ('When winter covers the Alban countryside with layers of snow'); but Maecenas' expectations are aroused only to have them sharply disappointed:

> *Ad mare descendet vates tuus, & sibi parcet,*
> *Contractusque leget ...* (11–12)

(your own poet will go down to the sea, take care of himself, wrap up warm, and read)

The play of tone here is very enigmatic: Horace is '*vates tuus*' ('your own poet'), but the three verbs announcing his intentions are unambiguous future indicatives. At once, however, Maecenas is called '*dulcis amice*' ('dear friend'), whom Horace announces he will revisit along with the *first* swallow ('*hirundine prima*'). But the '*si concedes*' ('if you don't mind') is somewhat challenging perhaps.

It is the subtlety of the tones, blending together warmth of feeling and boldness of address, that makes this opening arresting. In lines possibly addressed to Bolingbroke Pope imagines himself in Horace's position:

> 'Tis true, my Lord, I gave my word,
> I would be with you, June the third;
> Chang'd it to August, and (in short)
> Have kept it – as you do at Court.
> You humour me when I am sick,
> Why not when I am splenatick?
> In town, what Objects could I meet?
> The shops shut up in every street,
> And Fun'rals black'ning all the Doors,
> And yet more melancholy Whores:
> And what a dust in ev'ry place!
> And a thin Court that wants your Face,
> And Fevers raging up and down,
> And P–x and P* both in town!
>   "The Dog-days are no more the case,"
> "Tis true, but Winter comes apace:
> Then southward let your Bard retire,
> Hold out some months 'twixt Sun and Fire,
> And you shall see, the first warm Weather,
> Me and the Butterflies together.   (1–20)

Horace's enigmatic hyperboles are beautifully re-expressed, in a perfect blend of warmth and detachment:

> And you shall see, the first warm Weather,
> Me and the Butterflies together.   (19–20)

Pope also plays on Bolingbroke's position as a 'Lord': in one sense Bolingbroke is a courtier, hence the joke 'Have kept it – as you do at Court'; but in another sense Bolingbroke is himself most decidedly absent from court circles, and to Pope it is 'a thin Court that wants your Face.' Horace's exaggerated allusion to the anxiety of parents for their children inspires in Pope a nice touch of the macabre:

> And Fun'rals black'ning all the Doors,
> And yet more melancholy Whores ...   (9–10)

Pope's Imitation is clearly an astringent study of his own independence from Bolingbroke seen as Maecenas, and in his imitation of the next passage he makes sardonic remarks on what patrons can be like. Horace, having shown to Maecenas both his affection and his independence, now openly compliments Maecenas on the kind of gifts he gives and the way in which he gives them. The compliment comes in the form of the antithesis to an instance of emotional blackmail, one of Horace's little gems:

> Non quo more pyris vesci Calaber jubet hospes,
> Tu me fecisti locupletem: "Vescere sodes.
> Jam satis est. "At tu quantum vis tolle. Benigne.
> "Non invisa feres pueris munuscula parvis.
> Tam teneor dono quam si dimittar onustus.
> "Ut libet: haec porcis hodie comedenda relinques.
> Prodigus & stultus donat quae spernit & odit:
> Haec seges ingratos tulit, & feret omnibus annis,
> Vir bonus & sapiens dignis ait esse paratus;
> Nec tamen ignorat quid distent aera lupinis.   (14–23)

(When you made me rich, you were not acting like the Calabrian urging a guest to eat his pears. 'Eat them, please.' – 'I've had enough.' – 'Well, take as many as you like.' – 'No thank you.' – 'If you take them they'll make lovely presents for your children.' – 'I'm as grateful as if you'd sent me off with a load of them.' – 'Please yourself: what you leave will go straight to the pigs to eat.' The spendthrift fool bestows on others what he himself despises and rejects: that field has always borne a harvest of ingratitude, and always will. The good and wise man proclaims his readiness to help the worthy; but he also knows the difference between imitation money and the real thing.)

Maecenas has genuinely made Horace rich ('*locupletem*'), and has not sought appreciation by lavishly giving away what he himself despises and dislikes. Pope presents a more searching set of issues here. He compliments Bolingbroke on his capacity to distinguish in his favours between those who are deserving and those who are not but also sees in Horace's story a moral about compliments. On the one hand the compliments of fools never please; on the other, the ingratitude of Fops is just, because an intelligent man cannot himself care for the favours he scatters on such people. Horace's elegant compliment becomes here much more ambiguous, indeed, more attacking:

> My lord, your Favours well I know;
> 'Tis with Distinction you bestow;
> And not to every one that comes,
> Just as a Scotsman does his Plumbs.
> "Pray take them, Sir, – Enough's a Feast:
> "Eat some, and pocket up the rest–'
> What rob your Boys? those pretty rogues!–
> "No Sir, you'll leave them to the *Hogs*."
> Thus Fools with Compliments besiege ye,
> Contriving never to oblige ye.
> Scatter your Favours on a Fop,

> Ingratitude's the certain crop;
> And 'tis but just, I'll tell you wherefore,
> You give the things you never care for.
> A wise man always is or should
> Be mighty ready to do good;
> But makes a diff'rence in his thought
> Betwixt a Guinea and a Groat.   (21–38)

By transferring the line '*Non invisa feres pueris munuscula parvis*' ('If you take them they'll make lovely presents for your children') from the giver to the receiver Pope intensifies the idea that such gifts are worthless:

> What rob your Boys? those pretty rogues!–
> "No Sir, you'll leave them to the *Hogs*."   (27–8)

After complimenting Maecenas in this way Horace assures Maecenas that he will match, in his own way, the fame of Maecenas' good deeds; but at once he implies that if Maecenas asks the impossible, then Horace will ask it too:

> *Dignum praestabo me etiam pro laude merentis.*
> *Quod si me noles usquam discedere, reddes*
> *Forte latus, nigros angusta fronte capillos,*
> *Reddes dulce loqui; reddes ridere decorum, &*
> *Inter vina fugam Cynarae maerere protervae.*   (24–8)

(I shall show myself worthy, as my benefactor's generosity demands. But if you want me never to leave you, you'll have to give me back a sound chest, black hair, a low brow; give me back pleasant talk, innocent merriment, and drowning my sorrows at wanton Cynara's desertion.)

Horace not only reminds Maecenas of his age and loss of powers; he also poignantly alludes to that time of youth when one can indeed be wholly involved with others, and he remembers the pleasures and the sadnesses that such complete involvement brings. The repetition of '*reddes … Reddes … reddes*' ('you'll have to give back') wistfully emphasizes Horace's memory of those past experiences and the loss of being their loss involves:

> *Non sum qualis eram, bonae*
> *Sub regno Cynarae …*   (*Ode* IV.i. 3–4)

(I am not the man I was under the rule of good Cynara)

Pope here emphasizes not the gratitude for great gifts, but his own virtues as a frank and candid companion; and in a wry allusion to his physical weakness and illness, suggests that if Bolingbroke wants to have him constantly present, he would be well advised to return to him the health and charm he used to have as a younger man and the poet, indeed, of the *Rape of the Lock*:

> Now this I'll say, you'll find in me
> A safe Companion, and a free;
> But if you'd have me always near –
> A word, pray, in your Honour's ear.
> I hope it is your Resolution
> To give me back my Constitution!
> The sprightly Wit, the lively Eye,
> Th'engaging Smile, the Gaiety,
> That laugh'd down many a Summer's Sun,
> And kept you up so oft till one;
> And all the voluntary Vein,
> As when Belinda rais'd my Strain.   (39–50)

With a fresh start Horace tells another fable with an obvious moral, and Pope follows suit:

> *Forte per angustam tenuis nitedula rimam*
> *Repserat in cumeram frumenti; pastaque rursus*
> *Ire foras pleno tendebat corpore frustra:*
> *Cui mustela procul, Si vis, ait effugere istinc,*
> *Macra cavum repetes arctum, quem macra subisti.*   (29–33)

(A thin dormouse had once squeezed through a narrow crack into a cornbin. He ate his fill, then tried to get back out with his belly full – without success. A weasel came up to him and said, 'If you want to get out of there, you'll have to be lean enough to return through the crevice you were lean enough to enter by.')

> A Weasel once made shift to slink
> In at a Corn-loft thro' a Chink;
> But having amply stuff'd his skin,
> Cou'd not get out as he got in:
> Which one belonging to the House
> ('Twas not a Man, it was a Mouse)
> Observing, cry'd, "You scape not so,
> "Lean as you came, Sir, you must go."   (51–8)

But Horace's story is, we see at once, preparation for his clearest and strongest statement of his position in the lines that Shaftesbury found so compelling:

> *Haec ego si compellor imagine, cuncta resigno:*
> *Nec somnum plebis laudo, satur altilium, nec*
> *Otia divitiis Arabum liberrima muto.*
> *Saepe verecundum laudâsti; rexque paterque*
> *Audisti coram; nec verbo parcius absens:*
> *Inspice si possum donata reponere laetus.*
>   . . .
> *Parvum parva decent: mihi jam non regia Roma,*

Sed vacuum Tibur placet, aut imbelle Tarentum.
Strenuus & fortis rebusque Philippus agendis, & c.   (34–42)

(If you apply the parable to my case, I renounce everything. I don't praise the poor man's sleep when I've stuffed myself with capons; nor would I exchange perfect peace for the riches of Arabia. You've often praised my modesty. I've called you 'lord and master' to your face – and I'm no less fulsome in your absence. See if I can lay down your gifts, and be content.

...

Little things suit little men: what I enjoy nowadays is not the might of Rome, but the quiet of Tibur, or the peacefulness of Tarentum. That tireless, energetic barrister Philippus, etc.)

Horace states twice in unequivocal terms that he is prepared to return all that Maecenas has given him: '*Haec ego si compellor imagine, cuncta resigno*' ('If you apply the parable to my case, I renounce everything'). One assertion, indeed, is in the form of a bold challenge: '*Inspice si possum donata reponere laetus*' ('See if I can lay down your gifts, and be content'). The asterisks in the Horatian text show that Pope has left out four lines praising Telemachus for his polite but forceful reply to Menelaus, refusing the gift of horses and a chariot on the grounds that rugged Ithaca is not suitable for them. This leads to Horace's cryptic assertion '*Parvum parva decent*' ('Little things suit little men'); and his concluding point that at his time of life his delight is not in queenly Rome ('*regia Roma*') but quiet Tiber ('*vacuum Tibur*') or 'peaceful Tarentum' ('*imbelle Tarentum*'). In the complete Horatian poem the story of Philippus and Volteius follows directly.

As Shaftesbury asserts, therefore, Horace sees in the story of the dormouse something of himself; Pope refuses to accept any such suggestion.[2] In a powerful contrast he insists that he is, on the contrary, 'indebted to no Prince or Peer alive' (*Imitation of Epistle II.ii.*, 69):

> Sir, you may spare your Application
> I'm no such Beast, nor his Relation;
> Nor one that Temperance advance,
> Cramm'd to the throat with Ortolans:
> Extremely ready to resign
> All that may make me none of mine.
> South-sea Subscriptions take who please,
> Leave me but Liberty and Ease.
> 'Twas what I said to Craggs and Child,
> Who prais'd my Modesty, and smil'd.
> Give me, I cry'd, (enough for me)
> My Bread, and Independency!
> So bought an Annual Rent or two.
> And liv'd – just as you see I do;

> Near fifty, and without a Wife,
> I trust that sinking Fund, my Life.
> Can I retrench? Yes, mighty well,
> Shrink back to my Paternal Cell,
> A little House, with Trees a-row,
> And like its Master, very low,
> There dy'd my Father, no man's Debtor,
> And there I'll die, nor worse nor better.
>   To set this matter full before you,
> Our old Friend Swift will tell his Story.
> "Harley, the Nation's great Support,"–
> But you may read it, I stop short.   (59–84)

Horace says that he would not 'exchange perfect peace for the riches of Arabia' (*'nec / Otia divitiis Arabum liberrima muto'*); and Pope remembers his own indifference to the South-sea subscriptions Craggs gave to him:

> South-sea Subscriptions take who please,
> Leave me but Liberty and Ease.
> 'Twas what I said to Craggs and Child,
> Who prais'd my Modesty, and smil'd.   (65–8)

But Horace remembers proudly that Maecenas has often praised his moderation (*'verecundum'*); to Craggs and Child Pope's indifference to wealth was evidently rather eccentrically naive. Pope's situation is not quite Horace's: the only financial security Pope has is what he calls, with dry irony, 'that sinking Fund, my Life'. Horace has called Maecenas *'rexque paterque'* ('lord and master'); this reminds Pope of his *real* father, the truest image of himself. He will have to 'Shrink' to his 'Paternal Cell', the symbol, however, of a quite appropriate place in which to die. Horace's *'Parvum parva decent'* ('Little things suit little men') was obviously written with Pope in mind:

> A little House, with Trees a-row,
> And like its Master, very low ...   (77–8)

but in that place of miniatures Pope experiences humility before death, tragic loneliness, and heroic self-absorption. Writing to Ralph Allen on 2 August 1739, about the 'Vanities' of having his garden improved with paths and ornaments, Pope said: 'Indeed I think all my Vanities of this sort are at an end; & I will excuse them to the Connoisseurs by setting over my door, in conclusion of them, *Parvum Parva decent*' (*Corr.* IV, p. 191).

Short though it is, this Imitation is arresting: to imitate Horace's poem at all shows a willingness to recognise the difficulties and problems Horace himself sees as being inherent in the 'Horace/

Maecenas' relationship. There has always been a tendency to senti-mentalize that famous relationship. Swift in his version of the end of the epistle, and Pope in his imitation of the beginning show the strains and difficulties of this type of friendship. In doing so they, like Horace himself, make the 'Horace/Maecenas' relationship into a living symbol, full of suggestion and possibility, rather than a static image of perfection. But Pope's treatment of both the 'Horace/ Maecenas' relationship and his own independence is much more astringent and intense than Swift's. In Pope's address to his 'patron', and in his lines on his lonely life, we find some of the power and idealism that Shaftesbury saw in these poems. For that reason we must see this poem in relation to Pope's last major Imitation, *The Imitation of Epistle I.i.* There we find Pope writing directly to Bolingbroke as Maecenas yet again, and there we find Pope wrestling again with the problems of idealism and scepticism, isolation and involvement.

11

The Stoic self:
The Imitation of Epistle I.i.

My poetical affairs drawing toward a fair period, I hope the day will shortly come when I may honestly say
>   Nunc versus et caetera ludicra pono,
>   Quid *verum* atque *decens*, curo et rogo et omnis in hoc sum.

That *caetera ludicra* is very comprehensive: it includes visiting, masquerading, play-hanting [*sic*], sauntering, and indeed almost includes all that the world calls living.

Pope to Caryll, 4 February 1718

POPE'S *Imitation of Epistle I.i.*, addressed to Bolingbroke, is an extremely paradoxical poem. From one point of view this is a very public poem, a vigorous and daring attack on the city and the court, written at a time of mounting political tension, and boldly addressed to Bolingbroke as the government's long-standing enemy. In March 1738, when the poem was published, Bolingbroke was in retirement in France, but due back in England imminently. There were even suggestions that at this critical juncture, he should again be the leader of the Tories. To address a poem to Bolingbroke at this time was indeed 'a calculated affront' (Mack, 1969, p. 168), and taken as such by the government newspapers (*TE*, IV, p. xxxviii–ix). But from another point of view this is a very personal work, a poem about retirement in which Pope speaks to Bolingbroke as his close friend about his own inner spiritual yearnings, weaknesses, and failures.

Criticism of this Imitation has tended to emphasize one side or other of this paradox, whereas what really seems important is the paradox itself, and confirmation for this comes from the fact that the whole Horatian epistle is built around just these tensions. At the simplest level they provide the basic structure of the Horatian poem: Horace begins by talking about himself, moves to satire on Roman society, but ends by talking about himself again. More subtly, however, we can see that the epistle is actually an exploration of the relationship between himself and his society. Indeed we can say that this poem springs from something deep in the Horace of the first book of epistles – his capacity to see himself imaginatively in relation to other people.

Addressing Maecenas at the beginning of the epistle he speaks of the desire which has newly grown in him to attend to what is truly right and fitting in life (*'Quid* verum *atque* decens'), and makes us feel that such thoughts will eventually come to every thinking person. But at once he insists he does not follow any particular school of philosophy; and then he goes on to show that his attempt to know himself and attend to his true needs in fact sets him apart from most of his contemporaries. Their whole attitude to life is different: they rush frantically to India to flee poverty, build larger and larger fortunes, are carried by sheer whim from one fashionable resort to another in a maze of inconsistencies, while he stands back, asking if these desperate attempts to achieve fulfilment will really satisfy their needs. Yet after ridiculing others for their insanity, Horace then identifies himself with everyone else, and with challenging irony admits his own inconsistencies and his own inner discontent. At the end of the epistle we have an engaging picture of Horace as much in need of his own wisdom as everyone else; and for this he chastises Maecenas, claiming that he should help his friend to escape from the folly of such contradictions. But in the very last lines Horace changes tack again, and, with a lively pun ridiculing the extreme claims of Stoic idealism, ends his epistle on a note of buoyant confidence in himself and his own, very individual, moral vision.

Modern interpretations of this Horatian poem tend to stress the fine blend of confidence and scepticism achieved in this subtle structure which itself can be seen as a reflection of Horace's distinctive moral vision. They note that while this moral earnestness is crucial to the poem, it is tempered throughout by a wry scepticism about the actual possibilities of moral achievement: Horace is careful not to make too many claims for the lasting effect of the high ideals to which he is drawn himself and advocates for everyone else. They emphasize the importance of Horace's eclecticism in philosophy as set out in lines 13–19 (*'Nullius addictus jurare in verba Magistri'*, 'I have sworn an oath of allegiance to no master'), and the positive strength of Horace's admission of his own failings at the end of the poem (see, for example, Fraenkel, 1957, pp. 255, and 308–9, and Brower, 1959, pp. 178–9). These critics concentrate on the questioning character of Horace's poem, and Horace's confident wit and irony as he satirizes the extravagant claims of the strict philosophical schools, his own moral pretensions, and his own moral failings.

And yet we might say that with this poem Horace quite consciously makes us think again about the strengths and potential weaknesses of his famous eclecticism and of his free and flexible

poetic forms which can hold together so happily such radical inconsistencies. We might feel that here he studies with alarm the depth of
his inner contradictions, and explores with concern the uncertain
nature of himself. If Horace can see the weakness in his contemporaries he can also see them with unnerving clarity in himself. Is the
self capable of unity, or is the self only contradiction? Is Horace's
relationship with himself and his society more complex in this
respect than it may seem? Eighteenth-century readings of this poem
offer different views on these questions, and help us look afresh at
Pope's Imitation.

DACIER, SHAFTESBURY, GEORGE OGLE

Dacier, like many Renaissance and seventeenth-century commentators, gives Horace's *Epistle* i.i. a special place in his commentary, for
its moral teaching about the value of virtue and for Horace's
expression of his own desire to attend to the moral life. Furthermore,
as we would expect, Dacier sees this work very much in autobiographical terms. Whereas G. Williams uses the opening of this
poem to introduce his study of the 'problems and difficulties' of the
autobiographical interpretation of Latin literature (1968, pp. 1–7),
Dacier takes the poem literally as evidence of a significant change in
Horace's whole approach to his life and to himself: 'Il luy dit donc
qu'à l'âge où il est, ces vains amusemens qui l'ont occupé pendant ses
jeunes années, ont fait place à des soins plus utiles & plus pressons,
qu'il n'a plus d'amour que pour la Philosophie, qui seule peut luy
enseigner la verité, & former ses moeurs' (Dacier, VIII, p. 22).

Even more important, however, is Dacier's interpretation of the
nature of that change, for, as Maresca has noted, Dacier unquestionably stresses the spiritual character of the wisdom or philosophy
which Horace claims to be seeking in this poem (1966, pp. 151–93).
Throughout his commentary Dacier refers to the needs of the soul
('l'ame') rather than the mind, and he interprets Horace's metaphors
of cultivation and purgation repeatedly in terms of spiritual purifi-
cation: 'Quand nostre ame est purgée & dégagée de toutes les
passions' (Dacier, VIII, p. 35) and 'Et cela convient fort bien à la
Philosophie, qui redonne la vie à l'ame en la purgeant de ses vices'
(p. 63). It would be a mistake, however, to see this simply in
Christian terms: in fact Dacier appeals to a wide range of Socratic,
Platonic, Stoic, Old Testament, and New Testament thought to
explain what this spiritual cultivation means, and for Dacier the
classical traditions are just as important as the Christian traditions.

This stress on spiritual needs affects the way in which Dacier responds to the poem's satire. Whereas we might think of the poem's central section simply in terms of a powerful attack on avarice and amused ridicule of inconsistency, Dacier sees that avarice as a perverted form of ambition and that inconsistency as evidence of a profound spiritual disorder. Indeed, comparing this first epistle with Horace's first satire, he asserts that Horace is here exploring the relationship between the themes of that satire, avarice and inconsistency, and this new theme of ambition:

Il ne faut pas oublier une chose qui me paroist tres remarquable; c'est que cette premiere Epistre répond directement à la premiere Satire, où il a aussi traité de l'inconstance & de l'avarice. Icy il ajoûte à ces deux déreglemens de l'ame celuy de l'ambition, parce qu'à le bien prendre l'ambition n'est qu'une branche de l'inconstance, & qu'une espece d'avarice plus rafinée que l'avarice ordinaire.

(Dacier, VIII, p. 24)

All this helps us to understand Dacier's emphasis on the isolated position of the 'le Sage' in his society. Commenting on Horace's description of the differences between his attitudes to life and those of his fellow Romans (lines 70–80, complete text), Dacier stresses that the wise man is completely detached from both the ordinary people and its government. He admires neither riches nor honours and, like Socrates, is deeply suspicious of kings and princes (Dacier, pp. 92–4). As we shall see, Dacier's explicitly political interpretation of the story of the fox and the lion is very significant in this respect. Here Shaftesbury's 'third period' Horace and Dacier's Horace come together, and, of course, produce just the opposite of Weinbrot's court sycophant. Thus, whereas modern critics tend to stress Horace's common humanity Dacier emphasises his aloof detachment.

Finally Dacier emphasizes throughout the moral confidence of this Horace and this Horatian epistle. He plays down the poem's general spirit of inquiry and he does not concentrate on Horace's admission of his own inconsistency and inner confusion in the final passage. On the contrary, Dacier presents the poem as one written from a position of moral conviction and moral authority. Final evidence of this, indeed, is what Dacier sees as Horace's clear stand on Stoicism throughout the poem: Dacier stresses far more than modern editors the strongly Stoical tenor of Horace's moral idealism in this poem, quoting, to support this interpretation, Epictetus and Cicero, among others (see, for example, pp. 63–9 and 119–22). But at the same time he emphasizes Horace's basic eclecticism and his firm detachment from the excesses of Stoic philosophy. Dacier notes this in his prefatory remarks (p. 24) and, as we shall see, regards Horace's final joke as proof of Horace's fundamental independence.

Next to Dacier's reading we can place two others, those of Shaftesbury which in some ways is similar to Dacier's, and that of George Ogle which seems to offer a striking contrast to both. Shaftesbury, of course, sees the poem as yet another expression of Horace's resolve to leave Maecenas and the 'Court' of Augustus so that he can 'study quietly for his mind's sake': 'Here you will see his struggle and hard labour to get clear of Court pleasures' (Shaftesbury, 1900, pp. 364–5). As we shall see he interprets the story of the lion and fox specifically in terms of court corruption. It is striking, here, that Shaftesbury asserts that Horace was now fully committed again to the 'rigid philosophy' of 'the old Socratic academy' but disguises it with raillery. With Horace's famous passage on his eclecticism in mind, presumably, he asks Pierre Coste 'to see how artfully Horace (as in his first epistle of Bk. 1.) covers his rigid philosophy, which ere this he in reality was returned to, but would give it an air of raillery' (Shaftesbury, 1900, p. 364). Finally, it is likely that Shaftesbury would have found Horace's criticism of Maecenas at the end of this epistle very significant, indicative of Maecenas' concern for the superficial but not the essential self.

George Ogle's Imitation of this poem, which was published in 1735, and which Pope presumably would have known is, however, much more arresting. It is done in his usual style, generally expanding the original and turning it into sententious rhetoric; but it is interesting for three reasons. First, in his imitation of Horace's eclecticism passage he turns Horace's contrast between the Stoic and Cyrenaic schools of philosophy into a contrast between, on the one hand, Shaftesbury himself and, on the other, Mandeville. Shaftesbury as 'Philocles' represents the Stoic life, encouraging both the thoughtful exploration of philosophical certainties ('The golden Mines of *Order* to explore', p. 7) and the active life which requires selfless devotion to all that Shaftesbury means by 'Virtue':

> The rigid Post, the hard Defence I take;
> For *Virtue* I contend, for *Virtue*'s Sake.   (p. 8)

Horace's Aristippus becomes the Mandeville or 'the Fabled Hind' who doubts the nature of the self, refuses to accept that instincts and emotions are intrinsically moral, and questions the distinction between 'Virtue' and 'Vice':

> Of *Self* I doubt; if well or ill defin'd?
> If *Free* and *Sordid* share one common Mind?
> If from one *Seed* both *Love* and *Hatred* came?
> And differ, *Vice* and *Virtue* but in Name?   (p. 8)

Ogle, of course, is alluding to the whole debate between Shaftesbury's moral idealism and Mandeville's moral scepticism, to which Mandeville himself contributed in 'A Search into the Nature of Society' (Mandeville, 1728, pp. 371–428). The power of Ogle's contrast lies in the fact that if Shaftesbury could appropriate Horace, then Mandeville could have done so as well, for Ogle could well have had in mind those famous Horatian passages which raise just such searching questions:

> ... *utrumne*
> *Divitiis homines, an sint virtute beati:*
> *Quidve ad amicitias, usus rectumne trahat nos?*
> *Et quae sit natura boni, summumque quid ejus?*
> (*Satire* II.vi. 73–6; Pope's Latin text which presents
> these lines as questions)

(... whether wealth or virtue makes men happy; does expediency or 'right' draw us to friendship? And what is the nature of the 'good' and what is its highest form?)

Pope's own imitation of these lines emphasizes the genuinely questioning nature of such Horatian inquiry:

> Which is the happier, or the wiser,
> A Man of Merit, or a Miser?
> Whether we ought to chuse our Friends,
> For their own Worth, or our own Ends?
> What good, or better, we may call,
> And what, the very best of all?
> (*Imitation of Satire II.vi.* 147–52)

The Mandevillian view of the immoral self would, of course, be in accord with the egotistical and corrupt view of the self and society we found in Pope's *Sober Advice*. These passages can also be compared with Ogle's powerful Imitation of Horace's *Satire* II.v., in which he uses Horace's satire on legacy hunting to attack that same sordid form of money-making in the England of his time; *Of Legacy-Hunting. The Fifth Satire of the Second Book of Horace Imitated. A Dialogue between Sir Walter Raleigh, and Merlin the Prophet* (1737).

The second point of interest is that in his imitation of Horace's passage on the Roman people Ogle expands Horace's satire on materialism into an intense rhetorical attack on the pursuit of gold in his own society. His poem becomes here a powerful study of public corruption, and the passage deserves careful comparison with Pope's, as we shall see. Third, Ogle concludes his Imitation with a greatly expanded, though not very successful, version of Horace's sketch of the Stoic man. Weak though it is, the passage represents an attempt to conclude the Imitation with a full study of what that Stoic man might actually be like.

Seen in this eighteenth-century context Pope's *Imitation of Epistle I.i.* seems to raise a group of fundamental problems. We will need to consider how far Pope emulated the Horatian poem which Dacier offered him with its strong spiritual vision, and how far he deliberately turned away from that interpretation to give the Imitation a strong political character. Relevant here is the question of whether Pope's Imitation is a powerful expression of personal moral confidence or an expression of Pope's inner doubt and uncertainty at this time of tension. Does Pope's poem assume Shaftesbury's view that there is an order in the self which can be expressed in the inner harmony of the poem, or does it betray doubts about such an order which would be expressed in tensions and ambiguities, the doubts of a Mandeville? Finally, we must consider Pope's attitude to the Stoicism in this poem, particularly his exploration of inconsistency and what it reveals about the nature of the self.

HORATIAN RETREAT

The first third of this Imitation is about Horatian retreat, and here we see Pope emulating Horace's famous resolve to give up poetry in order to attend to philosophy, and, by implication, to the needs of the self. What is so striking in Pope's Imitation, however, is the tension between spiritual longing and involvement in the world. This seems to involve a very fine appreciation of the Horatian text: Pope is alive to Dacier's philosophical and religious reading of Horace's text, but is at the same time highly responsive to the subtleties of feeling and nuances of tone in the Horatian play of wit and irony. To appreciate these passages fully we must see the distinctively Horatian idea of self-discovery blending with the Christian ideal of inner spiritual wisdom in the context of the England of 1738.

> *Prima dicte mihi, summâ dicende Camenâ!*
> [2]*Spectatum satis, & donatum jam rude, quaeris*
> *(Maecenas) iterum antiquo me includere ludo?*
> *Non eadem est aetas, non mens.* [3]*Vejanius Armis*
> [4]*Herculis ad postem fixis, latet abditus agro,*
> *Ne populum* [5]*extremâ, toties, exoret arenâ.*
> [6]*Est mihi, purgatam crebro qui personet aurem;*
> *"Solve* [7]*senescentem mature sanus equum, ne*
> *"Peccet ad extremum ridendus, & ilia ducat."*

Nunc itaque, & ⁸Versus & caetera ludicra *pono,*
Quid ⁹verum atque decens, *curo & rogo,* & omnis *in hoc sum.*
¹⁰Condo & compono quae mox *depromere possim.*   (1–12)

(Maecenas – I praised you in my first poetry and I must praise you now in my last
– I've won distinction enough in the ring, they've presented me with the dummy
sword; are you trying to confine me again in the old training-camp? I'm an older
man; my heart's not in it. Veianius has nailed his gear to the doorpost of
Hercules' temple, and hidden himself in the depths of the country, rather than,
again and again, beg the crowd for mercy at the arena's edge.

One there is who speaks loud and clear in my receptive ear: 'Be wise in time,
and turn loose the ageing horse before it's too late, or else in the end he'll collapse,
a laughing-stock, flanks heaving.'

So now I am putting aside poetry and suchlike trifles: I ponder and meditate
Truth and Right and this claims all my thought. I am putting aside and stowing
away stores I can draw on by and by.)

This is the quintessential Horatian poetry of Horace's first book of
epistles, notable for the depth of its concerns and its subtle play of
tone and irony. Horace begins by telling Maecenas, his patron, he
cannot write any more poems for the time has come for him to think
about himself. The first line is impressively phrased: '*Prima ...
summâ*' ('first ... last'), '*dicte ... dicende*' ('I praised ... I must
praise'); '*Camenâ*' (a spring goddess) for the Muse is a poetic touch;
and the vocative '*(Maecenas)*' is respectfully and impressively
delayed until the third line. In one simple, haunting statement
Horace describes his condition '*Non eadem est aetas, non mens*'
('I'm an older man; my heart's not in it'). But there is dry irony in the
sustained comparison with the old gladiator Veianius who has had
the sense to leave the arena so as not to have to plead with the crowd
again and again ('*toties*'). After this Horace's self-deprecation
becomes more overt: the inner voice is amusingly insistent and loud
('*personet*' – 'speaks loud and clear'), and Horace as an ageing horse
bursting his wind is comic but also pathetic. But then Horace's tone
shifts again as he makes his central assertion, that he now intends to
study '*Quid* verum *atque* decens' ('Truth and Right'). If the 'caetera
ludicra' ('such like trifles') is amusing, the 'omnis *in hoc sum*' ('this
claims all my thought') suggests how absorbed Horace is in this
pursuit; and by using pairs of verbs he takes us deeply into that very
activity of thought: '*curo & rogo*' ('I ponder and meditate'), '*Condo
& compono*' ('I am putting aside and stowing away'). The metaphors are from harvesting – storing and arranging for future use.[1]

Some of Dacier's comments on these lines will show how he
interprets this type of poetry in terms which are both classical and
Christian. He asserts that the voice Horace hears is a divine inspiration: 'Horace imite icy les manieres de Socrate, qui dit dans le

Theagés, que par une grace particuliere des Dieux il avoit toûjours avec luy un genie qui l'accompagnoit depuis son enfance: que ce genie estoit une voix divine' (Dacier, VIII, p. 32). On 'Nunc itaque, & Versus' he comments: 'Voilà une obeïssance bien prompte, & c'est l'effect & la suite du mot *purgatam aurem*. Quand nostre ame est purgée & dégagée de toutes les passions, & que rien ne l'empesche d'estre penetrée des avis salutaires qu'on nous donne, elle obeït sans hesiter' (p. 35). He explains 'verum' by alluding to Plato's view of truth in the *Republic*, 'decens' by referring to Cicero's *Offices*, and the phrase 'omnis in hoc sum' by referring again to Socrates: 'C'est à cela que toute la vie de Socrate a esté uniquement occupée' (pp. 35–7).

In Pope's Imitation we find something quite different, but which all the same draws upon and blends all these Horatian tones and all these possibilities of meaning. In March 1738 Bolingbroke was in France but due back in England imminently, and Pope was almost fifty.

> ST JOHN, whose love indulg'd my labours past
> Matures my present, and shall bound my last!
> Why [2]will you break the Sabbath of my days?
> Now sick alike of Envy and of Praise.
> Publick too long, ah let me hide my Age!
> See modest [3]Cibber now has left the Stage:
> Our Gen'rals now, [4]retir'd to their Estates,
> Hang their old Trophies o'er the Garden gates,
> In Life's cool evening satiate of applause,
> Nor [5]fond of bleeding, ev'n in BRUNSWICK's cause.
>   [6]A Voice there is, that whispers in my ear,
> ('Tis Reason's voice, which sometimes one can hear)
> 'Friend Pope! be prudent, let your [7]Muse take breath;
> 'And never gallop Pegasus to death;
> 'Lest stiff, and stately, void of fire, or force,
> 'You limp, like Blackmore, on a Lord Mayor's horse.'
>   Farewell then [8]Verse, and Love, and ev'ry Toy,
> The rhymes and rattles of the Man or Boy:
> What [9]right, what true, what fit, we justly call,
> Let this be all my care – for this is All:
> To lay this [10]harvest up, and hoard with haste
> What ev'ry day will want, and most, the last.   (1–22)

We seem to be here in another world of poetry and feeling. In the address to Bolingbroke the formality of Horace's opening line is carefully re-created, though 'St John' comes impressively first. Horace's '*Non eadem est aetas, non mens*' ('I'm an older man; my heart's not in it') now carries haunting religious overtones:

> Why will you break the Sabbath of my days?
> Now sick alike of Envy and of Praise,
> Publick too long, ah let me hide my age!   (3–5)

But to balance this there is a superb touch of dry irony: 'See modest Cibber now has left the stage.' Cibber had officially retired from the theatre four years before, but unlike Horace's gladiator kept returning periodically for the next eleven years. The *brevitas* is Horatian, and the calm surface of the poetry unruffled. Developing Horace's '*latet abditus agro*' ('he has hidden himself in the depths of the country'), Pope speaks of Peterborough's retirement at Southampton, and this is given depth by the fact that Peterborough had in fact been dead for three years. Even the final political note is nicely subdued; 'Nor fond of bleeding, ev'n in BRUNSWICK's cause'. Originally it was the even finer 'Br – s', which could have been simply 'Britain's'.

The relationship between depth of feeling and ironic wit here is beautifully Horatian, but what follows is more Horatian than Horace himself. Horace says his inner voice pesters him; Dacier claims this is a divine inspiration; in Pope there is a much subtler self-deprecating irony:

> A Voice there is, that whispers in my ear,
> ('Tis Reason's voice, which sometimes one can hear) ... (11–12)

For '*personet*' ('speaks loud and clear') there is 'whispers', and for '*purgatam ... aurem*' ('receptive ear') the sardonic 'which sometimes one can hear.' For a moment Pope moves into the contemporary world with sarcastic allusions to Blackmore and the Lord Mayor's horse. But at once he takes us into another realm of thought with a fine version of Horace's famous resolve. If that 'caetera ludicra' 'almost includes all that the world calls living' then here we have it: 'Farewell then Verse, and Love, and ev'ry Toy.' Dwelling deeply on the 'omnis' of Horace's '& omnis *in hoc sum*', Pope makes us remember not only Horace and Socrates, but St Paul: 'whatsoever things are true, whatsoever things are honest, whatsoever things are just ... think on these things (*Philippians* 4.8; quoted Maresca, 1966, p. 176).

> What right, what true, what fit, we justly call,
> Let this be all my care – for this is All.   (19–20)

Significantly Pope ends by changing Horace's wisdom stored away to be used some day ('mox') to spiritual strength that will be needed most at death: 'What ev'ry day will want, and most, the last.'

Having stated that he has turned from poetry to philosophy, Horace now makes his important point that he is not bound to any one school. In the subtlest modulations of tone, he shows us what it means to be one man who can adopt two very different roles:

> *Ac ne forte roges,* [11]*quo me duce, quo* Lare *tuter?*
> *Nullius addictus jurare in verba Magistri,*
> [12]*Quo me cunque rapit tempestas, deferor* Hospes.
> *Nunc* agilis *fio, & mersor* [13]*civilibus undis,*
> *Virtutis verae Custos,* [14]*rigidusque satelles.*
> *Nunc in Aristippi* [15]*furtim praecepta relabor*
> *Et mihi res, non me rebus, submittere conor.* (13–19)

(In case you ask, who is my leader, under whose roof I shelter, I have sworn an oath of allegiance to no master: wherever the storm drives me, I seek hospitality. Sometimes the man of action, I plunge into the waves of public life, true Virtue's champion, her unbending servant. Sometimes I slink back furtively to the teachings of Aristippus, and attempt to subject the world to me, not myself to the world.)

Horace is sometimes a vigorous Stoic, active in the world ('*Nunc agilis fio, & mersor* civilibus undis'), a rigid follower of virtue ('*Virtutis verae Custos,* rigidusque satelles'); but then he slips back ('relabor') secretly ('furtim') to join the quite different Aristippus who believed momentary pleasure to be the highest good, and accepted a little more flexibility ('*Et mihi res, non me rebus, submittere conor*' – 'attempt to subject the world to me, not myself to the world').[2]

Pope's version of these lines is fascinating: whereas Shaftesbury asserts that Horace is really only a Stoic, Pope finds a whole host of contradictory commitments; whereas Horace moves with eloquent ease between his two positions, Pope presents a far more complex series and moves between a whole range of possibilities:

> But ask not, to what [11]Doctors I apply?
> Sworn to no Master, of no Sect am I:
> As drives the [12]storm, at any door I knock,
> And house with Montagne now, or now with Lock.
> Sometimes a [13]Patriot, active in debate,
> Mix with the World, and battle for the State,
> Free as young Lyttelton, her cause pursue,
> Still true to Virtue, [14]and as warm as true:
> Sometimes, with Aristippus, or St. Paul,
> Indulge my Candor, and grow all to all;
> Back to my [15]native Moderation slide,
> And win my way by yielding to the tyde. (23–34)

This can be interpreted in many different ways: Pope is sometimes a rigid thinker (Locke), sometimes a loose thinker (Montaigne); sometimes a politically committed Opposition 'Patriot'; sometimes utterly impartial ('all to all'); sometimes a moderate yielding to the tide. But for Pope *each* position is double-edged: for Horace '*Virtutis verae Custos,* rigidusque satelles' ('true Virtue's champion, her

unbending servant') is enough; Pope demands even more, 'Still true
to Virtue, and as warm as true.' For Aristippus, Pope looks through
Horace to Horace's *Epistle* I.xvii.23: 'omnis Aristippum decuit color
et status et res' ('To Aristippus every form of life was fitting, every
condition and circumstance'). To blend that social sophistication
with St Paul's earnest 'Even as I please all men in all things ... that
they may be saved' (1 *Cor.* 10.33) was deeply contradictory, and to
some very offensive (see Pope, *Works*, ed. Warton, 1822, IV, p. 109).
Was this not the language suitable for a Wharton himself?

> Grown all to all, from no one vice exempt,
> And most contemptible, to shun contempt ...
>
> (*Epistle to Cobham*, 194–5)

How significant that Pope's last line completely reverses Horace's 'I
attempt to subject the world to me, not myself to the world': 'And
win my way by yielding to the tyde.' Do we find here some of the
tensions between the idealist and the sceptic, and found in the
Horace itself when underlined by Ogle? It is significant that the
writer of *Horace to Scaeva. Epist. XVII. Book I. Imitated* (1730)
used Horace's passages about Aristippus to satirize the relationship
between changes of ecclesiastical dress and changes of moral position (pp. 22–6).

But if this seems to point to sceptical, worldly Horace, the next
passages completely reverse that impression. Nowhere in all the
poetry of Pope's *Imitations* do we feel we are so close to Shaftesbury's Horace, not the Horace who has achieved wisdom, but the
inward Horace who yearns so deeply to know his true self, that
private self as yet undiscovered:

> [16]*Ut nox longa quibus mentitur amica, diesque*
> *Longa videtur* opus debentibus, *ut piger annus*
> *Pupillis, quos dura premit custodia matrum:*
> *Sic mihi tarda* [17]*fluunt* ingrataque *tempora, quae spem*
> *Consiliumque* morantur *agendi gnaviter* [18]*id, quod*
> *Aeque* pauperibus *prodest,* locupletibus *aeque,*
> *Aeque neglectum* pueris, senibusque *nocebit.*   (20–6)

(As the night is long to the man whose mistress plays him false, and the day long
to men obliged to toil, and the year lags for wards oppressed by mothers' harsh
control: just as sluggish and irksome are any passing hours that defer my hope
and firm intent, strenuous application to that work which brings equal profit to
poor and rich, and neglect of which will injure young and old alike.)

> [16]Long, as to him who works for debt, the Day;
> Long as the Night to her whose love's away;
> Long as the Year's dull circle seems to run,
> When the brisk Minor pants for twenty-one;

> So slow th' [17]unprofitable Moments roll,
> That lock up all the Functions of my soul;
> That keep me from Myself; and still delay
> Life's instant business to a future day:
> That [18]task, which as we follow, or despise,
> The eldest is a fool, the youngest wise;
> Which done, the poorest can no wants endure,
> And which not done, the richest must be poor. (35–46)

Pope here recreates the long, slow rhythm of Horace's lines, with their touches of wit and pathos. He calmly echoes Horace's movement from '*nox*' to '*dies*' to '*annus*', and sympathetically gives prominence to the man whose work is an obligation ('opus debentibus' – 'men obliged to toil'). But the key lies in his rendering of '*Sic mihi tarda fluunt* ingrataque *tempora*' ('just as sluggish and irksome are any passing hours'):

> So slow th'unprofitable Moments roll,
> That lock up all the Functions of my soul;
> That keep me from Myself ...   (39–41)

This gives sudden depth to the passage, and is at once perfectly Horatian and beyond 'Horace'. Horace is of course *the* poet of those moments and those places in which we sense a return to ourselves: '*Vilice silvarum et mihi me reddentis agelli*', *Epistle* I.xiv.I. ('Bailiff of my woods and of the little farm which makes me my self again'). But for Pope that self seems entirely different from the self that is active in the world and in those moments which 'lock up all the Functions of my soul': it is something else, unknown. Pope's version of Horace's final lines is thoughtful and pointed, echoing Horace's careful turning on words ('*Aeque* pauperibus *prodest*, locupletibus *aeque*' – 'which brings equal profit to poor and rich') with its repeated '*aeque*'. But again there are tensions: Horace is calm and consoling while Pope is more aggressive and more idealistic. His superlatives are at once more paradoxical and more visionary: 'eldest ... youngest', 'poorest ... richest'.

Yet Pope, for all his moral idealism, is also aware of the limits of this wisdom, and in the very next passage we see how much he has internalized Horace's wry scepticism and sardonic irony. Horace points out that even if our physical potentialities are not remarkable, we still care for ourselves when ill, and asks dryly if the same might not apply to our moral life. In a single line he states his own position, that he will at least try to 'govern and inform' ('*regam, solerque*') himself with the simple beginnings; and then he slips subtly into the ambiguous second-person singular, addressing himself, Maecenas, and the general reader:

[19]Restat, *ut his ego me ipse regam,* [20]*solerque,* Elementis.
  [21]*Non possis oculo quantum contendere Lynceus,*
Non tamen idcirco contemnas lippus inungi:
Nec, quia desperes invicti membra Glyconis,
Nodosâ corpus nolis prohibere chiragrâ.
Est quâdam prodire [22]*tenus, si non datur ultra.*
  [23]*Fervet Avaritia, miseroque Cupidine pectus?*
Sunt verba & voces, *quibus hunc lenire dolorem*
Possis, & [24]*magnam morbi deponere partem.*
Laudis amore tumes? sunt [25]certa piacula, *quae te*
Ter *pure lecto poterunt recreare libello.*
[26]*Invidus, iracundus, iners, vinosus,* [27]Amator,
Nemo [28]*adeo* ferus *est ut non mitescere possit,*
Si modo culturae patientem commodet aurem. (27–40)

(Meanwhile, I must use these first lessons to govern and inform my own life. Your eyes may not match Lynceus': yet you wouldn't for that reason refuse to put ointment on them when sore; again, you couldn't hope for the physique of Glycon, the unconquered: still, you don't fail to protect your frame from crippling gout. Some progress is possible, even if further advance is denied us. Does your heart seethe with Avarice and the misery of Desire? There are formulae to ease that pain and get rid of the worst of the disorder. Are you swollen with love of praise? There are infallible remedies that can make a new man of you if you read the pamphlet three times and don't go wrong. Envious, hot-tempered, lazy, alcoholic, a lecher – no one is too wild to be tamed if only he will lend a willing ear to therapy.)

The move from '*ego*' ('I') to '*Non possis*' ('Your [eyes] may not') is very neat: this is the Horace of subtle questioning who is at once consoling and satirical. The reference to Lynceus, the Argonaut famed for his keen eyesight, and Glycon, a famous contemporary athlete, are dryly ironical; and Horace's promises of moral cures are satirically qualified by words like '*lenire*' ('ease'), '*magnam ... partem*' (the order of the words is so neat, 'the worst ... part'), 'Ter' (the magical number), and the amusing '*mitescere*' ('tame').

Pope here shows he understands perfectly this distinctively Horatian blending of calm assurance with irony, but he disarms us completely at first by taking Horace's metaphors about physical weakness quite literally. The intense, inward Horace is now Pope himself with his poor eyesight and persistent headaches:

[19]Late as it is, I put my self to school,
And feel some [20]comfort, not to be a fool.
[21]Weak tho' I am of limb, and short of sight,
Far from a Lynx, and not a Giant quite,
I'll do what MEAD and CHESELDEN advise,
To keep these limbs, and to preserve these eyes.
Not to [22]go back, is somewhat to advance,
And men must walk at least before they dance.

258

Say, does thy [23]blood rebel, thy bosom move
With wretched Av'rice, or as wretched Love?
Know, there are Words, and Spells, which can controll
([24]Between the Fits) this Fever of the soul:
Know, there are Rhymes, which ([25]fresh and fresh apply'd)
Will cure the arrant'st Puppy of his Pride.
Be [26]furious, envious, slothful, mad or drunk,
[27]Slave to a Wife or Vassal to a Punk,
A Switz, a High-dutch, or a Low-dutch [28]Bear –
All that we ask is but a patient Ear.   (47–64)

These remarkable lines are pure Horace, touched at every point by
Pope, and in them the tensions between Pope and Horace become
extremely subtle. Pope's 'you' is nicely ambiguous, but Pope speaks
directly of himself. The allusions to Lynceus and Glycon in Horace
enhance the pathos of these lines, and for a moment Pope is exposed
and vulnerable. There is an almost childlike play on words in his little
pun on '*Lynceus*', 'Far from a Lynx'. A haunting moment comes in
the imitation of Horace's wry but consoling '*Est quâdam prodire
tenus, si non datur ultra*' ('Some progress is possible, even if further
advance is denied us'):

> Not to go back, is somewhat to advance,
> And men must walk at least before they dance.   (53–4)

Horace is so simple; Pope is so paradoxical and contorted, with a
greater awareness of human limitation and greater yearning towards
perfection.

Pivoting on that couplet, Pope becomes 'Horatian' again. He
calmly echoes the phrasing of Horace's assurances: '*Sunt* verba &
voices ... *sunt certa* piacula' ('There are formulae ... There are
infallible remedies') – 'Know, there are Words, and Spells ... Know,
there are Rhymes.' And, at the same time, he captures the scepticism
in touches like: 'controll', '(Between the fits)', and '(fresh and fresh
apply'd)'. But at the end he modulates again. Horace's extraordinary
line, '*Invidus, iracundus, iners, vinosus*, Amator' ('Envious, hot-
tempered, lazy, alcoholic, a lecher'), resolves to a positive conclusion
with just a touch of mild irony:

> *Nemo adeo* ferus *est ut non mitescere possit,*
> *Si modo culturae patientem commodet aurem.*   (39–40)

(No one is too wild to be tamed if only he will lend a willing ear to therapy.)

In place of these elegant tones, we hear the first notes of the attacking
political satirist. The 'Amator' ('lecher') produces a double-edged
thrust, the 'ferus' ('wild') becomes a new kind of animal, and the dry
'*patientem ... aurem*' sparks off aggressive sarcasm:

Be furious, envious, slothful, mad or drunk,
Slave to a Wife or Vassal to a Punk,
A Switz, a High-dutch, or a Low-dutch Bear –
All that we ask is but a patient Ear.   (61–4)

THE POWERS OF EVIL

In the first part of this Imitation Pope writes in a new Horatian style about his yearning to know himself afresh, a style which fuses Horatian meditation with moments of spiritual intensity in keeping with Dacier's and Shaftesbury's reading of Horace. Horace is indeed his model here, but there are also in Pope desires and visions which are more paradoxical and intense than Horace's: a deeper yearning to be more perfect than he is, a stronger feeling of the separation of inner and outer self, the stirrings of a more intense moral idealism, and a greater sense of human limitation. We find these tendencies in Pope's attitude to himself, and we find them also in Pope's attack on his society at the centre of his poem.

Here, however, the relationship between these two poems seems to change. If we read the poetry of the first part of the Imitation next to Horace's we feel that Horace is something like a guide; in the middle part of the Imitation we find something very different as another side of Pope, felt only under the surface before, emerges. Pope begins an impassioned attack on the city and the Court, and here his poetry moves with its own self-generating energy. A new Pope, confident and bitter, emerges, as he turns Horace's satire on Roman materialism into a tremendous attack on contemporary corruption and its inner forces of evil.

The relationship between Pope's poetry and Horace's in this central section is many-sided. From one point of view this satiric poetry is quite different in character from Horace's, for the satire of Horace's central section is finely attuned to his poem's general spirit of questioning. Indeed the subtlety of the satire in the epistles springs from this, as Horace encourages us to think and speculate, asking which of two alternatives is a better way to live. Here is Dryden's Horace, who 'is teaching us in every Line, and is perpetually Moral' ('Discourse', p. 62). Horace shows what pressures men are under to make money; but he tries also to show the real strength of moral independence. Who advises best, Horace asks: the man who urges obsessively '"*Rem facias, rem, / Si possis, recte, si non, quocunque modo rem*"' (lines 62–3, 'make money, money by fair means if you can, if not, any way at all, make money'), or the man who urges you to be your own master and actually helps you to be a free, independent person? –

An, ⁴⁵qui Fortunae te responsare superbae
Liberum & erectum, ⁴⁶praesens hortatur, & aptat?   (65–6)

(Or the other who stands at your side urging and enabling you to confront arrogant fortune, free and unbowed?)

Pope takes all this and throws it into a contemporary political mould. Pope is no longer the man seeking retirement, nor a Horace asking questions, but an Opposition poet attacking the city and court in some of his most daring lines. Throughout, the very word 'Virtue', Horace's *'virtus'*, is charged with the political connotations given it by the Opposition of the 1730s. Here, at last, we might feel, is Dryden's impassioned Juvenalian satirist, or Dryden's Persius deeply committed to Stoic philosophy (see 'Discourse', pp. 56–7; and Weinbrot's reading of this middle section, 1982, pp. 292–5). And indeed the moral idealism of Pope's poetry is very striking. To the man fleeing frantically to India to escape poverty Horace says simply:

Ne cures ³²ea quae stulte miraris & optas
Discere, & audire, & meliori credere non vis?   (47–8)

(But yet, to lose your obsession with the things you stare at and crave, will you not learn, listen, trust one better than you?)

Verbs of foolish caring (*'miraris & optas'* – 'stare at and crave') are set against calming verbs of learning (*'Discere'*), hearing (*'audire'*) and trusting (*'credere'*). Here, as it were, is the soothing answer to the problems of 'Nil admirari'. For Pope this is an opportunity for the high rhetoric:

> Wilt thou do nothing for a nobler end,
> Nothing, to make Philosophy thy friend?
> To stop thy foolish views, thy long desires,
> And ³²ease thy heart of all that it admires?   (73–6)

But from another point of view this poetry reflects precisely the Stoic idealism which Dacier found in the Horatian poem itself.[3] It is vital to realize, in this respect, that Dacier's comments on the middle section of Horace's epistle in no way suggest a stance of spiritual withdrawal as Maresca tends to imply throughout his study (1966, Chapter 5); on the contrary they present a dynamic confrontation between the voices of Wisdom and the voices of Folly: set against the call to make money and gain honour are the voices of Wisdom, children, and the Sage. A host of details show just how closely Pope modelled his attack on his own society on Dacier's reading of Horace at this point. Following Dacier's comments (but not his Latin text)

Pope sets out Horace's contrast between Wisdom and Folly in terms of actual voices in the Horatian text itself:[4]

> "[33]*Vilius argentum est auro, virtutibus aurum –*
> "[34]*O cives, cives! quaerenda Pecunia primum est,*
> "*Virtus post nummos – Haec* [35]Janus summus *ab* imo
> *Prodocet: haec recinunt juvenes dictata, senesque,*
> [36]*Laevo suspensi loculos tabulamque lacerto.* (49–53)

('Silver is cheaper than gold, gold than virtue.' 'O citizens, citizens, seek money first, virtue after cash' – this Janus high proclaims, and Janus low; this is the lesson both young and old recite in unison, their slates and satchels slung over the left shoulder.)

On the first of these lines Dacier comments; 'C'est ce que la Sagesse crie aux hommes'; on the second he asserts, 'Si la Sagesse crie d'un costé aux hommes, *la vertu vaut mieux que l'or*; la folie leur crie d'un autre costé *l'or vaut mieux que la vertu*'; and to underline the point he quotes Scriptural passages on wisdom and riches (Dacier, VIII, pp. 76–7). Pope presents just this confrontation in contemporary London:

> Here, Wisdom calls: [33]"Seek Virtue first! be bold!
> "As Gold to Silver, Virtue is to Gold."
> There, London's voice: [34]"Get Mony, Mony still!
> "And then let Virtue follow, if she will."
> This, this the saving doctrine, preach'd to all,
> From [35]low St. James's up to high St. Paul;
> From him whose [36]quills stand quiver'd at his ear,
> To him who notches Sticks at Westminster. (77–84)

Horace ridicules his fellow Romans for judging merit only by cash, and then asserts that children at play are wiser and seem to realise that a clear conscience is the best protection a person can have:

> [39]*At pueri ludentes,* "*Rex eris (aiunt)*
> "*Si recte facies.*" *Hic* [40]*murus aheneus esto,*
> *Nil* conscire *sibi, nullâ pallescere culpâ!* (56–8)

(And yet children at play cry 'If you do right, you shall be king'. Let this be your wall of bronze, to have no sin on your conscience, no guilt to turn you pale.)

Dacier alludes to Christ's assertion about the wisdom of children, quotes from Plato's account of children's games in which the winner is made 'king', and commenting on 'murus aheneus' ('wall of bronze') refers to 'des Soldats armez de pied en cap, qui couvrent les autres' (Dacier, VIII, pp. 81–4). Playing on 'Rex' and 'murus aheneus', Pope produces a brilliant jibe at Walpole's 'screening':

> Yet every [39]child another song will sing,
> "Virtue, brave boys! 'tis Virtue makes a King."
> True, conscious Honour is to feel no sin,
> He's arm'd without that's innocent within;
> Be this thy [40]Screen, and this thy Wall of Brass;
> Compar'd to this, a Minister's an ass.   (91–6)

When Horace finally asserts that his whole way of life is fundamentally different from that of the people of Rome, and tells the
story of the fox and the sick lion, Dacier emphasises both the noble
isolation of 'le Sage' and finds a political meaning of the story:

> [47]*Quod si me Populus Romanus forte roget, cur*
> *Non, ut* [48]*porticibus, sic judiciis fruar iisdem,*
> *Nec sequar aut fugiam, quos diligit ipse, vel odit?*
> *Olim quod* [49]*Vulpes aegroto cauta Leoni*
> *Respondit, referam: "Quia me vestigia terrent*
> *"Omnia te adversum spectantia, nulla retrorsum.*   (67–72)

(Should the Roman people perhaps ask me why I don't share their views as I
share their walks, why I don't pursue what they love and shun what they loathe: I
shall answer with the reply of the canny fox to the sick lion in the fable: I'm afraid
of the footprints: they all point towards you, none away.')

'Quand le peuple vante le bonheur des Princes & des Rois, le Sage,
comme dit tres-bien Socrate, croit entendre vanter le bonheur d'un
Berger qui tire beaucoup de laict de son troupeau, avec cette difference pourtant que le Berger trait un bestail doux & apprivoisé, &
que les Princes ont à traire un animal feroce & dangereux' (Dacier,
VIII, p. 93–4). 'Le Lion c'est la Republique, & le Gouvernement; les
animaux ce sont les particuliers; le Renard c'est le Sage' (Dacier, VIII,
p. 95):

> If [47]such a Doctrine, in St. James's air,
> Shou'd chance to make the well-drest Rabble stare;
> If honest S*z take scandal at a spark,
> That less admires the [48]Palace than the Park;
> Faith I shall give the answer [49]Reynard gave,
> "I cannot like, Dread Sir! your Royal Cave;
> "Because I see by all the Tracks about,
> "Full many a Beast goes in, but none comes out."
> Adieu to Virtue if you're once a Slave:
> Send her to Court, you send her to her Grave.   (110–19)

Horace's ideal of personal independence now means freedom from
Walpole and the corruption of his age. Shaftesbury too saw these
lines in political terms:

Are the courts or even the senates, parliaments, and public stations, the passages
to virtue and true honour, as well as to fame, fortune, and honour of another
kind? – *Vestigia nulla retrorsum.*

If they once went in honest, how are they come out? Where are the footsteps? What are they changed to soon when there? Is this, then, the world? (Shaftesbury, 1900, p. 68; see also his letter to Locke, p. 306)

But if, in these lines, Pope is heroically confident and motivated by an impassioned commitment to virtue, he can also be darkly sceptical and intensely pessimistic. When he does turn to the 'People' he produces the real climax to the central section of his poem. Horace says it is impossible to follow his fellow Romans anyway, because they are all so different; and to illustrate this he sardonically caricatures a few different, sordid ways of making money:

> [50]Bellua multorum *est* capitum, *nam quid sequar aut quem?*
> Pars hominum gestit [51]conducere Publica. Sunt qui
> [52]Crustis & Pomis, Viduas venentur avaras,
> Excipiantque Senes quos in vivaria mittunt.
> [53]Multis *occulto crescit res foenore* –   (73–7)

(The people is a many-headed beast: what, and whom, am I to follow? Some are agog to take on public contracts. Some with crusts and apples set traps for stingy widows, or net old men to stock their pools. For many, unseen and unheard, money simply grows – by usury.)

We see here Horace's talent for creating in just a few lines a grotesque comic vision: '*gestit*' ('are agog') conveys how deeply some enter into degrading ways of making money, and bizarre images and metaphors bring other weird activities to life: hunting ('*venentur*') miserly widows with titbits and fruits ('*Crustis* & Pomis'), and catching ('*Excipiant*') old men to put into pools ('*vivaria*') like fish. In the last sinister line, money literally grows for many ('Multis') through the secret power of interest ('*foenore*').

Dacier says very little about these few lines, but George Ogle had seen their potentiality:

> *Some* for their Country lay the bolder Train;
> And build, on Public Ruin, Private Gain.
> *Some* by Extortion, blind to Right or Wrong!
> Raise Ore; that gathers as it rolls along.
> *Some* for weak Widows weave the pious Snares;
> And teach religiously to cheat their Heirs.
> With trifling Gifts, rich Neighbours, *Some* beset;
> And slily tickle till they take the Net.
> Whole Shoals are caught, unable to withstand
> The lureing Splendor of the baited Hand;
> And strait, in proper Ponds securely stor'd,
> Are fed with Care; but fed, to serve the Board.
>   (Ogle, 1735, pp. 21–2)

But Pope goes far beyond this. Taking the hint from Horace's 'Publica' and 'Multis', he turns all this into an intense vision of inner corruption on a national scale:

> Well, if a King's a Lion, at the least
> The [50]People are a many-headed Beast:
> Can they direct what measures to pursue,
> Who know themselves so little what to do?
> Alike in nothing but one Lust of Gold,
> Just half the land would buy, and half be sold:
> Their [51]Country's wealth our mightier Misers drain,
> Or cross, to plunder Provinces, the Main:
> The rest, some farm the Poor-box, some the Pews;
> Some keep Assemblies, and wou'd keep the Stews;
> Some [52]with fat Bucks on childless Dotards fawn;
> Some win rich Widows by their Chine and Brawn;
> While with the silent growth of ten per Cent,
> In Dirt and darkness [53]hundreds stink content.   (120–33)

There is nothing like this in Horace's poem, indeed nothing like it in the whole of Horace, except in the last Roman ode (*Odes*, III.vi.). The moral fervour and bitter cynicism here are all Pope's own. If Horace's poem is about perverted ambition as Dacier argues, this is the perverted ambition of England in 1738. Horace is coolly detached from the grotesque absurdities of avarice he portrays; but Pope is utterly gripped by the profound corruptions of the heart he discovers in the sinister association of avarice and sexual desire – 'one Lust of Gold'. Everything is a perversion of sexuality: 'Just half the land would buy, and half be sold'. 'Some keep Assemblies, and wou'd keep the Stews'; and Horace's '*Crustis* & Pomis' ('titbits and fruits') becomes 'Some win rich Widows by their Chine and Brawn.' Here the deepest human desires have been perverted by the power of evil, the driving forces of human experience have been tainted, and the purpose of life has been lost.

CONSISTENCY AND THE SELF

After this extraordinary passage it must have been hard for Pope to be Horatian again, and indeed these lines cast their shadow over the rest of Pope's poem. But in fact Pope does return to a more Horatian style once more. When Horace turns from avarice, or ambition, to inconsistency Pope follows suit with sardonic humour:

> – [54]*Verum*
> *Esto, aliis alios rebus, studiisque teneri:*
> *Iidem eadem possunt horam durare probantes?*   (77–9)

(But granted that individuals are swayed by different aims and interests; are men capable of holding on to the same opinion for a single hour?)

> Of all these ways, if each [54]pursues his own,
> Satire be kind, and let the wretch alone.

But show me one, who has it in his pow'r
To act consistent with himself an hour.   (134–7)

In Horace's dry poetic language '*aliis alios*' ('different [aims], different [individuals]') sit next to each other, and then '*Iidem eadem*' ('the
same [opinion] . . . a single [hour]'); and this leads to some searching
satire on the inconsistencies of human desires, opinions, and actions,
found alike in the rich and the poor:

> [55]"*Nullus in orbe locus* Baiis *praelucet amaenis:*"
> *Si dixit* Dives, [56]*lacus & mare* sentit *amorem*
> Festinantis *heri. Cui si* [57]*vitiosa* Libido
> Fecerit auspicium, *cras* "*ferramenta* Teanum
> "*Tolletis, fabri!* –
> – [58]*Lectus genialis in aula est?*
> *Nil ait esse prius, melius nil caelibe vita:*
> [59]*Si non est, jurat bene solis esse maritis.*
> [60]*Quo teneam vultus mutantem Protea nodo?*
> *Quid* [61]*pauper? ride: mutat* [62]*caenacula, lectos,*
> *Balnea,* [63]*tonsores; conducto* [64]*navigio, aequè*
> *Nauseat ac locuples, quem ducit priva triremis.*   (80–90)

('Nowhere in the world outshines lovely Baiae.' No sooner has the rich man said
this, than lake and sea are forced to endure the advances of their bustling master.
But if a perverse caprice is taken for an omen, tomorrow it's 'Up tools, builders,
and off to Teanum.'
Is the marriage-couch in the hall? Nothing, he says is finer, nothing better than
the single life: if it's not, he swears that only the married are happy. What knot
can I use to hold this face-changing Proteus? What about the poor man? You can
only laugh: he changes his lodgings, bed, baths, barber; when he hires a boat he is
just as sick as the rich man who sails his private yacht.)

Baiae was a fashionable resort on the sea, and Teanum an inland
town; the marriage-couch being in the hall meant the man was just
about to be married.

What amuses here in Horace is the depth of the contradictions, as
wishing for, achieving, or doing anything, lead at once to the
contrary wish and action. Such satire is very searching: does this
simply show inconsistencies which could be controlled or resolved,
or does it point to deeper contradictory needs of the self which
cannot be fulfilled in singleness of action? What, indeed, is the
relationship between these desires and the self? Is the self found in
embracing those contradictions, or in resisting them in the name of
the Stoic ideal of unity of being, 'semper eadem'? Do these inconsistencies merely point to the ultimate truth which lies beneath the inner
aimlessness of human lives?[5] Again we think of the haunting ironies
of Horace's *Nil Admirari*.

Dacier takes this passage very seriously indeed, arguing that these passions, whims, and fancies are in fact disorders of the soul. Indeed he stresses the 'religious' implications of the story of the man who wishes to be at Baiae only until he gets there. He tries to explain Horace's seemingly strange idea that the 'perverse caprice' ('*vitiosa Libido*') is taken for a religious omen ('*auspicium*'). Within such apparently random passions there is a force which seems as necessary as the religious impulses they parody:

Voilà un desir vicieux, parce qu'il ne vient pas de la nature. Et comme tous les desirs qui viennent de nostre corruption nous sont plus chers, & ont plus de force que ceux qu'excite la vertu, l'amour propre nous les déguise sous des apparences trompeuses, & nous leur obeïssons comme à une necessité, ou plûtost comme à une autorité absoluë qui prend dans nostre coeur la place de la Religion.

(Dacier, VIII, p. 102)

Pope picks out these words in the Latin and explores Dacier's interpretation:

> Sir Job [55]sail'd forth, the evening bright and still,
> "No place on earth (he cry'd) like Greenwich hill!"
> [56]Up starts a Palace, lo! th'obedient base
> Slopes at its foot, the woods its sides embrace,
> The silver Thames reflects its marble face.
> Now let some whimzy, or that [57]Dev'l within
> Which guides all those who know not what they mean
> But give the Knight (or give his Lady) spleen;
> "Away, away! take all your scaffolds down,
> "For Snug's the word: My dear! we'll live in Town."
>   At am'rous Flavio is the [58]Stocking thrown?
> That very night he longs to lye alone.
> [59]The Fool whose Wife elopes some thrice a quarter,
> For matrimonial Solace dies a martyr.
> Did ever [60]Proteus, Merlin, any Witch,
> Transform themselves so strangely as the Rich?
> "Well, but the [61]Poor" – the Poor have the same itch:
> They change their [63]weekly Barber, weekly News,
> Prefer a new Japanner to their shoes,
> Discharge their [62]Garrets, move their Beds, and run
> (They know not whither) in a Chaise and one;
> They [64]hire their Sculler, and when once aboard,
> Grow sick, and damn the Climate – like a Lord.   (138–60)

On the one hand Pope alludes persistently to that inner uncertainty and emphasizes the universal need for direction. Speaking of the common people he had asked:

> Can they direct what measures to pursue,
> Who know themselves so little what to do?   (122–3)

Now, characterizing Sir Job, he alludes to

> ... some whimzy, or that Dev'l within
> Which guides all those who know not what they mean ...   (143–4)

and points to the poor who

> Discharge their Garrets, move their Beds, and run
> (They know not whither) in a Chaise and one ...   (157–8)

On the other hand Pope is also aware of the profound paradoxes of the self, of wish and counter wish, which seem to point to the necessity of contradiction:

> At am'rous Flavio is the Stocking thrown?
> That very night he longs to lye alone.
> The Fool whose Wife elopes some thrice a quarter,
> For matrimonial Solace dies a martyr.   (148–51)

We appreciate the full power of such satire, and indeed the force of the conclusions of these two poems, only if we understand the Stoic attitude to such deep inconsistency. The *locus classicus* for this is Seneca's *Epistle to Lucilius*, cxx. A man is great, Seneca argues, when all the actions of his life show him to be one man. He quotes one of Horace's many passages on inconsistency (*Satire* I.iii. 11–17) and draws his moral with considerable wit:

Homines isti tales sunt, qualem hunc describit Horatius Flaccus, numquam eundem, ne similem quidem sibi; adeo in diversum aberrat ... Sic maxime coarguitur animus inprudens; alius prodit atque alius et, quo turpius nihil iudico, impar sibi est. Magnam rem puta unum hominem agere. Praeter sapientem autem nemo unum agit, ceteri multiformes sumus. Modo frugi tibi videbimur et graves, modo prodigi et vani. Mutamus subinde personam et contrariam ei sumimus, quam exuimus. Hoc ergo a te exige, ut, qualem institueris praestare te, talem usque ad exitum serves. Effice ut possis laudari, si minus, ut adgnosci. De aliquo, quem here vidisti, merito dici potest: "hic qui est?" Tanta mutatio est. VALE.

The men I speak of are of this stamp; they are like the man whom Horatius Flaccus describes – a man never the same, never even like himself; to such an extent does he wander off into opposites ... That is how a foolish mind is most clearly demonstrated: it shows first in this shape and then in that, and is never like itself – which is, in my opinion, the most shameful of qualities. Believe me, it is a great rôle – to play the rôle of one man. But nobody can be one person except the wise man; the rest of us often shift our masks. At times you will think us thrifty and serious, at other times wasteful and idle. We continually change our characters and play a part contrary to that which we have discarded. You should therefore force yourself to maintain to the very end of life's drama the character which you assumed at the beginning. See to it that men be able to praise you; if not, let them at least identify you. Indeed, with regard to the man whom you saw but yesterday, the question may properly be asked: 'Who is he?' So great a change has there been! Farewell.   (ed. Gummere, 1925, III, pp. 394–5)

'Magnam rem puta unum hominem agere' ('Believe me, it is a great rôle – to play the rôle of one man'). The supreme manifestation of virtue, Seneca argues in this essay, is achieved when a man is so trained in constancy that he cannot but do right:

Praeterea idem erat semper et in omni actu par sibi, iam non consilio bonus, sed more eo perductus, ut non tantum recte facere posset, sed nisi recte facere non posset. Intelleximus in illo perfectam esse virtutem.

Besides, he has always been the same, consistent in all his actions, not only sound in his judgement but trained by habit to such an extent that he not only can act rightly, but cannot help acting rightly. We have formed the conception that in such a man perfect virtue exists.   (ed. Gummere, 1925, III, pp. 386–9)

In August 1723, in a letter Bolingbroke and Pope wrote jointly to Swift, Bolingbroke quoted from Seneca's *Epistle to Lucilius*, cxx this statement about the highest manifestation of virtue, and claimed that this was precisely what he learned from his fall from power, serene detachment, 'Perfect Tranquillity', and concern only for the solemn 'Vows' of friendship:

I am under no apprehensions that a Glut of Study and Retirement should cast me back into the Hurry of the World; on the contrary, the single Regret which I ever feel, is that I fell so late into this Course of Life: My Philosophy grows confirmed by Habit, and if you and I meet again I will extort this Approbation from you, I am *consilio bonus, sed more eo productus, ut non tantum recte facere possim, sed nil non recte facere non possim.* The little Incivilities I have met with from opposite Sets of People, have been so far from rendring me violent or sour to any, that I think myself obliged to them all; some have cured me of my Fears, by shewing me how impotent the Malice of the World is; others have cured me of my Hopes, by shewing how precarious popular Friendships are; all have cured me of Surprize; in driving me out of Party, they have driven me out of cursed Company; and in stripping me of Titles, and Rank, and Estate, and such Trinkets, which every Man that will may spare, they have given me that which no Man can be happy without.

Reflection and Habit have rendred the World so indifferent to me, that I am neither afflicted nor rejoiced, angry nor pleased at what happens in it, any farther than personal Friendships interest me in the Affairs of it, and this Principle extends my Cares but a little Way: Perfect Tranquillity is the general Tenour of my Life; good Digestions, serene Weather, and some other mechanic Springs, wind me above it now and then, but I never fall below it; I am sometimes gay, but I am never sad; I have gained New Friends, and have lost some Old ones; my Acquisitions of this kind give me a good deal of Pleasure because they have not been made lightly: I know no Vows so solemn as those of Friendship, and therefore a pretty long noviciate of Acquaintance should methinks precede them; my Losses of this kind give me but little Trouble, I contributed nothing to them, and a Friend who breaks with me unjustly is not worth preserving.

(*Corr.* II, pp. 187–8)

The conclusions to these two poems explore just such obligations of friendship. After encouraging us to laugh at the inconsistencies of others, Horace now admits his *own* inner contradictions. At first we can hardly believe he is talking about himself: he uses a generalized 'I' and an ambiguous 'you'. We accept it only as we gradually realize that he is actually talking not to us, but, of course, to Maecenas, his closest friend. The whole passage is masterful:

> [65]*Si curtatus* inaequali *tonsore capillos*
> *Occurro, rides; si forte subucula pexae*
> *Trita subest tunicae, vel si toga* dissidet impar,
> *Rides: quid?* [66]*mea cum pugnat* Sententia *secum,*
> *Quod petiit, spernit; repetit quod nuper omisit;*
> [67]*Aestuat, & Vitae disconvenit ordine toto;*
> [68]*Diruit, aedificat, mutat quadrata rotundis?*
> [69]*Insanire putas solennia me; neque rides,*
> Nec [70]Medici *credis, nec* Curatoris *egere*
> A Praetore *dati? rerum* [71]*Tutela mearum*
> *Cum sis, & pravè sectum stomacheris ob unguem,*
> *De* te pendentis, te suspicientis, Amici.   (91–102)

(If the barber's cropped my hair unevenly and I meet you, you laugh; if perhaps I have a threadbare shirt beneath a new tunic or my toga sits lopsided, you laugh. But what when my mind fights with itself, scorns what it has been seeking, seeks again what it has just cast aside; when it ebbs and flows, and is in disarray throughout the whole pattern of life, destroys, constructs, exchanges round for square? You think my madness is normal, you don't laugh, you don't think I need a doctor or a guardian appointed by the court, do you? – even though you are the protection of my affairs and you are annoyed even at a badly cut nail of the friend who depends upon you and reveres you.)

Horace's self-criticism here is at once amusing and pointed; the Horace who delighted us with his clever eclecticism at the beginning of the poem, is now absurdly at variance with himself. The '*rides . . . Rides*' ('you laugh . . . you laugh') is persistent. How brilliantly this follows on from '*Quid* pauper? *ride*' (line 88 – 'What about the poor man? You can only laugh'). Dacier implies in fact that Horace speaking to the rich Maecenas *is* that 'pauper' (Dacier, VIII, p. 108–9). Horace's mind fights itself ('*pugnat*'); conflicting verbs of desire and rejection fall upon each other, '*Quod petiit, spernit; repetit quod nuper omisit*' ('scorns what it has been seeking, seeks again what it has just cast aside'); and '*quadrata*' ('square') and '*rotundis*' ('round') are pushed together. In tones that are ambiguous, amused but also sharp, he chastises Maecenas for criticizing his superficial failings, but accepting his real inner madness as merely normal ('*solennia*').The final note is beautifully controlled; '*stomacheris*' ('you are annoyed') is amusing yet also critical, but then, with the Latin syntax hanging upon the ill-pared nail ('the nail of the friend'), comes that appealing, personal last line. The suspended possessives and repeated 'te' ('te pendentis' – 'who depends upon you'; 'te suspicientis' – 'reveres you') prepare for the perfectly placed, warm '*Amici*'. At the beginning of this elaborate period Horace is 'everyone', in the middle he is a man critical of Maecenas, at the end he is 'Horace', who needs Maecenas as a friend. Dacier offers a very emotional interpretation of these lines:

C'est un reproche plein de douceur & de tendresse. Vous estes mon protecteur & mon Dieu tutelaire ... La veritable amitié doit porter les hommes à supporter les defauts de leurs amis, & à combatre leurs vices: & vous faites tout le contraire, vous souffrez mes vices, & vous combattez mes defauts'

but on the last line he notes,

Horace adoucit les reproches qu'il fait à Mecenas, par la maniere tendre avec laquelle il parle de l'attachment qu'il a pour luy.

(Dacier, VIII, pp. 116–17)

But at once Horace breaks off, asserts that indeed the Stoics are right about the wise man, and then ends with a sudden witty joke:

> Ad summam, Sapiens uno [72]minor est Jove! [73]Dives!
> [74]Liber! [75]honoratus! [76]pulcher! –
>   – [77]Rex denique regum!
> Praecipue sanus –
>   – [78]Nisi cum pituita molesta est.　　　　(103–5)

(In short, the wise man is second only to Jove! Rich, free, honoured, handsome! Indeed, a king of kings! above all, healthy – except when he has a nasty cold.)

The rapid list of Stoic terms ('Sapiens', '*Dives*', '*Rex denique regum*') leads straight to a neat pun on '*sanus*' ('sane', but also 'healthy') and a quick thrust at the Stoic wise man. This joke is quintessential Horace; it is both a final reminder of the need to recognize human limitation, and a witty assertion of his own eclecticism. Dacier gives full weight to Horace's list of Stoic terms, filling each one out with passages from Epictetus and Cicero, but on this ending he acutely remarks: 'Et le ridicule qu'il donne par là aux Stoïciens, prouve encore ce qu'il a dit au commencement de cette Epître, qu'il n'époussoit les sentimens d'aucune secte ... *Nullius addictus jurare in verba Magistri*' (Dacier, VIII, p. 123). We can only smile at those last words ('*pituita molesta est*' – 'except when he has a nasty cold') and delight in Horace's flash of detachment.

Pope's imitation of this conclusion is one of his most imaginative strokes in all the *Imitations of Horace*. Both Dacier's full explication of each of Horace's Stoic terms and George Ogle's expansion of each word in his imitation of Horace's conclusion could have inspired Pope's expansion of the final section of his conclusion.[6] But nothing prepares us for the intensity of Pope's address to Bolingbroke and the imaginative transformation of the two Horatian passages into one continuous whole:

> [65]You laugh, half Beau half Sloven if I stand,
> My Wig all powder, and all snuff my Band;
> You Laugh, if Coat and Breeches strangely vary,
> White Gloves, and Linnen worthy Lady Mary!
> But when no [66]Prelate's Lawn with Hair-shirt lin'd,
> Is half so incoherent as my Mind,
> When (each Opinion with the next at strife,
> One [67]ebb and flow of follies all my Life)
> I [68]plant, root up, I build, and then confound,
> Turn round to square, and square again to round;
> [69]You never change one muscle of your face,
> You think this Madness but a common case,
> Not [70]once to Chanc'ry, nor to Hales apply;
> Yet hang your lip, to see a Seam awry!
> Careless how ill I with myself agree;
> Kind to my dress, my figure, not to Me.
> Is this my [71]Guide, Philosopher, and Friend?
> This, He who loves me, and who ought to mend?
> Who ought to make me (what he can, or none,)
> That Man divine whom Wisdom calls her own;
> Great without Title, without Fortune's bless'd,
> Rich [73]ev'n when plunder'd, [75]honour'd while oppress'd,
> Lov'd [76]without youth, and follow'd without power,
> At home tho' exil'd, [74]free, tho' in the Tower.
> In short, that reas'ning, high, immortal Thing,
> Just [72]less than Jove, and [77]much above a King,
> Nay half in Heav'n – [78]except (what's mighty odd)
> A Fit of Vapours clouds this Demi-god.   (161–88)

The power of this passage springs from the intensity of his feelings for Bolingbroke, and from his yearning that Bolingbroke should make *him* into the Stoic wise man of Horace's poem, and from his resentment that Bolingbroke does not even think of doing such a thing. How much was Pope here thinking back to their joint letter to Swift of 1723 in which Bolingbroke asserted 'I know no Vows so solemn as those of Friendship'? Horace is amusing, and critical: *'Insanire putas solennia me; neque rides'* ('You think my madness is normal, you don't laugh'); but Pope is emotionally demanding in that criticism:

> You never change one muscle of your face,
> You think this Madness but a common case ...   (171–2)

> Careless how ill I with myself agree;
> Kind to my dress, my figure, not to Me.   (175–6)

> Is this my Guide, Philosopher, and Friend?
> This, He who loves me, and who ought to mend? (176–7)

He insists that if Bolingbroke really loves him he ought to *make* him into 'That Man divine whom Wisdom calls her own.' Indeed he makes a point of saying that only Bolingbroke could achieve this, '(what he can, or none)'. I think this image of the Stoic man is more than light raillery (*pace* Dixon, 1968, pp. 160–1; and Røstvig, 1962, II, pp. 62–3): there is irony in this self-characterization but there is also emotional involvement, for this ideal figure is a composite image of Pope and some of his closest friends, men he has known and loved, Atterbury, Oxford, and most importantly Bolingbroke himself. Pope builds the rhetoric to a climax only to cut it short with calculated sarcasm:

> Nay half in Heav'n – except (what's mighty odd)
> A Fit of Vapours clouds this Demi-god. (187–8)

The immediate contrast with Horace here is of course very impressive; Horace's lively joke directed at the Stoics is so different from Pope's sharp ridicule of *himself*: Horace ends on a note of buoyant confidence, Pope on a note of anguished personal failure.[7] But the whole ending is different, really because Pope's relationship with Bolingbroke is much more ambiguous, even confused, than Horace's relationship with Maecenas. Pope forms the final section of his poem around the idea that Bolingbroke as his friend must try to make him into a great person, but at the same time recognize the complexity of his nature and the inevitability of his failure. The subtle demands that Horace makes on Maecenas are justly famous – we think again of *Epistle* I.vii – but he never makes such demands as Pope is making here, for such intensities are not part of Horace's idea of friendship. Indeed Horace's ultimate need in friendship is freedom from such demands; above all else Horace requires independence, and his expressions of affection are normally very restrained. Critics of Pope's Imitation usually give a positive account of the role of Bolingbroke in this poem (see for example Weinbrot, 1982, pp. 295–8); and certainly Pope's appeal to Bolingbroke bears witness to his deep admiration for his 'Guide, Philosopher, and Friend'. But does it express also Pope's resentment for this man of 'mechanic Springs' he so admired? A recent study of Pope's relationship with Bolingbroke by B. S. Hammond (1984) would tend to suggest this possibility.

Pope's ending is also striking in that it contains a confession of personal failure which seems extraordinary after the tremendous confidence of the Imitation's central section. His poem's overall

Horatian structure can hardly contain such tensions. But here we see the differences between these two poems. Horace's poem is about his own desire for inner fulfilment, but it shows also what he has in fact achieved: his calm wisdom, his wit, his idealism, and his subtle flexibility in moral outlook. In the free movement of his poem Horace holds together his scepticism and his confidence, his sense of himself and his sense of others, his recognition of high moral demands and his acceptance of the limitations of human achievement. Interpretations of the poem can stress either the confidence of openness or the strength of conviction.

Pope's poem is much more paradoxical: it is at once more passionate and more disillusioned, more idealistic and more deeply sceptical. In Pope's poem a powerful yearning for improvement struggles much harder against inner doubt and the fear of failure. This troubled work is less unified than Horace's epistle, and less rounded; but it is in some ways a stronger poem than Horace's. Pope can re-create Horace's poetry of the private self, but he shows also that he recognizes the limitations of Horace's vision. The dark moments of Pope's poem give it a depth Horace's epistle does not have, its idealism and its intensities of feeling are more compelling. It questions more deeply the nature of the self, and undermines the very ideals it so passionately advocates.[8]

Seen in this light the contrast between Horace's *Epistle* I.i. and Pope's last two complete Imitations is particularly moving. Horace's *Epistle* I.i. is the fresh beginning of a book which suggests throughout that with thought and imagination it is possible to be a sane, whole person, more or less in control of circumstances and oneself. Pope's last two Imitations imply that in 1738 the forces which drive men are greater than the men themselves, more deeply corrupting, and yet strangely fulfilling. No wonder the poet's relationship with this society is strained, his public roles as satirist and idealist are ambiguous, and his image of his inner being is disturbed and unsettled. Exploring the contradictions of Horace Pope has discovered the even greater contradictions of himself.

Epilogue

It may be that one strong poet's work expiates for the work of a precursor. It seems more likely that later visions cleanse themselves at the expense of earlier ones. But the strong dead return, in poems as in our lives, and they do not come back without darkening the living. The wholly mature strong poet is particularly vulnerable to this last phase of his revisionary relationship to the dead. This vulnerability is most evident in poems that quest for a final clarity, that seek to be definitive statements.   Harold Bloom, *The Anxiety of Influence* (pp. 139–40)

The point of view which I am struggling to attack is perhaps related to the metaphysical theory of the substantial unity of the soul: for my meaning is, that the poet has, not a 'personality' to express, but a particular medium, which is only a medium and not a personality, in which impressions and experiences combine in peculiar and un-expected ways.

T. S. Eliot, 'Tradition and the Individual Talent' (pp. 19–20)

THE *Imitation of Epistle I.i.* forms a very striking conclusion to Pope's *Imitations of Horace*, but it is not in fact entirely the end of the story. The two 'Dialogues' written very shortly after it, and eventually to be called the *Epilogue to the Satires*, offer another and very different conclusion. The first, published only two months after the Imitation in May 1738, was entitled simply, *One Thousand Seven Hundred and Thirty Eight. A Dialogue Something like Horace*. The second came out in July, as *One Thousand Seven Hundred and Thirty Eight. Dialogue II*. Although this is not the place to engage in a detailed analysis of these two poems, without some comment on them the drama of Pope's relationship with Horace would be incomplete, and the 'story' of 1738 would be unfinished.

If the strains and paradoxes of the *Imitation of Epistle I.i.* show Pope at his most complex and vulnerable in response to the events of 1738, then these poems reveal Pope at his most heroic and defiant, overriding, in the impassioned language of satire at least, the Opposition's failure to defeat Walpole. By May 1738 it was evident to all that the old wizard had miraculously weathered the storm, and that

Vice, as the Opposition liked to put it, was now triumphantly secure again. The first of the 'Dialogues' records that triumph, and registers Pope's personal contempt for the patently immoral world it raised to eminence; the second demonstrates, as it attempts to justify, Pope's use of powerful personal satire, and culminates in his dramatic assertions that his poetic visions of truth, the product of moral fervour, would prove more lasting than the deeply ingrained corruption achieved by others in the England of his time.

To look at these two works from the point of view of the *Imitations* is extremely interesting. On the one hand they seem to represent a dramatic turning away from Horace, a passionate breaking of the Horatian tie in the direction of Juvenalian fervour, and this is how they are usually regarded (see, for example, Weinbrot, 1982, pp. 310–30). On the other hand, they represent, after so many epistles, a return to the dramatic dialogue form of the very first Imitation, and constitute fresh and lively developments of that language of self-dramatization and self-assertion. In terms of form and concern the point of departure for these poems would seem to be Pope's own interpretation of Horace's *Satire II.i.* Once again Pope attempts to explain and justify personal satire, and once again tries to explore the nature and significance of what he feels to be a profound commitment to 'Virtue'. Once again Pope tries to re-create in the poetry of dramatic debate those instinctive moral and emotional responses which he feels give rise to the energies of satire. Once more we recognize the extreme moral ambiguities of the whole activity of writing satire, and see how difficult Pope finds it to justify his personal satire and its lethal attacking power. The paradoxes present Pope at his most intense:

> Truth guards the Poet, sanctifies the line,
> And makes Immortal, Verse as mean as mine.
> (*Epilogue to the Satires. Dialogue II*, 246–7)

And once again we sense in the poetry the presence of a whole, complex, contradictory personality – an '*omnis ... vita senis*', older but if anything more imaginatively and morally vigorous than ever before.

In fact, these are poems of self-assertion and self-questioning, modelled on Horace's *Satires* II.iii. and vii. In one sense we feel they have been 'set up' so that Pope can defend his satire and attack the age in which it is so deeply embedded: in each dialogue it is Pope who dominates and who has the last triumphant word. This contrasts with Horace's two poems of self-criticism, where the adversaries are allowed to dominate, though hardly to 'win'. But on the other hand,

Pope is using this Horatian form to do more than simply defend himself. He uses it, as Horace did, to explore the complexities of his subject and to portray the nature of both speakers. If we are impressed by Pope's singular energy and passion, we are to be interested also in the intelligent responses of a typically cautious, morally lax, but quite acute, contemporary. His comments on Pope and current reactions to his poetry are not stupid or irrelevant.

In this respect it is fascinating to see how this 'Friend' interprets not only Pope but Horace, and here Pope presents us with a passage of masterful irony. He uses as his point of departure for *Dialogue I* the Friend's accusation that the *Imitations* have all been just cribbed from Horace:

> Why now, this moment, don't I see you steal?
> 'Tis all from *Horace: Horace* long before ye
> Said, "Tories call'd him Whig, and Whigs a Tory;"
> And taught his Romans, in much better metre,
> "To laugh at Fools who put their trust in *Peter*."   (6–10)

After these disparaging allusions to Pope's first Imitation, the Friend contrasts Pope's aggressive outspokenness with what he takes to be Horace's elegant delicacy:

> But *Horace*, Sir, was delicate, was nice,
> *Bubo* observes, he lash'd no sort of *Vice*:
> *Horace* would say, Sir Billy *serv'd the Crown*,
> Blunt *could do Bus'ness*, H–ggins *knew the Town*,
> In *Sappho* touch the *Failing of the Sex*,
> In rev'rend Bishops note some *small Neglects*,
> And own, the *Spaniard* did a *waggish thing*,
> Who cropt our Ears, and sent them to the King.
> His sly, polite, insinuating stile
> Could please at Court, and make AUGUSTUS smile:
> An artful Manager, that crept between
> His Friend and Shame, and was a kind of *Screen*.
> But 'faith your very Friends will soon be sore;
> *Patriots* there are, who wish you'd jest no more ...   (11–24)

As far as the Friend is concerned, Horace is admirable because he is so bland he offends no one, slyly ingratiates himself with the Court and Augustus, and protects his friends from the sense of shame. He quotes with approval 'Bubo's' conventional observation that Horace does not meddle with Vice, and he finds his own sly forms of words to illustrate what he takes to be Horace's delicate avoidance of direct comment: '*Sir* Billy *serv'd the Crown*', 'Blunt *could do Bus'ness*', 'And own, the *Spaniard* did a *waggish thing*.' This is hardly the Horace we have seen in the *Imitations*, and it is significant that, at this stage, Pope draws such a contrast between his own writing and this conventional, one-sided, view of Horace. The idea that Horace was just trying to please Augustus does not square with Pope's reading of the *Epistle to Augustus*, and in none of his poems does Horace attempt to shield his friends from shame. Harold Bloom might say that Pope's poetic vision here is attempting to cleanse itself at the expense of Horace. But in fact, the effect of these lines is very complex: they make us feel that Pope is indeed more biting, passionate, and moral than this Horace, but also that this is simply not the Horace that Pope has been imitating or that we have been reading.

And yet they offer a view of Horace which cannot be ignored: indeed they challenge and disorientate us. In doing so they achieve what Pope's *Imitations of Horace* as a whole achieve in their relationship to Horace. The most striking thing about this group of poems is its sustained energy and dynamism in the approach to the Horatian texts: every Imitation is different from every other, and each one is in itself a new departure. In this regard Pope's respect for the individuality of each Horatian text is impressive: far from reducing all his Horatian texts to any one formula or style, he constantly takes his lead from Horace and makes something new from each individual Horatian achievement. It is because of this that the *Imitations* as a group are so alive: the whole pattern of Pope's relationship with Horace over these five years involves constant change and imaginative development.

And yet this movement seems to contain within it a counter movement. We witness also a darkening struggle between two authors as they live within their texts. By honestly presenting his poems with their sources, by openly wrestling with one of his great predecessors in satire, Pope perhaps comes to know more consciously than most poets what Harold Bloom has called the 'anxiety of influence'. The overall movement from the buoyant confidence of the *Imitation of Satire II.i.*, through the depth of vision in the Imitations of the epistles of Book II, to the final portrayal of personal failure in the *Imitation of Epistle I.i.*, is a pattern of increasing strain and anxiety. The energy of Pope's development in the whole pattern of the *Imitations* must be set against this darkening of vision, both in Pope's perception of Horace and of himself and his time.

In this development Pope's Imitations argue for the plurality of 'Horace' and his texts, and for the necessary, and perhaps desirable, relativity of all interpretations of these Horaces. In the twelve Horatian poems Pope imitated we have twelve 'Horaces', not one;

and each Horatian text does what a poem so often does, it at once confirms and undermines our sense of what 'Horace' is. Whereas Shaftesbury tries to draw all the varied threads of Horace's late poetry to one vision ('All mean that same thing. If you have the moral of one, you have it all', Shaftesbury, 1900, p. 362), Pope's *Imitations* underline the diversity of these poetic achievements. In this diversity Pope finds opportunities to explore radically different views of Horace, who is now the moral teacher, now the immoral satirist, now the poetic visionary, now the aloof sceptic.

In addition, Pope's attitude to the details of Horace's classical texts is highly dynamic. Pope does not regard these classical texts as fixed, closed works; rather they are seen as being alive with suggestion, the catalysts of new meanings and new ideas. The *Imitations* do not merely allude to a Horace in the past: through the parallel texts and through the energy of intense linguistic detail they actively bring that Horace into the present, transformed by that process and newly alive. Indeed after we have read Horace's poems next to Pope's, those Horatian works can never be quite the same again. In the *Imitations* Pope has in a sense appropriated these Horatian poems, put them in a new order, and given them a new significance. *Epistle I.i.* is now not the fresh beginning of a book, but the troubled ending of a sequence. Furthermore, Pope's *Imitations* seem to raise new and fundamental questions about Horace and his poetry. How important is emotion, indeed passion, in the epistle form, usually prized for its display of control and urbanity? How far does Horace's vision of moral serenity spring from his own uncertainty and anxiety? Would Horace's texts be appropriately studied in terms of discontinuity rather than inner harmony?

We might ask, finally, whether Pope's *Imitations of Horace* do not question fundamentally the relationship between the 'self' and its poetry, and the problem of the 'origins' of that poetry. It is significant that when Eliot was drawn to reconsider the relationship between the 'individual talent' and 'tradition' he was forced to question 'the substantial unity of the soul', suggesting that in fact the poet had only a 'medium' and not a personality to express, a medium 'in which impressions and experiences combine in peculiar and unexpected ways' (1951, p. 20). More recently Roland Barthes has alluded to the radically plural nature of the 'Text', which exists in terms of an intertextual weave of 'citations, references, echoes, cultural languages (what language is not?), antecedent or contemporary' that make it impossible to identify for a 'Text' any simple 'source', 'influence', or, indeed, 'Author' (1977, p. 160).

This could be related to the paradoxes of the 'self' in both Horace's poetry and Pope's. In so many ways these are poets of 'self-portrait-ure', and critics have generally assumed that, as Eliot would say, these poets have personalities to express; and yet both Horace's poetry and Pope's seem to question the very idea of 'self' while they assert or imply it. Focusing so intently on human inconsistency and contradiction both Pope and Horace hint that 'self' is an ideal to be achieved and rarely attained, that desires and passions have 'identi-ties' of their own, and that the energies of the whole self – conscious and unconscious – cannot be contained in the fixed ideals of mor-ality, the received forms of poetry, or rigid conceptions of personal identity. Looking at the parallel texts of Pope's *Imitation of Horace* it is difficult to say if 'self' is the origin of poetry, or its goal, or rather, as Eliot would say, that from which the poet is attempting to escape.

Appendix:
Imitations of Horace Published 1730–40

(Dates and authors for anonymous works as suggested by Foxon, 1975)

1730

(13 May?) anon. [John Savage], *Horace to Scaeva. Epist. XVII. Book I. Imitated.*
Swift, *Horace Book I. Ode XIV ... Paraphrased and Inscribed to Ir – d*, [Dublin.]

1731

5 Feb. [James Miller], *Harlequin-Horace: or the Art of Modern Poetry.*

1732

(1732) anon. [?Charles Carthy], *An Ode in Imitation of the Third Ode of the Third Book of Horace. Address'd to the City of Dublin*, [Dublin].

1733

15 Feb. Pope, *The First Satire of the Second Book of Horace, Imitated in a Dialogue between A. Pope of Twickenham ... on the one Part, and his Learned Council on the other.*

2 March 'Guthry', *The First Satire of the Second Book of Horace, Imitated in a Dialogue between Mr. Pope and the Ordinary of Newgate.*

7 June anon., *The Satirist: in Imitation of the Fourth Satire of the First Book of Horace.*

1734

4 July Pope, *The Second Satire of the Second Book of Horace Paraphrased.*

21 Dec. anon. [Pope], *Sober Advice from Horace to the Young Gentlemen about Town. As Deliver'd in his Second Sermon.*

— anon., *Horace to Fannius* [an Imitation of Ode II.viii.].

1735

Feb. anon. [– Minshull], *The Miser, a Poem: From the First Satire of the First Book of Horace. Inscrib'd to H. Walpole.*

20 March George Ogle, *Epistles of Horace Imitated* [Epistles I.i. and I.iv.].

(April) Joseph Mitchell, *A Curse upon Punch, in Imitation of the Third Epode of Horace.*

Nov. George Ogle, *The Second Epistle of the First Book of Horace Imitated.*

12 Nov. James Miller, *Seasonable Reproof, a Satire in the Manner of Horace (Imitated from the Third and Fourth of the First Book of his Sermons).*

Appendix

1736

7 April   anon. [W. Melmoth], *Two Epistles of Horace* [*Epistles* i.xviii. and ii.i.].

1737

(Jan.)   anon. [Henry Hyde], *An Ode to the Earl of Chesterfield, Imploring his Majesty's Return. In Imitation of Horace, Ode II, Book IV.*
9 March   Pope, *Horace his Ode to Venus. Lib. IV. Ode I.*
28 April   Pope, *The Second Epistle of the Second Book of Horace, Imitated.*
20 May   Pope, *The First Epistle of the Second Book of Horace, Imitated.*
June   [George Ogle], *Of Legacy-Hunting. The Fifth Satire of the Second Book of Horace Imitated. A Dialogue between Sir Walter Raleigh, and Merlin the Prophet.*
1 Nov.   George Ogle, *The Miser's Feast; the Eighth Satire of the Second Book of Horace Imitated; a Dialogue between the Author and the Poet Laureate.*
—   [William Hamilton], *The Eighteenth Epistle of the Second Book of Horace, to Lollius, Imitated* (Edinburgh).

1738

23 Jan.   Pope, *The Sixth Epistle of the First Book of Horace Imitated.*
Feb.   anon. [F. Manning], *The Two First Odes of Horace Imitated.*
Feb.   George Ogle, *The Eleventh Epistle of the First Book of Horace Imitated.*
1 March   Pope, *An Imitation of the Sixth Satire of the Second Book of Horace.*
7 March   Pope, *The First Epistle of the First Book of Horace Imitated.*
March   J. Turner, *The First Epistle of the First Book of Horace Imitated.*
(18 April)   anon. [Robert Dodsley], *The Art of Preaching; In Imitation of Horace's Art of Poetry.*
April   George Ogle, *The Second Epistle of the First Book of Horace Imitated.*
May   anon., E. W.[alpole?], *The Sixth Satire of the First Book of Horace Imitated.*
26 Oct.   George Ogle, *Third Epistle of the First Book of Horace Imitated.*
—   George Ogle, *The Fifth Epistle of the First Book of Horace Imitated.*

1739

March   anon., *Epidemical Madness: A Poem in Imitation of Horace* [*Satire* ii.iii.].
(15 March)   [George Ogle], *The Eighth and Ninth Epistles of the First Book of Horace Imitated.*
May   anon. [?George Ogle], *Three Odes from the Second Book of Horace Imitated.*
May   anon., *The Sixteenth Epode of Horace Imitated: and Addressed to the People of England.*
28 June   anon. [Sir E. Turner], *An Imitation of Horace's 16th Epode.*
August   anon., *Men and Measures Characterised from Horace. Being an Imitation of the XVIth Ode of his Second Book.*
October   James Miller, *Art of Life. In Imitation of Horace's Art of Poetry. In Two Epistles. Epistle the First.*
(12 Dec.?) George Ogle, *The Twelfth Epistle of the First Book of Horace Imitated.*

— Richard West, *An Epistle to a Friend, In Imitation of the Second Epistle of the First Book of Horace.*

1740

Jan.   anon., *Horace's Instructions to the Roman Senate. (Imitated and Addressed to the House of Commons) and Character of Caius Asinius Pollio. In Two Odes* [III.ii. and II.i.].

April   J. Chase, *The Sixth Epistle of the First Book of Horace.*

Oct.   anon., *Horace, Book IV. Ode V Imitated.*

(1740)   anon., *An Imitation of the 22d. Ode in the First Book of Horace.*

Notes

PREFACE

1 The exact nature of Pope's Horatian text remains uncertain. Scholarship to date suggests that Pope's is an eclectic Horatian text, that he used Heinsius (1629) as a constant base, and that he emended it partly in the light of Bentley (1711) and Cunningham (1721*a* and *b*), as argued by L. Bloom, (1948), and partly in the light of other contemporary editions, including Baxter (1701), as implied by Rodgers (1949). My own research confirms this view, and in particular that Pope could have taken his emendations from many sources. I have spoken about Pope's Horatian text on that assumption; but until there is a complete study of the whole problem it can only be regarded as a plausible working hypothesis.

2 The Twickenham edition (IV) reproduces Pope's typography in the Horatian poems but does not print these index numbers. I have taken them from the first editions, occasionally adding and correcting from Pope's *Works*, 1743. The first edition of the *Imitation of Epistle II.i.* had only 39 index numbers generally referring to the initial line of each paragraph of the Latin poem printed at the bottom of the page; when Pope first printed the Latin in full in the octavo editions of 1738, he inserted 136 index numbers. It is interesting, however, that he did not increase the number in the corresponding case of the *Imitation of Epistle II.ii.*, which had 29 in the first edition and only one more when the Latin poem was printed in full. There are no index numbers for *Sober Advice*, the Imitations of Odes IV.i. and ix., and the *Imitation of Epistle I.vii.* The *Imitation of Satire II.vi.* had 24 index numbers in the first edition of 1738, but for some reason they were dropped in the *Works*, 1740 and 1743.

3 J. W. Tupper (1900), Reuben A. Brower (1959, Chapters VI and IX), G. K. Hunter (1960), Aubrey L. Williams (1963), and John M. Aden (1969) were the first modern critics to focus on these issues. Thomas E. Maresca (1966) attempted the first full historical study of the interpretation of Horace in the seventeenth and eighteenth centuries in relation to Pope's *Imitations*, but he presented a one-sided view of a 'Christianized' Renaissance Horace and a distorted view of the *Imitations* in the light of that. Maren-Sofie Røstvig in her comprehensive work on the 'beatus ille' tradition (1962) emphasized the Horace of retreat and contemplation, as did Maynard Mack (1969) in his study of retirement and politics in Pope's later poetry. Howard D. Weinbrot in a valuable but polemical work on the image of Augustus in 'Augustan' England (1978) raised again the whole question of the interpretation and evaluation of Horace, now stressing the disparagement of Horace as a political poet when compared with Juvenal. This too offered a one-sided view of Horace. Weinbrot has explored these themes further in a study of Pope (1982), but whereas he emphasizes the importance of Juvenal for Pope, my book stresses Pope's sustained interest in Horace. Weinbrot's whole approach

assumes that the eighteenth century's own generalizations about Horace and Juvenal provide adequate terms to describe the nature of Pope's *Imitations*, an assumption which I question. My own approach is much more in line with that of Howard Erskine-Hill (1983) who stresses the complexity and richness of the 'Augustan' and 'Horatian' traditions in English literature, and who interprets Pope's *Imitations* very sensitively within those contexts (Chapters 11 and 12).

4 The value of such a questioning approach to classical literature has been urged by D. R. Shackleton-Bailey (1962, p. 115) and reiterated by Penelope Wilson (1982, p. 87). Charles O. Brink (1981) has stressed the need for a revaluation of Horace's satires and epistles, particularly the epistles of Book 1, which, he asserts, 'need much fuller and deeper treatment than they have yet received' (p. 17).

1 INTERPRETING HORACE

1 J. W. Johnson (1967, Chapter 7) provides the best general introduction to the work of the Dutch scholars, particularly Heinsius, Scaliger, and Casaubon. Davies (1954) discusses the development of the Elzevir texts, and Sellin (1968) the importance of Heinsius in Stuart England. Weinbrot (1966) shows the popularity of Dacier's edition of Horace in England; while Marmier (1962), discussing Dacier and Desprez, points out that in France Dacier's edition was criticised by contemporaries such as Boileau for its literalism (pp. 50–1). For Pope's admiration of Dacier's *Horace*, however, see his letter to the Duke of Buckingham on 1 September, 1718 (*Corr.* I, p. 492). Shackleton-Bailey (1962) and Brink (1981) discuss the significance of Bentley's *Horace*. Maresca (1966, esp. Chapter 1) discusses these and other Renaissance editions of Horace, but he gives a distorted account of what he asserts is their 'Christian' bias. For the larger context of seventeenth-century classical scholarship see Sandys (1903–8, II) and Pfeiffer (1976).

2 It is important to note that Dryden is talking about Horatian satire. Horace's odes and epodes provided imitators with opportunities to portray corruption and vice beyond the scope of the Horatian satire and epistle. Early examples of these are the anonymous *Englands Sin, and Shame: In a Paralel between the Degenerate Estate of Old Rome & Great Britain. Or, Hor. Lib. 3. Ode 6.* (1672) and *The Causes of Scotland's Miseries* (1700) based on the same ode. In 1739, when Whitehead was turning to Juvenal and Persius to portray, appropriately, *The State of Rome, Under Nero and Domitian*, the anonymous *Men and Measures Characterised from Horace. Being an Imitation of the XVIth Ode of his Second Book* attacked Walpole's ministry in bitter irony, and the anonymous *Sixteenth Epode of Horace Imitated: and Addressed to the People of England* urged the nation in the most impassioned tones to reject the corruption that was making it the image of Rome.

3 Modern classicists have strongly criticized Dryden's account of the different historical contexts which, according to Dryden, gave rise to the different satire of Horace and Juvenal: see Harold Guite (1971) and Niall Rudd (1966, pp. 258–73) who argues that 'as far as Horace and Juvenal are concerned, Dryden's essay is wrong or misleading on almost every major point' (p. 273). Dryden's account was, however, extremely influential as can be seen, for example, in the essays on satire by Dennis (1721) and Knox (1779). For eighteenth-century accounts of the Roman Republic and Empire see particularly Vertot, *The History of the Revolutions That Happened in the Govern-*

ment of the Roman Republic, trans. John Ozell, 1723–4 (Pope is known to have had this book: see Mack, 1977, p. 303), and Blackwell, *Memoirs of the Court of Augustus*, 1753–63.

4 It is significant that modern critics have been divided on this crucial issue: in his studies of Horace's *Epistles* I. (1910, and most importantly, 1914) E. Courbaud stresses the importance of what he regarded as Horace's 'conversion' to Stoicism as recorded in those works. N. W. DeWitt (1937) and M. N. Porter Packer (1941), however, argue for his 'consistent Epicureanism'. But various forms and degrees of eclecticism are emphasized by W. S. Maguiness (1938), La Penna (1949), Fraenkel (1957, pp. 253–7, for example on *Odes* I, xxxiv), and McGann (1969, esp. pp. 9–32) who nevertheless stresses the importance of Panaexus for *Epistles* I.

5 The most comprehensive and suggestive study of both the 'Epicurean Horace' and the 'Stoic Horace' in the seventeenth and eighteenth centuries is in Røstvig (1962, *passim*); see also Earl Miner's short study of the influence of Stoicism in the seventeenth century (1970). The Horatian emblem books based on Oto van Veen's engravings of Horatian passages were an important part of this tradition (see, for example, Veen, 1612, and Veen, *Theatro Moral*, 1669). In general these works give a strongly Stoic interpretation of Horace, emphasizing the importance of moral choice, the strength but isolation of the Stoic wise man, the vanity of material things, and the ultimate triumph of the spirit set against haunting images of death. Røstvig reproduces four characteristic engravings (1962, I, facing pages 18, 26, 28, 38). For Pope's knowledge of these emblem books see Spence, ed. Osborn (1966, I. p. 228) and Cedric D. Reverard II (1980), who reproduces two engravings of Virtue.

6 Critics of Pope's *Imitation* have tended to concentrate on other aspects of form: the structural character of formal verse satire (Mary Claire Randolph, 1942), the debate format (Aden, 1962), and the distinction in purpose and tone between satire and epistle (Weinbrot, 1969, Chapter 6).

2 IMITATION

1 George C. Fiske's (1920) study of Horace as an imitator of Lucilius is a classic work in this area. The essays in *Creative Imitation and Latin Literature* (ed. David West and Tony Woodman, 1979) are very stimulating studies of such 'inter-textuality'. Both provide striking comparisons with Pope's practice in the *Imitations*, the latter especially in that so many of the essays stress the minute particularities of language involved in this 'creative' imitating of earlier, or other, Latin and Greek texts. Gordon Williams' *Tradition and Originality in Roman Poetry* (1968) is also very relevant, particularly Chapter 5, 'The Blending of Greek and Roman'.

2 Spingarn (Introduction to *Critical Essays of the Seventeenth Century*, 1908, I, pp. xlviii-lviii) discusses the influence of French theorists on this tradition. Brooks (1949) stresses the importance of the theory of free translation, while Weinbrot (1966) the role of the Restoration parodists. Weinbrot (1969) studies the whole tradition up to Johnson, and (1970) examines the 'role of the original'. Moskovit (1968) compares Pope's practice with that of his predecessors, particularly Swift. My account of this tradition is indebted to these studies.

3 Peterson (1975) discusses well the ambiguity of Johnson's attitudes to the 'classics' which can be compared with Pope's vigorous treatment of his Horatian texts. Weinbrot (1969, Chapters 7 and 8) stresses the significance of

Johnson's modifications of Juvenal, as do E. and L. Bloom (1970) in their study of the relationship between *London* and its Juvenalian texts. Mason (1962) uses Johnson to question whether Juvenal is a 'moral' writer.

4 More recent linguistic studies of translation suggest that *all* translation, in fact, undermines any such clear-cut categories (see a valuable collection of essays on translation ed. Brower, 1966). Dryden himself, of course, uses them with caution. It is likely, however, that the whole Restoration debate about different kinds of translation should be reconsidered from a linguistic point of view. The most recent, and most detailed, study of Oldham's Imitations of Horace shows how difficult it is to distinguish between close translation and free imitation (Paul Hammond, 1983, Chapter 4).

5 These questions should be seen in the context of the important critical debate in the eighteenth century about particular and general truth: see Scott Elledge's essay on this debate (1947) and Jeffrey Hart's further reflections on Elledge's work (1970). R. Wittkower (1965) offers fine inter-disciplinary views on the subject considering both fine art and literature in theory and practice in the eighteenth century.

3 RAILLERY AND ENERGY: *THE IMITATION OF SATIRE II.I.*

CRITICISM

The best modern general studies of Horace's satires are Rudd (1966) and Fraenkel (1957, Chapters 3 and 4). Lejay's edition of the *Satires* (1911) contains a detailed introduction to each poem. Campbell (1924, Chapter 6) provides a general introduction to Horatian satire, and there are valuable general essays by Anderson (1963) and McGann (1973).

On *Satire* II.i. in particular Fraenkel (1957, pp. 145–53) explores what he sees as Horace's profound revaluation of Lucilius. Rudd (1966, pp. 124–31) considers it in the context of Horace's other satires about Lucilius (*Satires* i.iv. and x.) and stresses its wit and irony. Lejay (1911, pp. 285–95) discusses the Roman laws against libel to which the poem alludes.

Hunter (1960) analyses the 'Romanticism' of Pope's image of himself in the Imitation. Maresca (1966, pp. 37–72) sees it as Pope's appeal to a higher vision of truth and order; but Mack (1969, pp. 66–9 and 177–87) stresses the poem's local political innuendo. Edwards (1963, pp. 80–95) and Weinbrot (1969, pp. 154–7) offer dark readings of this apparently triumphant poem, interpretations challenged by Reverard (1980). Erskine-Hill (1981, and 1983, pp. 292–301) considers in detail the complexity of Pope's response to Horace's poem; while Weinbrot (1982, Chapter 7) analyses Pope's fusion of Horatian and Juvenalian modes. Mack (1984) reproduces the manuscript of this Imitation.

1 See also Juvenal, *Satire* I. 165–7, for Lucilius as the satirist who reveals secret hypocrisy. For the importance of such views of Lucilius in seventeenth- and eighteenth-century England, see Weinbrot (1978, pp. 139–40; 1980; and 1982, pp. 45–51).

2 For a new assessment of the relevance of this type of Stoic retreat for Horace see McGann (1969, pp. 24–30) where he quotes this same passage from Seneca's 'De Tranquillitate Animi'.

3 Pope's Latin text of the two lines is the old version, found in Heinsius, Dacier, Desprez, and Baxter, and used in Creech's standard translation. Bentley, followed by Cunningham, repunctuated the lines in what is now the accepted way giving the last line to Trebatius:

Opprobriis dignum laceraverit, integer ispe?
Solventur risu: tu missus abibis.
Pope let this 'discrepancy' between his Latin text and his Imitation stand in all
subsequent editions of the poem. In the 1751 edition of the *Works*, Warburton,
rightly or wrongly, changed Pope's Latin text to follow Bentley's reading.

4 Gordon Williams (1968, Chapter 7) offers an excellent study of the autobiographical form as used by Horace and other Roman poets; pp. 443–59 on
Lucilius and Horace are very relevant to this whole discussion. Mack in a
classic essay (1951) explored Pope's use of the satirists' traditional 'stances';
and more recently he (1978) has studied the subtle relationship between
Pope's 'deformity' and his poetry. Dustin Griffin (1978) also explores this
theme and emphasizes the contradictions of Pope's full personality (see
particularly pp. 218 and 277).

5 Of course not all the responses to Pope's Imitation were so positive: they
include the immediate counter attack from Lady Mary Wortley Montague and
Lord Hervey, *Verses Address'd to the Imitator of the First Satire of the Second
Book of Horace* (1733), and a satiric attack on Pope by Mr 'Guthry' which
turns Pope's whole poem against itself, *The First Satire of the Second Book of
Horace, Imitated in a Dialogue between Mr. Pope and the Ordinary of
Newgate* (March 1733). But see also the anonymous *The Satirist: in Imitation
of the Fourth Satire of the First Book of Horace* (June, 1733) which praised
Pope as a satirist, and, later, the anonymous Imitation, *The First Satire of the
Second Book of Horace, Imitated* (1745) which was clearly modelled on
Pope's poem as well as the original. On these and other responses to Pope's
Imitation, see Weinbrot (1979) and (1982, pp. 233–6 and 339–40).

4 HORACE, MORAL: *THE PARAPHRASE OF SATIRE II.II.*

CRITICISM

Rudd (1966, Chapter 6) discusses the three diatribes of *Satires* II (ii, iii, vii) and
provides a valuable account of the Roman *mores* to which Horace alludes in this
satire. Lejay (1911, pp. 311–27) sets out the Stoic and Epicurean background of
the poem which provides a useful context for Dacier's reading.

Aden (1969, pp. 27–46) analyses Pope's Imitation in terms of its use of the
prolocutor. Erskine-Hill (1975, pp. 309–17) sets the poem in the rich context of
the country house tradition. Weinbrot (1982, pp. 277–83) finds ' Horatian
dominance' in this work, despite some Juvenalian undercurrents, a view shared
by Brower (1959, pp. 292–3).

1 Pope uses Heinsius' text as his base for this poem, but substantially abbreviates the work for his own purposes, reducing Horace's poem from 136 lines
to 116 in the following ways:

(a) From the first 48 lines Pope leaves out, at various points, 14 full lines and
parts of 9 others, thereby making this part of Ofellus' reported speech sharper
and terser. Pope leaves out parts of lines 8, 9, and 10 of the original; all of lines
11, 12, 13; parts of lines 15 and 16; parts of line 20 and all of 21 and 22; all of
25 and 26; part of line 28, all of lines 29–32, and part of line 33; all of line 38;
part of line 46, and all of lines 47 and 48.

Some of the gaps are indicated by asterisks or dashes; other lines are
'silently' dropped. In three cases broken lines are spliced together to create
pastiche 'Horatian' lines:

(1) Pope's line 8 is made from 'Dicam si potero –' of the original line 8, ' –
leporem sectatus, equove' of line 9, and 'Lassus' from line 10.

(2) His line 10 puts together 'Sperne cibum vilem' of line 15 and 'foris est promus, & atrum' of line 16.

(3) His line 18 brings together 'Quam laudas, pluma?' from line 28 and 'laudas insane trilibrem' from line 33.

The effect of these changes is that Ofellus' images and ideas are juxtaposed in new and striking ways. The Imitation, of course, also emphasizes this.

(b) From the description of Ofellus at the end of the poem, Pope silently, but significantly, drops line 115 of the original, the allusion to Ofellus' sons ('Cum pecore & gnatis, fortem mercede colonum' – 'with his cattle and his sons, a sturdy tenant farmer'). This would follow Pope's line 96.

(c) Finally, from Ofellus' speech he omits from lines 119–20 in the original the allusion to the bad weather which stops work ('gratus conviva per imbrem / Vicinus' – 'if in rainy weather a welcome neighbour paid me a visit'). The result is that his line 100 is another spliced line:

Sive operum vacuo, &c. – bene erit, non piscibus urbe petitis.

2 For Pope's relationship with Hugh Bethel see Aden (1969, pp. 33–6) and Erskine-Hill (1975, pp. 309–17). Dixon comments well on Pope's raillery of Bethel in this poem (1968, pp. 34–8), though this needs to be set against Dacier's more positive characterization of Ofellus.

3 George Ogle explores this Horatian theme of the paradoxical fusion of avarice and prodigality in his portrait of Nasidienus in The Miser's Feast; The Eighth Satire of the Second Book of Horace Imitated; a Dialogue between the Author and the Poet Laureate (1737).

4 Such works include Satire II.vi., especially 1–15, and 59–76; Epistle I.xiv.; Epistle I.xvi., especially 1–16; Epistle I.xviii., especially 96–112.

5 To appreciate Pope's success in creating a poetry of Horatian inner contentment we need only compare this passage with George Ogle's attempts to portray Horatian retreat in The Second Epistle of the First Book of Horace Imitated (1738) or mental serenity in The Eleventh Epistle of the First Book of Horace Imitated (1738). The anonymous Sixth Satire of the First Book of Horace Imitated (1738) by 'E. W.' is, however, more successful in this vein:

> Then Home to sup, one Servant brings to eat
> Olives and Celary my usual Treat:
> My earthen Urns are plac'd in wooden Tray,
> No silver Cistern casts a dazling Ray,
> Nor marble Slabs my shining Salvers bear,
> My Plates are Delft, the rest is Tunbridge Ware.   (165–70)

6 For a valuable discussion of the significance of this phrase in Epistles I, see McGann (1969, pp. 19–20) where he suggests that 'aequus' translates the concept of euthymia central to the doctrines of Democritus and Panaetius in which 'the ideas of balance and consistency, if not of joy, ... are essential.' He stresses the distinction between 'aequus animus' and 'tranquillitas' in this respect. Baxter, interestingly, sees in the 'aequus' of Satire II.i. 70 something of this: 'dicitur cui mens in sede manet suâ, & per hoc, dulcis & pacatus' (1701, p. 316).

5 HORACE, IMMORAL: THE IMITATION OF SATIRE I.II. (SOBER ADVICE)

CRITICISM

Fraenkel (1957, pp. 76–86), who uses this poem to introduce his chapter on Satires I, emphasizes its trenchant personal satire and the sophistication of its literary allusions and parodies. Rudd (1966, Chapter 1), discussing the poem along with the other 'diatribes' of *Satires* I (i. and iii.), assesses Horace's attitudes to contemporary Cynic, Epicurean, and Stoic thought. Lejay (1911, pp. 29–37) is also very illuminating on this.

Pope's Imitation has been unnecessarily maligned and unconvincingly defended. Brower (1959) finds it a 'fairly nasty imitation' (p. 293); while Moskovit (1965) and Aden (1969, pp. 47–68) in different ways attempt to justify it. Edwards (1963), more shrewdly, argues that it 'explores the perversity of cultivated lust' (p. 84).

1 Contrary to his normal practice of using Heinsius as his base, Pope here uses Bentley's text with all its emendations. He does not use index numbers in this Imitation. The words in capital letters are, of course, Pope's addition; but they are, in fact, modelled on Bentley's practice: Bentley places 'LEPOREM' and 'MEUS' in capitals to signal in lines 105–8 the quotation from Callimachus, and Pope prints them too, which nicely confuses the issue.

2 A fascinating analogue to Pope's parody of Bentley's notes is an anonymous work, *The Odes of Horace in Latin and English; with a translation of Dr. Bentley's Notes. To which are added, Notes upon Notes, Done in the Bentleian Stile* (1712–13). On the one hand, the writer satirizes the fusion of arrogance, scholarly fetishism, and salaciousness in Bentley's notes, but, on the other, he has to admit that all too often the Doctor is right in his interpretation of erotic passages. Commenting on Bentley's note on 'male pertinaci' (*Ode* I.ix. 24) describing a coy girl who teasingly feigns resistance, he asserts: 'The Dr. is extremely concern'd for some sowr Morose Criticks, who, as he says, would make *male pertinaces* [*sic.*] signifie an *utter refusal* and a *resolute holding out against all Attacks*, and he will by no means allow of that severe Interpretation. He is resolv'd the Girls shall yield: and I verily believe *Horace* was of his Mind. The truth of it is, *Horace* describes the Pleasure in so luscious and alluring a manner, that it is a very hard matter to peruse him with a feeling Intimacy, as the Dr. does, without becoming insensibly drawn into the same soft and tender Sentiments' (Part III, p. 12). I am indebted to Penelope Wilson for drawing my attention to this work (see her discussion of it, 1982, pp. 84–5). For another contemporary reaction to Bentley's *Horace* see Jean Le Clerc (1713). There is a useful account of the reception of Bentley's edition in Monk (1830). Thomas Bentley (Richard's nephew) in *A Letter to Mr. Pope, Occasioned by Sober Advice from Horace* (1735) actually admits that many readers found that Pope's *Imitations* revealed more of Horace than 'A Cartload of Commentaries' (p. 15).

3 In terms of Horace's satiric attacks on his friends Pope's reading of Horace is more challenging than Dacier's: Dacier tries to argue against the assumption that the satire on Malthinus in line 25 is a direct comment on Maecenas' effeminacy (VI, pp. 123–5). Pope, in effect, implies it was by making Horace's Sallust (lines 48–54) into a satiric portrait of Bolingbroke (lines 61–70). Bolingbroke certainly took it as such, as he indicated to Swift, 27 June–6 July, 1734: 'he has sent it [the Imitation] me, but I shall keep his secret, as he desires, & shall not I think return him the copy, for the Rogue has fixed a ridicule upon me, which some events of my life would seem perhaps to justify him in doing' (*Corr.* III, p. 414).

6 LYRIC VISION: *THE IMITATIONS OF ODES IV.I. AND IV.IX.*

CRITICISM

Fraenkel (1957) discusses Horace's *Odes* IV in Chapter 9, and considers IV.i., pp. 410–14, and ix. pp. 423–6. Commager (1962) analyses IV.i., pp. 291–7 and ix., pp. 321–2. Leishman (1956) provides a valuable introduction to Horace's odes for the general reader. This and Storrs (1959) are the best studies of the problems of translating Horatian odes into English.

Mack (1945) considers the two versions of Pope's *Imitation of Ode iv.i.*, and Erskine-Hill (1983, pp. 315–16) offers a brief analysis.

1 For contemporary studies of Horace's metres see the anonymous translation of A. P. Manutius' *A Treatise of the Several Measures Used by Horace in His Odes and Epodes* (1718) and E. Manwaring, *Stichology: or, a Recovery of the Latin, Greek and Hebrew Numbers, Exemplified in ... the Reduction of all Horace's Metres* (1737). The edition of Horace by David Watson and S. Patrick (1760) underlines Horace's poetic word order by printing the Latin words in the margin 'ranged in their Grammatical Order', although, of course, this was done to facilitate reading and translation.

2 The earliest English verse translations of Horatian Odes were by John Ashmore (1621), Sir Thomas Hawkins (1627, enlarged editions in 1631, 1635, and 1638); Henry Rider (1638; 2nd edn 1644); John Smith (1649); Sir Thomas Hawkins and Barton Holyday (1650–2); Sir Richard Fanshawe (1652); Barton Holyday (1653); and the various contributors to *The Poems of Horace*, ed. Alexander Brome (1666, 2nd edn 1671). For a short study of these see Valerie Edden (1973) who points out that Holyday attempted to reproduce Horace's classical metres in English, and that, more successfully, Fanshawe was the first to use a variety of different English metres in an attempt to convey the effects of Horace's different metrical patterns. Between 1660 and 1750 the most important verse translations of the odes were by John Harington (1684), Thomas Creech (1718), Henry Coxwell (1718), W. Duncombe, *Carmen Seculare* (1721), Roscommon *et al.* (1721), J. Hanway (1730), T. Hare (1737) and P. Francis (1747).

3 It is significant that G. Williams (1962) argues that the emotion in Roman poetry of this type is always fictional. He uses the treatment of homosexuality in this ode to show that 'the autobiographical form in Roman poetry is a poetic convention' (p. 40), and that the passion for Ligurinus is itself a convention. For a full discussion of this position with reference to Roman love poetry, see G. Williams (1968, Chapter 8, on 'Truth and Sincerity').

4 Ben Jonson's translation of this poem (*Underwood* 86), unlike Pope's Imitation, keeps the Roman setting. Jonson also translated *Odes* III.ix. (*Underwood* 87) and *Epode* II (*Underwood* 85). His deliberate literalism contrasts markedly with Pope's imaginative freedom. For a study of Jonson's interest in Horace, see Pierce (1981) and Erskine-Hill (1983, particularly pp. 169–74).

7 THE HORATIAN EPISTLE: *THE IMITATION OF EPISTLE II.II.*

CRITICISM

Brink (1982) offers the most complete commentary on *Epistle* II.ii. discussing particularly well the poem's 'diversity and unity' (pp. 513–22). Brink (1963, pp. 183–90), stressing that the poem is a literary treatise, comments primarily on the central passage about poetic language (lines 106–25). McGann (1954) studies how the poem's various themes are woven together and the problems this poses for interpretation.

A. L. Williams (1963) analyses the relationship between Pope's Imitation and Horace's epistle, stressing the importance of the metaphors of loss and time in Pope. Maresca (1966, pp. 117–49) unconvincingly argues that Pope's poem is about the conflict between the human and the divine views of life; while Erskine-Hill (1983, pp. 317–24) emphasizes the inwardness of this autobiographical poem. Weinbrot (1982, pp. 283–7) points to the darkening of Pope's own earlier Horatian vision in this work.

1 Cf. McGann's (1969) comment that 'the *Epistles* [of Book I] form a space, not a line' (p. 97, n. 2). His approach to the place of ethical principles within *Epistles* I is also valuable: 'What Horace has created is a self-contained world of the imagination in which ethical principles are paramount. It is for us to enter and explore this world, experiencing its texture and finally grasping it in all its complex harmony. The principles are integral to this final and total experience of the poem, in which we apprehend them not as a precept directed to us in our everyday lives, but as a vision of morality transfigured by the poetic imagination' (p. 100). Brink (1982) also considers these issues (see particularly pp. 451–63).

2 Brink (1963) stresses the emotional character of this 'literary' Horatian epistle. Noting that it is a 'poem of refusal' he asserts: 'The literary criticism of the letter is fitted into this psychological setting with great skill. The malaise of Roman poetry and the demand for new standards are part of Horace's present disenchantment. It is this personal emotion which causes him to make his critical points' (p. 185). In this respect *Spectator* essay no. 618 on the nature of the epistle provides interesting terms of reference with which to view this Imitation, and indeed all the Imitations that follow. The essay suggests that the passions and emotions expressed in the Heroic epistle, of Ovid for example, are not generally to be found in the Horatian epistle, which on the contrary is characterized by urbanity, wit, and detachment. In this sense, Pope has used that Horatian form to express an 'inappropriate' degree of feeling; but in doing so has perhaps seen more in Horace's language than his contemporaries were accustomed to perceive. Levine's (1962) valuable account of the verse epistle before Pope would seem to confirm the view that Pope's epistles were unusual in this respect.

3 Both McGann (1954, p. 354) and Brink (1963, p. 185) comment on the disorientating effect of the sequence of passages at the 'centre' of this poem. The debate turns on the question of the role of the passage on poetic language in the poem as a whole.

4 James Miller's *Art of Life* (1739), an Imitation of the *Ars Poetica* which turns it into a moral essay on the need for order, harmony, virtue, and sincerity in life, could be seen as an unintentional parody of Horace's ideas. For yet another Imitation relating art and life see George Ogle's *Third Epistle of the First Book of Horace Imitated* (1738). Both poems are merely conventional and throw into relief Pope's originality.

5 Cf. McGann's (1969) comment on Horace's satire on the various sources of human happiness in *Epistle* I.vi.: 'There is irony in this but there is present also an important element in Horace's philosophic position, his awareness of the importance of the individual human nature and his willingness to tolerate it in all its variety' (p. 47).

6 'L'âge adoucit nos humeurs ... Les réflexions & l'expérience des années passées contribuent à nous rendre meilleurs; voila pourquoi le poète joint

ensemble *lenior & melior* ... Un vieillar, qui ne chancelle point encore sous le poids des années, est comme un arbre fruitier dans le tems de l'autone: il conserve encore ses feuilles, voila pour l'agrément; & il est outre cela chargé de fruits, voila pour le profit' (1728, II, pp. 389–90. Quoted also by A. Williams, 1963, p. 320).

8 POETRY AND POLITICS; *THE IMITATION OF EPISTLE II.I.* ('TO AUGUSTUS')

CRITICISM

The best modern studies of *Epistle* II.i. are by Fraenkel (1957, Chapter 8) who concentrates on its central themes and artistic design; Brink (1963, pp. 191–209) who focuses on the poem's literary criticism; G. Williams (1968, pp. 71–5) who re-assesses the poem's structure of argument, suggesting that its real theme is the value of non-dramatic poetry; and Brink (1982) who offers a full commentary and critical analysis.

Brower (1959, pp. 305–9) presents the traditional reading of the Imitation's ironic attack on George II, which has been challenged by Weinbrot (1978, Chapter 6) arguing that in many ways the eighteenth century would have seen the Roman Augustus as similar to, not different from, George II. This interpretation is supported by Levine (1967), Schonhorn (1968 and 1980), and Kelsall (1976); but it is seen as one-sided by Erskine-Hill (1983, pp. 324–34). Russo (1972, pp. 215–28) comments particularly well on the poem's literary criticism.

1 It is uncanny that an anonymous Imitation of Horace's *Epistle* II.i. was published in April 1736 which was addressed to Pope, and presents *him* as Horace's Augustus. The poem laments the weakness of contemporary poetry and drama, and asks for Pope's guidance in improving artistic standards (see anon., *Two Epistles of Horace Imitated*).

2 As an example of the kind of panegyric Pope is satirizing we might consider the Imitation of Horace which had appeared in January 1737 expressing concern at the King's absence from a sympathetic point of view, *An Ode to the Earl of Chesterfield, Imploring his Majesty's Return. In Imitation of Horace, Ode II., Book IV.* The author had compared the King's imagined return to Augustus' return from what Horace presents as a campaign against the Sygambri, a German tribe (cf. Page, 1967, p. 404):

> Applauding Senates shall record his Fame,
>   And hail the Arbiter of *Europe* home;
> Him haughty *Gallia's* Dread they shall proclaim;
>   From him the *Turk* and *Tartar* wait their Doom.

> Fate never gave a King so great before;
>   A King so good no Nation shall behold;
> For Him the grateful Realm shall Heav'n adore,
>   For Him, whose Reign revives the Age of Gold.   (p. 10)

This, of course, is an imitation of the very passage from *Ode* IV.ii. that Dacier uses to provide a contrast with the 'decorum' of the epistle style. One of the nice ironies about this Imitation is that it presents Pope as the Pindar whose poetry might be able to summon the King home.

3 The imaginative power of Pope's approach to the relationship between poetry in politics in the Horatian poem and in his own society emerges from comparison with a later anonymous Imitation, *Horatii Ep. I. Lib. II. ad*

Augustum. The First Epistle of the Second Book of Horace Imitated. To the Right Honourable Philip, Lord Hardwicke, Lord High-Chancellor of Great-Britain, 1749. Whereas Pope seems to enter Horace's epistle, the author of this work merely skims along the surface of the argument.

4 For a general discussion of eighteenth-century views on tragedy see J. W. Johnson (1967, Chapter 8). His analysis of Cato as a Republican hero and his discussion of Pope's letter about the emotional power of Addison's *Cato* (pp. 99–100) are also relevant.

5 It is interesting to compare Pope's satire on contemporary theatre with James Miller's most successful Imitation of Horace, *Harlequin-Horace: or The Art of Modern Poetry* (1731) in which Miller uses the passages on the theatre in the *Ars Poetica* to satirize contemporary opera, pantomime, and mock Coronations. This work may, indeed, have influenced Pope's satire.

6 Howard Erskine-Hill (1983) comments well on Pope's manner of addressing 'George Augustus' throughout this poem, noting how it relates to Horace's own achievement: 'The idiom of the Epistle brings poet and ruler together in one sustained, serious, amusing and familiar act of communication. This is true of both poems. But in Pope's Epistle the false ruler is at the beginning and end, thrust out of this ideal dialogue into bold relief by the obtrusion of an extravagant and un-Augustan irony' (p. 334).

7 The anonymous *Remarks* on Carthy's translation (1731) emphasizes the importance of the metaphors in this poem, and notes the force of this 'coffin' metaphor in the poem's concluding passage (p. 20).

9 IDEALISM AND SCEPTICISM: THE IMITATION OF EPISTLE I.VI.

CRITICISM

The best modern study of *Epistles* I as a whole is by McGann (1969) who sees the epistles as conscious works of art rather than as the products of 'real' situations. In this respect Morris (1931) is also useful. Courbaud (1914) gives a full account of each epistle in Book I, but his approach is rather simplistic, while the formal studies by Stégen (1960 and 1963) are very wooden. Fraenkel (1957, Chapter 6) offers fine analyses of individual works; while West (1967, pp. 15–55) offers a refreshing view of Horace's use of imagery in the epistles. G. Williams (1968, Chapter 1) uses *Epistles* I to illustrate 'Some Characteristic Problems and Difficulties' of interpreting Roman poetry and in doing so provides a fine introduction to *Epistles* I itself. There is a valuable general essay on the Horatian epistle by Dilke (1973).

Courbaud (1914, pp. 105–16) gives a very Stoical reading of *Epistle* I.vi.; but McGann (1969, pp. 46–8) is more representative in speaking of its 'tolerant irony' and 'off-hand permissiveness'. Brower (1959, 179–80) stresses well the force of that irony.

Tupper (1900, pp. 212–13) contrasts Horace's cynical 'indifference' with Pope's strong commitment to virtue, and Aden (1969, pp. 69–84) sees this in relation to the poem's political commitments. Price (1965, pp. 168–71), however, emphasizes the poem's own inner contradictions of 'choice' and vision. Weinbrot (1982, pp. 287–92) discusses the poem in terms of the satiric stances of Persius and Juvenal; while Erskine-Hill (1983, pp. 334–9) analyses it in terms of the development of independent judgement.

1 McGann (1969) argues that this virtue is specifically the Stoic virtue: 'As the austerity of *fortis omissis deliciis* suggests, Horace is speaking of the Stoic

pursuit of virtue, against which he has already, while recommending *nil admirari*, issued a warning (15.f.)' (p. 47). Dacier and Shaftesbury, of course, do not make this distinction.

2 The point is that this kind of passionate but self-questioning rhetoric is different from the simpler 'sublimity' which Carnochan (1970) and Weinbrot (1982, Chapter 1) show was associated with Juvenal in the eighteenth century. I am suggesting that the century's own distinction between 'Horatian' and 'Juvenalian' is not able to account adequately for this type of poetry in either Horace or Pope.

10 FABLES OF THE SELF: *THE IMITATIONS OF SATIRE II.VI. AND EPISTLE I.VII.*

CRITICISM

Rudd (1966, Chapter 9) sees *Satire* II.vi. as 'a poem about wishes' (p. 243) and stresses its vision of contentment. So do Brower (1959, pp. 168–78) and Lejay (1911, pp. 512–23), who emphasize its praise of country life. Brink (1965), however, analyses the complexity of the 'seeming unity' of the poem and the contradictions in its attitudes to town and country and to Maecenas.

Fraenkel (1957, pp. 327–39) offers a detailed analysis of *Epistle* I.vii., commenting valuably on the ethics of benefaction as discussed by Aristotle, Cicero, and Seneca. McGann (1969, pp. 48–56) discusses the problems of friendship, particularly in the story of Philippus and Mena. On that story and Horace's relationship with Maecenas, see also Hiltbrunner (1960), Reckford (1959), and Weinbrot (1982, pp. 51–9).

Aden (1969, Chapter 5) analyses Pope's 'Swiftian' style and stresses the political allusions in both these Imitations, suggesting that 'In the Manner of Dr. Swift' does mean not 'stylistically' but 'politically' (p. 105).

1 Shaftesbury was not alone in the eighteenth century in criticizing easy Horatian 'contentment' and what Røstvig (1962, II, *passim*) shows to be the soft version of Horatian retreat. She points out that Thomas Nevile in his *Imitations of Horace* (1758) and Pope in the *Essay on Man* (IV, 168–70) were sharply critical of 'The whole fashionable creed of rural "simplicity"' which was in fact based on money (p. 146). The anonymous *Horace to Scaeva. Epist. XVII. Book I. Imitated* (1730) is notable for its satire on the life of the country parson it offers as an alternative to more fashionable advancement in the Church. Horace's own ironic description of himself in retreat seems all too apt:

> "Amen, I cry,
> Wallow, good Pig, in thy own Sty;
> And caring for thy self alone,
> Live to the World, an useless Drone".   (p. 21)

2 For a short study of other seventeenth- and eighteenth-century translations of the fable of the 'Weasel' and its 'application', see Ogilvie (1981).

11 THE STOIC SELF: *THE IMITATION OF EPISTLE I.i.*

CRITICISM

Courbaud (1914, pp. 60–79) interprets *Epistle* I.i. in terms of what he takes to be Horace's conversion to Stoicism; Stégen (1960, pp. 8–35), emphasizing Horace's commitment to Stoic ideals and his failure to achieve its ideals, offers a darker reading of the poem. McGann (1969, pp. 33–7) sees the poem as designed to introduce some of the central concerns of the book as a whole, and emphasizes its wit and irony, particularly in the 'flippant' final line.

Maresca (1966, Chapter 5) is unusual in seeing Pope's Imitation as an inner spiritual drama culminating in a vision of Pope's spiritual triumph. Lauren (1975) argues that 'Pope's concerns are above all political' (p. 419), a view questioned by Erskine-Hill (1983, pp. 339–44). Weinbrot (1982, pp. 292–8) suggests that Bolingbroke is seen positively by Pope and that his presence helps keep the poem 'Horatian'; whereas B. S. Hammond (1984, Chapter 7) sees the work as being critical of Bolingbroke and stresses Pope's feelings of failure. My chapter is a substantially revised and enlarged version of an article that appeared in *The Art of Alexander Pope*, see Stack (1979).

1 For two stimulating readings of the opening passages of this epistle see West (1967, pp. 22–8) and G. Williams (1968, pp. 1–7).

2 As McGann (1969) points out, these famous lines are a somewhat deceptive introduction to *Epistles* 1: 'While both the Stoicism of the *sapiens* and extreme hedonism are represented (the latter not very seriously), neither plays an important part, and the book as a whole displays a substantially coherent, though by no means monolithic, outlook lying between these extremes' (p. 9).

3 Furthermore, one modern critic has found Platonic influence in this part of Horace's epistle; see Heller (1964).

4 In order to keep the tone raised here Pope silently cuts lines 49–51 from the complete Horatian text.

5 On the importance of the theme of inconsistency in Horace, particularly in *Epistles* 1, see McGann (1969, pp. 12–13; 21 ff.; and 56–7). The last is particularly relevant in that McGann discusses Horace's utterly contradictory views of himself in *Epistles* I.vii. and viii. See also *Satire* I.i. 15 ff.; *Satire* I.iii. 1 ff.; and *Satire* II.vii. 6 ff.

6 Like Pope, Ogle expands on each word in Horace's list of Stoic terms which, as the index numbers show, he rearranges into his own order:

> To close [166]the Scheme I labor to support;
> (Nor long to grieve the Fair, or spoil the Court)
> What'er our State, Necessity or Wealth;
> Retir'd or Rais'd; Infirmity or Health;
> In *virtuous Order* true *Perfection* lies:
> Inferior [167]but to GOD, is *Good* and *Wise!*
> *Felicity*, from this pure Fountain, springs!
> Hence! *Man,* [170]is *Lord of Lords,* and *King* [172]of *Kings!*
> *Participates,* of Heav'n, if not *Possest!*
> Is only [171]*Beauteous,* and is only *Blest!*
> Is [168]*Rich* and [169]*Free,* tho' *Plunder'd* and *Confin'd!*
> Is *Sound* [173]of *Body,* and is *Sound* of Mind! – – – – – –
> "But hold (you cry) [174]*Not Sound,* when rack'd with *Pain,*
> "(If yet an *English* Feeling he retain!)
> "Or when molested with the *Nervous-Ill,*
> "He gulps *Crude-Silver,* or the *Wardian Pill.*

> *Ad summam,* [166]———
> ——— ——— *sapiens uno minor est* JOVE, [167]———
> ——— ——— ——— ——— *dives,* [168]
> *Liber,* [169] ———
> ——— *honoratus,* [170] ———

—— —— —— *pulcher,* [171]——
—— —— —— —— —— *rex denique regum;* [172]
Praecipuè sanus, [173] ——
—— —— —— *nisi cum pituita molesta est.* [174]

(1735,pp. 31–2)

7 I am assuming Dacier's reading of Horace's final line which is in accord with most modern interpretations. It is however interesting that Stégen's (1960) comments on the Stoic sage (pp. 10 ff.) and on Horace's sense of failure in the last passages (pp. 23 ff.) offer a view of Horace's epistle which is closer to Pope's Imitation. Stégen's interpretations are simply dismissed by McGann (1969, p. 36, n.4, and p. 37, n.1).

8 My reading of this Imitation is very much in line with Goldberg's essay on Pope's poetry of the 1730s and 1740s, 'Integrity and Life in Pope's Poetry' (1976). Goldberg is particularly suggestive on Pope's awareness of human inconsistency and his struggle to form some adequate conception of human 'integrity'. Relevant also is Shaftesbury's attempt to understand how '*Opinions*', '*Fancy*', '*Humours*', '*Passions*' relate to the '*Self*' (see for example, 1714, I, pp. 293–7). Shaftesbury's powerful studies of 'Artificial Self or Economical Self' and 'Natural Self' in 'The Philosophical Regimen' (1900, pp. 124–39) are fascinating in this respect.

Bibliography

A. WORKS WRITTEN BEFORE 1800

anon., *Englands Sin, and Shame: In a Paralel between the Degenerate Estate of Old Rome and Great Britain. Or, Hor. Lib. 3. Ode 6. Ad Romanos de Moribus sui soeculi corruptis. Occasionally Paraphrased, and applyed for the 30th of January, 1672. Being the Anniversary of the Murder of that Blessed Martyr King Charles I*, London, 1672.

anon., 'From J. S. to C. S.', *The Innocent Epicure, or, the Art of Angling. A Poem* [Imitation of *Epistle* i.x.], [ed. Nahum Tate], London, 1697.

anon., *The Causes of Scotland's Miseries: a poem, in Imitation of the vi. Ode of the Third Book of Horace*, Edinburgh, 1700.

anon., *The Odes of Horace in Latin and English; with a Translation of Dr. Bentley's Notes. To which are added, Notes upon Notes, Done in the Bentleian Stile*, 24 parts, London, 1712–13.

anon., *The Fifth Ode of the Fourth Book of Horace Imitated: and Inscrib'd to the King*, London, 1714.

anon., *The First Ode of the Second Book of Horace Paraphras'd, and address'd to Richard St[ee]le, Esq.*, London, 1714.

anon., *A Dialogue Between a Secretary of State and a Connaught Squier; or, a Satyr in Imitation of Horace, Ibam forte via &c.*, Dublin, 1714.

anon., *An Imitation of the Prophecy of Nereus, from Hor. L.I. Od. 15.*, [?Edinburgh, 1715].

anon., *An Allusion to Horace's "Integer vitae, &c." Book I. Ode XXII.*, London, 1716.

anon., *Horace, Lib. II. Ode IV. Imitated Ne sit Ancillae, ... The Lord G– to the E. of S–*, London, [?1718].

anon., *The Loyalist's Wish, or Horace's 5th Ode, Book 4, to Augustus, Paraphras'd in English prose*, [?London], 1719.

anon., *In Imitation of the 5th Ode of Horace.* [Book IV] [A Jacobite ballad], [?1720].

anon., *To Robert Ch[e]ster, Esq.; in Imitation of the First Ode* [of Book I] of *Horace*, London, [1720].

anon., *Horace to Scaeva. Epist. XVII. Book I. Imitated*, London, 1730.

anon., *A Translation of Horace's Epistle to Augustus in Imitation of Lord Roscommon's Stile in the Art of Poetry*, Dublin, 1730.

anon., *Some Remarks on Mr. Carthy's Translation of the First Epistle of the Second Book of Horace*, Dublin, 1731.

anon., *The Satirist: in Imitation of the Fourth Satire of the First Book of Horace*, London, 1733.

anon., *An Ode in Imitation of the Third Ode of the Third Book of Horace. Address'd to the City of Dublin*, [?Dublin, 1733; Foxon suggests 1732].

anon., *Horace to Fannius*, [an Imitation of *Ode* ii.viii.], 1734.

anon., *The Miser, a Poem: From the First Satire of the First Book of Horace. Inscrib'd to H. Walpole*, London, 1735.

anon., *Two Epistles of Horace [Ep. I.xviii. and II.i.] Imitated*, London, 1736.

anon., *An Ode to the Earl of Chesterfield, Imploring his Majesty's Return. In Imitation of Horace, Ode II., Book IV*, London, 1737.

anon. (E. W.), *The Sixth Satire of the First Book of Horace Imitated*, London, 1738.

anon., *Men and Measures Characterised from Horace. Being an Imitation of the XVIth Ode of his Second Book*, London, 1739.

anon., *The Sixteenth Epode of Horace Imitated: and Addressed to the People of England*, London, 1739.

anon., *Epidemical Madness: A Poem in Imitation of Horace [Satire II.iii.]*, 1739.

anon., *An Imitation of the 22d. Ode in the First Book of Horace*, London, [?1740].

anon., *Horace's Instructions to the Roman Senate. (Imitated and Addressed to the House of Commons) And Character of Caius Asinius Pollio. In two Odes* [III.ii. and II.i.], London, 1740.

anon., *The Art of Architecture; a Poem in Imitation of Horace's Art of Poetry*, London, 1742.

anon., *The First Satire of the Second Book of Horace, Imitated*, London, 1745.

anon., *The Art of Stock-jobbing: a Poem, in Imitation of Horace's Art of Poetry. By a Gideonite*, London, 1746.

anon., *Horatii Ep. I. Lib. II. ad Augustum. The First Epistle of the Second Book of Horace Imitated. To the Right Honourable Philip, Lord Hardwicke, Lord High Chancellor of Great-Britain*, London, 1749.

Ashmore, J., trans. *Certain Selected Odes of Horace, Englished and their Arguments Annexed*, London, 1621.

Baxter, W., ed., *Q. Horatii Flacci Eclogae*, London, 1701.

Bentley, R., ed., *Q. Horatius Flaccus ex Recensione et cum Notis atque emendationibus Richardi Bentleii*, Cambridge, 1711.

Bentley, Thomas, *A Letter to Mr. Pope, Occasioned by Sober Advice from Horace*, 1735.

Blackwell, Thomas, *Memoirs of the Court of Augustus*, 3 vols., Edinburgh and London, 1753–1763.

Bolingbroke, Henry St John, First Viscount, *The Works of the Late Right Honourable Henry St. John, Lord Viscount Bolingbroke*, ed. D. Mallet, London, 5 vols., 1754.

Boileau-Despréaux, N., *The Works of Monsieur Boileau made English ... by Several Hands*, 3 vols., London, 1711–13.

Satires, ed. Albert Cahen, Paris, 1932.

Epistres, ed. Albert Cahen, Paris, 1937.

Bond, J., ed., *Quinti Horatii Flacci Poemata, Scholiis sive annotationibus, à Ioanne Bond illustrata*, 6th edn, London, 1630.

[Bramston, James,] *The Art of Politicks, in Imitation of Horace's Art of Poetry*, London, 1729.

Brome, A., ed., *The Poems of Horace, consisting of Odes, Satyres, and Epistles, rendered in English verse by several persons*, London, 1666; 2nd edn, 1671.

Burnet, Alexander, and Guthry, –, *Achilles Dissected: Being a Compleat Key of the Political Characters in that New Ballad Opera, Written by the late Mr. Gay ... by Mr. Burnet ... to which is added, The First Satire of the Second Book of Horace, Imitated in a Dialogue between Mr. Pope and the Ordinary of Newgate* [signed: Guthry], London, 1733.

Carthy, Charles, *A Translation of the Second Book of Horace's Epistles, Together with Some of the Most Select in the First, with Notes*, Dublin, 1731.

Casaubon, Isaac, *De Satyrica Graecorum poesi et Romanorum satira libri duo*, Paris, 1605.

Auli Persii Flacci Satirarum liber. I. Casaubonus recensuit, & commentario libro illustravit, Paris, 1605.

Chesterfield, Philip Dormer Stanhope, Earl of, *The Letters of Philip Dormer Stanhope, 4th Earl of Chesterfield*, ed. Bonamy Dobrée, 6 vols., London, 1932.

Cotton, Charles, *Scarronides ... Being the First Book of Virgils Aeneis in English, Burlésque*, 1664.

Scarronides ... In Imitation of the Fourth Book of Virgils Aeneis in English, Burlésque, 1665.

Cowley, Abraham, *Pindarique Odes*, London, 1656.

Coxwell, Henry, trans., *The Odes of Horace. Translated into English Verse*, Oxford, 1718.

Creech, Thomas, trans., *The Works of Horace in Latin and English*, 5th edn, 2 vols., London, 1718.

Cruquius, J., ed., *Q. Horatius Flaccus cum commentariis & enarrationibus commentatoris veteris, et J. Cruquii*, Ex Officina Plantiniana, Lugduni Batavorum, 1597.

Cunningham, Alexander, ed., *Q. Horatii Flacci Poemata, ex antiquis codd. et certis observationibus emendavit, variasque ... lectiones adjecit A. Cunningamius*, London, 1721a.

Animadversiones in Ricardi Bentleii Notas et emendationes ad Q. Horat. Flaccum, The Hague, 1721b.

Dacier, André, ed., *Remarques Critiques sur les Oeuvres d'Horace, avec une nouvelle traduction*, 10 vols., Paris, 1683–97.

Oeuvres d'Horace en Latin et en François, avec des remarques, 3rd edn, 10 vols., Paris 1709.

Dacier, André, and Sanadon, P., eds., *Oeuvres d'Horace en Latin, traduites en François*, 8 vols., Amsterdam, 1735.

Dennis, John, 'To Matthew Prior, Esq; Upon the Roman Satirists' (1721) in *The Critical Works of John Dennis*, ed. Edward Niles Hooker, 2 vols., Baltimore, 1939–43, II, 218–20.

Desprez, L., ed., *Q. Horatii Flacci Opera ... illustravit L. Desprez*, London, 1694.

Diaper, William, *An Imitation of the Seventeenth Epistle of the First Book of Horace, Address'd to Dr. S[wi]ft*, London, 1714.

[Dodsley, R.] *The Art of Preaching; In Imitation of Horace's Art of Poetry*, London, [?1735; Foxon suggests 1738].

Drant, T., trans., *A Medicinable Morall, that is the two Bookes of Horace his Satyres Englyshed according to the prescription of saint Hierome*, London, 1566.

Horace his Art of Poetrie, pistles and satyrs Englished and to the Earl of Ormounte by T. Drant addressed, London, 1567.

Dryden, John, trans., *The Satires of D. J. Juvenalis. Translated into English verse. By Mr. Dryden, and ... other eminent hands. Together with the Satires of A. Persius Flaccus. Made English by Mr. Dryden*, London, 1693.

Essays of John Dryden, selected and edited, W. P. Ker, 2 vols., Oxford, 1926.

Poems 1693–1696, The Works of John Dryden, IV, ed. A. B. Chambers, William Frost, and Vinton A. Dearing, Berkeley and Los Angeles, 1974.

Duncombe, W., trans., *The Carmen Saeculare of Horace*, London, 1721.

Dunster, S., *The Satires and Epistles of Horace, Done into English* [prose], *with notes. 2nd ed. To which is now added, His Art of Poetry*, London, 1712.

Fanshawe, Sir Richard, *Il Pastor Fido; the Faithful Shepheard*, [translated from the Italian of B. Guarini,] *with ... divers other poems*, London, 1648.

Selected Parts of Horace, Prince of Lyricks, London, 1652.

Francis, P., trans., *A Poetical Translation of the Works of Horace: with the Original Text, and Notes collected from the best Latin and French Commentators*, 2nd edn, 4 vols., London, 1747.

Gay, John, *Poetry and Prose*, ed. Vinton A. Dearing and Charles E. Beckwith, 2 vols., Oxford, 1974.

Glanville, J., *Some Odes of Horace Imitated. With Relation to his Majesty and the Times*, London, 1690.

'Guthry, — ', see Burnet, Alexander.

[Hamilton, William,] *The Eighteenth Epistle of the Second Book of Horace, To Lollius, Imitated*, Edinburgh, 1737.

Hanway, J., *Translations of several Odes, Satyres, and Epistles of Horace*, London, 1730.

Hare, T., trans., *A Translation of the Odes and Epodes of Horace into English verse*, London, 1737.

Harington, John, trans., *The Odes and Epodon of Horace*, London, 1684.

Hawkins, Sir T., trans., *Odes of Horace*, 4th edn, London, 1638.

Hawkins, Sir T. and Holyday, B., trans., *Horace, the best of Lyrick Poets ... Together with A. Persius Flaccus his Satyres*, 2 parts, London, 1650–2.

Heinsius, D., ed., *Q. Horatius Flaccus. Accedunt nunc D. Heinsii de Satyra Horatiana libri duo*, Ex officina Elzeviriana, Lugduni Batavorum, 1629.

Holyday, B., trans., *All Horace his Lyrics, or His Four Books of Odes and His Book of Epodes Englished*, London, 1653.

Decimus Junius Juvenalis and Aulus Persius Flaccus translated and Illustrated, Oxford, 1673.

Horneck, A., *A Votive Ode for the Happy Delivery of ... the Princess of Wales ... Imitated from the Carmen Seculare of Horace*, London, 1716.

Hurd, Richard, ed., *Q. Horatii Flacci Ars Poetica. Epistola ad Pisones. With an English Commentary and Notes*, London, 1749.

Q. Horatii Flacci Epistolae ad Pisones et Augustum: with an English Commentary and Notes. To which are added Two Dissertations: the one, on the Provinces of the several Species of Dramatic Poetry; the other, on Poetical Imitation, 2nd edn, 2 vols., London, 1753.

Jonson, B., *Q. Horatius Flaccus: his Art of Poetry. Englished by Ben: Jonson. With other works of the Author never printed before*, London, 1640.

Ben Jonson, ed. C. H. Herford and Percy [and Evelyn] Simpson, 11 vols., Oxford, 1925–52.

Johnson, Samuel, *London: a Poem, in Imitation of the Third Satire of Juvenal*, London, 1738.

The Vanity of Human Wishes. The Tenth Satire of Juvenal, Imitated by Samuel Johnson, London, 1749.

Lives of the English Poets, ed. George Birkbeck Hill, 2 vols., Oxford, 1905.

Poems, The Yale Edition of the Works of Samuel Johnson, VI, eds. E. L. McAdam, Jr, with George Milne, New Haven and London, 1964.

[King, William,] *The Art of Cookery; a Poem, in Imitation of Horace's Art of Poetry*, London, 1708.

Knox, Vicesimus, 'On Satire and Satirists' in *Essays Moral and Literary*, 2nd edn, 2 vols., London, 1779, II, 147–55.

Le Clerc, Jean, *Mr. Le Clerc's Judgement and Censure of Dr. Bentley's Horace*, London, 1713.

Locke, John, *Two Treatises of Government* (1689), ed. Peter Laslett, 2nd impression, Cambridge, 1964.

Lyttelton, George, Lord, *Dialogues of the Dead*, London, 1760.

Mandeville, B., *The Fable of the Bees: or, Private Vices, Publick Benefits*, 5th edn, London, 1728.

Manilius, M., *The Five Books of M. Manilius, Containing a System of the Ancient Astronomy and Astrology; Together with the Philosophy of the Stoicks. Done into English Verse* [by Thomas Creech], London, 1697.

Manutius, A. P., *A Treatise of the Several Measures Used by Horace in His Odes and Epodes*, London 1718.

Manwaring, E., *Stichology: or, a Recovery of the Latin, Greek and Hebrew Numbers, Exemplified in the Reduction of all Horace's Metres, and the Greek and Hebrew Poetry*, London, 1737.

Miller, James, *Harlequin-Horace: or the Art of Modern Poetry*, London and Dublin, [1731].

Seasonable Reproof, a Satire in the Manner of Horace (Imitated from the Third and Fourth of the First Book of his Sermons). To be Continued Occaisionally as a Poetical Pillory, London, 1735.

Art of Life. In Imitation of Horace's Art of Poetry. In Two Epistles. Epistle the First, London, 1739.

Milton, John, *The Poetical Works of John Milton*, ed. Helen Darbishire, London, 1958.

Mitchell, J., *A Curse upon Punch, in Imitation of the Third Epode of Horace*, [?1735].

Montague, Lady Mary Wortley and Lord Hervey, *Verses Address'd to the Imitator of the First Satire of the Second Book of Horace*, London, 1733.

Montaigne, M., *Montaigne's Essays, John Florio's Translation*, ed. J. I. M. Stewart, 2 vols., London, 1931.

Nevile, T., *Imitations of Horace* [i.e. of select satires and epistles with the Latin original], London, 1758.

Ogle, George, *Epistles of Horace Imitated* [*Epistles* I.i. and I.iv.], London, 1735.

Of Legacy-Hunting. The Fifth Satire of the Second Book of Horace Imitated. A Dialogue between Sir Walter Raleigh, and Merlin the Prophet, London, 1737.

The Miser's Feast; the Eighth Satire of the Second Book of Horace Imitated; a Dialogue between the Author and the Poet Laureate, London, 1737.

The Second Epistle of the First Book of Horace Imitated, London, 1738.

Third Epistle of the First Book of Horace Imitated, London, 1738.

The Fifth Epistle of the First Book of Horace Imitated, London, 1738.

The Eleventh Epistle of the First Book of Horace Imitated, London, 1738.

The Eighth and Ninth Epistles of the First Book of Horace Imitated, London, [1739].

The Twelfth Epistle of the First Book of Horace Imitated, London, [1739].

Oldham, John, *Some New Pieces never before publisht*, London, 1681.

Poetical Works, ed. Robert Bell, London, 1854.

Oldisworth, W., trans., *The Odes, Epodes, and Carmen Seculare of Horace in English verse ... Translated from Dr. Bentley's Latin edition*, 2nd edn, London, 1719.
Pine, John, ed., *Quinti Horatii Flacci Opera*, 2 vols., London, 1733–37.
Pope, Alexander, *The First Satire of the Second Book of Horace, Imitated in a Dialogue between A. Pope of Twickenham ... on the one Part, and his Learned Council on the other*, London, 1733.
The First Satire of the Second Book of Horace Imitated in a Dialogue between A. Pope ... and His Learned Council. To which is added, The Second Satire of the Same Book. By the Same Hand. London, 1734.
The Second Satire of the Second Book of Horace Paraphrased, London, 1734.
Sober Advice from Horace to the Young Gentlemen about Town. As Deliver'd in his Second Sermon. Imitated in the Manner of Mr. Pope. Together with the Original Text, as restored by the Revd. R. Bentley Doctor of Divinity. And some Remarks on the Version, London, [1734].
Horace his Ode to Venus. Lib. IV. Ode. I. London, 1737.
The Second Epistle of the Second Book of Horace, Imitated, London, 1737.
The First Epistle of the Second Book of Horace, Imitated, London, 1737.
The Sixth Epistle of the First Book of Horace Imitated, London, 1737 [actually published 23 January 1738].
The First Epistle of the First Book of Horace Imitated, London, 1737 [actually published, March 1738].
The Works of Alexander Pope, 4 vols., London, 1743.
The Works of Alexander Pope, ed. William Warburton, 9 vols., London, 1751.
The Works of Alexander Pope, ed. Joseph Warton, 9 vols., London, 1822.
The Works of Alexander Pope, ed. W. Elwin and W. J. Courthope, 10 vols., London, 1871–86.
The Twickenham Edition of the Poems of Alexander Pope, general ed. John Butt, 11 vols., London and New Haven, 1939–69.
The Correspondence of Alexander Pope, ed. George Sherburn, 5 vols., Oxford, 1956.
Pope, Horatian Satires and Epistles, ed. H. H. Erskine-Hill, Oxford, 1964.
Pope, Alexander and Swift, Jonathan, *An Imitation of the Sixth Satire of the Second Book of Horace. Hoc erat in votis, etc. The first Part done in the Year 1714, by Dr. Swift. The latter Part now first added*, [by A. Pope], London, 1738.
Prior, Matthew, *An Ode, in Imitation of the Second Ode of the Third Book of Horace*, London, 1692.
Horace Lib. I. Epistle the Ninth ... To the Right Honourable R[obert] H[arley], Esq., [London, 1711].
Rider, H., *et al*, trans., *All the Odes and Epodes of Horace, Translated into English verse*, London, 1638.
Rochester, John Wilmot, Earl of, *The Works of John Earl of Rochester*, London, 1714.
The Complete Poems of John Wilmot, Earl of Rochester, ed. David M. Vieth, New Haven and London, 1968.
Roscommon, Wentward Dillon, Earl of, *et al*, *The Odes and Satyrs of Horace, That have been done into English By the most Eminent Hands, ... with his Art of Poetry, by the Earl of Roscommon*, London, 1721.
An Essay on Translated Verse (1685) *and Horace's Art of Poetry made English* (1684), Menston, 1971.

Sagittarius, Thomas M. *Horatius Christianus, sive parodiae sacrae ad Horatii ductum noviter accommodatae*, Jenae, 1615.

Sanadon, R. P., ed., *Les Poésies d'Horace, disposées suivant l'ordre chronologique, et Traduites en François: avec des remarques et dissertations critiques*, 2 vols., Paris, 1728.

Seneca, *Ad Lucilium Epistulae Morales*, ed. and trans. Richard M. Gummere, 3 vols., London and New York, 1917–25.

Moral Essays, ed. and trans. J. W. Basore, 3 vols., London and New York, 1928–1935.

Shaftesbury, Anthony Ashley Cooper, 3rd Earl of, *Characteristics of Men, Manners, Opinions, Times*, 2nd edn, 3 vols., 1714.

The Life, Unpublished Letters, and Philosophical Regimen of Anthony, Earl of Shaftesbury, ed. Benjamin Rand, London and New York, 1900.

Smart, Christopher, *The Horatian Canons of Friendship: being the Third Satire of the First Book of Horace Imitated* [in English Verse] by Ebenezer Pentweazle [pseud.], London, 1750.

S[mith], J[ohn], *The Lyrick Poet, Odes and Satyres translated out of Horace into English verse*, Southwark, 1649.

The Spectator, ed. Donald F. Bond, 5 vols., Oxford, 1965.

Spence, Joseph, *Polymetis: Or, an Enquiry concerning the Agreement Between the Works of the Roman Poets, and the Remains of the Ancient Artists*, London, 1747.

Observations, Anecdotes, and Characters of Books and Men, Collected from Conversation, ed. James M. Osborn, 2 vols., Oxford, 1966.

Spingarn, J. E., ed., *Critical Essays of the Seventeenth Century*, 3 vols., Oxford, 1908–9.

Swift, Jonathan, *T[o]l[a]nd's Invitation to Dismal to dine with the Calves-Head Club ... Imitated from Horace Epist. 5. Lib. I.* [with the text], [London, 1712].

Parts of the Seventh Epistle of the First Book of Horace Imitated, and address'd to a Noble Peer [Robert Harley], London, 1713.

To his Excellency John, Lord Carteret, Lord Lieutenant of Ireland. An Imitation of Horace, Ode. IX. Lib. IV., Dublin, 1729.

Horace Book I. Ode XIV ... Paraphrased and Inscribed to Ir−d., Dublin, 1730.

The Poems of Jonathan Swift, ed. Harold Williams, 2nd edn, 3 vols., Oxford, 1958.

The Correspondence of Jonathan Swift, ed. Harold Williams, 6 vols., Oxford, 1963–.

Talbot, J., ed., *Q. Horatii Flacci Opera ad optimorum exemplarium fidem recensita*, Cambridge, 1699.

Torrentius, L., ed., *Q. Horatius Flaccus cum erudito L. Torrentii commentario nunc primum in lucem edito* [by B. Moretus], Ex officinâ Plantinianâ, Antwerp, 1608.

Towers, Matthew, ed., *The Odes of Horace's Dispos'd According to the Chronologic Order by P. Sanadon, With an English translation, in Poetic-prose ... To which are Prefix'd, Sanadon's Life of Horace ... and a Critical Preface ... by Mathew Towers*, 2 vols., Dublin, 1744.

Turner, –, *The First Epistle of the First Book of Horace Imitated*, London, 1738.

Veen, Otto van, *Q. Horatii Flacci Emblemata*, Antwerp, 1612.

Theatro Moral de Toda la Philosophia de los Antiquos y Modernos, con el

Enchiridion de Epicteto [Emblems from Horace illustrated by one hundred engravings on steel from O. Vaenius], 3 vols., Brussels, 1669–73.

Vertot, René Aubert de, *The History of the Revolutions That Happened in the Government of the Roman Republic*. trans. John Ozell, 3rd edn, 2 vols., London, 1723–4.

Warmington, E. H., ed. and trans., *Remains of Old Latin*, 4 vols., London and Cambridge, Mass., 1936–40.

Warton, Joseph, *An Essay on the Genius and Writings of Pope*, 2nd edn, 2 vols., London, 1762–82.

Watson, David, and Patrick, S., eds., *The Works of Horace, Translated into English Prose, As near as the Propriety of the Two Languages will admit. Together with the Original Latin from the Best Editions. Wherein the Words of the Latin Text are ranged in their Grammatical Order ... with Notes ...*, 4th edn, 2 vols., London, 1760.

West, Richard, *An Epistle to a Friend, In Imitation of the Second Epistle of the First Book of Horace*, 1739.

Whitehead, Paul, *The State of Rome, Under Nero and Domitian: A Satire. Containing a List of Nobles, ... Ministers of State, &c. &c. &c. By Messrs. Juvenal and Persius* [Extracts from their satires, with a free translation], London, 1739.

Wollaston, William, *The Religion of Nature Delineated* (1724), Delmar, New York, 1974.

Wood, Thomas, *Juvenalis Redivivus, or the First Satyr of Juvenal Taught to Speak Plain English*, [London], 1683.

B.   WORKS WRITTEN AFTER 1800

Aden, John M., 'Pope and the Satiric Adversary', *Studies in English Literature*, 2 (1962), 267–86.
  Something Like Horace: Studies in the Art and Allusion of Pope's Horatian Satires, Kingsport, Tennessee, 1969.

Alden, Raymond M., *The Rise of Formal Satire in England*, Philadelphia, 1899.

Anderson, W. S., 'The Roman Socrates: Horace and his Satires', *Critical Essays on Roman Literature, Satire*, ed. J. P. Sullivan, London, 1963, 1–37.

Barthes, Roland, *Image-Music-Text*, Essays selected and translated by Stephen Heath, Fontana, 1977.

Bennett, C. E., ed. and trans., *Horace, The Odes and Epodes*, Cambridge, Mass. and London, 1914, rev. edn, 1927.

Bloom, Edward A. and Lillian D., 'Johnson's *London* and its Juvenalian Texts', *Huntington Library Quarterly*, 34 (1970), 1–23.

Bloom, Harold, *The Anxiety of Influence*, New York, 1973; paperback edn, 1975.

Bloom, Lillian D., 'Pope as a Textual Critic: A Bibliographical Study of His Horatian Text', *Journal of English and Germanic Philology*, 47 (1948), 150–5.

Brink, C. O., *Horace on Poetry: Prolegomena to the Literary Epistles*, Cambridge, 1963.
  On Reading a Horatian Satire. An Interpretation of Sermones II.6, Sydney, 1965.
  Horace on Poetry: The 'Ars Poetica'. Cambridge, 1971.
  'Horatian Poetry. Thoughts on the Development of Textual Criticism and

Interpretation', in *Geschichte des Textverständnisses am Beispiel von Pindar und Horaz*, ed. Walther Killy, Wolfenbütteler Forschungen, Band 12, Munich, 1981, 7–17.

Horace on Poetry: Epistles Book II: The Letters to Augustus and Florus, Cambridge, 1982.

Brooks, Harold F., 'The "Imitation" in English Poetry, Especially in Formal Satire, Before the Age of Pope', *Review of English Studies*, 25 (1949), 124–40.

Brower, R. A., *Alexander Pope: The Poetry of Allusion*, Oxford, 1959.

Brower, R. A., ed., *On Translation*, New York, 1966.

Campbell, A. Y., *Horace, A New Interpretation*, London, 1924.

Carnochan, W. B., 'Satire, Sublimity, and Sentiment: Theory and Practice in Post-Augustan Satire', *PMLA*, 85 (1970), 260–7.

Clark, A. F. B., *Boileau and the French Classical Critics in England (1660–1830)*, Paris, 1925.

Clifford, Frederick B., *Horace in the Imitations of Alexander Pope*, Lexington, 1954.

Commager, Steele, *The Odes of Horace: a Critical Study*, New Haven and London, 1962.

Courbaud, E., 'Sur l'Épître I 1', *Mélanges Émile Chatelain*, Paris, 1910, 354–66.

Horace, sa vie et sa pensée à l'époque des épîtres: étude sur le premier livre, Paris, 1914.

Davies, D. W., *The World of the Elsevires, 1580–1712*, The Hague, 1954.

DeWitt, N. W., 'The Epicurean Doctrine of Gratitude', *American Journal of Philology*, 58 (1937), 320–8.

'Epicurean Doctrine in Horace', *Classical Philology*, 34 (1939), 127–34.

Dilke, O. A. W., ed., *Horace: Epistles Book I*, 2nd edn, London, 1961.

'Horace and the Verse Letter', in *Horace*, ed. C. D. N. Costa, London and Boston, 1973, 94–112.

Dixon, Peter, *The World of Pope's Satires: An Introduction to the Epistles and Imitations of Horace*, 1968.

Dobrée, Bonamy, 'Pope's Horace', *TLS*, August 12, 1939, p. 479.

Draper, J. W., 'The Theory of Translation in the Eighteenth Century', *Neophilologus*, 6 (1921), 241–54.

Edden, Valerie, 'The Best of Lyrick Poets', in *Horace*, ed. C. D. N. Costa, London and Boston, 1973, 135–59.

Edwards, Thomas R. *This Dark Estate: A Reading of Pope*, Berkeley and Los Angeles, 1963.

Eliot, T. S., 'Tradition and the Individual Talent' (1919) in *Selected Essays*, 3rd edn, 1951, 13–22.

Elledge, Scott, 'The Background and Development in English Criticism of the Theories of Generality and Particularity', *PMLA*, 62 (1947), 147–82.

Elkin, P. K., *The Augustan Defence of Satire*, Oxford, 1973.

Empson, William, *Some Versions of Pastoral*, London, 1935.

Erskine-Hill, Howard, 'Augustans on Augustanism: England, 1655–1759', *Renaissance and Modern Studies*, 2 (1967), 55–85.

'Courtiers out of Horace: Donne's *Satyre IV*; and Pope's *Fourth Satire of Dr John Donne of St. Paul's Versifyed*', in *John Donne: Essays in Celebration*, ed. A. J. Smith, London, 1972, 273–307.

The Social Milieu of Alexander Pope, New Haven and London, 1975.

'Satire and Self-Portrayal: The First Satire of the Second Book of Horace, Imitated and Pope's Reception of Horace's in *Geschichte des Textverständ-*

nisses am Beispiel von Pindar und Horaz, ed. Walther Killy, Wolfenbütteler Forschungen, Band 12, Munich, 1981, 153–71.

'Alexander Pope: The Political Poet in His Time', *Eighteenth-Century Studies*, 15, no. 2 (Winter, 1981–2), 123–48.

The Augustan Idea in English Literature, London, 1983.

Fairclough, H. Rushton, ed. and trans., *Horace, Satires, Epistles and Ars Poetica*, London and Cambridge, Mass., rev. edn, 1929.

Fiske, George C. *Lucilius and Horace, A Study in the Classical Theory of Imitation*, Madison, Wisconsin, 1920.

Foxon, D. F., *English Verse 1701–1750: A Catalogue of Separately Printed Poems*, 2 vols., Cambridge, 1975.

Fraenkel, Eduard, *Horace*, Oxford, 1957.

Frost, William, 'Dryden and "Satire"', *Studies in English Literature*, 11 (1971), 401–16.

Freud, Sigmund, *Jokes and their Relation to the Unconscious*, (1905), trans. James Strachey, Pelican Freud Library, 6, Harmondsworth, 1976.

Gabriner, Paul, 'Pope's "Virtue" and the Events of 1738', *Scripta Hierosolymitana*, 25 (1973), 96–119.

Gaskell, Philip, 'Printing the Classics in the Eighteenth Century', in *The Book Collector*, 1 (1952), 98–111.

Goad, Caroline, *Horace in the English Literature of the Eighteenth Century*, New Haven, 1918.

Goldberg, S. L., 'Integrity and Life in Pope's Poetry', in *Studies in the Eighteenth Century, III, Papers presented at the Third David Nichol Smith Memorial Seminar, Canberra 1973*, ed. R. F. Brissenden and J. C. Eade, Canberra, 1976, 185–207.

Griffin, Dustin H., *Alexander Pope: The Poet in the Poems*, Princeton, 1978.

Griffith, R. H., *Alexander Pope: a Bibliography*, 2 vols., London, 1962.

Guilhamet, Leon M., 'Imitation and Originality in the Poems of Thomas Gray', in *Proceedings of the Modern Language Association Neoclassicism Conferences 1967–1968*, ed. Paul J. Korshin, New York, 1970, 35–52.

Guite, Harold, 'An 18th-Century View of Roman Satire', in *The Varied Pattern: Studies in the 18th Century*, ed. Peter Hughes and David Williams, Toronto, 1971, 113–20.

Hammond, Brean S., '"Old England's Genius": Pope's *Epistle to Bolingbroke*' in *British Journal for Eighteenth-Century Studies*, 3, no. 2 (Summer, 1980), 107–26.

Pope and Bolingbroke, A Study of Friendship and Influence, Columbia, Missouri, 1984.

Hammond, Paul, *John Oldham and the Renewal of Classical Culture*, Cambridge, 1983.

Hart, Jeffrey, 'Particular and General Truth: Some Speculative Footnotes to Scott Elledge', in *Proceedings of the Modern Language Association Neoclassicism Conferences 1967–1968*, ed. Paul J. Korshin, New York, 1970, 71–82.

Heller, J. L., 'Horace, *Epist.* i, 1, 47–54', *American Journal of Philology*, 85 (1964), 297–303.

Highet, Gilbert, *The Classical Tradition, Greek and Roman Influence on Western Literature*, Oxford, 1949.

Hiltbrunner, O., 'Volteius Mena: Interpretationen zu Hor. epist. i, 7', *Gymnasium*, 62 (1960), 289–300.

Hughes, R. E., 'Pope's *Imitations of Horace* and the Ethical Focus', *Modern Language Notes*, 71 (1956), 569–74.

Hunter, G. K., 'The "Romanticism" of Pope's Horace', *Essays in Criticism*, 10 (1960), 390–404.

Jack, Ian, 'Pope and The Weighty Bullion of Dr. Donne's Satires', *PMLA*, 66 (1951), 1009–22.

Augustan Satire, Oxford, 1952.

Jebb, R. C., *Bentley*, London, 1882.

Johnson, J. W., 'The Meaning of "Augustan"', *Journal of the History of Ideas*, 19 (1958), 507–22.

The Formation of English Neo-Classical Thought, Princeton, 1967.

Kelsall, Malcolm, 'Augustus and Pope', *Huntington Library Quarterly*, 39 (1976), 117–31.

Kupersmith, William, 'Pope, Horace and the Critics: Some Reconsiderations', *Arion*, 9 (1970), 205–19.

La Penna, A., 'Schizzo di una interpretazione di Orazio, partendo dal primo libro delle Epistole', *Annali della Scuola Normale di Pisa*, 18 (1949), 14–48.

Lauren, Barbara, 'Pope's *Epistle to Bolingbroke*: Satire from the Vantage of Retirement', *Studies in English Literature*, 15 (1975), 419–30.

Leishman, J. B., *Translating Horace*, Oxford, 1956.

Lejay, Paul, ed., *Oeuvres d'Horace, Satires*, Paris, 1911 (repr., Librairie Hachette, Paris, 1966).

Levine, Jay Arnold, 'The Status of the Verse Epistle before Pope', *Studies in Philology*, 59 (1962), 658–84.

'Pope's *Epistle to Augustus*, Lines 1–30', *Studies in English Literature* 7 (1967), 427–51.

Mack, Maynard, 'Pope's Horatian Poems: Problems of Bibliography and Text', *Modern Philology*, 41 (1943), 33–44.

'A Manuscript of Pope's Imitation of the First Ode of the Fourth Book of Horace', *Modern Language Notes*, 60 (1945), 185–8.

'The Muse of Satire', *Yale Review*, 41 (1951), 80–92.

'Secretum Iter: Some Uses of Retirement Literature in the Poetry of Pope', in *Aspects of the Eighteenth Century*, ed. Earl R. Wasserman, Baltimore and London, 1965, 207–43.

The Garden and the City: Retirement and Politics in the Later Poetry of Pope 1731–1743, Toronto and London, 1969.

'Pope's Books: A Biographical Survey with a Finding List', in *English Literature in the Age of Disguise*, ed. Maximillian E. Novak, Berkeley and London, 1977, 209–305.

'Pope: The Shape of the Man in His Work', *Yale Review*, 67, no. 4 (Summer 1978), 493–516.

Mack, Maynard, ed., *The Last and Greatest Art, Some Unpublished Poetical Manuscripts of Alexander Pope*, Newark, N.J., London and Toronto, 1984.

Maguinness, W. S., 'Friendship and the Philosophy of Friendship in Horace', *Hermathena*, 51 (1938), 29–48.

'The Eclecticism of Horace', *Hermathena*, 52 (1938), 27–46.

Maresca, Thomas E., 'Pope's Defense of Satire: *The First Satire of the Second Book of Horace Imitated*', *Journal of English Literary History*, 31 (1964), 366–94.

Pope's Horatian Poems, Columbus, Ohio, 1966.

Marmier, Jean, *Horace en France, au dix-septième siècle*, Paris, 1962.

Mason, H. A., 'Is Juvenal a Classic?', *Arion*, I., no. 1 (Spring, 1962), 8–44; and I, no. 2 (Summer, 1962), 39–79.

McGann, M. J., 'Horace's Epistle to Florus (Epist. 2.2)', *Rheinisches Museum für Philologie*, 97 (1954), 343–58.

Studies in Horace's First Book of Epistles, Collection Latomus 100, Brusseles, 1969.

'The Three Worlds of Horace's *Satires*', in *Horace*, ed. C. D. N. Costa, London and Boston, 1973, 59–93.

Miner, Earl, 'Patterns of Stoicism in Thought and Prose Styles, 1530–1700', *PMLA* 85, (1970), 1023–34.

Monk, J. H., *The Life of Richard Bentley*, London, 1830.

Morris, Edward P., 'The Form of the Epistle in Horace', *Yale Classical Studies*, 2, 1931, 81–114.

Moskovit, Leonard A., 'Pope's Purposes in *Sober Advice*', *Philological Quarterly*, 44 (1965), 195–99.

'Pope and the Tradition of the Neoclassical Imitation', *Studies in English Literature*, 8, no. 3 (1968), 445–62.

Newman, J. K., *Augustus and the New Poetry*, Collection Latomus 88, Brussels, 1967.

Nisbet, R. G. M., 'Notes on Horace, *Epistles* I', *Classical Quarterly*, n.s. 9 (1959), 73–6.

Ogilvie, Robert M., 'Translations of Horace in the 17th and 18th Centuries', in *Geschichte des Textverständnisses am Beispiel von Pindar und Horaz*, ed. Walther Killy, Wolfenbütteler Forschungen, Band 12, Munich, 1981, 71–80.

Orelli, J. G. and Baiter, J. G., eds., *Quintus Horatius Flaccus*, 3rd edn, 2 vols., Turici, 1850.

Page, T. E., ed., *Q. Horatii Flacci, Carminum Libri IV, Epodon Liber*, London, 1895 (repr. 1967).

Palmer, Arthur, ed., *The Satires of Horace*, London, 1st edn 1883 (repr. 1964).

Perret, Jacques, *Horace*, Paris, 1959.

Peterson, Richard, 'Johnson at War with the Classics', *Eighteenth-Century Studies*, 9 (1975), 69–86.

Pfeiffer, R., *History of Classical Scholarship from 1300 to 1850*, Oxford, 1976.

Pierce, Robert B., 'Ben Jonson's Horace and Horace's Ben Jonson', *Studies in Philology*, 78, no. 1 (Late Winter, 1981), 20–31.

Porter Packer, M. N., 'The consistent Epicureanism of the first book of the *Epistles* of Horace', *Transactions of the American Philological Association*, 72 (1941), xxxix–xl.

Price, Martin, *To the Palace of Wisdom, Studies in Order and Energy from Dryden to Blake*, New York, 1965.

Purpose, Eugene R. 'The "Plain, Easy, and Familiar Way": The Dialogue in English Literature, 1660–1725', *Journal of English Literary History* 17 (1950), 47–58.

Randolph, Mary Claire, 'The Structural Design of Formal Verse Satire', *Philological Quarterly*, 21 (1942), 368–84.

Reckford, K. J. 'Horace and Maecenas', *Transactions of the American Philological Association*, 90 (1959), 195–208.

Revenand, Cedric D., II, '*Ut Pictura Poesis*, and Pope's "Satire II, i"', in *Pope: Recent Essays*, ed. Maynard Mack and James A. Winn, Brighton, Sussex, 1980, 373–91.

Rodgers, Robert W., Review of Lillian D. Bloom, 'Pope as a Textual Critic: A Bibliographical Study of His Horatian Text', *Philological Quarterly*, 28 (1949), 397–8.

The Major Satires of Alexander Pope, Urbana, 1955.

Røstvig, Maren-Sofie, *The Happy Man: Studies in the Metamorphoses of a Classical Idea*, 2nd edn, 2 vols., Oslo and New York, 1962.

Rudd, Niall, *The Satires of Horace*, Cambridge, 1966.

Horace: Satires and Epistles. Persius: Satires, Harmondsworth, 1979.

'Pope and Horace on Not Writing Poetry: A Study of *Epistles* II.2', in *English Satire and the Satiric Tradition*, ed. Claude Rawson, Oxford, 1984, 167–82.

Russo, John Paul, *Alexander Pope, Tradition and Identity*, Cambridge, Mass., 1972.

Sandys, John Edwin, *A History of Classical Scholarship*, 3 vols., Cambridge, 1903–8.

Schonhorn, Manuel, 'The Audacious Contemporaneity of Pope's *Epistle to Augustus*', *Studies in English Literature*, 8 (1968), 431–43.

'Pope's *Epistle to Augustus*: Notes Toward a Mythology', in *Pope: Recent Essays*, ed. Maynard Mack and James A. Winn, Brighton, Sussex, 1980, 546–64.

Sellin, Paul R., *Daniel Heinsius and Stuart England*, London, 1968.

Shackleton-Bailey, D. R., 'Bentley and Horace', in *Proceedings of the Leeds Philosophical and Literary Society*, 10 (1962), 105–15.

Stack, Frank, 'Pope's *Epistle to Bolingbroke* and *Epistle I. i*', in *The Art of Alexander Pope*, ed. Howard Erskine-Hill and Anne Smith, London, 1979, 169–91.

Stégen, G., *Essai sur la composition de cinq épîtres d'Horace*, Namur, 1960.

L'unité et la clarté des Épîtres d'Horace, Namur, 1963.

Storrs, Ronald, *Ad Pyrrham, A Polyglot Collection of Translations of Horace's Ode to Pyrrha, Book I, Ode 5*, London, 1959.

Thomson, J. A. K., *The Classical Background of English Literature*, London, 1948.

Classical Influences on English Poetry, London, 1951.

Tupper, J. W., 'A Study of Pope's *Imitations of Horace*', PMLA, 15 (1900), 181–215.

Villeneuve, François, ed., *Horace, Satirae*, Paris, 1946.

Horace, Épîtres, Collection G. Budé, 3rd edn, Paris, 1955.

Weinbrot, Howard D., 'The Pattern of Formal Verse Satire in the Restoration and the Eighteenth Century', PMLA, 80 (1965), 394–401.

'André Dacier in "Augustan" England: Towards the Reclamation of His Horace', *Romance Notes*, 7 (1966), 155–60.

'Translation and Parody: Towards the Genealogy of the Augustan Imitation', *Journal of English Literary History*, 33, no. 4 (1966), 434–47.

The Formal Strain, Studies in Augustan Imitation and Satire, Chicago and London, 1969.

'Augustan Imitation: The Role of the Original' in *Proceedings of the Modern Language Association Neoclassicism Conferences 1967–1968*, ed. Paul J. Korshin, New York, 1970, 53–70.

'Lyttelton and Pope's "Balanc'd World": The "Epistle to Augustus", Lines One and Two', *N&Q*, 216 (1971), 332–33.

'History, Horace, and Augustus Caesar: Some Implications for Eighteenth-Century Satire', *Eighteenth-Century Studies*, 7 (1974), 391–414.

Augustus Caesar in "Augustan" England, The Decline of A Classical Norm, Princeton, 1978.

'Such as Sir Robert Would Approve? Answers to Pope's Answer from Horace', *Modern Language Studies* 9 (1979), 5–14.

'The Conventions of Classical Satire and the Practice of Pope', *Philological Quarterly*, 50 (1980) 317–37.

Alexander Pope and the Traditions of Formal Verse Satire, Princeton, 1982.

West, David, *Reading Horace*, Edinburgh, 1967.

West, David and Woodman, Tony, eds., *Creative Imitation and Latin Literature*, Cambridge, 1979.

Whitford, R. C., 'Juvenal in England 1750–1802', *Philological Quarterly*, 7 (1928), 9–16.

Wickham, E. C. and Garrod, H. W., eds., *Q. Horati Flacci Opera*, Oxford, 1901, repr. 1963.

Wilkins, Augustus S. *The Epistles of Horace*, London, 1939, repr. 1965.

Wilkinson, L. P. *Horace and his Lyric Poetry*, 2nd edn, Cambridge, 1951.

Williams, Aubrey L., 'Pope and Horace: *The Second Epistle of the Second Book*', in *Restoration and Eighteenth-Century Literature*, ed. Carroll Camden, Chicago, 1963, 309–21.

Williams, G., 'Poetry in the Moral Climate of Augustan Rome', *Journal of Roman Studies*, 52 (1962), 28–46.

Review of C. O. Brink, *Horace on Poetry, Journal of Roman Studies*, 54 (1964), 186–96.

Tradition and Originality in Roman Poetry, Oxford, 1968.

Horace, New Surveys in the Classics, no. 6., Oxford, 1972.

Wilson, Penelope, 'Classical Poetry and the Eighteenth-Century Reader', in *Books and their Readers in Eighteenth-Century England*, ed. Isabel Rivers, Leicester, 1982, 69–96.

Wittkower, R., 'Imitation, Eclecticism, and Genius', in *Aspects of the Eighteenth Century*, ed. Earl R. Wasserman, Baltimore and London, 1965, 143–61.

Index

313

1